Informatik-Fachberichte 116

Herausgegeben von W. Brauer
Im Auftrag der Gesellschaft für Informatik (GI)

Recent Trends
in Data Type Specification

3rd Workshop on Theory and Applications
of Abstract Data Types
Selected Papers

Edited by H.-J. Kreowski

Springer-Verlag Berlin Heidelberg GmbH

Editor

Hans-Jörg Kreowski
Universität Bremen, Fachbereich Mathematik und Informatik
Postfach 330 440, 2800 Bremen 33, FRG

CR Subject Classifications (1984): F.3, F.4.1, F.4.2, D.2.1, D.3.1, D.4.5

ISBN 978-3-540-16077-9   ISBN 978-3-662-09691-8 (eBook)
DOI 10.1007/978-3-662-09691-8

PREFACE

    This volume contains the major part of the contributions to the 3rd Workshop on Theory and Applications of Abstract Data Types held in Bremen (Germany) from November 13 to November 16, 1984.

    The workshop, as both its predecessors (Sorpesee, 1982 and Passau, 1983), brought together many researchers interested in algebraic specifications and related topics. It provided an opportunity to present the latest, even unfinished, work and to discuss the future trends and research problems. The remarkable progress of the field reported at the workshop provoked this volume.

    The present collection of papers documents the recent developments and trends in data type and software specification in theory and in practice. The theoretical contributions pursue four objectives: the liberation of the specification methods from the underlying logic (Sannella and Tarlecki; Maibaum and Sadler), the extension of the algebraic theory of data types to meet adequately the semantics of imperative programming languages and the idea of observability (Wagner; Hennicker and Wirsing; Möller and Dosch; Streicher), the adaption of stepwise-refinement techniques to specifications with loose semantics (Beierle and Voss) and error and exception handling (Gogolla; Poigné). The papers oriented more towards practice are harder to classify. Two contributions open new, promising applications to the specification of services and protocols in open system interconnections and of database schemata (Ehrich; Hasler and de Meer). In two other contributions, prototyping and efficient evaluation of algebraic specifications are studied by means of translations into Prolog and of conditional term rewriting respectively (Kaplan; Petzsch). The four remaining papers supplement software engineering methodology related to algebraic specifications by introducing a new specification language, by designing a specification environment, by discussing a formal approach to user interfaces, and by translating interfaces in Ada into formal (Anna) specifications (Lermen and Loeckx; Bidoit, Choppy and Voisin; Ehrig, Fey and Hansen; Krieg-Brückner).

    But there is no reason to get euphoric about the state of the semantical understanding of software development and about the extent to which theory helps in practice and to which practice produces the proper, reliable results. To underline my warning, I will recall a well-known function which is extremely simple to specify, but about which we can tell bafflingly little inside and outside the algebraic approach to data types.

PLEASE ANSWER THE RIDDLE

Usually, the (algebraic) specification of a function is not the only knowledge you have. But the situation may be different in a riddle.

Let us assume we have a correct (equational) specification of natural numbers including a constant I, unary operations SUCC, PRED and SQUARE as well as binary operations ADD, MULT and SUBTRACT all of them with the ordinary meaning (i.e. SUCC(n)=n+I, PRED(I)=I, PRED(n+I)=n, SQUARE(n)=n^2, ADD(m,n)=m+n, MULT(m,n)=m·n, SUBTRACT(m,n)= =if m≤n then I else m-n).

In the next step, we add the following equations defining four unary functions A, B, C and RIDDLE

A(n) = PRED(SUBTRACT(SQUARE(SUCC(n)),SQUARE(n)))
B(n) = SUBTRACT(MULT(SUCC(I),A(n)),PRED(MULT(n,SUCC(I))))
C(n) = ADD(I,MULT(B(n),SUCC(SUCC(I))))

RIDDLE(I) = SUCC^{12}(I)
RIDDLE(n) = RIDDLE(A(n))
RIDDLE(B(n)) = RIDDLE(C(n)) .

Please notice that A, B and C are simple derived operations. The riddle is RIDDLE. If you recognize the function, the game is over. And I must apologize for being so bad in hiding functions.

Otherwise the more interesting part may start.
(1) Is there an interpreter running on your computer ? You may test RIDDLE.
(2) Is there any other tool running ? You may try it.
(3) Your favorite approach to data type specification probably provides notions like enrichment, extension, consistence, completeness, persistence, etc. Do they help ?
(4) Do you investigate the specification of partial functions ? Is RIDDLE partial ?
(5) Are you interested in exception handling ? Does RIDDLE need it ?
(6) Is RIDDLE correct (with respect to, e.g., RIDDLE(13)=13) ?
(7) Can you implement RIDDLE ?

A remark is necessary concerning the structure of the volume. The paper by Eric G. Wagner was an invited contribution in honor of his being one of the promoters of the algebraic theory of data types. Three short notes were invited to allow the reader a better survey of the important trends even if some of them are not properly emphasized by full papers. All other contributions passed a refereeing process. I am very grateful to L. Bonsiepen, M. Broy, H.-D. Ehrich, H. Ehrig, B. Hoffmann, B. Krieg-Brückner, J. Loeckx, B. Mahr, P. Padawitz, C. Schumann, H. Weber and A. Wilharm for their help. By the way, I would like to acknowledge that the Department of Mathematics and Computer Science at the University of Bremen sponsored the workshop and that the editing of this volume was partly done during my stay at the IBM Thomas J. Watson Research Center in Yorktown Heights, New York. Last but not least, I would like to thank Karin Limberg and Anne Wilharm who helped me, untiringly, in organizing the workshop.

H.-J. Kreowski

CONTENTS

Preface

CATEGORICAL SEMANTICS, OR EXTENDING DATA TYPES TO INCLUDE MEMORY

Eric G. Wagner
Computing Technology Department
IBM Thomas J. Watson Research Center
Yorktown Heights, New York 10598 / USA

1. Introduction

This paper extends the algebraic theory of data types so that it can deal with issues, such as those involving memory, that can not be easily treated within the usual algebraic specification framework. The result is a simple, uniform, mathematical framework in which we can treat, not only data types and their operations, but also, the semantics of imperative languages with assignment, conditionals, while-do's, and elementary exception handling.

The approach is to introduce just a bit more category theory into the treatment of data types. Specifically, we employ algebras in which certain carriers are restricted to being products or coproducts of other carriers, and to consider the related mediating morphisms as derived operators (the needed definitions from category theory are reviewed in section 4).

All our examples could be carried out within **Set**, the category of sets, using specific products and coproducts. However, by treating the products and coproducts abstractly we maintain, and extend, that fundamental idea of data abstraction, that everything is only defined (at most) up to isomorphism.

The paper begins with a short introduction to the the algebraic approach to abstract data types. We then point out some of the shortcomings of this theoretical and conceptual framework. All these shortcomings deal with the interface between abstract data types and the fundamental ideas of imperative programming languages -- namely such concepts as variable, location, environment, store, and assignment. Then, in section 4, we introduce the basic categorical concepts, the necessary notation, and some examples. Section 5 shows how to treat RECORDs (resp. VARIANTs) as products (resp. coproducts) and gives some basic examples. Next, in section 6, we exploit products to provide a treatment of memory (environments) and assignment. Then, in section 7, we, in turn, employ coproducts to treat conditionals (IF-THEN-ELSE), and iteration (WHILE-DO). In section 8 we take a quick look at exception handling and, in section 9 we give a treatment of ARRAY's. Section 10 contains some concluding remarks concerning extensions of this material.

This paper only includes two out of the three parts of the talk [3] given at the Data Types workshop. More precisely, we deal here only with statically declared data types. The material on dynamically declared data types will appear in a subsequent paper.

2. The Algebraic Approach to Abstract Data Types

The underlying idea of the algebraic approach to abstract data types is very simple. A data type, or more accurately, a family of data types, is viewed as a collection of named sets together with a collection of named operations between these sets. For example,

sets: INTEGER, BOOLEAN, CHAR__STRING

operations: 0, +, *, -, $Equal_{Int}$, True, False, 'A', 'B',...,'Z', Concat, Empty, $Equal_{Char\_String}$

Such a collection of named sets together with a collection of named operations between them is a *many-sorted algebra* or a *homogeneous algebra*. What makes this significant is not the fact that we have a name for it, but that much is known about such algebras that can be exploited for computer science purposes. In particular, we can exploit certain simple ideas from category theory to help in defining, and working with, data types.

Before briefly reviewing what has been done, let us give a precise definition of a many-sorted algebra in order to establish terminology and notation.

An *S-sorted Σ-algebra* A is consists of a set S (of *sorts*, (intuitively the names of the sets)) together with an $(S^* \times S)$-indexed set

$$\Sigma = < \Sigma_{w,s} \mid w \epsilon S^*, s \epsilon S >,$$

(intuitively, the names of the operations), and for each $s \epsilon S$ there is given a set A_s, and for each $\sigma \epsilon \Sigma_{w,s}$ there is given a function

$$\sigma_A : A^w \to A_s$$

where, if $w = s_1...s_n$, then

$$A^w = A_{s_1} \times ... \times A_{s_n}.$$

A first example of what this mathematical framework can do for us is that we can easily go from the notion of a data type (family) as an algebra to the concept of an *abstract data type*. The intuitive idea of an abstract data type is that it is a representation independent, and implementation independent, version of a data type. That is, in the above example, we really were talking in terms of abstract data types, we didn't say anything about the representation of the integers, or how to carry out the integer operations +, * and - in terms of this representation. And while we may tend to think of integers in decimal notation, it does not matter that computers "think" of them in binary notation. This "independence" is captured in the algebraic framework by defining an *abstract data type* to be an isomorphism class of algebras.

Recall that a *homomorphism* between two S-sorted Σ-algebras A and B is an S-indexed family of functions

$$h = < h_s : A_s \to B_s \mid s \epsilon S >$$

such that, for each $\sigma \epsilon \Sigma_{w,s}$, with $w = s_1...s_n$,

$$h_s(\sigma_A(a_1,...,a_n)) = \sigma_B(h_{s_1}(a_1),...,h_{s_n}(a_n))$$

Two algebras, A and B, are *isomorphic* if there exist homomorphisms $h : A \to B$ and $h^{-1} : B \to A$ such that

$$h \cdot h^{-1} = 1_A \text{ and } h^{-1} \cdot h = 1_B$$

The S-sorted Σ-algebras, together with all the homomorphisms between them, form a *category* (see section 4, or [2], for definitions).

Using properties of algebras together with the concepts and language of elementary category theory it has been possible to make great strides in the development of a theory of data types. A well-known example of this is the algebraic specification of data types by means of equations or conditional-axioms (Horn sentences). Given an S-sorted signature Σ and a set E of axioms such as

$$\text{Concat}(s, \text{Empty}) = s$$
$$\text{Concat}(s_1, \text{Concat}(s_2, s_3)) = \text{Concat}(\text{Concat}(s_1, s_2), s_3)$$
$$\cdots$$

there exists a class of all Σ-algebras which satisfy these axioms. This collection of algebras, together with the homomorphisms between them, will again turn out to be a category. The particular class of such algebras that correspond to an abstract data type can be characterized as the class of *initial algebras* in such a category. Where an algebra A is said to be *initial in a category* **Alg** if for each algebra B in **Alg** there is exactly one homomorphism $h_B : A \rightarrow B$. This not only provides a characterization of the desired abstract data type, but it provides the basis for techniques for proving the correctness of specifications, [1].

By exploiting other algebraic and categorical concepts theorists have developed treatments of a large number of other data type concepts including Modularization (specification of data types up to behavioral equivalence), Parameterized data types (e.g., specifying FINITE__SETS__OF__(D) in a way that will work for many choices of D), and a number of abstract approaches to the implementation of Data Types.

3. Some Shortcomings of the Old Approach

The view of a data type as an algebra emphasizes the operations on the data type objects. This lends itself very well to a functional programming approach. However most programming languages are not functional, but imperative. As such they intuitively viewed having an underlying memory (or state, or environment, or store). Consider the following piece of a program:

```
VAR A:INTEGER;
A:=3;
A:=A+1;
```

The first line introduces, or declares, A to be the name of a variable (a memory location) in which we can store an integer; the second line places the integer 3 into that location; the third line says to take the contents of the location, add 1 to it, and put it back in the location.

This obviously involves the data type INTEGER, but it is not explained by the data type INTEGER, that is, by the algebra with, say, sets: INTEGER, BOOL

operations: +, *, -, Equal, ≥, ...

Now the "traditional" approach by data type theorists is to say, "Not to worry, all that assignment and location stuff is really independent of the data type concept." But it is very easy to produce examples where the usual programmers point of view is rather different than the data type theorists. For example, consider the data type ARRAY__(1..n)__OF__INTEGERS. In the usual algebraic model we have something like:

sets: INTEGERS, BOOL, ARRAY__OF__INTEGERS, INDICES-(1..n)

operations: +, *, -, 0, Equal, Access, Update, Initial

Here the ARRAY operations have the following sources and targets

$$\text{Initial:} \rightarrow \text{ARRAY}$$
$$\text{Update: ARRAY} \times \text{INDICES} \times \text{INTEGERS} \rightarrow \text{ARRAY}$$
$$\text{Access: ARRAY} \times \text{INDICES} \rightarrow \text{INTEGERS}$$

Now consider the program
```
VAR A:ARRAY_(1..n)_OF_INTEGER;
A[i]:=A[i]+1;
```
The semantics of the assignment, as given in terms of the above description of the data type ARRAY, must be, "Take the contents α (an ARRAY) of A from memory location A, perform the operation Update(α, i, Access(α, i)+1), put the resulting ARRAY back into memory location A." But most programmers would probably describe the meaning of the assignment as, "Take the contents of A[i], add 1 to it, and put it back in A[i]" That is, we intuitively regard A[i] as a location rather than as an INTEGER, in particular A[i] is regarded as a location that can hold an INTEGER. This "lack of locations" and the consequent problems with ARRAYs are the first shortcoming of the data type theory which we will seek to remedy.

One might argue that there is no real problem here, that if we do not want to regard an ARRAY__(1..n)__OF__INTEGERS as an

(1..n)-indexed set of INTEGERS,

but rather as an

(1..n)-indexed set of INTEGER__holding__locations

then we can capture this within the existing algebraic framework as follows:

sets: INTEGERS, ARRAYS, INT__VARS, STATES, INDICES

operations: Fetch, Put, Access

where here, in contrast to the earlier treatment

$$\text{Fetch: STATE} \times \text{INT\_\_VAR} \rightarrow \text{INTEGER}$$
$$\text{Put: STATE} \times \text{INTEGER} \times \text{INT\_\_VAR} \rightarrow \text{STATE}$$
$$\text{Access: ARRAY} \times \text{INDICES} \rightarrow \text{INT\_\_VAR}$$

Here the INT__VARs (INTEGER__VARIABLES) are, intuitively, locations which can hold INTEGERS, the STATEs are different assignments of INTEGERS to locations, and an ARRAY is viewed, as desired, as an indexed set of INTEGER__VARIABLES.

This is fine as far as it goes. That is, it is clear that we can look at the "memory" in algebraic terms, however,

1) It is not at all clear that we want to define the desired algebra by means of the standard approaches of algebraic data typery, that is, by using axioms and initial (or terminal) semantics. Certainly it can be done. For example, we can define a memory model with INTEGERs, BOOLEANs, INTEGER__VARIABLEs, and STATEs and operations

$$fetch:STATE \times INT\_\_VAR \rightarrow INTEGER$$
$$put:STATE \times INTEGER \times INT\_\_VAR \rightarrow STATE$$
$$if\_\_then\_\_else:BOOLEAN \times INTEGER \times INTEGER \rightarrow INTEGER$$
$$equal: INT\_\_VAR \times INT\_\_VAR \rightarrow BOOLEAN$$
$$empty: \rightarrow STATE \text{ (starting state - "empty memory")}$$

Then the "key" axioms are simple:

$$fetch(empty, V) = 0 \text{ (or whatever integer you want for default)}$$
$$fetch(put(S, I, V_1), V_2) =$$
$$if\_\_then\_\_else(equal(V_1, V_2), I, fetch(S, V1))$$
$$if\_\_then\_\_else(true, I_1, I_2) = I_1$$
$$if\_\_then\_\_else(false, I_1, I_2) = I_2$$
$$equal(V, V) = true$$

HOWEVER, many additional axioms are needed to specify the rest of the "equals" operation, i.e., to state that for each pair, v_1, v_2, of distinct INT__VARs that,

$$equal(v_1, v_2) = false$$

(it would appear that if, say, V has 1000 elements then we will need something on the order of 1,000,000 axioms). This "equals" operation, which is a "hidden function" in the sense that it is probably not wanted as part of the USER-language, cannot be avoided, or made simpler, without putting additional structure on the INT__VARs.

2) It seems wrong that STATES, VARIABLES, and Assignment, despite their central importance in imperative languages, are treated just like an ordinary data type. That is, this treatment does not give them any distinguishing properties despite the fact that they play a distinguished role in programming languages.

This unsatisfying treatment of "memory" is the second shortcoming of the existing theory of data types.

We now come to the third of the shortcomings considered here. The problem of TAGGED__VARIANTS. What is a TAGGED__VARIANT? For those of you familiar with ALGOL'68, they are very similar to a UNION of MODES. For those of you familiar with PASCAL, they are very similar to a tagged-variant part of a RECORD. Intuitively, a TAGGED__VARIANT is a "location" that can hold any one of a fixed set of types and it's contents are always tagged so that you can tell exactly which type of object it contains.

PASCAL users should note that PASCAL variant records don't quite fit this definition as it is possible, in PASCAL, to cheat on the tags in various nefarious (if possibly useful) ways, that for better, or for worse, make it possible to get around the apparent type correctness in PASCAL.

An example of a possibly useful TAGGED__VARIANT might be the following:

```
VAR ANS:TAGGED_VARIANT
      name : CHAR_STRING
      quant: INTEGER≥0
END
```

One might encounter this VARIANT as the form of the data you get back from a request to a data base for "name of the item satisfying a certain predicate", where:

if there is exactly one item satisfying the predicate you get the CHAR__STRING (tagged *name*) which is its name.

otherwise you get back an INTEGER (tagged *quant*) specifying the quantity of items satisfying the predicate. The problem with a TAGGED__VARIANT is how to ensure that it is never used in such a way as to violate type correctness. That is, in terms of the above example, if the TAGGED__VARIANT A "contains"

$$(quant, 3)$$

then we don't want to end up printing out "3" as the name of the desired item. This problem shows up in its purest form if we just try to do the TAGGED__VARIANT as a data type (as an algebra). Since we clearly want to "get things in and out" of the TAGGED__VARIANT it might seem reasonable, as a first attempt, to try

sets: INTEGERS, CHAR__STRINGS, VARIANT

operations: Name__in, Name__out, Quant__in, Quant__out

where

Name__in:CHAR__STRING → VARIANT

Name__out:VARIANT → CHAR__STRING

Quant__in:INTEGERS → VARIANT

Quant__out:VARIANT → INTEGERS

The obvious problem here is what to do with expressions such as

```
Name_out(Quant_in(3))
```

Of course there are "mathematical solutions", such as going to partial or pointed algebras, or introducing special "error-" or "exception-elements" into the sets INTEGER and CHAR__STRING. However, if we are really interested in strong typing, we might take a completely different approach and do something akin to what is done in ALGOL'68, namely, to have operations such as Name__in and Quant__in above, for reading data into TAGGED__VARIANTS, but to introduce a special kind of CASE__STATEMENT for "taking information out of TAGGED__VARIANTS. For example, a CASE__STATEMENT that might be employed with the above TAGGED__VARIANT would be

```
CASE_STATEMENT:  ANS
     (case name)  : PRINT ANS;
     (case quant) : IF ANS=0 THEN PRINT 'No such items';
          ELSE PRINT 'There are' ANS 'such items. Refine
             your query';
END
```

The significant aspect of this solution, is that it falls outside of our present algebraic framework. For the CASE__STATEMENT is a statement, that is, a function from STATES to STATES, and, as such, does not seem to fit into the algebra with the INTEGERS, CHAR__STRINGS, and TAGGED__VARIANT.

If we are not really worried about strong typing but only about type correctness then we need not introduce such a CASE__STATEMENT but we will have to deal with the same question (the same consideration of cases) some-where else in the semantics.

Note further that this problem can not be simply solved by introducing a new sort, STATES into our algebra, be-cause the CASE__STATEMENT takes STATEMENTS as arguments (one for each case). Now we could probably get around this by introducing yet another sort, called STATEMENTS with appropriate additional operations. For example, we would need an operation for constructing CASE__STATEMENTS from other STATEMENTS and then an operation for applying STATEMENTS to STATES. Etc. This is a perfectly feasible program, but seems only too obvious that it is rather *ad hoc*, and that, if mathematics is really able to capture the essence of things, then there must be a way to do it that captures more of the essence of the situation.

We've now seen three shortcomings of the current data type theory. All involve problems with the interface be-tween the current algebraic view of data types and the states, statements, variables, assignment operations, etc. of imperative languages. In the remainder of the paper we show how these shortcomings may be remedied (in reverse order) by means of a relatively simple extension of the algebraic approach.

4. Some Basic Concepts from Category Theory

Definition 4.1. A *category* is a collection of *objects* together with a collection of *morphisms* such that each morphism h "goes from some object (its *source*) to another object (its *target*) (we write h:A→B for "h is a morphism with source A and target B"); that if h:A→B and g:B→C then they have a *composite* h•g:A→C, and this *composition operation* "•" is associative; finally, for each object A there exists an *identity morphism* 1_A:A→A such that h•1_A = h, and 1_A•g = g for all h and g such that the composite is defined. □

The most familiar example of a category, and the important one for this paper, is the category **Set** of sets, in which the objects are all sets and the morphisms are all functions.

Definition 4.2. Let C be a category, I be a set, and K = <k_i | i∈I > be an I-indexed family of objects from C then a *product* for K is a pair consisting of an object, $\prod$K, in C together with an I-indexed family < π_i: $\prod$K→k_i | i∈I >, of morphisms, with the property that if X is any other object in C and F = < α_i:X→k_i | i∈I > is an I-indexed family of morphisms then there exists a unique morphism α:X→$\prod$K such that

$$\alpha \bullet \pi_i = \alpha_i$$

for all i∈I. The morphisms π_i are called the *(product) projections*. The morphism α is called the *(product) mediating morphism* for F. When I is finite we will use special notation, for I = {t_1,...,t_n} we may write the mediating morphism as

$$< t_1 \Leftarrow \alpha_{t_1}, ..., t_n \Leftarrow \alpha_{t_n} >,$$

we may write the product projections as $t_1, ..., t_n$, and, at the risk of some ambiguity, we may write $k_{t_1} \times ... \times k_{t_n}$ rather than $\prod <k_t \mid t \in I >$ for the product object, and write the mediating morphism without the tags, i.e., the mediating morphism given above would be written as $< \alpha_{t_1}, ..., \alpha_{t_n} >$. $\square$

Fact 4.3. In **Set**, given a set T (of *tags*) and a T-index family of sets $<A_t \mid t \in T >$, then a product $\prod <A_t \mid t \in T >$ can be defined as the set of all mappings $p:T \to \bigcup <A_t \mid t \in T >$ such that $p(t) \in A_i$ for each $t \in T$, together with the projection mappings

$$\pi_t: \prod <A_t \mid t \in T > \to A_t$$
$$p \mapsto p(t).$$

$\square$

In category theory every concept, such as product, that is defined in terms of morphisms (arrows) has a corresponding dual concept associated with it, which is defined by reversing all the arrows. The dual to product is coproduct:

Definition 4.4. Let **C** be a category, I be a set, and $K = <k_i \mid i \in I >$ be an I-indexed family of objects from **C** then a *coproduct* for K is a pair consisting of an object, $\bigsqcup K$, in **C** together with an I-indexed family $< \iota_i:k_i \to \bigsqcup K \mid i \in I >$, of morphisms, with the property that if X is any other object in **C** and $F = < \alpha_i:k_i \to X \mid i \in I >$ is an I-indexed family of morphisms then there exists a unique morphism $\alpha: \bigsqcup K \to X$ such that

$$\iota_i \bullet \alpha = \alpha_i$$

for all $i \in I$. The morphisms ι_i are called the *(coproduct) injections*. The morphism α is called the *(coproduct) mediating morphism* for F. When I is finite we will use special notation, for $I = \{t_1, ..., t_n\}$ we may write the mediating morphism as

$$[t_1 \Rightarrow \alpha_{t_1}, ..., t_n \Rightarrow \alpha_{t_n}],$$

we may write the coproduct injections as $t_1, ..., t_n$, and, at the risk of some ambiguity, we may write $k_{t_1} + ... + k_{t_n}$ rather than $\bigsqcup <k_t \mid t \in I >$ for the coproduct object, and write the mediating morphism without the tags, i.e., the mediating morphism given above would be written as $[\alpha_{t_1}, ..., \alpha_{t_n}]$. $\square$

Fact 4.5. In **Set**, given a set T (of *tags*) and a T-indexed family of sets $<A_t \mid t \in T >$, then a coproduct $\bigsqcup <A_t \mid t \in T >$ can be defined as the set

$$\bigcup <\{t\} \times A_t \mid t \in T >$$

together with the injection mappings

$$\iota_t:A_t \to \bigsqcup <A_t \mid t \in T >$$
$$a \mapsto <t, a>$$

$\square$

The following notation is both conventional and useful, given binary products

$$A_1 \xleftarrow{\pi_{A_1}} A_1 \times A_2 \xrightarrow{\pi_{A_2}} A_2$$

and

$$\begin{array}{ccc} \pi_{B_1} & & \pi_{B_2} \\ B_1 \xleftarrow{\hspace{1cm}} & B_1 \times B_2 & \xrightarrow{\hspace{1cm}} B_2 \end{array}$$

and given maps $f_i: A_i \to B_i$, $i = 1, 2$, we write

$$f_1 \times f_2$$

for the mediating morphism

$$< \pi_{A_1} \bullet f_1; \ \pi_{A_2} \bullet f_2 >.$$

Similarly, given binary coproducts

$$\begin{array}{ccc} \iota_{A_1} & & \iota_{A_2} \\ A_1 \xrightarrow{\hspace{1cm}} & A_1 + A_2 & \xleftarrow{\hspace{0.5cm}} A_2 \end{array}$$

and

$$\begin{array}{ccc} \iota_{B_1} & & \iota_{B_2} \\ B_1 \xrightarrow{\hspace{1cm}} & B_1 + B_2 & \xleftarrow{\hspace{0.5cm}} B_2 \end{array}$$

and given maps $f_i: A_i \to B_i$, $i = 1, 2$, we write

$$f_1 + f_2$$

for the mediating morphism

$$< f_1 \bullet \pi_{A_1}; \ f_2 \bullet \pi_{A_2} >.$$

Most of our development will be restricted to algebras over categories in which products and coproducts satisfy the following

Distributivity Requirement: For all objects A, B and C

$$(A \times C) + (B \times C) \cong (A + B) \times C.$$

☐

Fact 4.7. The above distributivity requirement is satisfied in **Set**. Indeed, given a coproduct injections

$$\begin{array}{ccc} \iota_A & & \iota_B \\ A \xrightarrow{\hspace{1cm}} & A + B & \xleftarrow{\hspace{0.5cm}} B \end{array}$$

for $A + B$, the desired isomorphism is

$$[\iota_A \times 1_C; \ \iota_B \times 1_C]$$

or, equivalently

$$\iota_A \times 1_C : A \times C \to (A + B) \times C$$

and

$$\iota_B \times 1_C : B \times C \to (A + B) \times C$$

are coproduct injections for $(A + B) \times C$.

Proof: This is easily seen by looking at the above concrete definitions of coproduct in **Set**, which, when the tags for the coproduct are t_1 and t_2 yield

$$(A \times C) + (B \times C) = (\{t_1\} \times (A \times C)) \cup (\{t_2\} \times (B \times C))$$
$$\cong ((\{t_1\} \times A) \cup (\{t_2\} \times B)) \times C = (A + B) \times C.$$

☐

5. Records and Variants

What is the appropriate way to view RECORDs and VARIANT? One answer is to be found in the folklore of theoretical computer science, namely, as I have most often heard it, "RECORDs are products and VARIANTs are disjoint sums." This is almost what we want but we can make it more precise, more general, and more useful, by re-phrasing it in terms of the elementary category theory concepts of product and coproduct.

Our first message then is that

Records are Products

In particular, given an S-sorted, Σ-algebra, some set I (of tags) and an I-indexed set K of elements of S, we extend A to a new algebra with an additional sort r (for record) with corresponding carrier, $A_r = \prod <A_{k_i} \mid i\epsilon I>$, and an additional operation

$$\pi_j : \prod <A_{k_i} \mid i\epsilon I > \rightarrow A_{k_j}$$

for each $j\epsilon I$. The intuition is that the product projection π_j is the operation for extracting an object of type k_j (ϵS) from the record field with tag j, and the mediating morphism for a family $F = < \alpha_i : X \rightarrow k_i \mid i\epsilon I >$ corresponds to to an operation for producing records from objects in X in such a way that the contents of the record field with tag j is given by the function α_j. (It may be that this is not the way you intuitively perceive records as being, but, as we will show, this is a useful way to look at them.)

It is easy to give examples of RECORDs since they are a familiar programming concept. If we start with given types(sorts) INTEGER, BOOLEAN, and CHAR__STRING, and operations indicated by the signature diagram in Figure 1., then the interpretation of the declaration

```
EMPL = RECORD
          name : CHAR_STRING
          num  : INTEGER
          age  : INTEGER
       END.
```

extends our original algebra A to an algebra B with an additional sort EMPL and additional operations name, num, and age, where

$$B_{INTEGER} = A_{INTEGER}$$

$$B_{BOOLEAN} = A_{BOOLEAN}$$

$$B_{CHARSTRING} = A_{CHARSTRING}$$

$$B_{EMPL} = A_{INTEGER} \times A_{BOOLEAN} \times A_{CHAR\_STRING}$$

and where the new operations are the evident projection functions. We will sometimes find it convenient to write RECORD declarations in the form

```
EMPL = < name : CHAR_STRING; num : INTEGER; age : INTEGER >
```

Another, surprisingly useful, RECORD type is the NULL type which is characterized by the property that its tag set is the empty set $\emptyset$. There is an alternative characterization of such empty products.

Fact 5.1. Let C be a category, then an object X in C is an ∅-indexed product iff for every object Y in C there is exactly one morphism $F_Y:\to X$, i.e., X is a *terminal* object in C.

Proof: This is a direct consequence of the definition of product. □

Not all categories have terminal objects, but **Set** does, indeed,

Fact 5.2. The terminal objects in **Set** are precisely the singleton sets (sets with exactly one element). □

An important property of terminal objects is the following

Fact 5.3. Let T be a terminal object in a category C, then for any object K in C
$$K \times T \cong K \cong T \times K.$$

Proof: We shall prove that $K \cong K \times T$. Let the product be given as as follows

$$K \xrightarrow{\;\;\pi_1\;\;} K \times T \xleftarrow{\;\;\pi_2\;\;} T$$

Now where $F_K:K\to T$ is the unique morphism from K to T, and $1_K:K\to K$ is the identity on K, we get a mediating morphism $<1_K, F_K>:K\to K\times T$. We claim this is the desired isomorphism, with inverse π_1. It is immediate from the definition of mediating morphism that
$$<1_K, F_K>\bullet\pi_1 = 1_K$$
Next consider $\pi_1\bullet<1_K, F_K>$. We have
$$\pi_1\bullet<1_K, F_K>\bullet\pi_1 = \pi_1\bullet 1_K = \pi_1$$
and
$$\pi_1\bullet<1_K, F_K>\bullet\pi_2 = \pi_1\bullet F_K$$
But $\pi_2:K\times T\to T$, and $\pi_1\bullet F_K:K\times T\to T$, so, since T is terminal, $\pi_1\bullet F_K = \pi_2$. Thus
$$\pi_1\bullet<1_K, F_K> = <\pi_1, \pi_2> = 1_{K\times T}$$
and so $<1_K, F_K>$ is an isomorphism. □

That is enough, for now on RECORDs and products. Let us turn now to our second message, namely that

Variants are Coproducts.

In particular, given an S-sorted, Σ-algebra, some set I (of tags) and an I-indexed set K of elements of S, we extend A to a new algebra with an additional sort v (for variant) with corresponding carrier, $A_v = \underset{i}{\coprod}<A_{k_i} \mid i\epsilon I>$, and an additional operation
$$\iota_j:A_{k_j}\to\underset{j}{\coprod}<A_{k_i} \mid i\epsilon I>,$$
for each $j\epsilon I$. The intuition is that the coproduct injection ι_j is the operation for putting an object of type k_j (ϵS) with tag j, into the variant, and the mediating morphism for a family $F = <\alpha_i:k_i\to X \mid i\epsilon I>$ corresponds to the case-statement where the desired behavior in the ith case is given by α_i. Note that the mediating morphisms are more

general than case-statements since they are not restricted to operating on the state (indeed, at this point we don't even have a state).

VARIANTs are typically used to produce variant fields in RECORDs (as in PASCAL) but, from a theoretical, if possibly impractical, point of view, they can be employed much more widely. To begin with, any finite type (together with its operations) can be defined as a VARIANT. We say a type is *finite* if there are only finitely many elements of the type (i.e., if the carrier is finite). A simple, but well-known, example of a finite type is the type BOOLEAN which, of course, has just two elements. We can define it as the VARIANT

```
BOOLEAN = VARIANT
            true  : NULL;
            false : NULL;
          END.
```

(where NULL is as defined above in the discussion of RECORDs), or, more compactly, we can write the declarations as

```
BOOLEAN = [ true : NULL; false : NULL ]
```

The usual BOOLEAN operations can be defined using appropriate mediating morphisms. For example negation is the mediating morphism, neg:BOOLEAN$\rightarrow$BOOLEAN

$$\text{neg} = [\text{ true} \Rightarrow \text{false; false} \Rightarrow \text{true].}$$

It is slightly more complicated to define operations with more that one argument, such as and:BOOLEAN$\times$BOOLEAN$\rightarrow$BOOLEAN. Let us write B for BOOLEAN, and 1_B for $1_{BOOLEAN}$ (the identity on BOOLEAN), then

$$\text{and} \quad = [\ (\text{true} \times 1_B) \Rightarrow [\ \text{true} \Rightarrow \text{true; false} \Rightarrow \text{false}]; (\text{false} \times 1_B) \Rightarrow \text{false }]$$
$$= [\ (\text{true} \times 1_B) \Rightarrow 1_B; (\text{false} \times 1_B) \Rightarrow F_B \bullet \text{false }].$$

The following diagram displays the whole construction

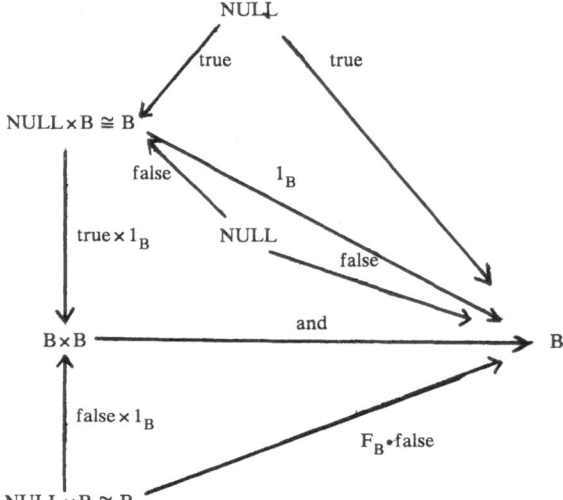

6. Memories and Assignments

Probably the simplest, "high-level" notion of memory is that in which a memory state is viewed as a mapping from "identifiers" to "values". In a context where there are values of different types then, in general, the "identifiers" are "typed" in the sense that the different states always map a given identifer to values of a fixed type. We will call such a simple memory an *environment*.

In a program an environment is built up by means of declaring (and initializing) the identifiers. Given an enviroment E, and a declared (and initialized) identifier I we have two operations: one, an operation "I", which fetches the value of I in E, and two, given an expression (term) e, an operation "$I:=e$" which yields a new environment which is the same as E except at I where it have the value of e as evaluated in E.

It doesn't take much thought to see that such an environment, together with its operations, is very much like a record (a product). Indeed, if if we have data types given by an S-sorted Σ-algebra A and we wish to declare an environment E where **Id** is the set of declared identifiers wherein $I_i \epsilon$**Id** is declared to be of type (i.e., sort) $\tau(I_i) \epsilon S$, then the set of memory states is exactly the same as the set of records with tag set **Id** = { $I_1,...,I_n$}, where the ith tag has type $\tau(I_i)$, the fetch operation for identifier I_i is exactly the product projection I_i: $\prod <A_{\tau(I_j)} \mid I_j \epsilon$**Id** $> \rightarrow A_{\tau(I_i)}$. Finally, a mediating morphism

$$< I_1 \Leftarrow e_1,...,I_n \Leftarrow e_n>$$

from $\prod <A_{\tau(I_j)} \mid I_j \epsilon$**Id** $>$ to itself corresponds to a *concurrent assignment*

$$I_1, I_2, ..., I_n := e_1, e_2, ..., e_n;$$

where, simultaneously, for all $i=1,...,n$, I_i is assigned the value of the "expression" e_i. *Ordinary assignment* (assignment to a single identifier or variable) is just a special case of this concurrent assignment. In particular, for $I \epsilon$**Id** and an appropriate "expression" e (i.é., an expression of the type corresponding to I), the assignment $I:=e$ is precisely the mediating morphism

$$< I_1 \Leftarrow e_1,...,I_n \Leftarrow e_n>: \prod <A_{\tau(I_j)} \mid I_j \epsilon$$**Id** $> \rightarrow \prod <A_{\tau(I_j)} \mid I_j \epsilon$**Id** $>$$

in which, if $I = I_i \epsilon$**Id** then $e_i=e$, and for $j \neq i$, $e_j=I_j$, the jth projection function.

In the preceeding section we showed how the "declaring" of RECORDs and VARIANTs could be viewed as a construction adding new sorts and operations to an algebra. The "declaring" of VARiables is again a construction on algebras, which introduces a new sort, the *environment*, an introduces a new operation (projection function) for each declared VARiable. We can also treat the "declaration" of CONSTants within our algebraic framework. The declaration of, say, an INTEGER CONSTant K of value 17, introduces a constant function K with value 17 (in effect the declaration adds a the constant symbol K and an axiom, K=17). For example, if we start from the algebra given in Figure 1, and make the following declarations:

```
TYPE ANS = [ quant:INTEGER; explan:CHAR_STRING ];
TYPE EMPL = < name:CHAR_STRING; age:INTEGER;
    num:INTEGER >;
VAR V1 : EMPL;
VAR V2 : INTEGER;
VAR V3 : INTEGER;
CONST K1 := 13;
CONST K2 := 'YeS';
```

Then the resulting algebra has the signature indicated in Figure 2. and, in addition to having the special properties associated with the definitions of RECORD, VARIANT, and environment, the new algebra also satisfies the two axioms K1 = 13 and K2 = 'YeS', which force the desired interpretation of the constants.

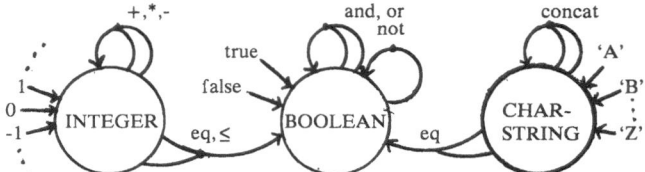

Figure 1. The Algebra Before the Declarations

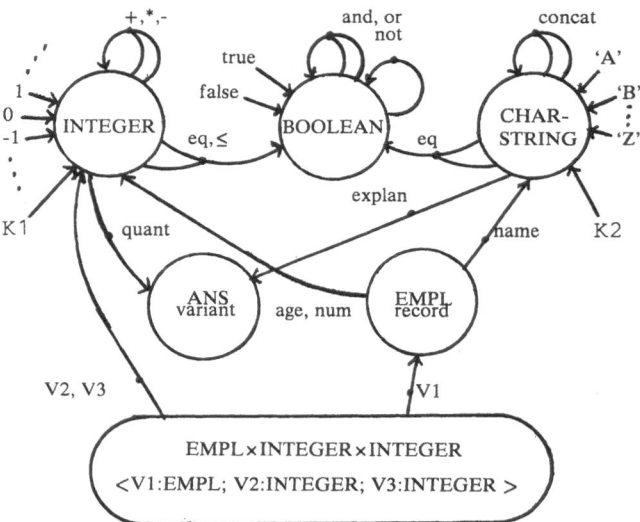

Figure 2. The Algebra After the Declarations

7. If–Then–Else and While–do

In the preceeding section we exploited the product to capture the notions of a environment and assignment operations on environments. This is enough to allow the writing of straight-line programs, but to get interesting programs we need to introduce some sort of conditional, and some form of iteration. These we can get by exploitation of the coproduct.

By a *statement* in a programming language we mean a function from the environment to itself. Consider the statement, "If P then F else G" where P is a predicate on the environment and F and G are statements. Assuming P is well-defined, we can partition the environment into two sets

$$E_P = \{ e \mid e\epsilon E \text{ and } P(e) \},$$

and

$$E_{\neg P} = \{ e \mid e\epsilon E \text{ and } \neg P(e) \}.$$

It is immediate that, $E = E_P \cup E_{\neg P}$, with the evident inclusion mappings ι_P and $\iota_{\neg P}$ as injections, is a coproduct. But then it follows that the coproduct mediating morphism

$$[\, \iota_P \bullet F;\ \iota_{\neg P} \bullet G \,]$$

is exactly the function we want as the semantics of "If P then F else G".

We do not need to restrict ourselves to statements (i.e., functions on the environment). Given any sets X and Y, a predicate P on X, the resulting partition of X into X_P and $X_{\neg P}$, and functions $F:X \rightarrow Y$ and $G:X \rightarrow Y$, the mediating morphism

$$[\, \iota_P \bullet F;\ \iota_{\neg P} \bullet G \,]$$

yields the desired conditional from X to Y.

Indeed there is a sense in which this works in an arbitrary category. Let X_1 and X_2 be objects in an arbitrary category and let $X_1 + X_2$ be their coproduct with injections $\iota_i:X_i \rightarrow X_1 + X_2$, i=1,2. Given $F_i:X_i \rightarrow Z$, i=1,2, let

$$H = [\, \iota_1 \bullet F_1;\ \iota_2 \bullet F_2 \,]$$

be the corresponding mediating morphism. Now given any other object K and morphism $f:K \rightarrow X_1 + X_2$ let us say f *is in* X_i iff there exists a mapping $g_i:K \rightarrow X_i$ such that $g_i \bullet \iota_i = f$. Then we have

Fact 7.1. Let H and f be defined as above, then f *is in* X_i implies

$$f \bullet H = f \bullet F_i.$$

Proof: We have

$$
\begin{aligned}
f \bullet H &= f \bullet [\, \iota_1 \bullet F_1;\ \iota_2 \bullet F_2 \,] && \text{def. H}\\
&= g \bullet \iota_i \bullet [\, \iota_1 \bullet F_1;\ \iota_2 \bullet F_2 \,] && \text{def. f}\\
&= g \bullet (\iota_i \bullet F_i) && \text{def. coproduct}\\
&= f \bullet F_i && \text{def. f}
\end{aligned}
$$

□

The difficulty here is, of course, that it may happen that f *is in* neither X_1 nor X_2. However, in the case the category is **Set**, is the category of sets, then taking K to be a singleton set makes f *is in* X_i the same as $f \epsilon X_i$, (identify f with the image, under f, of the one-and-only element of K).

Having captured If-Then-Else with the coproduct, we are in position to capture While-do by going only one step further. This time let us begin with the abstract setting, i.e., in an arbitrary category **C** let us be given objects, X_1 and X_2 together with their coproduct $X_1 + X_2$ and coproduct injections $\iota_i:X_i \rightarrow X_1 + X_2$, i=1,2, and another morphism $F:X_1 + X_2 \rightarrow X_1 + X_2$ Then we claim that a suitable semantics for "While [*in*] X_1 Do F" is any function W from $X_1 + X_2$ to itself such that

$$W = [\, \iota_1 \bullet F \bullet W; \quad \iota_2 \,]$$

As a first step toward establishing this claim we prove

Lemma 7.2. Let F and W be as above, then for all $n \geq 0$,

$$W = [\iota_1 \bullet F; \iota_2\,]^n \bullet W.$$

Proof: We have

W	$= [\, \iota_1 \bullet F \bullet W; \iota_2\,]$	def. W
	$= [\, \iota_1 \bullet F \bullet [\, \iota_1 \bullet F \bullet W; \iota_2\,]; \iota_2\,]$	def. W
	$= [\, \iota_1 \bullet F \bullet [\, \iota_1 \bullet F \bullet W; \iota_2\,]; \iota_2 \bullet [\, \iota_1 \bullet F \bullet W; \iota_2\,]\,]$	def. coproduct
	$= [\, \iota_1 \bullet F; \iota_2\,] \bullet [\, \iota_1 \bullet F \bullet W; \iota_2\,]$	factoring
	$= [\, \iota_1 \bullet F; \iota_2\,] \bullet W$	def. W

and we are done. $\square$

We now prove our main result which shows that our formal version of WHILE-DO captures our intuitive notion of WHILE-DO for "terminating cases".

Proposition 7.3. Let $W = [\, \iota_1 \bullet F \bullet W; \iota_2\,]$ as above. If $f : K \to X_1 + X_2$ such that $f \bullet F^k$ *is in* X_1 for $k = 0, 1, \ldots, n-1$, and $f \bullet F^n$ *is in* X_2 then

$$f \bullet W = f \bullet F^n.$$

Proof: We proceed by induction on n. To begin, let $n = 0$, then $f = f \bullet F^0$ *is in* X_2 so there exists $g_2 : K \to X_2$ such that $g_2 \bullet \iota_2 = f$, but then

$f \bullet W$	$= f \bullet [\, \iota_1 \bullet F \bullet W; \iota_2\,]$	def. W
	$= g_2 \bullet \iota_2 \bullet [\, \iota_1 \bullet F \bullet W; \iota_2\,]$	f in X_2
	$= g_2 \bullet (\iota_2)$	def. coproduct
	$= f$	def. f
	$= f \bullet F^0$	def. F^0

so the result is true for $n = 0$. Now assume that the result is proved for $n = t \geq 0$, and consider the case for $n = t+1$. Since $f \bullet F^j$ *is in* X_1 for all $j \leq t$, and $f \bullet F^{t+1}$ *is in* X_2, it follows that f *is in* X_1, so say $f = g_1 \bullet \iota_1$, then we have

$f \bullet W$	$= g_1 \bullet \iota_1 \bullet W$	def. f
	$= g_1 \bullet \iota_1 \bullet [\, \iota_1 \bullet F; \iota_2\,] \bullet W$	Fact 7.2
	$= g_1 \bullet (\iota_1 \bullet F) \bullet W$	def. coproduct
	$= (f \bullet F) F^t$	induction
	$= f F^{t+1}$	

and we are done. $\square$

Again, if the category being considered is **Set**, then taking K to be any singleton set makes f *is in* X_i the same as $f \epsilon X_i$, and so the above result yields the desired answer for WHILE-DO for all $f \epsilon X_1 + X_2$ where there exists n such that $xF^n \epsilon X_2$. The above result does not tell us about the value of fW if for all n, $fF^n \notin X_2$. It is easy to prove that there exists solutions in that case but they are not unique.

8. Exceptions and Exception Handling

If we wish, say, to define a division operation on INTEGERs then we have to cope with the problem of division by 0. One way to cope with such exceptions is to introduce an "new INTEGER", say `div-error`, to be the result of the computation in the case of division by 0.

This can be formalized by replacing the INTEGERs by

```
E-INTEGER = [ ordinary : INTEGER; div-error : NULL ];
```

that is, by using a **VARIANT** (a coproduct). The mediating morphisms provide a means for extending the original INTEGER operations to E-INTEGER operations. For example, we can extend the addition operation $+:\text{INTEGER} \times \text{INTEGER} \to \text{INTEGER}$ to a new operation

$$\oplus : \text{E-INTEGER} \times \text{E-INTEGER} \to \text{E-INTEGER}$$

defined by the mediating morphism

$$\oplus = [\ (\text{ordinary} \times 1_{\text{E-INT}}) \Rightarrow [\ (\text{ordinary} \times 1_{\text{INT}}) \Rightarrow +;\ (\text{div-error} \times 1_{\text{INT}}) \Rightarrow \text{div-error}\ ];$$
$$(\text{div-error} \times 1_{\text{E-INT}}) \Rightarrow \text{div-error}\ ]$$

which defines $\oplus$ so that it strictly preserves `div-error`.

We can, however, go even further in our current framework and specify the desired effect of such an "error" on the overall state. For example, consider the following program:

```
VAR A, B : INTEGER;
BEGIN
   A := 11;
   B := 0;
   A := A/B;
END.
```

What do we want the meaning to be of this program? Clearly we could introduce an "error state" into the environment in the same way as we introduced it into the INTEGERs and have the assignment A := A/B produce this "error state". However this is really not what happens in "real life". A much "realer" scenario would be to have a CHAR-STRING, such as

`'Exception raised: Division by Zero'`

appear on the console screen. We can capture this (specify this) easily in the current framework by adding to the environment E an additional component, `console` of type CHAR-STRING, and taking the defining the assignment so that it changes the contents of A to A/B when the exception is not raised (i.e., B≠0), but "writes" the string s = `'Exception raised: Division by Zero'` when the exception is raised. We can get the desired behavior within our formal framework as follows:

Let EI denote E-INTEGER, I denote INTEGER, N denote NULL, and let s and E be as above, then the desired function is $<A/B; 1_E> \cdot M$, where M is the mediating morphism indicated in the following diagram and π_1 and π_2 are the indicated projection functions.

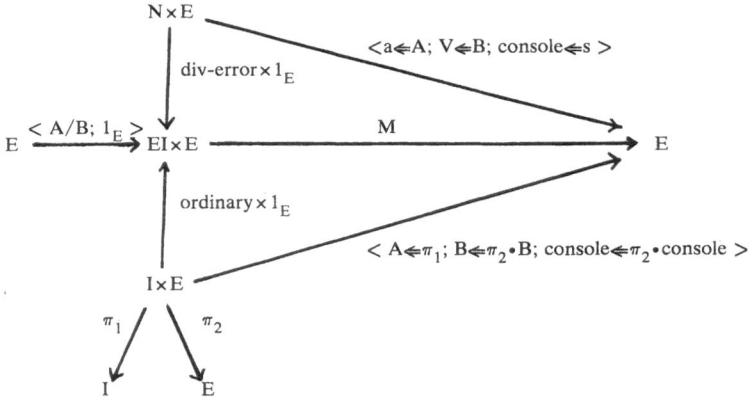

9. About those ARRAYs

In the earlier version of this material [3] presented at the 1984 Workshop on the Theory and Application of Abstract Data Types, the treatment of ARRAY's employed a more complex memory model than the one given here. (That model, which abstracts the notion of a store, rather than an environment, will be treated in a separate paper.) However it is perfectly possible to give a treatment of ARRAYs with the framework of environments. One way to do this is as follows:

A declaration of an ARRAY VARiable,

```
      VAR A : ARRAY (1..5) OF INTEGER;
```
will be regarded as an environment constructing operation which adds a factor of INTEGER×INTEGER×INTEGER×INTEGER×INTEGER and projection functions $A[1], \ldots, A[5]$, to the environment (product). Expressions of the form $A[3]:=7$ or $3+A[4]$ are then given meaning in the same way as we earlier gave meaning to expressions containing "declared identifiers". But more remains to be done, we need to be able to give meaning to expressions such as $A[I]$, where $I \in$ **Id**, in programs such as

```
      VAR J : INTEGER;
      VAR I : (1..5);
      VAR A : ARRAY (1..5) OF INTEGER;
      BEGIN
       I := 1;
       J := 1;
       WHILE I≤5 DO
        A[I] := I;
        J := J*A[I];
        I := I+1;
       END;
      END.
```

That is, how do we interpret the expression $A[I]$ on the left and right side of assignments.

There are other important problems here as well, such as, how do we interpret $(1..5)$ so that $I := I+1$ is meaningful, and what is the meaning, if any, of expressions such as $I+13$? We will deal, briefly, with these problems before we answer the question on ARRAY's.

Now $(1..5)$ could be viewed as a finite type with just five elements, and we could define special "INTEGER-like" operations on it, making *ad hoc* decisions respecting "exceptional situations" such as "5+1". However, our mathematical framework allows us to do better than this with very little work. Namely, we can view $(1..5)$ as the finite type given by the variant

$$(1..5) =$$
$$[\ 1\text{:NULL}; \ 2\text{:NULL}; \ 3\text{:NULL}; \ 4\text{:NULL}; \ 5\text{:NULL}; \ ex\text{-}(1..5)\text{:NULL} \ \ ]$$

which contains an exception tag, $ex\text{-}(1..5)$. Let EXT-INTEGER be the following extension of INTEGER
$$\text{EXT-INTEGER} = [\ \text{ordinary:INTEGER; ex-Int:NULL} \ ]$$
There is an obvious embedding of $(1..5)$ into EXT-INTEGER, which may be specificed by the mediating morphism
$$\text{In} = [\ 1{\Rightarrow}1; \ 2{\Rightarrow}2; \ 3{\Rightarrow}3; \ 4{\Rightarrow}4; \ 5{\Rightarrow}5; \ \text{ex-(1..5)}{\Rightarrow}\text{ex-Int} \ ]$$

There is also a morphism in the other direction
$$\text{Out} = [\ \{1\}{\Rightarrow}1; \ \{2\}{\Rightarrow}2; \ \{3\}{\Rightarrow}3; \ \{4\}{\Rightarrow}4; \ \{5\}{\Rightarrow}5; \ \{...\text{-}1, 0, 6, ...,\ \text{ex-Int}\}{\Rightarrow}\text{ex-(1..5)} \ ]$$

Using these operations In and Out we can interpret the above expression $"I+1$ as an abbreviation for
$$\text{Out(In}(I)+1)$$

(remember that, by the declaration in the program, I is a projection function from the environment (product) into $(1..5)$, so that the above expression is also a function from the environment to $(1..5)$ and so the assignment, $I := I + 1$ is well-defined (though the result may be "exceptional").

Now that we have $(1..5)$ well-defined, let us look at $A[I]$ on the right-side of an assignment statement. It seems clear that what we want for $A[I]$ is a function
$$A[I]: (1..5) \times E {\rightarrow} \text{EXT-INTEGER},$$
which yields the evident "ARRAY component" from E (or, when appropriate, yields $ex\text{-}Int$). The desired function is the following mediating morphism
$$[\ (1 \times 1_E){\Rightarrow} \ A[1]; (2 \times 1_E){\Rightarrow} \ A[2]; (3 \times 1_E){\Rightarrow} \ A[3];$$
$$(4 \times 1_E){\Rightarrow} \ A[4]; (5 \times 1_E){\Rightarrow} \ A[5]; (\text{ex-(1..5)} \times 1_E){\Rightarrow} \ \text{ex-Int} \ ]$$

(Note that we are exploiting the fact that $\text{NULL} \times E {\cong} E$.)

It remains to take care of appearences of $A[I]$ on the left-sides of assignment statements, i.e., to define assignment to $A[I]$. This obviously involves some decision on how to handle the exceptional cases. This can be done as in the preceeding section or however the reader chooses. But the basic assignment "$A[I] :=$" is a function

$$(A[I] :=) : (1..5) \times \text{EXT-INTEGER} \times E \rightarrow E$$

given by a mediating morphism

$$[(1 \times 1_{E\text{-}I} \times 1_E) \Rightarrow A[1] := \pi_1 ; (2 \times 1_{E\text{-}I} \times 1_E) \Rightarrow A[2] := \pi_1 ;$$
$$(3 \times 1_{E\text{-}I} \times 1_E) \Rightarrow A[3] := \pi_1 ; (4 \times 1_{E\text{-}I} \times 1_E) \Rightarrow A[4] := \pi_1 ;$$
$$(5 \times 1_{E\text{-}I} \times 1_E) \Rightarrow A[5] := \pi_1 ;$$
$$(ex\text{-}(1..5) \times 1_{E\text{-}I} \times 1_E) \Rightarrow \textit{reader's choice} \ > .$$

Where we identify $\text{NULL} \times E\text{-}I \times E$ with $E\text{-}I \times E$, and the indicated assignments "$A[i] := \pi_1$" are given the usual semantics for assignment to variables as explained in Section 6. Note that this mediating morphism is just a very precisely written conditional statement.

10. Some Concluding Remarks

All the program-pieces in the paper that were written in terms of mediating morphisms for coproducts can be rewritten in terms of conditionals. Thus one might ask, why not stick with the familiar If__the__else and forget the categorical notation. The answer is that mediating morphisms for coproducts and products (together with their associated injection or projection morphisms) have the advantage that they can be manipulated, in a well-established manner, to prove various results (e.g., the results given in Section 7). I suggest that the results given here only scratch the surface (if that) and that much more can be done, both in regard to making folklore mathematically precise and in regard developing useful program transformations.

We have shown in this paper how to present finite types in terms of coproducts (VARIANTs). It should be evident that one can go beyond this to recursive types defined in terms of $+$ and $\times$. Given both finite and recursive types we then have enough power to define, up to behavioral equivalence, types such as FINITE__SETS__OF__INTEGERs. Thus starting from only products and coproducts we can build up very powerful (i.e. expressive) languages.

Products (resp. coproducts) are special examples of limits (resp. colimits). This suggests that we ought be able to get an even richer framework by going to limits and colimits. Actually, we are almost there since, as is well-known, having all small limits is equivalent to having equalizers and all small products (and, of course, there is a corresponding result for colimits, coproducts and coequalizers). However having arbitrary limits permits us to define some interesting types such as "speadsheet"-like objects, i.e., classes of RECORDs in which there is some built-in relationship between certain fields (e.g., that one field is always the sum of all the others).

As noted in the Introduction, there was material in the original talk that is not contained in this paper. That material, on what we called *pointer algebras*, shows how to extend this approach to languages that have STOREs rather than ENVIRONMENTs, and thus allows us to treat such dynamic types as POINTERs.

11. Bibliography

[1]   ADJ (Goguen, J.A., Thatcher, J.W., Wagner, E.G.), "An Initial Algebra Approach to the Specification, Correctness, and Implementation of Abstract Data Types," in *Current Trends in Programming Methodology, Volume IV*, (R. Yeh, Editor), Prentice-Hall, Inc. Englewood Cliffs, NJ, 1978.

[2]   MacLane, S. *Categories for the Working Mathematician*, Springer-Verlag, New York, Heidelberg, Berlin, 1971.

[3]   Wagner, E.G., "Categorical Semantics, or Extending Data Types to Include Memory," presented at the 3rd Workshop on Theory and Applicatons of Abstract Data Types, in Bremen, West Germany, 12-16 November, 1984.

ALGEBRAIC (?) SPECIFICATION OF CONCEPTUAL DATABASE SCHEMATA
(Extended Abstract)

H.-D. Ehrich

Inst.f.Informatik, PF 3329, D-3300 Braunschweig

1. Introduction

This contribution does not present any technical results. Rather, it is an attempt to broaden the view towards specification problems and algebraic methods.

Algebraic specification of abstract data types is, by now, a well developed discipline. There are two comprehensive textbooks available [Kl83, EM85], and others are likely to follow. It is interesting to note that both textbooks call their subject just "algebraic specification", obviously assuming that there can be no doubt about <u>what</u> is to be specified. Indeed, up to now, interest exclusively concentrated on the specification of abstract data types, modelled as classes of many-sorted algebras, specified by signatures, axioms in some predicate calculus, and algebraic concepts like initiality, terminality, etc. to further constrain the class of models.

There are, however, other specification problems in software development. We claim that, for instance, the problem of specifying a conceptional database schema is different from that of specifying an abstract data type. We will also argue that algebraic concepts and techniques might prove usefull here, too. We have not in mind to model a conceptual database schema as an algebraic data type. This is possible in principle [EKW78, DMW82], but it seems to be inappropiate to do so. At least, this approach is incompatible with all data modelling approaches taken in the database field. The deeper reason is that algebraic data type specification is based on purely applicative concepts providing no means of directly modelling storage concepts like variables, etc., whereas concepts of storage are very central for databases.

2. Database Specification in Layers

Data modelling approaches (see [TL82] for a recent textbook) have a notion of "entity" or "object" that is not just a data element. While a data sort like bool, nat, int, text, etc. is naturally interpreted by a fixed set of data elements (taking, of course, the operations defined on them into account), an object sort like PERSON, PROJECT, etc. essentially denotes a time-varying collection of objects of that sort, and it is the objective of a database to store information about the objects "currently in" the database, like salary or age of a person, manager or set of employees in a project, etc.

Modelling this situation by means of abstract data types would require to add "database states" as an extra data sort, with operations like insert, delete, retrieve operating on it. This approach of viewing a database state as an atomic data element in an abstract data type looks strange to most database people. They are used to view a database state as a large, sometimes sophisticated structure. This view is nicely captured in a suggestion made in [GMS83] to consider database states as "possible worlds" in a modal system of algebras. We have taken up this approach [ELG84, LEG85], concentrating on dynamic database constraints expressed in a temporal logic. Updates and views are treated in [KMS85] using this approach. Temporal logic has been used before in database specification [Se80, CCF82, CF82, Ku84], following more or less the abstract data type point of view.

One of the main features of our modal approach is that the specification of data and objects in a conceptual database schema can be separated into two layers:

data layer: here we imagine a set of abstract data types like bool, int, etc., specified algebraically by one of the approaches advocated in the literature. The abstract data types have a fixed interpretation not changing in time. Thus, there is only one "fixed world of data elements" (that is part of every possible world constituting a database state).

object layer: here we have the objects, attributes and relation-
         ships that determine the structure of database
         states. Database states change in time, and it is the
         objective of the object specification to characterize
         the permissible states as "possible worlds" in a
         modal logic, together with the permissible state
         changes.

There is another layer on top of the object layer, specifying
the state-dependent operations or "transactions". These consist
of aggregate functions like average or minimal salary of persons
in the database state, and state changing operations like insert,
delete and update. We will not consider transactions here, but
concentrate on data and object layers.

Attributes and Relationships are uniformly modelled in the functional approach to data modelling [BF79, Sh81]. We adopt this
approach, since it opens the way for applying algebraic concepts
to the object level.

3. Object specifications

In order to make the above ideas precise, let $\Sigma_D=(S_D,\Omega_D)$ be a
data signature, where S_D is a set of data sorts, and Ω_D is an
$S_D^* \times S_D$-indexed family of data operators. We assume a fixed data
algebra A that serves as the standard interpretation of Σ_D in
each database state, thus building an invariant part of the
database.

An object signature Σ_O is a signature extension of the data
signature,

$$\Sigma_O = \Sigma_D + (S_O,\Omega_O).$$

S_O is a set of object sorts, and Ω_O is an $S^* \times S$-indexed set of
object functions, where $S=S_D \cup S_O$. A (database) state is an interpretation of Σ_O, i.e. a mapping σ associating a set $\sigma(s)$ with
each sort $s \in S$ and an operation $\sigma(f)$ with each operator $f \in \Omega = \Omega_D \cup \Omega_O$,
such that $\sigma(f) : \sigma(s_1) \times \ldots \times \sigma(s_n) \rightarrow \sigma(s_0)$ for each $f : s_1 \times \ldots$
$s_n \rightarrow s_0 \in \Omega$ and $\sigma|\Sigma_D=A$. In this sense, the object layer is "built
upon" the data layer. For $s \in S_O$, we call $\sigma(s)$ the set of "actual"
objects, and for $f \in \Omega_O$. we call $\sigma(f)$ the "actual" object function

in state σ. In order to constrain the class of possible states, we assume a set π(s) of "possible" objects for each s∈S_O, and σ(s)⊆π(s) for each s∈S_O. We call π(s) the <u>universe</u> of object sort s.

Thus, database states are algebras. It is also possible to extend the universe π by setting π(Σ_D)=σ(Σ_D)=A and also adding some meaningful object functions to it, so that universes are algebras, too. We will elaborate on this point in a forthcoming paper.

Attributes are object functions of the special form a:s->t, where s∈S_O and t∈S_D. An example is age : PERSON -> <u>nat</u>. "Object constants" v:->t of a data sort t∈S_D can serve as simple variables of sort t.

The <u>specification</u> of an object schema has to characterize the permissible states and the permissible state changes. For the data layer, this amounts to specifying the data algebra A, and this is the classical specification problem for abstract data types. Thus, we assume an algebraic specification D=(Σ_D,E_D), where E_D is a set of axioms (e.q. equations, initiality constraints, etc.), such that the semantics of D is A (up to isomorphism).

For the object layer, we have to extend the data specification D by Σ_O-axioms C_O,

$$O = D + (\Sigma_O,C_O) .$$

We call the axioms in C_O (object or database) <u>constraints</u>. C_O will contain <u>static</u> and <u>dynamic</u> constraints. Static constraints characterize the permissible states, and that can be coped with by giving a loose specification using some (first order) predicate calculus. In order to give dynamic constraints characterizing permissible state changes, however, we have to leave the grounds of conventional algebraic specification and extend our logic by temporal aspects.

Temporal Logic was originated in [RU71] and has been applied to the specification and verification of programs in [MP79]. Application of Temporal Logic to database specification was originated in [Se80] and developed in [CCF82, CF82, Ku84]. Our simplified

version of Temporal Logic uses two temporal quantifiers, <u>always</u>..
<u>until</u>.. and <u>sometimes</u>.. <u>before</u>.., as well as quantification $\forall$,
$\exists$ over actual objects (states) and $\underline{\forall}$, $\underline{\exists}$ over possible objects
(universes). Models of temporal formulas are sequences

$$\underline{\sigma} = (\sigma_0, \sigma_1, \sigma_2, \ldots)$$

of structures (states, in our case), thus modelling the development of a database in time.

Now, the objective of an object specification $O=D+(\Sigma_O, C_O)$ is to
characterize a class of permissible state sequences $\underline{\sigma}$:

$$[O] = \{ \underline{\sigma} \mid \underline{\sigma} \vDash C_O \}$$

The details of our Temporal Logic and its semantics can be found
in [LEG85], together with results how to enforce a special class
of temporal database constraints operationally, i.e. how to recognize as early as possible whether a given state sequence $\underline{\sigma}$ is
permissible, inspecting its prefixes $[\sigma_0, \ldots \sigma_n]$, $n \geq 0$.

4. Conclusions

Many problems are open in the field of conceptual database
specification. Of particular interest here is that it would be
nice to have an algebraic semantics for an object specification,
associating with it a fixed algebra (up to isomorphism) as a
standard universe, and characterizing the class of algebras that
can represent database states within this standard universe. The
class of permissible state sequences is then well defined by the
semantics of the Temporal Logic. Having a theoretically well
founded and usefull specification methodology for data and objects, however, is only a first step towards the ultimate goal of
establishing software correctness and reliability. The logical
next step is to elaborate the transaction layer and see how the
database constraints can be taken into consideration and, hope-
fully, be enforced there. Here again, we have another specification problem that might require different concepts and
techniques.

References

BF79   Buneman, P. / Frankel, R.E. : FQL - A Functional Query Language. Proc. ACM SIGMOD Int. Conf. on Management of Data 1979, 52-58

CCF82   Castilho, J.M.V. / Casanova, M.A. / Furtado, A.L. : A Temporal Framework for Database Specifications. Proc. 8th Int. Conf. on Very Large Data Bases, Mexico 1982

CF82   Casanova, M.A. / Furtado, A.L. : A Family of Temporal Languages for the Description of Transition Constraints. Proc. Workshop on Logical Bases for Data Bases, Toulouse 1982

DMW82   Dosch, W. / Mascari, G. / Wirsing, M. : On the Algebraic Specification of Databases. Proc. 8th Int. Conf. on Very Large Data Bases, Mexico City 1982

EKW78   Ehrig, H. / Kreowski, H.J. / Weber, H. : Algebraic Specification Schemes for Database Systems. Proc. 4th Int. Conf. on Very Large Data Bases, Berlin 1978

ELG84   Ehrich, H.-D. / Lipeck, U.W. / Gogolla, M. : Specification, Semantics, and Enforcement of Dynamic Database Constraints. Proc. 10th Int. Conf. on Very Large Data Bases, Singapore 1984

EM85   Ehrig, M. / Mahr, B. : Fundamentals of Algebraic Specification 1. Springer-Verlag, Berlin 1985

GMS83   Golshani, F. / Maibaum, T.S.E. / Sadler, M.R. : A Modal System of Algebras for Database Specification and Query /Update Language Support. Proc. 9th Int. Conf. on Very Large Data Bases, Florence 1983

Kl83   Klaeren, H. : Algebraische Spezifikation. Springer-Verlag, Berlin 1983

KMS85   Khosla,S. / Maibaum, T.S.E. / Sadler, M. : Database Specification. Proc. IFIP Working Conf. on Database Semantics, R. Meersman / T.B. Steel (eds.), North Holland, Amsterdam 1985

Ku84   Kung, C.H. A Temporal Framework for Database Specification and Verification. Proc. 10th Int. Conf. on Very Large Data Bases, Singapore 1984

LEG85   Lipeck, U.W. / Ehrich, H.-D. / Gogolla, M. :Specifying Admissibility of Dynamic Database Behaviours Using Temporal Logic. Proc. IFIP Working Conf. on Theoretical and Formal Aspects of Information Systems, A.Sernadas et al. (eds.), North Holland, Amsterdam 1985

MP79   Manna, Z. / Pnueli, A. : A Modal Logic of Programs. Proc. Conf. Automata, Languages and Programming. LNCS 19, Springer-Verlag, Berlin 1979

RU71   Rescher, N. / Urquhart, A. : Temporal Logic. Springer-Verlag, Berlin 1971

Se80   Sernadas, A. : Temporal aspects of Logical Procedure Definition. Inform. Sys. 5(1980), 167-187

Sh81   Shipman, D,W. : The Functional Data Model and the Data Language DAPLEX. ACM TODS 6(1981), 140-173

TL82   Tsichritzis, D.C. / Lochovsky, F.H. : Data Models. Prentice-Hall, Englewood Cliffs 1982

OBSCURE, A NEW SPECIFICATION LANGUAGE

Claus-Werner Lermen and Jacques Loeckx
Fachrichtung 10.2 Informatik
Universität des Saarlandes
6600 Saarbrücken   (FRG)

Recently several specification languages based on the use of abstract
data types have been proposed in the literature: CLEAR [BG 77, Sa 84],
ACT ONE [EM 85], OBJ2 [FGJM 85], ASL [SW 83], Extended ML [ST 85, Sa 85].
The specification language OBSCURE differs from these languages in the
following respects.

In the existing languages a specification is classically interpreted as
an algebra or a theory. The specification of elaborate abstract data
types is then performed "bottom-up" by putting algebras or theories
together. Instead, a specification in OBSCURE introduces "new" types
on the basis of not yet specified - so-called "global" - ones. More
formally, an OBSCURE specification is interpreted as a function mapping
an algebra (containing the global types) into an extension of this
algebra (containing in addition the new types). The specification of
elaborate abstract data types may therefore be performed "top-down"
by "stepwise refinement": for each global type introduced one constructs an specification introducing this type on the basis of other,
more "elementary" types. The final specification is obtained by "putting
together" these different specifications. Take, as an example, the
development of an interpreter for a programming language. First, the
type *program* is specified, on the basis of the types *input-data* and
output-data.This type contains in particular the operation *Interprete*
mapping programs and input data into output data. The next step consists in the specification of the type *input-data*, etc. The development
is completed when the remaining global types are "known" ones, for
instance types provided by a usual programming language.

As a further feature OBSCURE explicitly links program development to
program verification. This is reflected by the fact that an OBSCURE
implementation consists of a development module and a verification

module. This feature allows OBSCURE to provide, for instance, constructs transforming an algebra into a subalgebra or a quotient algebra. It is well-known that such transformations make sense only if certain (semantic) constraints are satisfied, viz. a closure condition in the case of a subalgebra and a congruence condition in the case of the quotient algebra (see e.g. [EM 85]). In OBSCURE the satisfaction of these constraints is proved with the help of the verification module.

OBSCURE is designed for interactive use. A specification in OBSCURE essentially consists of a sequence of elementary constructs. At each construct the development module of the OBSCURE implementation automatically checks the syntactic constraints. Moreover, it generates the theorems expressing the semantic constraints - such as those implied by the construct yielding a subalgebra or quotient algebra - and transmits them for proof to the verification module.

Finally, by performing type inferencing OBSCURE allows a mild form of polymorphism.

The original version of OBSCURE [Le 85] was developed for the algorithmic specification method [Lo 81, Lo 84]. According to this method an abstract data type is specified by a (constructively defined) model. The present version of OBSCURE is more general in that it is applicable to any specification method based on the use of a single model. It is, for instance, also applicable to the initial algebra specification method.

Essentially, an OBSCURE program consists of specifications and procedure declarations. A specification is a sequence of constructs. These constructs allow to create an algebra with the help of a model, to transform an algebra into a subalgebra or a quotient algebra, to forget (i.e. "hide") sorts or operations, to rename sorts or operations, to introduce constraints in the form of axioms, to put specifications together and to call procedures. A procedure declaration consists of a name, a list of formal parameters and a specification constituting the procedure body.

An informal introduction to OBSCURE may be found in [LL 85]. A complete formal description of OBSCURE in the style of [Sa 84] may be found in [Lo 85]. In addition to the description of the (context-free) syntax, the semantics and the context conditions, this report contains a detailed proof of the consistency of the description. By the way, the use

of a copy-rule semantics instead of a denotational semantics for the
parameter mechanism appears to lead to a substantially simpler description than those known from the literature.

REFERENCES

[BG 77] Burstall, R.M., Goguen, J.A., Putting theories together to
make specifications, *Proc. 5th Joint Conf. on Art. Int.*, Cambridge,
pp. 1045 - 1058 (1977)

[EM 85] Ehrig, H., Mahr, B., Fundamentals of Algebraic Specification,
Springer-Verlag, 1985

[FGJM 85] Gutatsugi, K., Goguen, J., Jouannaud, J.-P., Meseguer, J.,
Principles of OBJ2, *Proc. 12th POPL Conf.*, pp. 52 - 66 (1985)

[Le 85] Lermen, C.W., The specification language OBSCURE, Int. Rep.
A 85/11, Univ. Saarbrucken (1985)

[LL 85] Lermen, C.W., Loeckx, J., OBSCURE: A language for interactive
top-down specification, Int. Rep. A 85/16, Univ. Saarbrucken
(November 1985)

[Lo 81] Loeckx, J., Algorithmic specifications of abstract data types,
Proc. ICALP 81, LNCS 115 (1981), 129 - 147

[Lo 84] Loeckx, J., Algorithmic specifications: A constructive specification method for abstract data types, Int. Rep. A 84/03, Univ.
Saarbrucken (1984). To appear in *TOPLAS*

[Lo 85] Loeckx, J., A formal description of the specification language
OBSCURE, Int. Rep. A 85/15, Univ. Saarbrucken (November 1985)

[Sa 84] Sannella, D., A set-theoretic semantics for CLEAR, *Acta Inform.*
21, 5, 443 - 472 (1984)

[Sa 85] Sannella, D., The semantics of Extended ML, draft (May 1985)

[ST 85] Sannella, D., Tarlecki, A., Program specification and development in standard ML, *Proc. 12th POPL Conf.*, pp. 67 - 77 (1985)

[SW 83] Sannella, D., Wirsing, M., A kernel language for algebraic
specification and implementation, *Proc. Int. Coll. FCT*, LNCS 158,
413 - 427, 1983

SOME THOUGHTS ON ALGEBRAIC SPECIFICATION[1]

Donald Sannella and Andrzej Tarlecki[2]
Department of Computer Science
University of Edinburgh

Introduction

This paper presents in an informal way the main ideas underlying our work on
algebraic specification. The central idea, due to Goguen and Burstall, is that much work
on algebraic specification can be done independently of the particular logical system (or
institution) on which the specification formalism is based. We also examine the nature of
specifications and specification languages, the problem of proving that a statement follows
from a specification, the important notion of behavioural equivalence, and the evolution of
programs from specifications by stepwise refinement. Although many of the issues
discussed are motivated by technically complicated problems, in this paper the
technicalities have been suppressed in an attempt to make the ideas more accessible. The
same ideas are presented with full technical details in [ST 85c].

We assume that the reader is convinced as we are that formal specifications are not
only theoretically interesting but are also practically important. Throughout the paper we
also assume some familiarity with the basic concepts of algebraic specification, although
we do not rely on any specific technical knowledge.

Many of the ideas expressed here were evolved under the influence of Rod Burstall and
Martin Wirsing, but this remains a personal statement.

Generality and institutions

Any approach to algebraic specification must be based on some logical framework. The
pioneering papers [ADJ 76], [Gut 75], [Zil 74] used many-sorted equational logic for this
purpose. Nowadays, however, examples of logical systems in use include first-order logic
(with and without equality), Horn-clause logic, higher-order logic, infinitary logic, temporal
logic and many others. Note that all these logical systems may be considered with or
without predicates, admitting partial operations or not. This leads to different concepts of
signature and of model, perhaps even more striking in examples like polymorphic
signatures, order-sorted signatures, continuous algebras or error algebras.

There is no reason to view any of these logical systems as superior to the others; the
choice must depend on the particular area of application and may also depend on personal
taste.

The informal notion of logical system has been formalised by Goguen and Burstall
[GB 84], who introduced for this purpose the notion of *institution* (this generalizes the
ideas of "abstract model theory" [Bar 74]). An institution defines a notion of a signature
together with for any signature Σ a set of Σ-sentences, a collection of Σ-models and a

---

[1] This research has been supported by a grant from the (U.K.) Science and Engineering Research Council.

[2] Present address: Institute of Computer Science, Polish Academy of Sciences, Warsaw.

satisfaction relation between Σ-models and Σ-sentences. The only semantic requirement is that when we change signatures, the induced translations of sentences and models preserve the satisfaction relation. This condition expresses the intentional independence of the meaning of specifications from the actual notation. All the above logical systems (and many others) fit into this mould. For example, many-sorted equational logic constitutes an institution: take signatures to be many-sorted algebraic signatures and for any algebraic signature Σ let the set of Σ-sentences be the set of all equations between Σ-terms of the same sort, let Σ-models be just Σ-algebras and let satisfaction of a Σ-equation by a Σ-algebra be defined as usual. It is necessary to adopt some notion of signature morphism $\sigma{:}\Sigma{\to}\Sigma'$ such as defined e.g. in [BG 80] in order to provide for changing signatures, which induces the σ-translation of Σ-equations to Σ'-equations and of Σ'-algebras to Σ-algebras (σ-reduct).

Note that we can define institutions which diverge from logical tradition and have, for example, sentences expressing constraints on models which are not usually considered in logic, e.g. data constraints as in Clear [BG 80], which impose the requirement of initiality (cf. [Rei 80], [EWT 83]).

For purposes of generality, it is best to avoid choosing any particular logical system on which to base a specification approach, as suggested by Goguen and Burstall. We can instead parameterise our work (whatever it may be) by an *arbitrary* institution. We strongly believe that this is an appropriate level of generality on which to introduce and analyse concepts like specification, implementation, specification-building operations etc. It is possible to define specification languages which can be used to build specifications in any institution (examples are Clear [BG 80] and ASL [ST 85c]).

Of course, not everything can be done in an institution-independent way. For example, a theorem prover needs to know about the detailed structure of axioms. Fixing an institution or even fixing some part of an institution (say, the notion of signature and of model) opens possibilities for doing things which cannot be done at the completely general level. For example, part of a theorem prover (the part dealing with terms, substitutions, type checking etc.) could be built under the single additional assumption that signatures are standard many-sorted algebraic signatures. Striving to always work at the most general level possible results in reusable theories and tools. Typically (but not always) these can be adapted for use under a particular institution simply by providing some low-level details. For example, instantiating the underlying institution in the formal definition of Clear (and changing the low-level syntax accordingly) yields a family of Clear-like specification languages: equational Clear, error Clear, continuous Clear and so on.

Specifications and specification languages

What is a specification? Different views are possible, but one thing which is certain is that a specification is a description of a signature and a class of models over that signature (called the *models of the specification*).

We will not put any restrictions on the class of models described by a specification. Thus, specifications may be *loose* (having non-isomorphic models), so as to avoid premature design decisions. We do not even assume that the class of models of a specification is closed under isomorphism (see [ST 85c] for a brief discussion of this point). In contrast to many approaches (e.g. CIP-L [Bau 81]) we do not require models to be *reachable* (in the standard framework, an algebra is reachable if every element is the value of some ground term; for the generalisation to an arbitrary institution see [Tar 84]). On the other hand, these restrictions are not ruled out, and specification approaches may well contain some mechanism to allow such restrictions to be included in specifications when required (cf. [EWT 83], [ST 85c]).

There are other levels than the level of models at which specifications may be dealt with. For example, we can consider:

- textual level: a sequence of characters on paper,
- presentation level: a signature and a set of axioms over this signature (required to be finite or at least recursive or recursively enumerable),
- theory level: a signature and a set of axioms over this signature closed under logical consequence,
- model level: a signature and a class of models over this signature.

Each approach to specification needs the textual level for actually writing down specifications. The meaning of a specification text is determined by giving a mapping from the textual level to one of the other levels. For example, Clear maps to the theory level, ASL maps to the model level and ACT ONE [EFH 83] to both the presentation and the model level. There are natural mappings from presentations to theories and from theories to classes of models (a presentation maps to the smallest theory containing it, and a theory maps to the class of models satisfying its axioms); the second-level semantics of ACT ONE is actually redundant since it is just the composition of the first-level semantics with these natural mappings, as proved in [EFH 83]. However, not every class of models is the class of models of a theory, and not every theory has a (finite, recursive or recursively enumerable) presentation. In fact, Clear has no presentation-level semantics and ASL has neither a presentation- nor theory-level semantics.

But every specification language has a model-level semantics — and this is in the end all that really matters since the purpose of a specification is not to describe a presentation or a theory but rather to describe a class of models.[3]

Slogan: *A specification comprises (at least) a signature and a class of models over this signature.*

Everybody knows that big, monolithic specifications are difficult to understand and use. Thus it is important to build specifications in a structured way from small bits. We build specifications in this way using *specification-building operations* (examples: +, **derive**). The semantics of each of these operations is a function on classes of models, e.g. + in ASL corresponds to a function which when given a class of $\Sigma1$-models and a class of $\Sigma2$-models yields a class of $(\Sigma1\cup\Sigma2)$-models [SW 83].

A specification language may be viewed as a set of such operations, together with some syntax. Some operations correspond to functions at the presentation or theory level, but in general this need not be so — in any case they are described by functions at the model level.

In choosing the class of operations there is a trade-off between the expressive power of the language and the ease of understanding and dealing with the operations. One way to circumvent this problem is to first develop a *kernel* language which consists of a minimal set of very powerful operations. Such a kernel language is difficult to use directly. We can build higher-level languages on top of the kernel, so that each higher-level construct corresponds to a kernel-language expression. This is analogous to the way that high-level programming languages are defined in terms of machine-level operations. This approach has been taken in ASL; high-level languages built on top of ASL include PLUSS [Gau 84] and Extended ML [ST 85a].

Besides providing a certain collection of predefined specification-building operations, a

---

[3] Actually, the ultimate purpose of a specification is typically to describe a class of *programs*, but the notion of a model is chosen so as to precisely capture those aspects of programs which are relevant to the specification while abstracting away from those which are not. For example, in the standard framework algebras are chosen as models in order to abstract away from the syntactic and algorithmic details of programs while capturing their functional behaviour.

specification language usually provides a way for the user to define his own specification-building operations, i.e. a mechanism for constructing *parameterised specifications*. There are different approaches to parameterised specifications; the ones which seem most natural in our general framework are those which treat a parameterised specification as a function from specifications to specifications as in e.g. Clear, LOOK [ETLZ 82] or ASL. Such a parameterised specification normally has a certain domain of specifications to which it can be applied.

Proving things

In the framework of an arbitrary institution, any class of models determines a theory, that is the set of all sentences which are true in every model belonging to this class (note however that the class of models satisfying this theory may be bigger than the class of models we started with). So every specification determines the set of its logical consequences, the set of sentences which hold in all its models. These are exactly the properties of the specified object expressible in the given institution on which a user is allowed to rely.

In the above, we said nothing about how to effectively determine if a property (sentence) follows from a specification. Our basic notion is the satisfaction relation and model-theoretic (rather than proof-theoretic) consequence. All the same, it would be convenient to have some effective (=computational) way of proving that a sentence is a consequence of a specification, i.e. a *proof system*. This would provide an important tool for the practical use of formal specifications. As suggested by Guttag and Horning [GH 80], by proving that selected properties follow from a specification we can understand it and gain confidence that it expresses what we want. Moreover, in order to do any kind of formal program development or verification a theorem-proving capability is necessary.

Notation: $SP \vDash \varphi$ means that the sentence φ holds in all models of SP (φ is a semantic consequence of SP). $SP \vdash \varphi$ means that φ is provable from SP in a given proof system.

Any useful proof system must be *sound*, that is $SP \vdash \varphi$ must imply $SP \vDash \varphi$ (we must only be able to prove things which are true). Another pleasant property is *completeness*, i.e. $SP \vDash \varphi$ implies $SP \vdash \varphi$ (we can prove all true things). Unfortunately, for every practical specification approach no sound and complete effective proof system can exist; more precisely, this holds for every specification approach which is powerful enough to specify the natural numbers and in which equations can be expressed — see [MS 85] for a discussion of this problem. So we have to be content with a proof system which is sound but not complete. The same situation occurs in program verification; there is no (Cook-) complete Hoare-like proof system for any programming language with a sufficiently rich control structure [Cla 79]. This is too bad, but that's life.

Of course, we cannot expect to be able to construct an institution-independent proof system. We have to assume that we are given some (sound) proof system for the underlying institution, that is a proof system which allows us to deduce sentences from sets of sentences in the institution. This amounts to a proof system for any specification language where specification-building operations are defined at the level of presentations. However, this does not imply that such a semantics is required for doing theorem proving. It is possible to extend the proof system for the underlying institution to a proof system for the specification language in an institution-independent way. What we have to do is to devise an inference rule for every specification-building operation which allows facts about a compound specification to be deduced from facts about its components [SB 83], [ST 85b], [ST 85c]. A simple example of such a rule is:

$$SP \vdash \varphi \implies SP + SP' \vdash \varphi$$

This is another case where, due to the quest for generality via institutions, something (part of a theorem prover for a specification language) may be built once and for all.

Behavioural equivalence

A concept which has (not) been extensively (enough) studied in the context of algebraic specifications is that of the behaviour of a program or model. Intuitively, the behaviour of a program is determined just by the answers which are obtained from computations the program may perform. Switching for awhile to the usual algebraic framework, we may say informally that two Σ-algebras are *behaviourally equivalent* with respect to a set OBS of *observable sorts* if it is not possible to distinguish between them by evaluating Σ-terms which produce a result of observable sort. For example, suppose Σ contains the sorts *nat*, *bool* and *bunch* and the operations *empty*: → *bunch*, *add*: *nat,bunch* → *bunch* and ∈: *nat,bunch* → *bool* (as well as the usual operations on *nat* and *bool*), and suppose A and B are Σ-algebras with

$|A_{bunch}|$ = the set of finite sets of natural numbers
$|B_{bunch}|$ = the set of finite lists of natural numbers

with the operations and the remaining carriers defined in the obvious way (but B does *not* contain operations like *cons*, *car* and *cdr*). Then A and B are behaviourally equivalent with respect to {*bool*} since every term of sort *bool* has the same value in both algebras (the interesting terms are of the form $m \in add(a_1,...,add(a_n,empty)...))$. Note that A and B are not isomorphic.

Behavioural equivalence seems to be a concept which is fundamental to programming methodology. For example:

Data abstraction

A practical advantage of using abstract data types in the construction of programs is that the implementation of abstractions by program modules need not be fixed. A different module using different algorithms and/or different data structures may be substituted without changing the rest of the program provided that the new module is behaviourally equivalent to the module it replaces (with respect to the non-encapsulated types). ADJ [ADJ 76] have suggested that "abstract" in "abstract data type" means "up to isomorphism"; we suggest that it really means "up to behavioural equivalence".

Program specification

One way of specifying a program is to describe the desired input/output behaviour in some concrete way, e.g. by constructing a very simple program which exhibits the desired behaviour. Any program which is behaviourally equivalent to the sample program with respect to the primitive types of the programming language satisfies the specification. This is called an *abstract model specification* [LB 77] or *specification by example* [Sad 84]. In general, specifications under the usual algebraic approaches are not abstract enough; it is either difficult, as in Clear [BG 80] or impossible, as in the initial algebra approach of [ADJ 76] and the final algebra approach of [Wand 79] to specify sets of natural numbers in such a way that both A and B above are models of the specification. ASL provides a *behavioural abstraction* operation which when applied to a specification SP relaxes interpretation to all those algebras which are behaviourally equivalent to a model of SP. We want to stress that although the phrase "specification by example" suggests sloppiness, this is not the case; in this approach it is a precisely-defined, convenient and intuitive way to write specifications, and it is also an established technique in software engineering.

In the above we assume that the only observations (or experiments) we are allowed to perform are to test whether the results of computations are equal. In the context of an arbitrary institution we can generalise this and abstract away from the equational bias by allowing observations which are arbitrary sentences (logical formulae). This yields an institution-independent notion of *observational equivalence*. Two models are observationally equivalent if they both give the same answers to any observation from a prespecified set. Based on this general notion of observational equivalence we can define an institution-independent specification-building operation for observational abstraction (the behavioural abstraction operation mentioned above is actually only a special case of observational abstraction in the standard algebraic framework). The properties of this operation are more complicated than for other specification-building operations, but it is possible to overcome these difficulties and for example to provide proof rules for reasoning about specifications built using observational abstraction [ST 85b].

Implementation of specifications

The programming discipline of stepwise refinement suggests that a program be evolved by working gradually via a series of successively lower-level refinements of the specification toward a specification which is so low-level that it can be regarded as a program. For example, the specification

```
reverse(nil) = nil
reverse(cons(a,l)) = append(reverse(l),cons(a,nil))
```

is an executable program in Standard ML [Mil 84]. The stepwise refinement approach guarantees the correctness of the resulting program, provided that each refinement step can be proved correct. A formalisation of this approach requires a precise definition of the concept of refinement, i.e. of the *implementation* of one specification by another.

In programming practice, proceeding from a specification to a program (by stepwise refinement or by any other method) means making a series of design decisions. These will include decisions concerning the concrete representation of abstractly defined data types, decisions about how to compute abstractly specified functions (choice of algorithm) and decisions which select between the various possibilities which the specification leaves open. The following very simple formal notion of implementation captures this idea: a specification SP is implemented by another specification SP', written SP$\leadsto$SP', if SP' incorporates more design decisions than SP, i.e. any model of SP' is a model of SP (SP and SP' are required to have the same signature). We can adopt this simple notion in the context of a specification language incorporating an operation like behavioural abstraction (see [SW 83] for more discussion on this point).

This notion of implementation can be extended to give a notion of the implementation of parameterised specifications: P is implemented by P', written P$\leadsto$P', if for all specifications SP in the domain of P, SP is also in the domain of P' and P(SP) $\leadsto$ P'(SP).

An important issue for any notion of implementation is whether implementations can be composed *vertically* and *horizontally* [GB 80]. Implementations can be vertically composed if the implementation relation is transitive (SP$\leadsto$SP' and SP'$\leadsto$SP" implies SP$\leadsto$SP") and they can be horizontally composed if the specification-building operations preserve implementations (i.e. P$\leadsto$P' and SP$\leadsto$SP' implies P(SP) $\leadsto$ P'(SP')). The above notion of implementation has both these properties, provided that all specification-building operations are monotonic (with respect to inclusion of model classes) which is the case for the specification-building operations defined in e.g. Clear, LOOK and ASL. These two properties allow large structured specifications to be refined in a gradual and modular fashion. All of the individual small specifications which make up a large specification can be separately refined in several stages to give a collection of lower-level specifications (this should be easy because of their small size). When the low-level specifications are put back together, the result is guaranteed to be an implementation of the original specification. Note that other more complicated notions of implementation ([EKMP 82], just to take one example) do not compose vertically or horizontally in general.

Final remarks

In this note we put forward some of our thoughts and prejudices concerning algebraic specification. The theme which underlies most of our arguments is one of generality. We argued in favour of working at a high level of generality whenever possible, and against making unnecessary restrictions. The advantage of generality is (at least) the development of reuseable theories and tools; the problem with introducing even the most reasonable-seeming restriction is that we exclude something which we may need someday. An instance of this is the restriction to reachable models (the *generation principle* of [BW 82]) — see [SW 83] for an example which requires considering unreachable models. The result of (for example) fixing an institution at an early stage is that after years of work it is necessary to start again from scratch to introduce some enhancement like the ability to handle higher-order functions or imperative programs.

Practitioners may think we are dreamers because our interest in mathematical elegance and generality seems so far removed from the real world of programmers writing operating systems and payroll programs. But we believe that if practical formal program specification and development is ever to become a reality (and we are optimistic about this) it must be based on sound mathematical foundations. Foundations acceptable in the long term cannot contain restrictions adopted for short-term convenience, e.g. it is a mistake to forever limit yourself to equational specifications because you happen to have a Knuth-Bendix equational theorem prover running on your system. The eventual practical feasibility of all this depends on the existence of good tools for supporting formal program development; although we do not believe that program production will ever be automated, the right tools could reduce the burden of formal program development to an acceptable level.

References

[ADJ 76]   Goguen, J.A., Thatcher, J.W. and Wagner, E.G. An initial algebra approach to the specification, correctness, and implementation of abstract data types. IBM research report RC 6487; also in: Current Trends in Programming Methodology, Vol. 4: Data Structuring (R.T. Yeh, ed.), Prentice-Hall, pp. 80-149 (1978).

[Bar 74]   Barwise, J. Axioms for abstract model theory. Annals of Math. Logic 7, pp. 221-265.

[Bau 81]   Bauer, F.L. *et al* (the CIP Language Group) Report on a wide spectrum language for program specification and development. Report TUM-I8104, Technische Univ. München; see also: The wide spectrum language CIP-L. Springer LNCS 183 (1985).

[BW 82]   Bauer, F.L. and Wössner, H. Algorithmic language and program development. Springer.

[BG 80]   Burstall, R.M. and Goguen, J.A. The semantics of Clear, a specification language. Proc. of Advanced Course on Abstract Software Specifications, Copenhagen. Springer LNCS 86, pp. 292-332.

[Cla 79]   Clarke, E.M. Programming language constructs for which it is impossible to obtain good Hoare axiom systems. JACM 26, 1 pp. 129-147.

[EFH 83]   Ehrig, H., Fey, W. and Hansen, H. ACT ONE: an algebraic specification language with two levels of semantics. Report Nr. 83-03, Institut für Software und Theoretische Informatik, Technische Univ. Berlin; see also: Ehrig, H. and Mahr, B. Fundamentals of Algebraic Specification I: Equations and Initial Semantics.

38

EATCS Monographs on Theoretical Computer Science, Springer (1985), chapters 9-10.

[EKMP 82] Ehrig, H., Kreowski, H.-J., Mahr, B. and Padawitz, P. Algebraic implementation of abstract data types. Theoretical Computer Science 20, pp. 209-263.

[ETLZ 82] Ehrig, H., Thatcher, J.W., Lucas, P. and Zilles, S.N. Denotational and initial algebra semantics of the algebraic specification language LOOK. Draft report, IBM research.

[EWT 83] Ehrig, H., Wagner, E.G. and Thatcher, J.W. Algebraic specifications with generating constraints. Proc. 10th ICALP, Barcelona. Springer LNCS 154, pp. 188-202.

[Gau 84] Gaudel, M.-C. A first introduction to PLUSS. Draft report, Univ. de Paris-Sud, Orsay.

[GB 80] Goguen, J.A. and Burstall, R.M. CAT, a system for the structured elaboration of correct programs from structured specifications. Technical report CSL-118, Computer Science Laboratory, SRI International.

[GB 84] Goguen, J.A. and Burstall, R.M. Introducing institutions. Proc. Logics of Programming Workshop, Carnegie-Mellon. Springer LNCS 164, pp. 221-256.

[Gut 75] Guttag, J.V. The specification and application to programming of abstract data types. Ph.D. thesis, Univ. of Toronto.

[GH 80] Guttag, J.V. and Horning, J.J. Formal specification as a design tool. Proc. ACM Symp. on Principles of Programming Languages, Las Vegas, pp. 251-261.

[LB 77] Liskov, B.H. and Berzins, V. An appraisal of program specifications. Computation Structures Group memo 141-1, Laboratory for Computer Science, MIT.

[MS 85] MacQueen, D.B. and Sannella, D.T. Completeness of proof systems for equational specifications. IEEE Transactions on Software Engineering SE-11, pp. 454-461.

[Mil 84] Milner, R.G. A proposal for Standard ML. Proc. 1984 ACM Symp. on LISP and Functional Programming, Austin, Texas.

[Rei 80] Reichel, H. Initially restricting algebraic theories. Proc. 9th MFCS, Rydzyna. Springer LNCS 88, pp. 504-514.

[Sad 84] Sadler, M. Mapping out specification. Draft report, Dept. of Computing, Imperial College, London; presented at: Workshop on Formal Aspects of Specification, Swindon.

[SB 83] Sannella, D.T. and Burstall, R.M. Structured theories in LCF. Proc. 8th Colloq. on Trees in Algebra and Programming, L'Aquila, Italy. Springer LNCS 159, pp. 377-391.

[ST 85a] Sannella, D.T. and Tarlecki, A. Program specification and development in Standard ML. Proc. 12th ACM Symp. on Principles of Programming Languages, New Orleans, pp. 67-77.

[ST 85b] Sannella, D.T. and Tarlecki, A. On observational equivalence and algebraic specification. Report CSR-172-84, Dept. of Computer Science, Univ. of Edinburgh; extended abstract in: Proc. 10th Colloq. on Trees in Algebra and Programming, Joint Conf. on Theory and Practice of Software Development (TAPSOFT), Berlin. Springer LNCS 185, pp. 308-322.

[ST 85c] Sannella, D.T. and Tarlecki, A. Specifications in an arbitrary institution. Report CSR-184-85, Dept. of Computer Science, Univ. of Edinburgh; see also: Sannella, D.T. and Tarlecki, A. Building specifications in an arbitrary institution. Proc. Intl. Symposium on Semantics of Data Types, Sophia-Antipolis. Springer LNCS 173, pp. 337-356.

[SW 83] Sannella, D.T. and Wirsing, M. A kernel language for algebraic specification and implementation. Report CSR-131-83, Dept. of Computer Science, Univ. of Edinburgh; extended abstract in: Proc. Intl. Conf. on Foundations of Computation Theory, Borgholm, Sweden. Springer LNCS 158, pp. 413-427.

[Tar 84] Tarlecki, A. On the existence of free models in abstract algebraic institutions. Draft report, Univ. of Edinburgh.

[Wand 79] Wand, M. Final algebra semantics and data type extensions. JCSS 19, pp. 27-44.

[Zil 74] Zilles, S.N. Algebraic specification of data types. Computation Structures Group memo 119, Laboratory for Computer Science, MIT.

IMPLEMENTATION SPECIFICATIONS

Christoph Beierle, Angelika Voß
Fachbereich Informatik, Universität Kaiserslautern
Postfach 3049, 6750 Kaiserslautern, West Germany

Abstract

Loose specifications of abstract data types (ADTs) have many non-isomorphic
algebras as models. An implementation between two loose specifications
should therefore consider many abstraction functions together with their
source and target algebras. Just like specifications are stepwise refined to
restrict their class of models, implementations should be stepwise refinable
to restrict the class of abstraction functions. In this scenario
specifications and implementations can be developed interwovenly.
For example, we can consider implementations of sets by lists where the set
simulating list operations are still left open. They may be refined later on
so that an implementation of sets by arbitrary lists, by lists without
double entries, or by sorted lists is obtained, differing e.g. in the
efficiency of the set simulating operations.
We suggest to have implementation specifications analogously to loose ADT
specifications: Implementations have signatures, models, axioms and
sentences thus constituting an institution. Implementation specifications
are the theories of this institution and refinements between implementation
specifications are its theory morphisms.

1. Introduction

Fixed ADT specifications with only isomorphic models were studied before loose ADT
specifications with non-isomorphic models, and several implementation concepts have
been proposed, discussed, and revised for fixed specifications (e.g. [GTW 78], [Ehc
82], [EKP 78], [EKMP 82], [Ga 83]). By now there seems to be a basic consent that
such an implementation concept should incorporate the following notions:

- an abstract specification to be implemented,
- a concrete specification implementing the abstract one,
- a signature morphism from the abstract to the (possibly extended) concrete
  specification allowing to translate abstract terms to concrete ones, and
- an abstraction function from the concrete to the abstract algebra allowing to
  translate the concrete value of a concrete term back to an abstract value.
  Abstraction functions need not be totally defined, but must be surjective and
  homomorphic w.r.t. their domain of definition.

In contrast, so far only one implementation concept has been proposed for loose
specifications that generalizes the fixed case, namely the concept proposed by
Sannella and Wirsing in [SW 82]. Our own implementation concept generalizes that of
Sannella and Wirsing giving room to a refinement process between implementations.
Moreover, our approach abstracts from a particular ADT specification method by using
the notion of an institution ([GB 83]) which provides abstract characterizations of
signatures, models, sentences etc.

In Section 2 we outline the basic idea of our implementation concept. In Section 3 we
briefly state the assumptions about the underlying loose specifications which are
fundamental for our development. In Section 4 we introduce the institution of
implementation specifications. In Section 5 we illustrate how implementations of sets
by lists can be developed and refined stepwise hand in hand with the loose
specifications. Section 6 contains a summary and a comparison.

2. Basic idea

As compared to fixed specifications, in the loose case we still have specifications, signatures, signature morphisms, etc, the essential difference lying in the number of models being considered. Therefore, an implementation for loose specifications should at least consist of
- an abstract specification,
- a concrete specification, and
- a signature morphism translating the abstract signature to the (possibly extended) concrete signature.

Since a concrete specification can always be extended before giving the implementation, we will choose the technically simpler approach and omit any extension of the concrete specification as part of the implementation.

Having translated an abstract term into a concrete one we are faced with the following questions:

(1) In which concrete algebra shall the concrete term be evaluated, since there may be many non-isomorphic algebras?

(2) To which abstract algebra shall we translate the value of the concrete term, since there also may be many non-isomorphic algebras?

(3) Which abstraction function shall be used for the translation, since there may be different ones?

Having answered these questions we may further ask:

(4) How can we specify the selected concrete algebras, abstract algebras, and abstraction functions in an implementation?

In [SW 82] Sannella and Wirsing require that for every concrete model there should be some abstract model and an abstraction function connecting them. If such a complete set of triples exists, the concrete specification is said to implement the abstract one, otherwise it does not. This is an implicit, non-constructive approach which gives no room for a notion of refinement between implementations since there is no way to characterize and restrict the set of triples - e.g. by constraints on the concrete or abstract models - any further.

Since the idea of loose specifications is to consider at first an arbitrary large set of models and to restrict this set stepwise by refining the specification, we think the adequate idea of implementations between loose specifications is to accept all meaningful combinations of an abstract model, a concrete model, and an abstraction function and to restrict them stepwise by refining the implementation.

To realize these ideas and answering (1) - (3) we introduce the notion of implementation models:
    A simple implementation consisting of an abstract specification, a concrete one, and a signature translation between them denotes the set of all triples consisting of an abstract model, a concrete one, and an abstraction function from the concrete to the abstract model. Such a tripel is called an implementation model. As in the fixed case, the abstraction function may be partially defined and it must be surjective and homomorphic.

Now we extend these simple implementations to a concept incorporating a notion of

refinement between implementations. Such a refinement should restrict the set of implementation models which can be done componentwise by
- restricting the set of abstract models,
- restricting the set of concrete models,
- restricting the set of abstraction functions.

In the framework of loose specifications the set of models - like the abstract and the concrete ones - is restricted by adding sentences to the respective specification. Thus we solve problem (4) w.r.t. the algebras by allowing sentences over the abstract and the concrete signature to be given in an implementation.

Since the abstraction functions operate on both concrete and abstract carriers we propose to view them as algebra operations from concrete to abstract sorts. These operations can be restricted as usually by adding sentences over both the concrete and the abstract signatures extended by the abstraction operation names. Thus we solve problem (4) completely by admitting arbitrary sentences over the abstract and the concrete signatures extended by the abstraction operation names. These sentences will be called implementation sentences.

Summarizing we propose an implementation specification to be
- a simple implementation
- together with a set of implementation sentences and
- denoting all implementation models of the simple implementation which satisfy the implementation sentences.

Analogously to specifications which consist of a signature in the simplest case, a simple implementation will also be called an implementation signature.

We already claimed that an implementation should be refinable by adding more implementation sentences to it and thus reducing the class of implementation models. This idea is extended analogously to loose ADT specifications by admitting a change of signature: There, a specification morphism is a signature morphism such that the translated sentences of the refined specification hold in the refining specification.

Since an implementation contains two specifications, an implementation morphism should consist of two specification morphisms, an abstract one between the abstract specifications and a concrete one between the concrete specifications. With these two morphisms, the sentences of the refined implementation can be translated into sentences over the refining implementation by mapping the sorts and operations according to the two specification morphisms and by mapping the abstraction operation names to the corresponding abstraction operation names in the refining implementation.

Thus, a refinement between two implementations is given by an abstract and a concrete specification morphism such that the translated sentences of the refined implementation hold in the refining one.

3. The underlying institution of loose specifications

We only assume that the loose specifications have equational signatures with error constants, denote strict algebras, and are formally defined as the theories of an institution ([GB 83]).

Assumption: SPEC-institution := $\langle$ SIG, EAlg, ESen, $\models^e$ $\rangle$

is an institution where

- SIG is a category of equational signatures with an error constant error-s for each sort s.

- EAlg is a model functor mapping a signature Σ to all strict Σ-algebras, which have flat cpos as carriers, strict operations, and the error constants denoting the bottom element.

- ESen is a sentence functor mapping a signature Σ to a set of Σ-sentences.

- $|^{\underline{e}}$ is the strict satisfaction relation.

SPEC denotes the category of theories in the SPEC-institution which will be called (loose) specifications, and Sig: SPEC → SIG is the functor forgetting specifications to their signatures.

4. The institution of implementation specifications

In order to develop our implementation concept in the framework of institutions we will have to make precise the notions of
- implementation signatures (Section 4.1) and
- implementation models (Section 4.2).
Having determined these notions we will establish a connection between loose specifications and implementations in Section 4.3 which will be helpful to formalize in Section 4.4 the remaining notions of
- implementation sentences and
- satisfaction of an implementation sentence by an implementation model.
Section 4.5 contains a summary of the new institution.

4.1 Implementation signatures

The signature Σ of a loose specification SP = $\langle \Sigma, E \rangle$ may be viewed as a simple specification which has no sentences at all:
$$\Sigma \cong \langle \Sigma, \emptyset \rangle.$$
This suggested to define an implementation signature to be a simple implementation specification which has no sentences.

According to Section 2, such a simple implementation consists of an abstract specification SPa = $\langle \Sigma a, Ea \rangle$, a concrete specification SPc = $\langle \Sigma c, Ec \rangle$, and a signature morphism $\sigma: \Sigma a \to \Sigma c$ translating the abstract to the concrete signature. Thus, an implementation signature, or shorter i-signature IΣ is a triple
$$I\Sigma = \langle SPa, \sigma, SPc \rangle.$$

We already suggested that a refinement between two implementations should consist of two specification morphisms between the abstract specifications and between the concrete specifications. Since an implementation comprises in particular an i-signature, we obtain the notion of refinement or morphism between i-signatures:
An i-signature morphism
$$\tau: I\Sigma_1 \to I\Sigma_2$$
between two i-signatures IΣ_j = $\langle SPa_j, \sigma_j, SPc_j \rangle$ for $j \in \{1,2\}$ is a pair
$$\tau = \langle \rho a, \rho c \rangle$$
consisting of an abstract specification morphism $\rho a: SPa_1 \to SPa_2$ and a concrete specification morphism $\rho c: SPc_1 \to SPc_2$. The refinement requirement that the translated sentences of IΣ_1 must hold in IΣ_2 is trivially satisfied since IΣ_1 has no sentences at all.

However, another requirement should also be satisfied: Assume we have an i-signature from sets over arbitrary elements to extended lists over arbitrary elements, and another i-signature from sets over natural numbers to extended lists over natural numbers. Then it should not matter whether we first represent sets over arbitrary elements by lists over arbitrary elements and then refine to lists over natural numbers, or if we first refine the sets over arbitrary elements to sets over natural numbers and then represent them as lists over natural numbers.

In general that means that the specification morphisms ρa and ρc should be compatible with the signature morphisms σ_1 and σ_2. This in turn means that the diagram

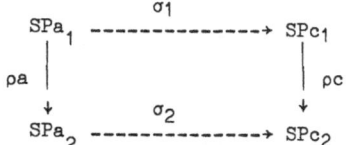

should commute viewing ρa and ρc as signature morphisms.

These notions of i-signatures and i-signature morphisms constitute a category. In fact, it is the comma category induced by the functor Sig forgetting specifications to their signatures.

<u>Definition 4.1</u> [ISIG, i-signature]

Given the forgetful functor Sig: SPEC → Sig, the comma category
    ISIG = (Sig↓Sig)
is the category of implementation signatures (i-signatures).

For an i-signature $I\Sigma$ = ⟨SPa,σ,SPc⟩ ε ISIG, SPa is called the abstract specificatation of $I\Sigma$, SPc the concrete specification, and σ the translation. For an i-signature morphism τ = ⟨ρa,ρc⟩: $I\Sigma_1$ → $I\Sigma_2$, ρa is called the abstract specification morphism and ρc the concrete one.

Since the category SIG is cocomplete and the functor Sig preserves all colimits, ISIG is cocomplete, too, by a general property of comma categories.

<u>Fact 4.2</u> [colimits]

ISIG is cocomplete.

<u>4.2 Implementation models</u>

In Section 2 we already discussed the meaning of a simple implementation. Thus, for an i-signature $I\Sigma$ an $I\Sigma$-implementation model should consist of a concrete SPc-algebra Ac, an abstract SPa-algebra Aa, and a partial, homomorphic, surjective abstraction function α from Ac to Aa. More precisely, for Σa = ⟨Sa,Opa⟩ α is an Sa-indexed family of functions α_s, each going into an abstract carrier Aa_s and starting from the corresponding concrete carrier $Ac_{\sigma(s)}$.

As in the fixed case, the concrete carriers and operations which are not needed for the translation can be forgotten along σ so that we obtain EAlg(σ)(Ac), i.e. Ac viewed as a Σa-algebra, as the source of the abstraction function α.

Now we could define α: EAlg(σ)(Ac) → Aa as a partial, surjective homomorphism. However, according to Section 2 we want to introduce abstraction operations as ordinary operations which are interpreted by abstraction functions and which can be restricted by ordinary sentences. Since in the framework of the SPEC-institution the algebra operations must be totally defined, we will also require that the abstraction operations are totally defined. This is no limitation because the algebras are cpos and there is an error constant for each sort denoting the minimum element. Thus $\alpha(x)$ is mapped to error whenever $\alpha(x)$ is meant to be undefined.

Doing so we must only suitably restrict the homomorphism requirement
$$\alpha(\sigma(op)(x)) = op(\alpha(x))$$
which under these circumstances need to hold only if $\alpha(x)$ is non-error.

Calling a family of functions partially homomorphic if it is homomorphic except for the error elements, we can define an abstraction function
$$\alpha: EAlg(\sigma)(Ac) \rightarrow Aa$$
to be a surjective, partially homomorphic family of functions. Thus an $I\Sigma$-implementation model, or just $I\Sigma$-i-model MA is a tripel
$$MA = \langle Ac, \alpha, Aa \rangle.$$

Note that in contrast to $I\Sigma$, where the first component is the abstract one and the third is the concrete one, we now have the abstract algebra in the third component and the concrete algebra in the first component. However, in both cases the first component contains the source and the third component the target of the function in the middle component.

Proceeding analogously to i-signature morphisms, we obtain a notion of i-model morphisms as a connection between two i-models. Given another $I\Sigma$-i-model
$$MB = \langle Bc, \beta, Ba \rangle$$
an i-model morphism from MA to MB should consist of
- an SPa-homomorphism ha: Aa $\rightarrow$ Ba and
- an SPc-homomorphism hc: Ac $\rightarrow$ Bc.

Analogously to i-signature morphisms the compatibility condition for i-model morphisms should express that it does not matter whether we first abstract Ac-elements with α to Aa-elements and then map them with hc to Bc-elements, or whether we first map the Ac-elements with hc to Bc-elements and then abstract them with β to Ba. This condition may be expressed graphically by requiring that the square

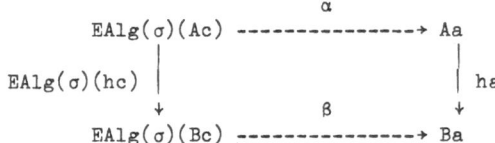

commutes. Note that we must forget hc along σ because we also forget its source and target along σ.

To formalize this description we first have to solve a technical problem: In order to require that the square above commutes the morphisms occurring in there must belong to the same category. However, hc and ha are homomorphisms while α and β as abstraction functions are functions which are surjective but which are only partially homomorphic in general.

Since every homomorphism is partially homomorphic, but is not necessarily surjective the appropriate category for the square should have strict algebras as objects and partially homomorphic functions as homomorphisms.

Definition 4.3 [Σ-p-homomorphism]

Let A, B ε EAlg(Σ) with Σ = <S,Op> ε SIG. An S-sorted family of functions
h = {h_s: A_s → B_s | s ε S }
is a partially-homomorphic Σ-homomorphism (or just Σ-p-homomorphism) iff
$\forall$ op: $s_1 \ldots s_n$ → s ε Σ .
$\quad \forall$ x_1 ε A_{s1} . ... $\forall$ x_n ε Asn .
$\quad\quad$ hs1(x_1) ≠ error-s1B & ... & hsn(x_n) ≠ error-s_{nB}
$\quad\quad\quad$ => h_s(op_A($x_1,\ldots,x_n$)) = opB(hs1(x_1),...,hsn(x_n))

Fact 4.4 [p-homomorphisms are closed under composition]

Let Σ = <S,Op> ε SIG and f: A → B, g: B → C be Σ-p-homomorphisms. Then their composition
$\quad$ g ∘ f := {g_s ∘ f_s | s ε S }: A → C
is a Σ-p-homomorphism.

Definition 4.5 [PEAlg]

The functor
$\quad$ PEAlg: SIG → CAT^{op}
maps a signature Σ to the category of strict Σ-algebras with Σ-p-homomorphisms, and it maps a signature morphism σ to the forgetful functor PEAlg(σ) which is defined analogously to EAlg(σ).

Definition 4.6 [Partial$_\Sigma$]

For Σ ε SIG
$\quad$ Partial$_\Sigma$: EAlg(Σ) → PEAlg(Σ)
is the inclusion functor.

Fact 4.7 [Partial is a natural transformation]

$\quad$ Partial: EAlg ==> PEAlg
is a natural transformation.

With PEAlg formalizing the property "partially homomorphic" we are now ready to define a preliminary model functor mapping an i-signature IΣ to the category of all tripels TA = <Ac,α,Aa> where α is p-homomorphic but not necessarily surjective. Morphisms in that category are pairs of homomorphisms such that they commute with the abstraction functions. Similar to i-signatures, this situation can be expressed neatly as a comma category.

Definition 4.8 [Tripel(IΣ)]

Let IΣ = <SPa,σ,SPc> be an i-signature with Sig(SPa) = Σa and Sig(SPc) = Σc. The comma category
$\quad$ Tripel(IΣ) := (Partial$_{\Sigma a}$ ∘ EAlg(σ)|EAlg(SPc) → PartialΣa|EAlg(SPa))
is called the category of IΣ-tripels.

For an IΣ-tripel TA = <Ac,α,Aa>, Aa is called the abstract (or implemented) algebra, Ac the concrete (or implementing) algebra, and α is the abstraction function of TA.

Similar to ordinary signatures, every i-signature morphism induces a forgetful functor between the respective model categories in the reverse direction. It is defined componentwise.

Fact 4.9 $[\text{Tripel}(\tau)]$

Let $\tau = \langle\rho a,\rho c\rangle\colon I\Sigma_1 \to I\Sigma_2 \in \text{ISIG}$.
   $\text{Tripel}(\tau)\colon \text{Tripel}(I\Sigma_2) \to \text{Tripel}(I\Sigma_1)$
defined on objects by
     $\text{Tripel}(\tau)(\langle Ac,\alpha,Aa\rangle) := \langle EAlg(\rho c)(Ac),PEAlg(\rho a)(\alpha),EAlg(\rho a)(Aa)\rangle$
and on morphisms by
     $\text{Tripel}(\tau)(\langle hc,ha\rangle) := \langle EAlg(\rho c)(hc),EAlg(\rho a)(ha)\rangle$
is a functor.

The observations above yield a prelimininary model functor Tripel: ISIG $\to$ CAT^{op}. We still have to restrict this functor to consider only tripels with surjective abstraction functions.

Definition 4.10 $[\text{IMod}(I\Sigma)]$

For every $I\Sigma \in \text{ISIG}$ the category of $I\Sigma$-implementation models (or just $I\Sigma$-i-models)
   $\text{IMod}(I\Sigma)$
is the full subcategory of $\text{Tripel}(I\Sigma)$ generated by all tripels with surjective abstraction function.

Fact 4.11 $[\text{IMod}(\tau)]$

For every $\tau\colon I\Sigma_1 \to I\Sigma_2$ the restriction and corestriction of $\text{Tripel}(\tau)$ to $\text{IMod}(I\Sigma_2)$ and $\text{IMod}(I\Sigma_1)$ exists. It is denoted by
   $\text{IMod}(\tau)\colon \text{IMod}(I\Sigma_2) \to \text{IMod}(I\Sigma_1)$.

Definition 4.12 $[\text{IMod}]$

     $\text{IMod}\colon \text{ISIG} \to \text{CAT}^{op}$
is the modelling functor for implementation signatures.

4.3 Relating implementation signatures to specifications

According to Section 2, implementation sentences over an i-signature $I\Sigma$ shall be expressed over the abstract signature Σa, the concrete signature Σc, and so-called abstraction operations to be interpreted as abstraction functions. In a first approach, implementation sentences will be all ordinary sentences over this vocabulary.

With this decision we can define the set of $I\Sigma$-implementation sentences to be the set of all ordinary $\psi(I\Sigma)$-sentences, where $\psi(I\Sigma)$ is a suitable equational signature combining Σa, Σc, and the abstraction operations.

We must define $\psi(I\Sigma)$ such that the sentences which are to restrict the abstract algebras do not affect the concrete ones and vice versa. Therefore, taking the set theoretic union of signatures is not suitable, since the abstract and the concrete signatures need not be disjoint. Thus we take the disjoint union (or coproduct). Moreover, for reasons of convenience we will use standard names for the abstraction operations:

Definition 4.13 $[\text{abs-operations}]$

For $I\Sigma = \langle\langle\Sigma a,Ea\rangle,\sigma,\langle\Sigma c,Ec\rangle\rangle \in \text{ISIG}$ and $\tau = \langle\rho a,\rho c\rangle\colon I\Sigma \to I\Sigma' \in /\text{ISIG}/$ we define:
   $\text{abs-operations}(I\Sigma) := \{\text{abs-s}_{I\Sigma}\colon \sigma(s) \to s \mid s \in \Sigma a\}$
   $\text{abs-operations}(\tau) := \{(\text{abs-s}_{I\Sigma}, \text{abs-}\rho a(s)_{I\Sigma'}) \mid s \in \Sigma a\}$.

Fact 4.14 $[\psi]$

$$\psi: \text{ISIG} \to \text{SIG}$$
defined on objects by
$$\psi(I\Sigma) := \Sigma a \uplus \Sigma c \uplus \text{abs-operations}(I\Sigma)$$
and on morphisms by
$$\psi(\tau) := \rho a \uplus \rho c \uplus \text{abs-operations}(\tau)$$
is a colimit preserving functor.

Having defined an $I\Sigma$-implementation sentence to be an ordinary $\psi(I\Sigma)$-sentence p we must determine whether an $I\Sigma$-i-model MA = $\langle Ac,\alpha,Aa \rangle$ satisfies p. Since the abstract symbols in $\psi(I\Sigma)$ shall be interpreted by the abstract algebra Aa, the concrete symbols by the concrete algebra Ac, and the abstraction operations by the abstraction function α, we can take the disjoint union of Aa, Ac, and α to obtain a $\psi(I\Sigma)$-algebra interpreting $\psi(I\Sigma)$.

Definition 4.15 $[\text{join}_{I\Sigma}(MA)]$

For an i-signature $I\Sigma = \langle SPa,\sigma,SPc \rangle$ and an $I\Sigma$-i-model MA = $\langle Ac,\alpha,Aa \rangle$
$$\text{join}_{I\Sigma}(MA) := Aa \uplus Ac \uplus \alpha$$
is the $\psi(I\Sigma)$-algebra A defined by
- for $s \in \text{Sig}(SPa)$: $A_s := Aa_s$
- for $s \in \text{Sig}(SPc)$: $A_s := Ac_s$
- for $op \in \text{Sig}(SPa)$: $opA := opAa$
- for $op \in \text{Sig}(SPc)$: $opA := opAc$
- for $\text{abs-}s \in \text{abs-operations}(I\Sigma)$: $\text{abs-}s_A := \alpha_s$.

The join operator can be extended to a functor from $I\Sigma$-i-models to $\psi(I\Sigma)$-algebras.

Fact 4.16 $[\text{join}_{I\Sigma}]$

Defining $\text{join}_{I\Sigma}$ on $I\Sigma$-i-model morphisms g = $\langle hc,ha \rangle$ by
$$\text{join}_{I\Sigma}(g) := \{ha_s \mid s \in \text{Sig}(SPa)\} \uplus \{hc_s \mid s \in \text{Sig}(SPc)\}$$
yields a functor
$$\text{join}_{I\Sigma}: \text{IMod}(I\Sigma) \to \text{EAlg}(\psi(I\Sigma)).$$

Generalizing over all i-signatures we obtain a natural transformation from the implementation model functor to the model functor of the SPEC-institution composed with the signature translation.

Fact 4.17

$$\text{join}: \text{IMod} ==> \text{EAlg} \circ \psi$$
is a natural transformation.

Now the question whether an $I\Sigma$-i-model MA satisfies an implementation sentence p has been reduced to the question whether $\text{join}_{I\Sigma}(MA)$ satisfies p in the framework of the SPEC-institution.

4.4 Implementation sentences and their satisfaction

According to the preceding section we define the set of $I\Sigma$-implementation sentences or just $I\Sigma$-i-sentences to be the set of all ordinary $\psi(I\Sigma)$-sentences. Such an $I\Sigma$-i-sentence p is satisfied by an $I\Sigma$-i-model MA exactly if MA viewed as the $\psi(I\Sigma)$-algebra $\text{join}_{I\Sigma}(MA)$ satisfies p.

Definition 4.18 [ISen]

The implementation sentence functor is given by
ISen := Sen ∘ ψ: ISIG → SET.

Definition 4.19 [$|\overset{i}{=}$]

Let $I\Sigma \in$ ISIG, $MA \in IMod(I\Sigma)$ and $p \in ISen(I\Sigma)$. MA satisfies p, written
$MA \mid\overset{i}{=}_{I\Sigma} p$
iff $join_{I\Sigma}(MA) \mid\overset{e}{=}_{\psi(I\Sigma)} p$.

Fact 4.20 [satisfaction condition]

∀ τ: $I\Sigma_1 \to I\Sigma2 \in$ ISIG .
∀ $MA \in IMod(I\Sigma_2)$.
∀ $p \in ISen(I\Sigma_1)$.
$MA \mid\overset{i}{=}_{I\Sigma2} ISen(\tau)(p)$ <=> $IMod(\tau)(MA) \mid\overset{i}{=}_{I\Sigma1} p$.

4.5 The institution

Since the satisfaction condition holds the notions defined above constitute an institution.

Definition 4.21 [IMP-institution]

IMP-institution := ⟨ISIG, ISen, IMod, $|\overset{i}{=}$ ⟩
is the institution of implementation specifications.

Like specifications are defined as the theories of the SPEC-institution, implementation specifications will be defined as the theories of this new institution.

Definition 4.22 [IMP]

IMP is the category of theories of the IMP-institution and it is called the category of implementation specifications.

Thus an implementation specification or just i-specification ISP is a pair
ISP = ⟨I\Sigma,IE⟩
consisting of an i-signature $I\Sigma$ and a set of $I\Sigma$-i-sentences IE, and an i-specification morphism is an i-signature morphism respecting the i-sentences.

Since ISIG is cocomplete, general institution properties tell us that IMP is cocomplete as well.

Fact 4.23 [colimits]

IMP is cocomplete.

5. Examples: developing imlementations of sets by lists

In our examples we will assume that the error constants are implicitly declared. As sentences we will use first order formulas where the bound variables are not interpreted as bottom elements. Besides we need some constraint mechanism to exclude unreachable elements (e.g. initial [HKR 80], data [BG 80], hierarchy [SW 82], or algorithmic constraints [BV 85]).

We will show how several well known implementations of sets by lists can be developed stepwise and hand in hand with the implementing specification.

On the abstract side we have the specification SET of sets with the empty set as constant, and operations to insert an element, to determine or remove the minimum element in a set, and to test for the empty set or for the membership of an element. Beside standard sets, there may be bags or unreachable elements of sort set. The set elements are described in the specification LIN-ORD which introduces a sort elem with an equality operation and an arbitrary reflexive linear ordering. The subspecification BOOL of LIN-ORD specifies the booleans.

On the concrete side the specification LIST extends LIN-ORD to standard lists with the constant nil, the operations cons, car, and cdr, and a test nil? for the empty list. All lists must be generated from the elements by nil and cons. LIST is extended to LIST-S by introducing names for the set simulating operations, but without restricting these operations in order to obtain a variety of different models.

```
spec BOOL =
    sorts bool
    ops    true, false: → bool
           not: bool → bool
           and, or: bool bool → bool
    sentences ...  〈 specifying the booleans 〉

spec LIN-ORD = BOOL u
    sorts elem
    ops    eq, le: elem elem → bool
    sentences ...  〈 specifying eq as equality and le as an arbitrary reflexive
                      linear ordering 〉

spec SET = LIN-ORD u
    sorts set
    ops    empty: → set
           insert: elem set → set
           min: set → elem
           remove-min: set → set
           empty?: set → bool
           in?: elem set → bool
    sentences ... 〈 specifying the set operations with their usual meaning, but not
                      necessarily excluding non-standard sets 〉

spec LIST = LIN-ORD u
    sorts list
    ops    nil: → list
           cons: elem list → list
           car: list → elem
           cdr: list → list
           nil?: list → bool
    sentences ... 〈 specifying standard lists over elem generated by nil and cons 〉

spec LIST-S = LIST u
    ops    l-insert: elem list → list
           l-min: list → list
           l-remove-min: list → list
           l-in?: elem list → bool
```

Figure 5.1 The ADT specifications in the implementation of sets by lists

Presentations of the specifications mentioned so far are given in Figure 5.1. The sentences parts are not elaborated since the necessary first order formulas are standard and since we did not want to go into the details of the constraint mechanism to be used, because our implementation concept abstracts from these details completely.

We can give a first simple i-specification I:SET/LIST-S from SET to LIST-S:

```
ispec I:SET/LIST-S =
      isig σ_S/LS: SET → LIST-S
```

with the signature morphism
```
σ_S/LS: Sig(SET) → SIG(LIST-S)
        set          → list
        empty        → nil
        empty?       → nil?
        insert       → l-insert
        in?          → l-in?
        min          → l-min
        remove-min   → l-remove-min
        x            → x          for x ε Sig(LIN-ORD)
```

It merely defines the signature morphism σS/LS translating sort set to list and translating the set operations to their simulating list operations without renaming the signatures of the common subspecifications LIN-ORD and BOOL. Since I:SET/LIST-S contains no i-sentences, its i-models comprise all possible implementations of sets by lists.

I:SET/LIST-S can be refined in various ways by adding i-sentences restricting the abstraction operations of sort set, such that e.g.

```
ispec IA:SET/LIST-S = I:SET/LIST-S u
       isentences
            (∀ x: list . ∀ e: elem.
                abs-set(cons(e,x)) = insert(abs-elem(e),abs-set(x)))

ispec IS:SET/LIST-S = I:SET/LIST-S u
       isentences
            (∀ e, e1, e2:elem . ∀ x: list .
                abs-set(cons(e,nil)) = insert(abs-elem(e),empty) &
                le(e1,e2) = true & eq(e1,e2) = false =>
                  abs-set(cons(e1,cons(e2,x))) =
                       insert(abs-elem(e1),abs-set(cons(e2,x)))  &
                le(e2,e1) = true & eq(e1,e2) = false =>
                abs-set(cons(e1,cons(e2,x))) = error-set         )

ispec IU:SET/LIST-S = I:SET/LIST-S u
       isentences
            (∀ e, e1, e2: elem . ∀ x: list .
                abs-set(cons(e,nil)) = insert(abs-elem(e),empty) &
                (in?(e,abs-set(x)) = true =>
                    abs-set(cons(e,x)) = error-set)              )

ispec ISU:SET/LIST-S = IU:SET/LIST-S u IS:SET/LIST-S
```

Figure 5.2 Some i-specifications implementing sets by lists

- all lists represent sets (IA:SET/LIST-S),
- only lists with unique entries may represent sets (IU:SET/LIST-S),
- only sorted lists may represent sets (IS:SET/LIST-S), or
- only sorted lists with unique entries may represent sets (ISU:SET/LIST-S).

The last i-specification refines not only I:SET/LIST-S, but also IU:SET/LIST-S and IS:SET/LIST-S. The i-specifications are given in Figure 5.2 where we use abs-s: $\sigma_{S/LS}(s) \rightarrow s$ as the abstraction operation name of sort s.

By restricting the abstraction operations these alternative i-specifications constrain their i-models not only w.r.t. the abstraction function of sort set, but also w.r.t. the set simulating list operations. Correspondingly, we can specify four refinements of the concrete LIST-S specification by adding sentences fixing the set simulating operations, such that they generate (and operate upon) exactly
- all lists (LIST-SA),
- all lists with unique entries (LIST-SU),
- all sorted lists (LIST-SS), or
- all sorted lists with unique entries (LIST-SSU).

To give an example we elaborate the specification LIST-SS:

spec LIST-SS = LIST-S u
    sentences
        l-min(nil) = error-elem
        l-remove-min(nil) = nil
        ($\forall$ e: elem . l-insert(e,nil) = cons(e,nil))
        ($\forall$ x: list . $\forall$ e: elem .
            l-min(cons(e,x)) = e   &
            l-remove-min(cons(e,cons(e.x))) = l-remove-min(cons(e,x)))
        ($\forall$ x: list . $\forall$ e1, e2: elem .
            le(e1,e2) = true =>
                l-insert(e1,cons(e2,x)) = cons(e1,cons(e2,x)) &
                l-in?(e1,cons(e2,x)) = eq(e1,e2))   &
            (eq(e1,e2) = false =>
                l-insert(e2,cons(e1,x)) = cons(e1,l-insert(e2,x)) &
                l-in?(e2,cons(e1,x)) = l-in?(e2,x)   &
                l-remove-min(cons(e1,cons(e2,x))) = cons(e2,x)   ))

Now we can in turn refine each of the i-specifications IX:SET/LIST-S for X ϵ {A, U, S, SU} by replacing the concrete specification LIST-S by its refinement LIST-XS and calling the resulting i-specifications IX:SET/LIST-SX. Since the abstraction operation of sort elem is not restricted, IX:SET/LIST-SX i-models have many non-isomorphic LIN-ORD implementations, e.g. the characters represented by the natural numbers or by the integers. However, for each LIN-ORD implementation there are only isomorphic IX:SET/LIST-SX i-models as extensions since the set simulating operations are fixed by now. Thus
- IA:SET/LIST-SA specifies the implementation of sets by all lists,
- IU:SET/LIST-SU specifies the implementation of sets by all lists with unique entries,
- IS:SET/LIST-SS specifies the implementation of sets by all sorted lists, and
- ISU:SET/LIST-SSU specifies the implementation of sets by all sorted lists with unique entries,

which are well known sets-by-lists implementations, differing in the time efficiency of the set simulating operations and in the amount of storage needed by the lists. As an example we give the i-specification IS:SET/LIST-SS:

ispec IS:SET/LIST-SS = IS:SET/LIST-S u
        isig σS/LS: SET → LIST-SS

The refinement relations between the specifications and i-specifications described above are depicted in Figures 5.3 and 5.4:

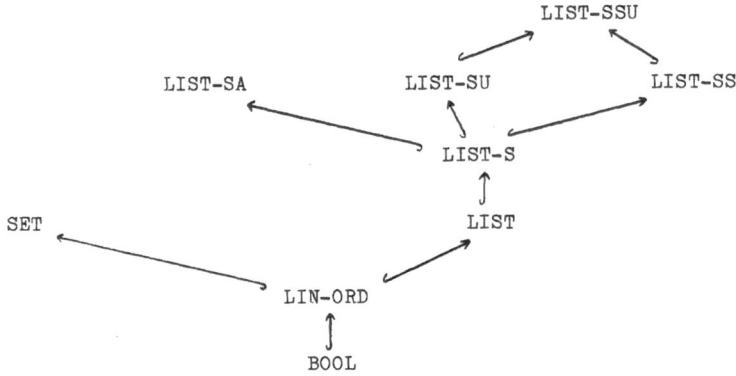

Figure 5.3   The relations between the specifications

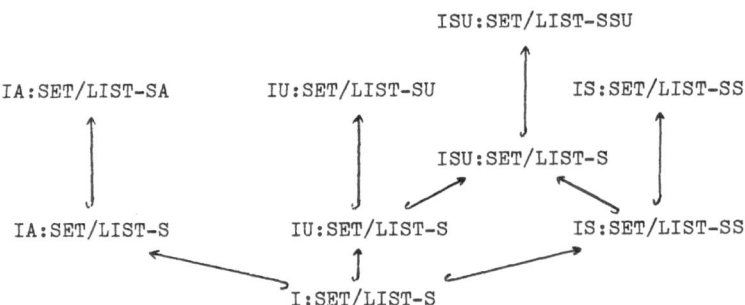

Figure 5.4   The relations between the i-specifications

6. Conclusions

We proposed an implementation concept for loose abstract data type specifications. It introduces the notions of implementation signatures, - models, and - specifications and it formalizes the transition from a more abstract to a more concrete specification including a change of the underlying data structures. By providing the notion of refinement between implementations it supports to develop specifications and implementations hand in hand. Moreover, using institutions our concept abstracts from the underlying ADT specification method and is applicable to different specification techniques.

Other implementation concepts for loose specifications lack the notion of refinement. An implementation in the approach for Clear-like specifications proposed in [SW 82] is - in our terminology - an i-signature with the semantic condition that for every abstract algebra there is a concrete one with an abstraction function in between. Concepts like those of [GM 82] and [Sch 82] are based on behavioural abstraction and have been proposed for modules. The implementation concept for the kernel language

ASL of [SW 83] merely requires that the abstract specification is included in the concrete one. This simple notion is based on the fact that, as a semantical language, ASL has very powerful specification building operations which however may not be present in a language for ADT specifications.

In [BV 85] the implementation concept proposed here is elaborated for a particular institution of ADT specifications. An effective procedure is given to convert an implementation specification to a normal form which essentially consists of an ordinary ADT specification. Referring to the normal forms associative vertical composition operations for implementations are defined compatibly on the syntactical and semantical levels. Horizontal composition and instantiation of parameterized implementations are compatible with vertical composition allowing to combine implementation specifications interchangeably in different directions with the same result.

References

[BG 80]   Burstall, R.M., Goguen, J.A.: The semantics of Clear, a specification language. Proc. of Advanced Course on Abstract Software Specifications, Copenhagen. LNCS Vol.86, pp. 292-332.

[BV 85]   Beierle, C., Voß, A.: Algebraic specifications and implementations in an integrated software development and verfication system. FB Informatik, Univ. Kaiserslautern (to appear 1985).

[Ehc 82]   Ehrich, H.-D.: On the theory of specification, Implementation and Parametrization of Abstract Data Types. JACM Vol. 29, No. 1, Jan. 1982, pp. 206-227.

[EKMP 82] Ehrig, H., Kreowski, H.-J., Mahr, B., Padawitz, P.: Algebraic Implementation of Abstract Data Types. Theor. Computer Science Vol. 20, 1982, pp. 209-254.

[EKP 78]   Ehrig, H.,Kreowski, H.J.,Padawitz, P.: Stepwise specification and implementation of abstract data types. Proc. 5th ICALP, LNCS Vol. 62, 1978, pp. 203-206.

[Ga 83]   Ganzinger, H.: Parameterized Specifications: Parameter Passing and Implementation with respect to Observability. ACM TOPLAS Vol. 5, No.3, July 1983, pp. 318-354.

[GB 83]   Goguen, J.A., Burstall, R.M.: Institutions: Abstract Model Theory for Program Specification. Draft version. SRI International and University of Edinburgh, January 1983.

[GM 82]   Goguen, J.A., Meseguer, J.: Universal Realization, Persistent Interconnection and Implementation of Abstract Modules. Proc. 9th ICALP, LNCS 140, 1982, pp. 265-281.

[GTW 78]   Goguen, J.A., Thatcher, J.W., Wagner, E.G.: An initial algebra approach to the specification, correctness, and implementation of abstract data types, in: Current Trends in Programming Methodology, Vol.4, Data Structuring (ed. R. Yeh), Prentice-Hall, 1978, pp. 80-144.

[HKR 80]   Hupbach, U.L., Kaphengst, H., Reichel, H.: Initial algebraic specifications of data types, parameterized data types, and algorithms. VEB Robotron, Zentrum für Forschung und Technik, Dresden, 1980.

[Sch 82]   Schoett, O.: A theory of program modules, their specification and implementation. Draft report, Univ. of Edinburgh.

[SW 82]   Sannella, D.T., Wirsing, M.: Implementation of parameterized specifications, Proc. 9th ICALP 1982, LNCS Vol. 140, pp 473 - 488.

[SW 83]   Sannella, D., Wirsing, M.: A kernel language for algebraic specification and implementation. Proc. FCT, LNCS Vol. 158, 1983.

The ASSPEGIQUE specification environment

Motivations and Design

Michel BIDOIT, Christine CHOPPY, Frédéric VOISIN

Laboratoire de Recherche en Informatique
Unité Associée au C.N.R.S. 410
Université Paris-Sud, Bât 490
F-91405 ORSAY Cédex
FRANCE

1. INTRODUCTION

In this paper we describe ASSPEGIQUE, an integrated environment for the development of large algebraic specifications and the management of a specification data base. We focus on what motivated us when designing this environment, some crucial design choices and the specific CIGALE parser tool which is extensively used in ASSPEGIQUE.

It is now widely agreed on the fact that specification languages and methods without supporting tools are not practical. Therefore, specific tools must be provided that support the use of algebraic specifications. The aim of the ASSPEGIQUE specification environment is to provide a "specification laboratory" where such tools are closely integrated.

Our goals in the design of ASSPEGIQUE were twofold : on the one hand, the environment should allow the design and management of large specifications ; this point is especially important as far as one is concerned with bridging the gap between research prototypes and the industrial use of specifications. On the other hand, the environment should be flexible enough in order to cope with various styles of specifications or even with various theoretical frameworks. This last point is justified by the fact that no specification language has been widely agreed on up to now. Indeed these algebraic specification languages are still under experiment, and will still evolve depending on the results of these tests. Moreover, specific formalisms may be required to deal with some difficult theoretical points, such as exception handling [BID 84, B&C 85a].

The main problems addressed in the design of ASSPEGIQUE are related to the previous motivations : dealing with modularity and reusability, providing ease of use, flexibility of the environment and user-friendly interfaces. It is moreover necessary to carefully identify the tools required in the environment to achieve these purposes and to determine their respective roles and interfaces. Other specification languages and/or environments have already been designed or are currently under development. The main ones are OBJ [GOG 81, GOG 83], AFFIRM [GER 81], the CIP Project [CIP 81] or the LARCH language [G&H 83]. But all these projects focus on some points and none of them fully integrate all the aspects referred to above.

A direct consequence of our concern in dealing with large specifications is the high degree to which ASSPEGIQUE allows specifications to be modularized. This modularization as well as the flexibility aspects mentioned above raise specific problems that were taken into account from the beginning of the design of the ASSPEGIQUE specification environment. Some of these problems are detailed in the next section.

2. MODULARITY AND REUSABILITY ASPECTS IN ASSPEGIQUE

The size of a specification clearly varies in accordance with the complexity of the system being specified. Therefore, specifications of large software systems cannot be managed as a whole. It is necessary to split them into smaller, hierarchized elementary units. Besides, a better modularity promotes the reusability of existing specification parts. Consequently, the design and management of large specifications require linguistic tools to structure and modularize the specifications while the problem of the reusability and integration of existing specification parts must also be addressed.

The ASSPEGIQUE specification environment supports the specification language PLUSS, where special care has been paid to the choice of specification-building primitives [GAU 84, B&C 85a]. Thus, at the ASSPEGIQUE level, the user only deals with elementary specifications which correspond, so to speak, to types of interest. A major role of the specification language is to assemble these elementary specifications into more complex ones.

One of the main characteristics of our environment is the high degree of flexibility it allows in the way (and in the order) the user may introduce the various components of a large specification into the specification data base. This means that the user is not constrained to use a specific development method, and may build a complex specification without following a strict top-down (or bottom-up) approach. Indeed, this choice was motivated by the fact that strict top-down or bottom-up specification development methods present serious drawbacks in the algebraic framework. The top-down approach leaves to the end the checks that the system must carry out : for example, the system cannot verify that the axioms of the topmost specification are well-formed terms before a lower specification (which eventually contains the definition of the required operations) has been defined. Leaving such checks to the end however means that errors may be discovered far too late. Unfortunately, a wholly bottom-up approach does not correspond more accurately to a natural way of specifying complex data structures, since the most primitive specifications are generally given last, and not first.

Another remark drawn from experiments when specifying real examples is that bottom-up and top-down approaches may lead to very different ways of specifying a given system. To compare the resulting specifications may be instructive, and anyway it is hard to decide which one is best beforehand. Moreover, it is not clear that either the bottom-up or the top-down approach facilitates the reuse of specifications. Mixed approaches seem to be more appropriate for this purpose.

Since the high degree of modularization of the specifications promotes their reuse, elementary pieces of specifications are likely to be shared by several complex specifications. However, modifying shared specification units leads to consistency issues in the specification data base. In fact, it may happen that, once modified, the shared unit is no longer convenient for some of the specifications that reuse it.

To solve the data base management problems raised by reusability and modularity, some relations should be provided in the data base : on the one hand, such relations allow the management of the consequences of a modification made on some elementary specification in the data base ; on the other hand, they allow the list of all the *required types* (i.e. those assumed to be predefined) of a given type of interest to be computed.

In order to provide a better understanding of the issues raised by modularity and reusability, and of the role of the relations in the data base, we describe below a simple but still fairly representative example. Let us specify a *DICTIONARY* as an instance of a (general-purpose) *SORTED-ARRAY[SORTED-THING]* parameterized specification, with *WORD* substituted to the formal parameter *SORTED-THING*. *WORD* will be itself defined as an instance of *SEQ[X]*, with *CHAR* substituted to *X*. The *DICTIONARY* specification looks like :

```
SPEC : DICTIONARY
        SORTED-ARRAY (SORTED-THING => WORD)
        RENAMING    Sorted-Array    INTO Dictionary
END DICTIONARY.
```

The *WORD* specification looks like :

```
SPEC : WORD
        SEQ (X => CHAR)
        RENAMING    Seq         INTO Word
                    cons _ _    INTO _ _
                    car _       INTO first of _
                    cdr _       INTO rest of _
END WORD.
```

As can be noticed in the above example, the syntax for operators has been derived from the one proposed by Goguen in the OBJ system [GOG 81]. The syntax of an operator is composed of strings of symbols and of the reserved symbol "_" (the *placeholder*), which stands for the position of an operand. All combinations of strings and placeholders are allowed, provided that there are as many sorts in the domain of the operator as occurrences of "_" in its syntax. A most typical example is the renaming of the prefix operation *cons* into the operation _ _.

Let us now define a new specification *COMPARABLE-WORDS* which enriches the *WORD* specification by providing a new operation *prefix of* which tests if a word is a prefix of another one :

    SPEC : COMPARABLE-WORDS
        WITH : WORD

    OPERATIONS :

        _ prefix of _ :   Word Word   -> Bool

    VARIABLES :

        w1, w2 :   Word
        c :   Char

    AXIOMS :

        prefix-1 :   empty prefix of w2 = true
        prefix-2 :   c w1 prefix of w2 = (c is first of w2) and (w1 prefix of rest of w2)

    END COMPARABLE-WORDS.

Operations that can appear amongst the axioms of *COMPARABLE-WORDS* are operations of *SEQ[X]* (instanciated and renamed), as well as operations of *WORD* or even operations of *CHAR* or *BOOL*. Thus, checks to be carried out on the axioms of *COMPARABLE-WORDS* (e.g. the fact that the right hand side of the axiom *prefix-2* is a well-formed term) cannot be done by just looking at the text of this piece of specification, neither can they be done before the other pieces are introduced in the data base (in our example, the term is well-formed as far as - at least - an infix operation _ *is* _ is defined in *CHAR*, with a suitable arity ...).

In our specification data base, elementary relations are associated to each specification-building primitive : *use* is associated to the enrichment primitive denoted by **WITH**, *parameterized by* relates a parameterized specification to its formal parameters, *instance of ... using ...* relates an instanciated specification to the parameterized specification from which it is derived and to its actual parameter(s), etc.

The figure on next page illustrates the relations induced by the example sketched above.

Two essential relations *requires* and *depends on* are defined by means of the elementary relations mentioned above. The relation *requires* will in particular allow the computation of the set of all the operations that may appear in an axiom of the specification considered. The relation *depends on* will allow the propagation of modification consequences in the specification data base. Such modification consequences may be quite tricky : a modified version of the *WORD* specification may no longer be a suitable actual parameter for *SORTED-ARRAY*, or conversely a modified version of the formal parameter *SORTED-THING* may lead to the rejection of a (previously) correct actual parameter ...

58

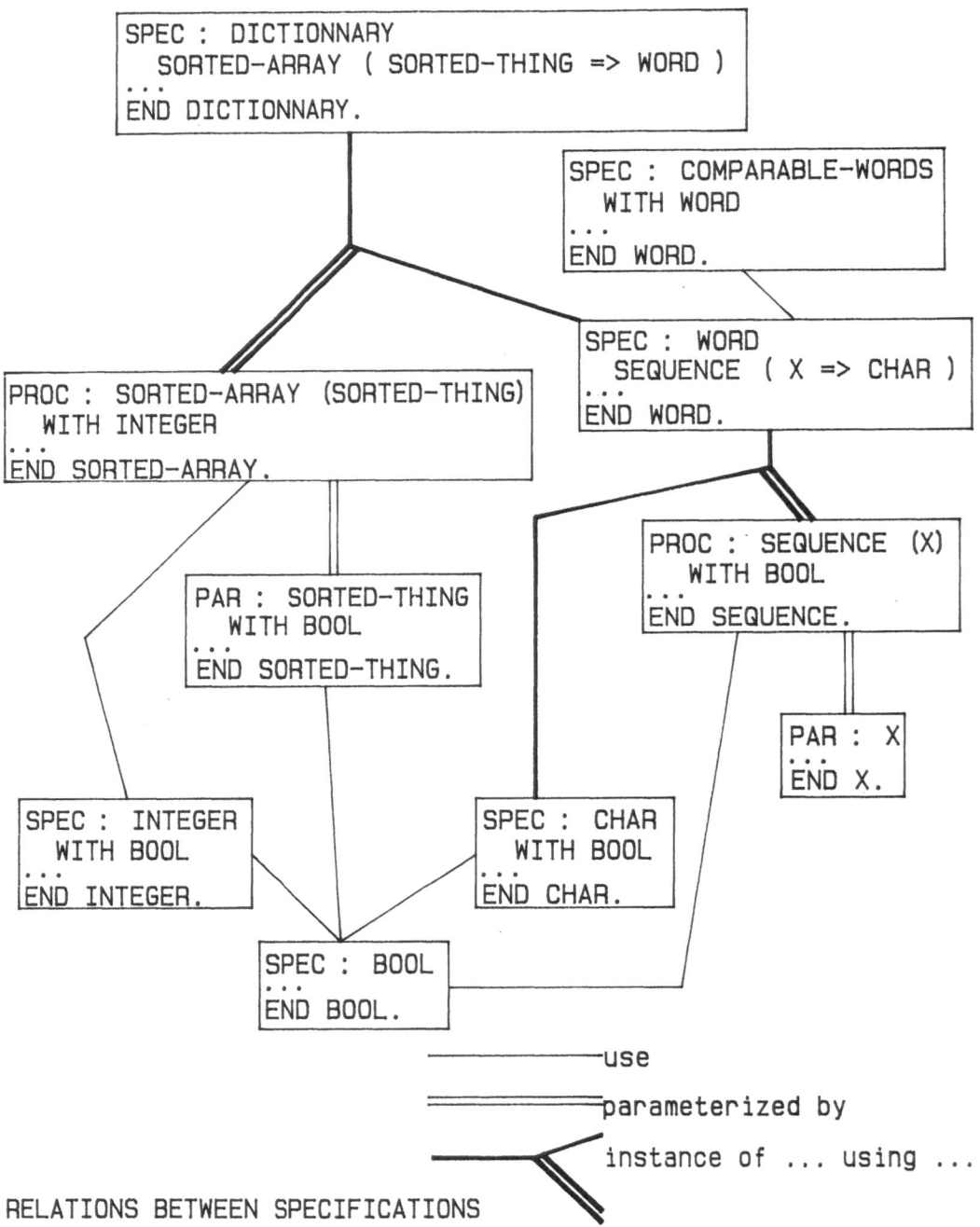

RELATIONS BETWEEN SPECIFICATIONS

Other relations are also used to store various pieces of informations, such as the fact that a specification is implemented by another one, or that test sets have been generated from it [BCFG 85], etc.

3. CIGALE : A parsing viewpoint

In an algebraic specification environment specifications must also be considered from a parsing viewpoint as one must check the syntactical correctness of operators, axioms or expressions to be reduced by the symbolic evaluator. It is important to notice that there are two notions of *language* and of *syntactical correctness*. The first one is defined by the specification language and is related to problems such as : what is the syntax to declare a specification or an axiom. The second language is the one implicitly defined by the operators of a specification and whose typical elements are the text of the axioms (and all what is usually called *terms*) ! In this section we consider only this second notion of language (the first one is taken into account by the specification editor, cf. Section 4) and we focus on the characteristics of parsing in an algebraic specification environment and on the parsing counterpart of the facilities provided by ASSPEGIQUE (interactivity, modularity...). We describe why these facilities lead to problems which are difficult to handle with classical methods and how they are handled by CIGALE, a system for incremental grammar construction, which is part of the ASSPEGIQUE kernel.

The main capabilities of CIGALE are :

- real simplicity for the definition of operators by an incremental construction of grammars ;
- efficient handling of modularity.
- complete support of algebraic data types specific notions such as coercion and overloading of operators ;
- a flexible and user-oriented way of defining operators.

Algebraic specifications as grammars and languages : from our very specific viewpoint, a specification is merely an enumeration of operators (the signature) and relations describing their mutual interactions, as well as the connection with operators of already defined specifications (the axioms). In a specification, each operator is described by its arity, its range and its syntax : its own way of combining operands and symbols. The introduction of an operator is similar to the declaration of a production in a context-free grammar, with the sorts standing for non-terminals. Thus to each specification corresponds a grammar, and we can define the language associated with a specification as the set of all terms composed of valid (w.r.t. the signature and syntax) combinations of operators from the specification or from the languages associated with the required specifications.

3.1. Syntax of operators

One way of offering simplicity of definition and use, and therefore a first step towards the **legibility** and **correctness** of specifications, consists in leaving a great flexibility in the choice of the operator's syntax. It should be possible to use the usual syntaxes (infixed, postfixed, prefixed) for standard operators, as well as to define new ones for other operators if they are more expressive or less error-prone.

We give below another example of specification (*POLYNOMIAL*), which illustrates the different possibilities for the syntax.

SPEC : POLYNOMIAL
      WITH : INTEGER

OPERATIONS :

_ X** _	: integer integer	-> monomial
_ + _	: polynomial monomial	-> polynomial
_	: integer	-> monomial
_	: monomial	-> polynomial
[_] _	: polynomial integer	-> integer

VARIABLES :

coef, exp, val :	integer
M :	monomial
P :	polynomial

AXIOMS

constant :	[coef] val = coef
zero-degree :	[coef X** 0] val = coef
other-monomial :	[coef X** succ(exp)] val = val × [coef X** exp] val
polynomials :	[P + M] val = [P] val + [M] val

END POLYNOMIAL

In the same way that users should not be constrained in the syntax of operators neither should they be limited in the choice of operators by parsing requirements. Typical methods (LL-like) may refuse, for example, left-recursive rules (the + operator on *POLYNOMIAL*) while others (LR-like) require global properties of the set of operators [AU 72]. In such cases the intuitive way of expressing operators has to be abandoned, and operators have to be rewritten in a different, and sometimes more obscure way to be accepted by the system.

Our claim, applied to CIGALE, is that, in the framework we consider, it is more important to offer maximum flexibility, and thus to allow any syntactical construction rather than to limit them because of parsing or for a better time performance. A more precise discussion on performance is presented in Section 3.5.

3.2. Incremental construction of the language

As mentioned in the second section, the main activity in an algebraic specification environment is the reuse of specifications already included in the data base. Users may enrich them by adding new operators and axioms, or they may suppress other ones which are not useful for the application on hand.

Even if it is difficult to decide which specification(s) can be reused, this is not the only problem we have to face : even the design of an isolated specification is also not an easy and direct task, and it may need some backtracking for defining operators. Typically, the specification design appears as a repetition of steps of :

- declaration of operators ;
- writing of axioms or expressions to reduce (and so using the language implicitly defined by the operators),
- and finally, modifications of the kernel of operators.

An example of a situation in which the set of operators to be used is not easy to find is the one of specifications with so-called **hidden** operators [MAJ 77], used to ease the setting of axioms. The need for hidden operators to design a specification may not be clear at the beginning !

Another way of modifying the kernel of operators is to change the syntax for operators. There are usually several possible syntaxes for a given operator, differing for example by the associativity or precedence they induce. Axioms may be more or less easy to express, depending on the syntax used and it is not obvious to find the right syntax at once !

In any case, the signature is an **evolving object**, through the list of operators, or through their syntax. It is therefore important to allow an **incremental** and **interactive** construction of the language. Thus the possibility to **add** or **delete** operators must be offered, while parsing must be available at any time to use the language defined.

This feature puts a requirement to the method used for parsing : to be really powerful, this incremental construction of the language must be performed efficiently. The complexity of the operations involved in adding or deleting operators to or from a given grammar is one important criterion for the choice of a method. All the methods (LR, Coke-Younger-Kasami [AU 72]...) that need some pre-computation on operators before parsing, are rather inadequate in this respect. Such typical pre-computations are the reduction to a normal form, systematic detection of ambiguities or computation of tables describing the different contexts that occur during parsing and the corresponding action to be executed.

Moreover, most of the restrictions that may be required when a language is stable, cannot be imposed on a user who incrementally defines a language.

3.3. Modularity

Another point related to the previous one is the ability to reflect the modularity, which is supported by ASSPEGIQUE. We have seen that with each specification is associated a grammar and a language. Grammars are usually defined independently of each other, and the specification data base may be viewed as a collection of grammars. The languages generated by these grammars may not be disjoint, if some specifications are shared (cf. the *DICTIONARY* example).

The environment must reflect and even induce modularity. The main requirements for our purposes are :

■ Parsing must be oriented towards separate compilation, to allow the modification or enrichment of basic specifications, without having to regenerate grammars for all the specifications that use them.

■ It is also useful to introduce the notion of a current parsing environment. This environment contains all the grammars associated with the specifications required for the work in progress, and the list of the operators that have been defined in the current piece of specification. The main facilities to be provided are the **addition** and **deletion** of (sub)languages in this parsing environment.

The efficiency constraint imposes that lengthy computations on grammars at integration time must be avoided as much as possible. Modularity also implies that some checks on operators (unicity of the declaration of an operator, detection of possible ambiguities in the language...) cannot be done when the specification is designed but must be postponed until (and done every time) it is used ! Such checks are related only to the **current** parsing environment.

A contrario, parsing can take advantage of the modularity for its own purposes : for example searching for an operand of a given sort in the appropriate grammar, rather than in a simple operators list composed of all the elementary grammars merged ! Operations related to the environment (visualization or protection against modifications of a given grammar...) are also simplified by this natural partition of grammars.

3.4. Coercion, overloading and ambiguity

Coercion and overloading are two specific notions of algebraic data types and programming languages. In addition to their semantical issues [GOG 78], these features also have some syntactical implications which we describe below.

Coercions (declared by a syntax composed of a unique "_") are associated with the definition of partial ordering over sorts. To define a coercion from a sort s to a sort t is, in short, to accept each term of sort s as a valid operand everywhere a term of sort t is required. Coercions may also be thought of, and used simply as implicit operators (i.e. without any visible call), and they may be used to solve some purely syntactical problems, e.g. as an easy way to terminate "recursive" definitions (see the *SEQ* specification in Section 4.)

An operator is said to be overloaded if there exist several operators that have the same syntax but different arity or range, as in the classical example of the three "+" operators in Pascal defined on *integer, real* or *sets*. Overloading may be extended to let operators share not only their syntax but also their domain, the range being the only way to distinguish between them. Its main use is the definition of several constants with the same syntax in different specifications. For example, a typical object included in the specification of *stacks, files, lists* is the object *empty*. It is more convenient to let several *empty* constants coexist in the data base, rather than to constrain the user to name them *empty-file, empty-stack* or *empty-list*. Another frequent example is the declaration of variables for axioms. From a parsing point of view these variables appear as constant operators ! The unicity of constant declaration would be thus a very stringent rule, the verification of which would, moreover, be difficult to achieve, due to modularity.

A simple expression such as *empty* becomes of course impossible to parse without the help of the user or without privileging one of the possible ranges, but the context of use will frequently raise the ambiguity. For example with these (non overloaded) operators :

$$push \ \_ \ on \ \ \_ \ : data \ stack \ \text{->} \ stack$$
$$append \ \_ \ to \ \ \_ \ : data \ file \ \text{->} \ file$$
$$x \ : \ \text{->} \ data$$

parsing of *empty* in terms such as *push x on empty* or *append x to empty* can be uniquely determined.

Coercion and overloading are present in modern programming languages and can be handled, in a restricted way, by conventional compilers. Unfortunately they are usually wired in the compiler and cannot be tailored to the user's needs. One exception is the ADA programming language [DoD 83] in which overloading may be introduced for literals and procedures or functions. A qualification mechanism may be used to make ambiguous cases clear.

The generalization of coercion and overloading in a system leads to inefficiencies during the parsing step, due to the ambiguity introduced in the language. In addition to the *syntactical* ambiguities caused by the syntax of operators our system must also deal with *type* ambiguities implied by coercions and overloading.

There is a difference between syntactical and type ambiguities : for expressions with syntactical ambiguities there is usually a most natural parsing among all those possible, which may be given by the user, for example by precedence or associativity indications. This parsing holds independently of the context. On the contrary type ambiguities are introduced on purpose by the user and cannot be solved statically.

In any case, choices must be made to handle such situations : the choice of an arbitrary parsing, the search for all parsings or other heuristics, etc. Some help in raising an ambiguity or in speeding up the parser may also be obtained from the user, thanks to the interactive nature of the environment.

3.5. Performances

The last point we want to consider in this discussion about the characteristic of parsing in an algebraic specification environment is the notion of performances to consider when evaluating a method :

- we mentioned earlier that one criterion to be taken into account was the performance of the operations needed to build the parsing environment : the addition or deletion of operators or grammars. This is a step usually hidden in other methods since it is performed once and for all (or it appears to be so, when the grammar is finally designed !). This step can be costly for standard methods, especially LR-like, and must be considered ;

- even if we restrict our analysis to the time required to parse an arbitrary expression, comparison may be difficult to perform since the length (number of operators) of our expressions is very short, w.r.t. the length of input usually fed into standard compilers. An axiom in a specification is only a small piece of knowledge about some operators and is not a very complex combination. For example, the biggest axiom included in the specification of a realistic application (a part of a telephone switching system [BIE 84]) only contains about 30 operators, one-third of which are constants. This property remains valid although less significant when we parse terms to be evaluated.

CIGALE is designed to handle the characteristics presented above. It offers the possibility to build incrementally the environment by adding or deleting operators to a specification or languages to the environment. There is no restriction on the syntax of operators, and coercion and overloading (even on the domain) are fully supported. The only restriction (put to conform with the partial ordering on sorts) is that coercions must define an acyclic relation over sorts.

3.6. Implementation

We can neither discuss standard methods w.r.t. these constraints, nor detail our parsing method here [VOI 84] [VOI 85], and we only give some insights :

Grammars : grammars are represented by **tries** : each specification is associated with a trie containing its operators. Coercions are represented implicitly by the graph on the sorts they induce. The trie structure allows a factorization of the steps of recognition of operators with a common prefix in a natural way, that is without modifying the productions as in an explicit factorization. The addition or deletion of operators in a trie are easy and fast algorithms. Overloading is also dealt with simply, as operators with overloading on the domain share a unique path of the trie.

Our current parsing environment is composed of a circular list of tries : one for each specification needed for the current work (every specification can also be accessed directly). The inclusion or deletion of grammars are easy operations, although some care must be taken, because of the possible inclusion of overloaded operators in different tries.

Parsing strategies : Parsing is achieved in a bottom-up manner. It is based on a recursive tree traversal (on the tries included in the circular list) with special routines handling the type-checking. An important choice is that we do not derive productions in a systematical way (as it is done by general non-deterministic algorithms) but we express the parsing steps in term of *strategies*, which may be understood and used by a user. For example, one characteristic of our tree traversal is that assignment of operands to placeholders is done as early as possible. This implies that all operators are assumed to be left-associative and have equal precedence. The strategies are additional functions that are used when the default traversal fails to parse a sentence. They are applied locally and correspond, in short, to the use of right-associativity and to the detection of *handles* in bottom-up parsing methods. The word "strategy" is used here to reflect that we dont try to resolve all parsing conflicts but we prefer to offer a simple (and understandable) characterization of the steps of parsing.

We claim that this notion of strategies is important in our context of parsing potentially (very) ambiguous sentences (due to coercions or overloading, or syntactical problems). It gives the user a good intuition of the way its input will be parsed, allows the parsing of most of the realistic cases, and it is thus a practical alternative to the handling of ambiguity by a systematical (and costly) search for all valid parsing that is used in other systems.

User indications : to parse terms which cannot be accepted by the main traversal and the recovery strategies, the user may give parsing informations by adding at will type-checking indications or by bracketing operands. This is maybe the best solution in an interactive environment, both for the user and for the system ! Such indications must also be systematically given in systems which search for all parsings.

The use of these natural strategies and the search for only one parsing yields to a system which is simple to use, in which few indications have to be given and is nevertheless powerful enough.

All the experiments made in the ASSPEGIQUE project have reinforced our conviction that great care must be focussed on these syntactical problems, to offer a really powerful environment to programmers. A parsing system is a significant part of the kernel module for an algebraic specification environment, and its possibilities greatly influence those of the whole environment. Without an efficient assistance for the manipulation of grammars and operators, many theoretical aspects (eg. coercion, overloading or modularity) cannot be fully used and remain theoretical features.

4. A GUIDED TOUR THROUGH ASSPEGIQUE

Besides the CIGALE incremental grammar generator and parser, the tools available in the ASSPE-GIQUE environment include : a **special purpose editor, modification tools, a compiler, a debugger, a symbolic evaluator and theorem proving tools.** They are available to the user through a **user interface** and access the specification data base through the **hierarchical library management tool** (see figure on next page).

Particular attention has been paid to the **interaction with the user** : all the tools are interfaced in a uniform way and make full use of full-screen multiwindow display and graphic facilities to provide a user-friendly interaction ; among others, this includes the use of on-screen and pop-up menus, and on-line help and documentation facilities, detailed according to the degree of expertise of the user. The graphic facilities may be used to display a graphic representation of a specification signature as explained below, but also to display the syntax tree produced by the CIGALE parser, or the logical structure of a proof made using the theorem proving tools, or the relations between the specifications stored in the data base, etc.

The role of the **hierarchical library management tool** is to maintain the specification data base coherence w.r.t. the relations between the specifications ; in particular, the management tool updates the library information file. The hierarchical library management tool also allows the user to obtain various informations about some specification, and to remove obsolete specifications from the data base.

The **specification editor** is syntax-directed which does not mean that the user has to deal with the internal representation of the specification : the *concrete views* available to the user are a *text representation* of the specification and a *graphic representation* of its signature. Thus, the originality of the editor is that, while offering all the flexibility in the use of a full-screen editor, it establishes links between the external concrete views (text, graphics) and the internal representation,

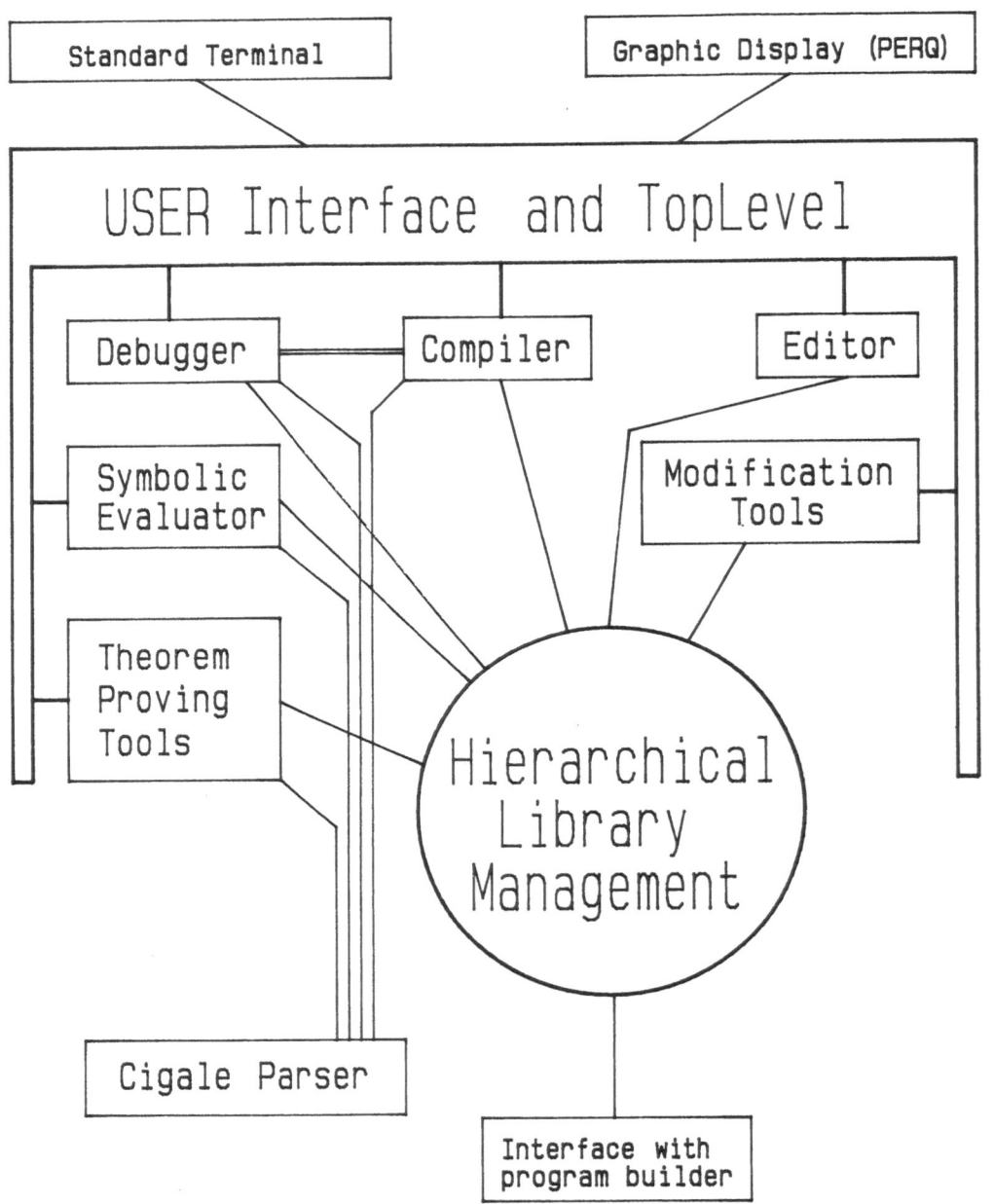

making it a syntax editor [EDS 83]. Therefore, any movement within the text or the graphic representation of the description is also a movement within the corresponding tree, and any modification is taken into account at both levels by means of a validation mechanism.

The part of the editor devoted to the specification text was developed as an extension of WINNIE [AMA 83], a full-screen multi-window editor. The graphical part of the editor was derived from a graphical interactive editor for Petri-nets, PETRIPOTE [BEA 83].

The editor displays a template which depends on the construction primitives (enrichment, formal parameter, parameterized type, etc.), and on the *style* of specification (basic, with error handling, etc.). For instance, the figure on next page shows how the screen looks at some stage of the edition of a specification *enriching* other ones, written in a *basic style*.

In what concerns the signature (sorts and operations), the user may either type in directly the text in the text view or use the PERQ graphical interface. In this case, (s)he just needs to select the appropriate command in the pop-up menu and draw, say, the operation, by pointing at the domains and codomain sorts (the operation arrows are then drawn automatically by the system).

The **specification compiler** may be a misleading appellation, since the compiler does not produce any executable code. A more appropriate name would perhaps be *specification integration tool*, but we have preferred the first name, due to some analogy with the work done by a compiler when separate compilation of modules is allowed. The specification compiler plays two roles :

- The first (and main) role is to carry out all the tests that cannot be done by the editor, due to the modularity and the flexibility of the environment.

  The compilation of a specification cannot take place before all specifications on which it depends are introduced and themselves compiled. Once this is done, the compiler is able to verify that all the terms used in the axioms are syntactically correct (well-formed), that all the sorts occurring in the operator arities are defined, etc. (remember the *COMPARABLE-WORDS* example of Section 2).

  Moreover, the compiler has to verify that the elementary, separate pieces of specifications put together by the specification being compiled are coherent. The compiler must also compute the grammar associated with the specification, and resolve the overloading conflicts. For all these tasks, the compiler makes extensive use of the incremental grammar generator and parser CIGALE described in Section 3.

- The second role of the compiler is to produce an internal form of the specification which will be directly usable by software accessing the library : symbolic evaluator, theorem prover, program construction assistance tool [BGG 83].

The internal form associated with a specification is made up of LISP property lists : this type of internal form is especially flexible, and proved itself to be very convenient for handling problems raised when interfacing ASSPEGIQUE with external tools.

The **specification debugger** is automatically loaded by the compiler when errors are detected ; it allows interactive debugging of the specification. In particular, and this is a contrast with the

```
28 Nov 84 20:41:09 L.R.I. -  Simulation du terminal TVI  -  V1.0  -
            WELCOME IN THE "ASSPEGIQUE"  SPECIFICATION  ENVIRONMENT !!!
+------------------------------------------------------------------------+
|SPEC : SEQUENCE                                                         |
|        WITH : BOOL                                                      |
|                                                                        |
|        SORTS :  Seq                                                    |
|------------------------------------------------------------------------|
|OPERATIONS : Use INS-* to edit operations and sorts trough the PERQ interface
|    empty :  -> Seq                                                     |
|    _ : X  -> Seq              " one-item list ! "                      |
|    cons _ _ : X Seq  -> Seq                                            |
|    car _ : Seq  -> X                                                   |
|    cdr _ : Seq  -> Seq                                                 |
|    _ append _ : Seq Seq  -> Seq                                        |
|    _ less than _: Seq Seq  -> Bool                                     |
|VARIABLES :                                                             |
|    s1, s2 : Seq                                                        |
|    x : X                                                               |
|AXIOMS :                                                                |
|    car-1 : car cons x s1 = x                                          |
|    cdr-1 : cdr cons x s1 = s1                                         |
|------------------------------------------------------------------------|
(ASSEDIQUE<mod>) Value : t
```

EDIT OPS

HELP !!!
OUT !
Add sort
Add sort of int.
Add operation
Delete sort/op
Rename sort/op
Local
Back to Spec.

Fenetre graphique - Menu

editor, the debugger is not loaded unless all required specifications do in fact exist (and have been compiled). The debugger consequently allows axioms to be debugged interactively, which is impossible at the general editing level.

The **symbolic evaluator** is a term rewriting system. However, the term rewriting system used in ASSPEGIQUE is especially powerful, since **conditional rewriting rules** are allowed. One should note that not all specifications may be *evaluated*, since any kind of axioms are allowed at the specification language level, and some of them may prevent the term rewriting system to terminate. Nevertheless, the class of specifications that may be *evaluated* using the symbolic evaluator is still fairly large, since the conditions required by the term rewriting system (**fairness**) are verified in most realistic examples (for a detailed discussion of this technical point, see [KAP 84a] and [KAP 84b]).

Theorem proving tools are obviously needed in an integrated environment such as ASSPEGIQUE. On the one hand, these tools may be used to verify that some desired properties are effectively consequences of the axioms of the specifications. On the other hand, theorem proving tools are necessary in order to prove that the instanciation of some parameterized specification is correct (i.e. that the actual parameter verifies the properties required by the formal one) or to prove that the implementation of one specification by another one is correct. The theorem proving tools implemented in ASSPEGIQUE use the techniques described in [BID 82], i.e. they assume that the specification is *fair* and they use an explicit induction rule, known as "constructor induction". An extension of these tools in order to take into account conditional axioms in the specifications is currently under development [B&C 85b].

Finally, the specification environment is provided with tools whose aim is to make operations easier and to maximize the possibilities for **re-using** specifications. Consequently, suitable tools allow a specification to be copied, to enrich it by adding new operations or axioms, or to rename an operation or an axiom, etc.

5. CONCLUSION

The tools integrated in ASSPEGIQUE range from a high-level syntax-directed editor to a symbolic evaluator and theorem proving tools ; therefore, ASSPEGIQUE is especially well-suited for rapid prototyping purposes [CHO 85]. Industrial sized experimentations on ASSPEGIQUE are currently under development, and will provide a firm basis for further versions.

A kernel system of ASSPEGIQUE consisting in the top-level and user-interface, the specification editor together with its graphic interface, a specification compiler, a symbolic evaluator, the special purpose grammar generator and the parser, theorem proving tools is implemented on VAX-UNIX and PERQ-POS. This system was demonstrated at the 7th International Conference on Software Engineering, Orlando, USA and at the 2nd AFCET Conference on Software Engineering, Nice, France.

6. ACKNOWLEDGEMENTS

This work is or has been partially supported by A.D.I. Contract No 639, the C.N.R.S. (Greco de Programmation) and ESPRIT Project 283 FOR-ME-TOO.

Special thanks are due to Stephane Kaplan, Marianne Choquer, Michel Beaudouin-Lafon who respectively made the symbolic evaluator, the theorem proving tools and the graphic interface.

7. REFERENCES

[AU 72]   Aho & Ullman : "The theory of parsing, translation and compiling" Prentice Hall Series in Automatic Computation 1972

[AMA 83]   Amar P., "Winnie : un éditeur de textes multifenêtres extensible", Actes des Journées BIGRE (Le Cap d'Agde), 1983.

[BEA 83]   Beaudouin-Lafon M., "Petripote: a graphic system for Petri-Nets design and simulation" Proc. of 4th European Workshop on Applications and Theory of Petri Nets, Toulouse, France, 1983.

[BID 82]   Bidoit M., "Proofs by induction in "fairly" specified equational theories" Proc. 6th German Workshop on Artificial Intelligence, Bad Honnef, Germany, Springer-Verlag IFB 58, 1982.

[BID 84]   Bidoit M., "Algebraic specification of exception handling and error recovery by means of declarations and equations", Proc. 11th ICALP, Antwerp, L.N.C.S. 172, Springer-Verlag, pp 95-108, 1984.

[B&C 85a]   Bidoit M., Choppy C., "ASSPEGIQUE : an integrated environment for algebraic specifications", Formal Methods and Software Developments, Proc. International Joint Conference on Theory and Practice of Software Development (TAPSOFT), Berlin, Mars 1985, Vol. 2 : Colloquium on Software Engineering (CSE), L. N. C. S. 186, Springer Verlag, pp 246-260.

[B&C 85b]   Bidoit M., Choquer M., "Preuves de formules conditionnelles par récurrence", Proc. 5ème Congrès AFCET Reconnaissance des Formes et Intelligence Artificielle, Grenoble, Novembre 85.

[BGG 83]   Bidoit M., Gresse C., Guiho G., "CATY : Un système d'aide au développement de programmes", Actes des Journées BIGRE 83 (Le Cap d'Agde), 1983.

[BGG 84]   Bidoit M., Gaudel M.-C., Guiho G. "Towards a systematic and safe programming of exception handling in ADA" Proc. of Ada-Europe/Ada TEC Conf., Brussels, 1984.

[BIE 84]   Biebow B. : "Application d'un langage de spécification algébrique à des exemples téléphoniques", Thèse de 3ème Cycle, Univ. Paris 6, fév. 1984.

[BCFG 85]   Bougé L., Choquet N., Fribourg L., Gaudel M.C., "Applications of Prolog to test sets generation from algebraic specifications", Formal Methods and Software Developments, Proc. International Joint Conference on Theory and Practice of Software Development (TAPSOFT), Berlin, Mars 1985, Vol. 2 : Colloquium on Software Engineering (CSE), L. N. C. S. 186, Springer Verlag, pp 261-275.

[CIP 81]   CIP language group "Report on a wide spectrum language for program specification and development", Rapport TUM-I8104 (Munich), 1981.

[CHO 85]   Choppy C., "Tools and techniques for building rapid prototypes", AFCET Workshop on "Prototypage, Maquettage et Génie Logiciel", Lyon, January 1985.

[DoD 83]   "The programming language ADA - Reference Manual" United States Department of Defense, January 1983.

[EDS 83]   "Les éditeurs dirigés par la syntaxe", Journées d'Aussois - INRIA Ed. (Rocquencourt - France), 1983.

[GAU 84]   Gaudel M.-C., "A first introduction to PLUSS", L.R.I. Research Report, Dec 1984.

[GER 81]   Gerhart S.L., "AFFIRM Reference Manual", UCS-Report (Marina del Rey), 1981.

[GOG 81]   Goguen J.A., Parsaye-Ghomi K., "Algebraic denotational semantics using parameterized modules", Tech. Report CSL-119, SRI International, UCLA, 1981.

[GOG 83]   Goguen J.A., "Parameterized Programming", Proc. Workshop on Reusability in Programming, Stratford CT, USA, 1983.

[G&H 83]   Guttag J.V., Horning J.J., "An introduction to the LARCH shared language", Proc. IFIP 83, R.E.A. Mason ed., North Holland Publishing Company, 1983.

[KAP 84a]   Kaplan S., "Fair Conditional Term Rewriting Systems : Unification, Termination and Confluence", in this volume.

[KAP 84b]   Kaplan S., "Conditional Rewrite Rules", Theoretical Computer Science, 1984.

[MAJ 77]   Majster M., "Limits of the algebraic specification of data types", SIGPLAN Notices 12, 1977.

[VOI 84]   Voisin F., "CIGALE : un outil de construction incrémental de grammaire et d'analyse d'expression", Thèse de 3ème cycle, Orsay (France), 1984.

[VOI 85]   Voisin F. : "CIGALE : a tool for interactive grammar construction and expressions parsing", Science of Computer Programming (to appear).

Towards Abstract User Interfaces
For Formal System Specifications

Hartmut Ehrig, Werner Fey, Horst Hansen

TECHNISCHE UNIVERSITÄT BERLIN
FACHBEREICH INFORMATIK (20)

Abstract

In this paper we propose the concept of an abstract user interface which is an abstract
version of some important parts of a user interface as known in software engineering.
The main advantage of an abstract user interface formulated in BNF-terms compared
with an ordinary user interface written in natural language is the possibility to
translate the abstract user interface into a formal specification of the corresponding
system. This is achieved by translating the formal parts of an abstract user interface into separate texts of the same formal specification language which is also
used for the executable system specification. We link these parts by a third specification text in the same language, which gives an interpretation of the user command
language in terms of the system specification. So the resulting executable specification is a prototype of the software system, equipped with an abstract user interface. We exhibit this method by an example, a simple screen-oriented editor.

Introduction

Although the benefit of formal specifications for software development is widely

accepted in the scientific community by now (see /Jo 80/, /Kr 80/), there are still

a number of problems concerning their use in practice. It is claimed, for example,

that there are large parts of programs which are beyond the scope of formal specifi-

cations, like details of man-machine interaction, formats of input and output data,

communication mechanisms with peripheral devices and software utilities (see /Fl 85/).

Most of these aspects are concerning the user interface of the software system.

Since the user interface is usually given in natural language it is difficult to

relate it to the formal specification of the system in some precise way.

The idea of the paper is to provide a new concept to bridge this gap. We propose to

consider the notion of an abstract user interface which contains some relevant

information about the user interface on an abstract level. On one hand this informa-

tion should be still understandable for the user, on the other hand it should be

precise enough to allow a formal relationship to the formal specification of the

system. In the simplest version, which is studied in this paper, we propose that an

abstract user interface comprises four parts: A command language, input/output

formats for I/O-data, an informal description of the meaning of commands, and formal

properties of commands which are relevant for the user of the system.

Starting with the command language and the I/O-formats of an abstract user interface,

which are given in some extended BNF-notation, we first translate the given context-

free grammar (resp. the context-free parts of the grammar) into an algebraic specification according to the ideas of initial algebra semantics in /ADJ 77/. In a second step we relate the specification of the user interface to the specification of the system. We accomplish this by a further specification, which includes both the specifications mentioned above and contains some additional operation symbols and equations, which interpret the command language into the system specification. The resulting specification is an operational specification (see /Za 84/), which is executable by an interpreter for algebraic specifications, if the system specification was executable. In this case we have reached a specification which essentially is a prototype of the system including a user interface. So the system designer and the user can experiment with both the system and its user interface at an early stage in the development process.

The concept of an abstract user interface will be studied in Section 1. In Section 2 we demonstrate this concept giving an abstract user interface and main parts of a formal specification for a simple screen editor. Neither we propose a new advanced editor nor an abstract user interface which is best suited for this application. Both are only intended to serve as examples and to show explicitly in Section 3 how they can be related to each other in a precise way. A conclusion of the paper is given in Section 4.

The specification language which we use to present our example is ACT ONE. This algebraic specification language is based on a small number of structuring concepts only, making specifications more easily understandable. The full language and its semantics can be found in /EM 85/, a previous version in /EFH 83/.

Acknowledgement

This paper is part of the DFG-project ACT (Algebraic Specification Techniques for Correct and Trusty Software Systems) at TU Berlin. We are most grateful to Paul Boehm, Christiane Floyd, Ulrich Grude, Klaus Peter Hasler, Michael Löwe and Michaela Reisin for several valuable discussions on the subject of this paper. Many thanks also to H. Barnewitz for excellent typing.

1. Abstract User Interfaces

In this first section we introduce the concept of an abstract user interface, which was sketched already in the introduction. Especially we want to relate it to the well-known concepts of a user interface on one hand and to the formal specification of the system on the other hand.

In software engineering (see /Ki 79/) a user interface comprises the following parts:

1. user commands
2. input/output formats of the system on the user's screen and/or printer,
3. operating instructions for the physical input- and output-devices,
4. sequences of actions to handle everday's work and instructions how to cope with exceptional situations,
5. performance requirements,
6. sociological environment of the system.

This concept of a user interface relates the software system to the user taking into account its software, hardware and sociological environment. Our concept of an abstract user interface is intended to depend only on the software but not on hardware and sociological environment. More precisely it should depend only on abstract software, i.e. on software specification. This means it will not comprise parts 3, 5 and 6 of a user interface above. In our first version of abstract user interfaces we concentrate on parts 1 and 2 which, however, could also be extended to handle part 4. Instead of part 4, however, we consider sequences of user commands yielding identical effects. This part will also be used to check formally the link of the abstract user interface and the system specification.

1.1 CONCEPT OF ABSTRACT USER INTERFACES

An abstract user interface consists of four parts:

1. a grammar in BNF-notation defining the user command language,

2. a grammar in BNF-notation defining the input/output formats of the system,

3. a description in natural language of the meaning of each user command, its parameters, and the input/output formats,

4. sequences of user commands yielding identical effects.

Parts 1 and 2 are clearly related to parts 1 and 2 of a user interface. Part 3 provides the necessary semantical information in natural language for the user, which, of course, is not intended to be a formal semantics.

A formal semantics of commands and input/output formats, however, will be given by a translation of these items into the formal specification of the system. This link between abstract user interface and formal system specification is intended to be comprehensible on the same level as the formal system specification, i.e. at least for the system designer, but not necessary for the user. This can be achieved by using the same specification language for the system specification and the translation, where the BNF-rules are reformulated as operation symbols in the signature of the formal specification of the command language (see /ADJ 77/).

In the list of pairs of sequences of user commands in part 4 some pairs of sequences of commands are given which are assumed to have the same effect. Since the command language is comprehensible for the user - which is not assumed for the specification language used for the formal specification of the system - he is able to learn about mutual effects of the commands in a precise way, although the description of the commands in part 3 is informal.

Once the abstract user interface is linked to the system specification these pairs of sequences of user commands become equations in terms of the formal specification and we are able to verify whether these equations are provable from the specification. In this case the abstract user interface is correctly linked to the system specification. It is important to note that we have a precise notion of correctness, although we don't have an explicit formal semantics for the abstract user interface. The reason is that we have an implicit formal semantics via the translation of the

command language into the system specification. This means the command language has
a "translation semantics" which is comparable to compiler semantics of programming
languages.

The main advantages of an abstract user interface compared with a usual user interface is that we are able to define a translation into the formal specification of
the system such that:

1. Each user command gets equipped with a formal semantics, thereby enabling the
system designer to answer all user questions concerning the effect of the command.

2. As the user interface is formalized using the same specification language which
is used for the system specification, a prototype of the system can easily be out-
fitted with an abstract user interface. This enables the user of the projected system
to check his intuitive ideas behind each command against the effects of the command
proposed by the software developer.

We think, however, that the parts 3 - 6 of user interfaces are important, too, but
they are not necessary for the link with the formal specification. Actually we would
like to propose that a user interface should extend an abstract user interface adding
parts 3 - 6 above.

2.   Screen Editor

In this section we give an abstract user interface and an algebraic specification for
a simple screen editor.

Using this editor the user can write and manipulate a text interactively. Such a
text consists of a sequence of lines of characters, with all lines having a certain
fixed length l. The system displays a window of w lines of the text around the
current line with the working position marked by the cursor. To transform a text,
the user invokes commands and the system displays parts of the changed text in the
window. The cursor can be moved explicitly in four directions.

2.1   ABSTRACT USER INTERFACE

The command language and the input/output formats are described in extended Backus-
Naur-Form where $\{<l>\}$ means a finite sequence of elements, $\{<l>\}^n$ a sequence of
length n of elements, $[<l>]$ the empty sequence or a sequence of one element of $<l>$
and line-length as well as window-length are natural numbers.

(1)   command language

        $\langle$command language$\rangle$::= EDITOR $[\langle$text$\rangle]$ line-length window-length $\{\langle$command$\rangle\}$ EXIT

        $\langle$command$\rangle$ ::= PRINT-TEXT $|$ WINDOW-LENGTH window-length $|$ NEW-LINE $|$

                           DELETE-LINE $|$ DELETE $|$ $[\langle$mode$\rangle]$ $\langle$character$\rangle$ $|$ $\langle$cursor$\rangle$

        $\langle$mode$\rangle$ ::= INSERT-MODE $|$ CHANGE-MODE

        $\langle$cursor$\rangle$ ::= $\rightarrow$ $|$ $\leftarrow$ $|$ $\downarrow$ $|$ $\uparrow$

        $\langle$character$\rangle$ ::= characters including SPACE

(2)   input/output formats text and window

$\langle\text{text}\rangle$ ::= $\{\langle\text{line}\rangle\}$

$\langle\text{line}\rangle$ ::= $\{\langle\text{character}\rangle\}^l$ where l = line-length

$\langle\text{window}\rangle$ ::= $\{\langle\text{line}\rangle\}^n \langle\text{current line}\rangle \{\langle\text{line}\rangle\}^m$ where n+m $\langle$ window-length

$\langle\text{current line}\rangle$ ::= $\{\langle\text{character}\rangle\}^r \{\langle\text{character}\rangle\}^s$ where r+s = line-length

(3)   informal description of the commands and input/output formats

EDITOR t l w   start the editor with text t, length of line l and length of window w.

EXIT   terminate the editor;

INSERT-MODE   set editor in insert mode;

CHANGE-MODE   set editor in change mode.

For each character char of a fixed character set (including a character SPACE) there is one command:

char   depending on the actual editor mode change or insert char into the working position and move the cursor to the right by one position;

DELETE   delete any character in the working position and set the character SPACE in the rightmost position of the current line, but don't move the cursor;

DELETE-LINE   delete the current line and move the cursor to the leftmost position of the line directly below. If there is no line below go to the line directly above. If there is also no line above create a new line.

NEW-LINE   if the cursor position is the leftmost position then insert a new line, i.e. a sequence of l SPACE character, directly before else directly below the current line and move the cursor to the leftmost position of this new line.

PRINT-TEXT   print the actual text;

WINDOW-LENGTH w   alter the window length to w.

There are commands to move the cursor:

$\longrightarrow$ move right one position;

$\longleftarrow$ move left one position;

$\downarrow$ move down one line;

$\uparrow$ move up one line.

By these four commands and also by char the cursor can only be moved within the actual text. If the intended move can not be done then cursor and text are not changed.

By the input/output format $\langle\text{text}\rangle$ a text is described as a finite sequence of lines where all the lines are sequences of characters of the fixed length line-length.

By the output format $\langle\text{window}\rangle$ a window of the actual text displayed by the system is described as consisting of
- a sequence of n lines (the n lines directly above the current line),
- a current line, i.e. the line with the cursor and
- a sequence of m lines (the m lines directly below the current line).

Only maximal window-length lines can be shown by such a window.

A current line described by $\langle\text{current line}\rangle$ consists of two sequences of characters: The one of length r (contains the characters left of the cursor) and the one of length s (contains the characters right of the cursor). The cursor is implicitly placed between the two sequences of characters of the current line. The working position is at the first character right of the cursor.

We also require properties of the screen editor by expressing that some command sequences of the command language must have identical effects (=): Two effects are identical, if they can not be distinguished on the output components window and text using the command language only (observable equivalent effects).

(4)   sequences of user commands yielding identical effects

- For all cursor of ⟨cursor⟩

     cursor PRINT-TEXT = PRINT-TEXT cursor,

   i.e. the actual text must not be changed by moving the cursor.

- For all char of ⟨character⟩

     DELETE INSERT-MODE char = CHANGE-MODE char INSERT-MODE,

   i.e. changing a character to char must be the same as first deleting that

   character and then inserting char.

- For all mode of ⟨mode⟩ , char, char' of ⟨character⟩ and command-sequence of

   {⟨command⟩} except of mode commands

      mode char command-sequence char' =

      mode char command-sequence mode char',

   i.e. the effect of character commands is depending on the latest given mode

   command.

Here we have given only some choice of properties. They all are assumed to be satisfied by the software system.

The notion of identical effects can be liberated by requiring that the effects must
be identical only on some defined components, e.g. on printed text ($=_t$) or the system
component ($=_s$). Then we can demand for example that

. NEW-LINE   DELETE-LINE   PRINT-TEXT $=_t$ PRINT-TEXT,
   i.e. first NEW-LINE then DELETE-LINE must not change the actual text.

. Our second command sequence given above can then be weakend by
   DELETE INSERT-MODE char $=_s$ CHANGE-MODE char
   i.e. changing a character to char must be the same on the system component as
   first deleting that character and then inserting char. Nothing is said about
   the other components especially the mode component, which must be different after
   application of the two sequences of commands (see their informal description in
   2.1 (3)).

To avoid trivial connections of the abstract user interface to our system specification we may also require that exactly every text can be generated by the command
language:

. For each text of ⟨text⟩ exists a command-sequence of {⟨command⟩} without
   PRINT-TEXT such that
   EDITOR line-length window-length command-sequence PRINT-TEXT $=_t$ text.

2.2   EDITOR SPECIFICATION

As software development includes the task to give a system specification for an

informally given problem, we give such a specification using the algebraic specifi-

cation language ACT ONE (see /EM 85/). In Section 3 this operational specification

will be related to the abstract user interface. For lack of space we only present

a shortened version of the full specification.

The ACT ONE specification text SCREEN-EDITOR is subdivided in the four specification

definitions EDITOR, EXTENDED-BASE-EDITOR, BASE-EDITOR, and 5-TUPLE (TEXT,WINDOW,TEXT,

NAT,NAT).

They are specified using from a library the predefined specifications TEXT for
sequences of lines of characters, WINDOW for sequences of lines of character with
cursor, NAT for natural numbers and 5-TUPLE(DATA5) for tuples of five formal
components.

In the definitions BASE-EDITOR and 5-TUPLE(TEXT,WINDOW,TEXT,NAT,NAT) the main data
structure consists of five components

> text front, i.e. the text above the window,

> window, i.e. the part of the text with cursor being displayed,

> text rest, i.e. the text below the window,

> line length and window length

with corresponding GET and SET operations to get and set each component.

In definition EXTENDED-BASE-EDITOR we only lift the GET and SET operation of the
window components

> window front above the current line, line front before the cursor

> line rest behind the cursor, and window rest below the current line

to the editor level such that we can on this level also manipulate the window
components.

In definition EDITOR the main editing operations are specified using the definition
EXTENDED-BASE-EDITOR.

These definitions are organized into the following ACT ONE specification text which
requires a top down succession of definitions.

```
act text {SCREEN-EDITOR}
  def EDITOR is
      EXTENDED-BASE-EDITOR
      opns INITIAL-EDITOR          : text nat nat       ⟶ editor
           INSERT                  : character editor   ⟶ editor
           DELETE,NEW-LINE,DELETE-LINE: editor          ⟶ editor
           ⟶ , ⟵ , ↓ , ↑          : editor             ⟶ editor
           MAKE-TEXT               : editor             ⟶ text
           ADJUST-WINDOW           : nat editor         ⟶ editor
      eqns for all t in text; line-length; window-length in nat:
      {E1} INITIAL-EDITOR(t,line-length,window-length) =
             SET-LINEREST(FIRST(t)),
             SET-WINDOWREST(FRONT(REST(t)),window-length - ONE),
             SET-TEXTREST(REST(REST(t)),window-length - ONE),
             SET-LINELENGTH(line-length ,
             SET-WINDOWLENGTH(window-length,EMPTY-EDITOR)))))
           for all ed in editor; char in character:
      {E2} INSERT(char,ed) =
             if LENGTH(GET-LINEFRONT(ed)) = GET-LINELENGTH(ed) then ed
             else SET-LINEFRONT(GET-LINEFRONT(ed) · char,
                  SET-LINEREST(FRONT(GET-LINEREST(ed)),ed))

             {*** only these examples of equations are given here ***}

  end of def
```

```
def EXTENDED-BASE-EDITOR is
    BASE-EDITOR

    {*** SET and GET operations for the four components of window are lifted to
        editor level ***}

end of def

def BASE-EDITOR is
    5-TUPLE(TEXT,WINDOW,TEXT,NAT,NAT) renamed by
    sortnames editor        for 5-tuple
    opnames EMPTY-EDITOR for CONST-5TUPLE
        SET-TEXTFRONT       for SET1    GET-TEXTFRONT       for PROJ1
        SET-WINDOW          for SET2    GET-WINDOW          for PROJ2
        SET-TEXTREST        for SET3    GET-TEXTREST        for PROJ3
        SET-LINELENGTH      for SET4    GET-LINELENGTH      for PROJ4
        SET-WINDOWLENGTH    for SET5    GET-WINDOWLENGTH    for PROJ5
end of def

def 5-TUPLE(TEXT,WINDOW,TEXT,NAT,NAT) is
    5-TUPLE(DATA5) actualized by TEXT and WINDOW and NAT using
    sortnames text for data1 opnames EMPTY-TEXT      for CONST-DATA1
              window for data2         EMPTY-WINDOW    for CONST-DATA2
                text for data3         EMPTY-TEXT      for CONST-DATA3
                 nat for data4         ZERO            for CONST-DATA4
                 nat for data5         ZERO            for CONST-DATA5
end of def

    uses from library TEXT,WINDOW,NAT,5-TUPLE(DATA5)
end of text   {SCREEN-EDITOR}
```

3.   Linking the Abstract User Interface to the System Specification

3.1   SPECIFICATION OF THE ABSTRACT USER INTERFACE

The context-free parts of the command language (see 2.1 (1)) and the input/output
formats (see 2.1 (2)) of the abstract user interface for the screen editor are translated to two ACT ONE specification texts SCREEN-EDITOR-COMMAND-LANGUAGE and INPUT/
OUTPUT-FORMATS.

Such translation from BNF to algebraic specifications has been put forward in
/ADJ 77/:

> For every nonterminal symbol we introduce a sort, for every rule an operation
> symbol, which takes its arguments from the sorts corresponding to the non-
> terminal symbols on the right-hand side of the rule, and delivers a result
> of the sort corresponding to the nonterminal symbol on the left-hand side.

Therefore, we get for each nonterminal of the grammar for the command language, i.e.
⟨command language⟩, ⟨command⟩, ⟨mode⟩, ⟨cursor⟩ and ⟨character⟩ corresponding ACT ONE
definitions COMMAND-LANGUAGE, COMMAND, MODE and CURSOR. For ⟨character⟩ and also for
the notation of sequences of data we use predefined specifications CHARACTER and
SEQUENCE-of-data from a library. In definition SEQUENCE(COMMAND) we actualize the
formal parameter data of SEQUENCE-of-data by the specification COMMAND and in definition COMMAND-SEQUENCE we rename the sort sequence to command-sequence and the sequence
EMPTY-SEQ to EMPTY-COMMAND-SEQ.

(1) command language

act text {SCREEN-EDITOR-COMMAND-LANGUAGE}
  def COMMAND-LANGUAGE is
        COMMAND-SEQUENCE and NAT and TEXT
    sorts command-language
    opns   EDITOR-EXIT: text nat nat command-sequence &longrarr; command-language
            EDITOR-EXIT: nat nat command-sequence   &longrarr; command-language
  end of def

  def COMMAND-SEQUENCE is
        SEQUENCE(COMMAND) renamed by
        sortnames command-sequence for sequence
        opnames EMPTY-COMMAND-SEQ for EMPTY-SEQ
  end of def

  def SEQUENCE(COMMAND) is
        SEQUENCE-of-data actualized by COMMAND using
        sortnames command for data
  end of def

  def COMMAND is
        MODE and CURSOR and CHARACTER
    sorts command
    opns PRINT-TEXT, NEW-LINE,
          DELETE-LINE,DELETE: &longrarr; command
          WINDOW-LENGTH   : nat   &longrarr; command
          ___   ___   : mode character &longrarr; command
              ___   : character   &longrarr; command
              ___   : cursor   &longrarr; command
  end of def

  def MODE is
    sorts mode
    opns INSERT-MODE: &longrarr; mode
          CHANGE-MODE: &longrarr; mode
  end of def

  def CURSOR is
    sorts cursor
    opns &longrarr; , &longlarr; , ↓, ↑ : &longrarr; cursor
  end of def

  uses from library TEXT,NAT,SEQUENCE-of-data,CHARACTER
end of text   {SCREEN-EDITOR-COMMAND-LANGUAGE}

In the following ACT ONE specification text INPUT/OUTPUT-FORMATS the context-free parts of the I/O-formats window and text of the abstract user interface for the screen editor are translated to algebraic specifications in a similar way. The definitions TEXT and WINDOW for texts and windows are already used in 2.2 as part of the system specification. So we have the same input/output-formats in the system specification and the abstract user interface.

(2) input/output formats

act text {INPUT/OUTPUT-FORMATS}
   def WINDOW is
      4-TUPLE(TEXT,LINE,LINE,TEXT) renamed by
  sortnames window   for 4-tuple
  opnames EMPTY-WINDOW   for CONST-4TUPLE
        SET-WINDOWFRONT for SET1 GET-WINDOWFRONT for PROJ1
        SET-LINEFRONT   for SET2 GET-LINEFRONT   for PROJ2
        SET-LINEREST   for SET3 GET-LINEREST   for PROJ3
        SET-WINDOWREST for SET4 GET-WINDOWREST for PROJ4
  end of def

   def 4-TUPLE(TEXT,LINE,LINE,TEXT) is
      4-TUPLE(DATA4) actualized by TEXT and LINE using
  sortnames text for data1   opnames EMPTY-TEXT for CONST-DATA1
         line for data2   EMPTY-LINE for CONST-DATA2
         line for data3   EMPTY-LINE for CONST-DATA3
         text for data4   EMPTY-TEXT for CONST-DATA4
  end of def

   def TEXT is
      SEQUENCE(LINE) renamed by
  sortnames text for sequence opnames EMPTY-TEXT for EMPTY-SEQ
  end of def

   def SEQUENCE(LINE) is
      SEQUENCE-of-data actualized by LINE using
  sortnames line for data   opnames EMPTY-LINE for CONST-DATA
  end of def

   def LINE is
      SEQUENCE(CHARACTER) renamed by
  sortnames line for sequence opnames EMPTY-LINE for EMPTY-SEQ
  end of def
  uses from library 4-TUPLE(DATA4),SEQUENCE-of-data,SEQUENCE(CHARACTER)
end of text {INPUT/OUTPUT-FORMATS}

3.2 INTERPRETATION OF THE COMMAND LANGUAGE

In this part we exhibit the relationship between the algebraic specification of the command language (see 3.1) and the system specification of the editor (see 2.2). The linkage between both specifications is achieved by the ACT ONE specification text INTERPRETATION, in which the command language terms and command sequence terms as well as command terms are interpreted in the ACT ONE specification EDITOR-STATE by appropriate equations. The specification text EDITOR-STATE is built using the definition EDITOR of the specification text SCREEN EDITOR (see 2.2) together with MODE and TEXT (see 3.1). Terms of sort state represent a complete description of the situation the editor is in: the actual text being edited with window and cursor, the current insert/change mode and the text representing the actual printout.

(1) editor state

<u>act text</u> {EDITOR-STATE}
  <u>def</u> STATE <u>is</u>
      TRIPLE(EDITOR,MODE,TEXT) <u>renamed by</u>

<u>sortnames</u> state	<u>for</u> triple				
<u>opnames</u> SET-EDITOR	<u>for</u> SET1	GET-EDITOR	<u>for</u> PROJ1		
SET-MODE	<u>for</u> SET2	GET-MODE	<u>for</u> PROJ2		
SET-PRINT	<u>for</u> SET3	GET-PRINT	<u>for</u> PROJ3		
INITIAL-STATE	<u>for</u> CONST-TRIPLE				

  <u>end of def</u>

  <u>def</u> TRIPLE(EDITOR,MODE,TEXT) <u>is</u>
      3-TUPLE(DATA3) <u>actualized by</u> EDITOR <u>and</u> MODE <u>and</u> TEXT <u>using</u>

<u>sortnames</u> editor	<u>for</u> data1	<u>opnames</u> CREATE-EDITOR	<u>for</u> CONST-DATA1	
mode	<u>for</u> data2	INSERT-MODE	<u>for</u> CONST-DATA2	
text	<u>for</u> data3	EMPTY-TEXT	<u>for</u> CONST-DATA3	

  <u>end of def</u>

  <u>uses from library</u> EDITOR,MODE,TEXT,3-TUPLE(DATA3)
<u>end of text</u> {EDITOR-STATE}

(2) interpretation

<u>act text</u> {INTERPRETATION}
  <u>def</u> LANGUAGE-INTERPRETATION <u>is</u>
      COMMAND-LANGUAGE <u>and</u> STATE <u>and</u> COMMAND-INTERPRETATION
    <u>opns</u>   INTERPRET: command-language   ⟶ state
            INTERPRET: command-sequence state ⟶ state
    <u>eqns for all</u> line-length,window-length <u>in</u> nat;
               com-seq <u>in</u> command-sequence:
    {I1}   INTERPRET(EDITOR-EXIT(line-length,window-length,com-seq)) =
            INTERPRET(EDITOR-EXIT(EMPTY-TEXT,line-length,window-length,com-seq))
        <u>for all</u> t <u>in</u> text; line-length,window-length <u>in</u> nat;
               com-seq <u>in</u> command-sequence:
    {I2}   INTERPRET(EDITOR-EXIT(t,line-length,window-length,com-seq)) =
            INTERPRET(com-seq,SET-EDITOR(INITIAL-EDITOR(t,line-length,window-length),
                                        INITIAL-STATE))
        <u>for all</u> s <u>in</u> state:
    {I3}   INTERPRET(EMPTY-COMMAND-SEQ,s) = s
        <u>for all</u> com <u>in</u> command; com-seq <u>in</u> command-sequence; s <u>in</u> state:
    {I4}   INTERPET(com ° com-seq,s) = INTERPRET(com-seq,INTERPRET(com,s))
  <u>end of def</u>

  <u>def</u> COMMAND-INTERPRETATION <u>is</u>
      STATE <u>and</u> COMMAND
    <u>opns</u>   INTERPRET: command state ⟶ state
    <u>eqns for all</u> s <u>in</u> state:
    {I5}   INTERPRET(PRINT-TEXT,s) =
               SET-PRINT(GET-PRINT(s) ° MAKE-TEXT(GET-EDITOR(s)),s)
        <u>for all</u> s <u>in</u> state:
    {I6}   INTERPRET(NEW-LINE,s) = SET-EDITOR(NEW-LINE(GET-EDITOR(s)),s)

        {*** similar equations for DELETE-LINE and DELETE ***}

        <u>for all</u> length <u>in</u> nat; s <u>in</u> state:
    {I9}   INTERPRET(WINDOW-LENGTH(length),s) =
               SET-EDITOR(ADJUST-WINDOW(length,GET-EDITOR(s)),s)

```
               for all m in mode; char in character; s in state:
{I10}       INTERPRET((m,char),s) =
               SET-EDITOR(IF m = INSERT-MODE
                          THEN INSERT(char,GET-EDITOR(s)),
                          ELSE INSERT(char,DELETE(GET-EDITOR(s))),
                          SET-MODE(m,s))
               for all char in character; s in state:
{I11}       INTERPRET((char),s) =
               IF GET-MODE(s) = INSERT-MODE
               THEN SET-EDITOR(INSERT(char,GET-EDITOR(s)),s)
               ELSE SET-EDITOR(INSERT(char,DELETE(GET-EDITOR(s))),s)
               for all s in state:
{I12}       INTERPRET(⟶ , s) = SET-EDITOR(⟶ (GET-EDITOR(s)),s)

               {*** similar equations for ⟵ , ↓ and ↑ ***}
end of def

uses from library COMMAND-LANGUAGE,COMMAND,STATE

end of text {INTERPRETATION}
```

We think that the function INTERPRET rather explicitly describes the function of the
projected software system:

After recognizing the command invoked by the user- which is formalized in the lefthand side of the corresponding equation in the specification text INTERPRETATION -
those routines (or subprograms) are executed, that constitute the right-hand side of
the equation. Thinking along these lines provides a way to connect the user commands
to the operations of the system specification.

It is obvious, that the function INTERPRET mainly depends on the 'distance' between
the user commands and the system operations:

If there is an operation directly corresponding to each user command, the specification of INTERPRET becomes rather trivial, but if the command language includes
commands for which there is no operation in the specification, then the function
INTERPRET must translate the command to a possibly rather complex sequence (term) of
operations from the specification.

3.3   CORRECTNESS OF THE LINK

We are going to prove that the abstract user interface (see 2.1) is correctly linked
to the system specification of the editor (see 2.2).

Therefore we have to translate the sequences of user commands of 2.1 (4) into
equations of terms of the definition LANGUAGE-INTERPRETATION (see 3.2 (2)) which is
straightforward:

For every command sequence we construct the corresponding term of the definition
COMMAND-LANGUAGE (see 3.1 (1)) and apply the operation symbol INTERPRET to each such
term and arbitrary editor states. Every pair of command sequences which should yield
identical effects so becomes an equation of terms of the specification INTERPRETATION.

(1) the translated sequences of user commands

–   For all c ∈ cursor, s ∈ state

      INTERPRET(c ° PRINT-TEXT,s) = INTERPRET(PRINT-TEXT ° c,s)

–   For all s ∈ state, c ∈ character

      INTERPRET(DELETE ° INSERT-MODE ° c,s) =

          INTERPRET(CHANGE-MODE ° c ° INSERT-MODE,s)

–   For all m ∈ mode, c,c' ∈ character, s ∈ state, cs ∈ command[*] without mode

      INTERPRET(m,c) ° cs ° c',s) =

          INTERPRET(m,c) ° cs ° (m,c'),s)

Although according to (2.1 (4)) we only would have to show that these terms are ob-servable equivalent we essentially will show a stronger property, i.e. that they are congruent w.r.t. the specification INTERPRETATION, which implies observable equivalence.

Before we can formulate our correctness theorem we need assumptions and a definition to clarify the notions of the theorem.

(2) assumptions and definition

We assume that all specifications in this paper are correct ACT ONE texts, which implies that all specifications are extensions of their named subspecifications. Furthermore the act specification INTERPRETATION is considered as an example of an interpretation as required in the following definition:

DEFINITION (correctness of the link)

The abstract user interface (see 2.1) is correctly linked to the system specification SCREEN-EDITOR (2.2), if the translated sequences of user commands (see 3.3 (1)) are provable in the definition LANGUAGE-INTERPRETATION (see 3.2 (2)).

(3) **THEOREM** (correctness of the link)

The abstract user interface is correctly linked to the system specification SCREEN-EDITOR.

Proof: We show that the translated equations (see 3.3 (1)) are provable in the definition LANGUAGE-INTERPRETATION for states which are generated by commands.
As an example we only prove the first equation here, using the equations in 3.2 (2) and (A) – (D) given below:

Let c ∈ cursor, s ∈ state:

    INTERPRET(c ° PRINT-TEXT,s) $\underset{=}{\text{I4}}$
    INTERPRET(PRINT-TEXT,INTERPRET(c,s)) $\underset{=}{\text{I12}}$
    INTERPRET(PRINT-TEXT,SET-EDITOR(c(GET-EDITOR(s)),s)) $\underset{=}{\text{I5}}$
    SET-PRINT(GET-PRINT(SET-EDITOR(c(GET-EDITOR(s)),s)) °
      MAKE-TEXT(GET-EDITOR(SET-EDITOR(c(GET-EDITOR(s)),s))),
              SET-EDITOR(c(GET-EDITOR(s)),s)) $\underset{}{\text{(A)}}$
    SET-PRINT(GET-PRINT(SET-EDITOR(c(GET-EDITOR(s)),s)) °
      MAKE-TEXT(GET-EDITOR(s)),SET-EDITOR(c(GET-EDITOR(s)),s)) $\underset{=}{\text{(B)}}$
    SET-PRINT(GET-PRINT(s) °
      MAKE-TEXT(GET-EDITOR(s)),SET-EDITOR(c(GET-EDITOR(s)),s)) $\underset{}{\text{(C)}}$
    SET-EDITOR(c(GET-EDITOR(s)),
      SET-PRINT(GET-PRINT(s) ° MAKE-TEXT(GET-EDITOR(s)),s)) $\underset{=}{\text{(D)}}$

```
SET-EDITOR(c(GET-EDITOR(
            SET-PRINT(GET-PRINT(s) ° MAKE-TEXT(GET-EDITOR(s)),s))),
            SET-PRINT(GET-PRINT(s) ° MAKE-TEXT(GET-EDITOR(s)),s))   I12
INTERPRET(c,SET-PRINT(GET-PRINT(s) ° MAKE-TEXT(GET-EDITOR(s)),s))  ═══  I5
INTERPRET(c,INTERPRET(PRINT-TEXT,s))  ═══  14
INTERPRET(PRINT-TEXT ° c,s)
```

The labels at the equation sign correspond to the application of the corresponding
equations in the specification INTERPRETATION (see 3.2 (2)), or they are explained
below:

(A) MAKE-TEXT(GET-EDITOR(SET-EDITOR(c(GET-EDITOR(s)),s))) =
        MAKE-TEXT(GET-EDITOR(s))

(B) GET-PRINT(SET-EDITOR(e,s)) = GET-PRINT(s)

(C) SET-PRINT(t,SET-EDITOR(e,s)) = SET-EDITOR(e,SET-PRINT(t,s))

(D) GET-EDITOR(SET-PRINT(t,s)) = GET-EDITOR(s).

The equations (B) to (D) are renamed equations of the specification 3-TUPLE(DATA3)
which is used from the ACT ONE library (see 3.2 (1)). Equation (A) expresses the
fact that moving the cursor does not change the content of the text worked on, which
is a provable property of the given system specification SCREEN-EDITOR.
The other translated equations of 3.3 (1) have been proved in a similar way. Because
of lack of space we omit those proofs here.   #

The proofs of the translated equations above are essentially depending on some
equations and properties of the system specification SCREEN-EDITOR, which is part of
the definition LANGUAGE-INTERPRETATION via STATE (see 3.2).

Our formal correctness notion of the link concerns only part (1), (2) and (4) of the
abstract user interface (see 2.1)   because part (3) is informal. But as our specification is essentially a prototype, the system designer and the user can test whether
the specified effects of the user commands conform to their informal description given
in part (3) of the abstract user interface.

4. Conclusion

We have demonstrated how to establish a close relation between the abstract user
interface and an algebraic specification of a software system, thereby connecting
two documents arising in the software design process which often are considered laying
far apart. The method proposed here allows system developers to design the abstract
user interface and the system specification rather independently, except for the in-
put/output formats, which should be identical. Of course we can define many different
command languages for a given system specification. The expense of fitting a command
language to a system specification depends on their similarity or dissimilarity.

This paper puts forward a first small example by which we tested our method.
Especially the grammar of the command language is extremely simple. (The corresponding
interaction diagram only has one node.) But the proposed technique in principal need
not be changed for larger grammars of more complex and advanced command languages.
To find out its drawbacks and merits in practical cases we need to apply our ideas

to larger examples.

In Section 3.1 we noted that we translate only the context-free parts of the grammars of the user command language and input/output formats to an algebraic specification. This restriction makes the translation straightforward and easily understandable. Kaphengst and Reichel /KR 77/ show that there is a more general translation which can be applied to context-sensitive grammars as well.

Furthermore it is necessary to generalize this approach to arbitrary abstract user interfaces and system specifications and lay ground for a formalized method which possibly could be useful bringing closer user and software-developer. We think that using a common language for the abstract user interface and the system specification is profitable in itself for the software-developer.

Of course specifications tend to grow enormously in size as the problems tackled do. So only an interactive specification environment which assists in writing (executable) algebraic specifications can encourage the use of the methods proposed. The ACT group at the TU Berlin has just started to design such a system for ACT ONE, including an editor and an interpreter, as well as a tool to assist in proving the correctness of the link. The interpreter provides the means to execute ACT ONE specifications.

In this paper we suppose the user commands to be given by a grammar in BNF-notation. Other authors advocate interaction diagrams instead, which they consider even more comprehensible. From formal language and automata theory the close connection between certain classes of formal languages and corresponding automata is widely known (cf. /HU 79/). We believe that interaction diagrams are a special kind of representation of language-recognizing automata thus enabling us to translate the interaction diagram to a corresponding grammar to which we can apply our method.

The proposed method can be seen as a first step to deal with part 4 of a user interface as well (see 1.). It shows how to formalize sequences of commands and gives their semantics from the systems point of view. By translating back the results of commands or command sequences into a description given in natural language we can provide very detailed information especially on those sequences of actions which are necessary to handle everydays work. Furthermore we can explicitly describe commands which must be used to cope with (and overcome) exceptional situations arising from inadequacies of the (hardware-/software) information processing system.

Studer considers in /St 84/ screen oriented user interfaces, too. In contrast to our approach, which stresses the connection of the abstract user interface and the system specification, he abstracts from concrete software systems behind the user interface as well as from specific command languages. Instead, he focusses on different realizations for the input of commands (via keystrokes or menues together with pointing devices) and for the output of data (via windows and forms).

Finally let us mention that our ideas can also be extended to the specification of modular systems in the sense of /WE 85/, where also the relationship between informal and formal parts of a specification are discussed but the problem of user interfaces is not explicitly mentioned.

5. References

/ADJ 77/   Goguen, J.A., Thatcher, J.W., Wagner, E.G., Wright, J.B.:
            Initial Algebra Semantics and Continous Algebras.
            JACM 24, 1, pp. 68-95

/EFH 83/   Ehrig, H., Fey, W., Hansen, H.: ACT ONE: An Algebraic Specification
            Language with Two Levels of Semantics, Techn. Report 83-03, TU Berlin,
            FB 20, 1983

/EM 85/   Ehrig, H., Mahr, B.:
            Fundamentals of Algebraic Specifications 1, Equations and Initial
            Semantics. EATCS Monograph Series Vol. 6, Springer 1985

/FH 84/   Fey, W., Hansen, H.:
            Linking Abstract User Interface and Formal System Specification;
            Techn. Report (draft version) TU Berlin, FB 20, August 1984

/Fl 85/   Floyd, Ch.: On the Relevance of Formal Methods to Software Develop-
            ment, LNCS 186, pp. 1-11

/HU 79/   Hopcroft, J., Ullman: Introduction to Automata Theory, Languages
            and Computation, Addison-Wesley, 1979

/Jo 80/   Jones, C.B.: Software Development: A Rigorous Approach;
            Prentice Hall International, 1980

/Ki 79/   Kimm, R. et al: Einführung in Software Engineering;
            De Gruyter, Berlin, 1979

/KR 77/   Kaphengst, H., Reichel, H.: Initial Algebraic Semantics for Non-
            Context-Free Languages, LNCS 56, pp. 120-126

/Kr 80/   Kreowski, H.-J.: Algebraische Spezifikation von Softwaresystemen.
            2. Treffen Gm. Chp. ACM, "Software Engineering - Entwurf und Spezifi-
            kation", Berlin 1980

/Pa 83/   Partsch, H.: On the Use of Algebraic Methods for Formal Requirements
            Definitions. In: Hommel, G., Kröning, D.(eds.): Requirements
            Engineering; Informatik-Fachberichte 74, Springer Verlag 1983

/St 84/   Studer, R.: Abstraction Concepts for Modeling Screen Oriented
            Dialogue Interfaces; LNCS 181, pp. 242-258

/WE 85/   Weber, H., Ehrig, H.: Specification of Modular Systems;
            Techn. Report Nr. 198, Universität Dortmund, 1985

/Za 84/   Zave, P.: The Operational Versus the Conventional Approach to Soft-
            ware Development, Com. ACM, Vol. 27, No. 2, pp. 104-118

A FINAL ALGEBRA SEMANTICS FOR ERRORS AND EXCEPTIONS

Martin Gogolla

Informatik B, TU Braunschweig

Postfach 3329, D-3300 Braunschweig

Federal Republic of Germany, March 1985

Abstract Algebraic specifications allowing equations and inequations are studied. A characterisation of the existence of models
and initial algebras as well as a criterion for the existence of
final algebras for such specifications are given. As an application it is shown, how the result can be applied to yield maximal
error propagation preserving error recovery in abstract data types.

Keywords Abstract data type, algebraic specification, equation,
inequation, initial and final algebra semantics, error and exception handling.

1. Introduction

Today the theory of abstract data type has been studied widely and
is considered as a promising tool for program specification. Since
interest in algebraic descriptions of data types has been initia-
ted by [LZ 74,Gu 75], at least two different approaches can be re-
cognised. The concept of initial algebra is favoured by [ADJ 78,
ADJ 81, EKMP 82, Eh 82, Kl 84], whereas final algebras and classes
of algebras are treated in [Wa 79, HR 80, BW 83, WPPDB 83, Ga 83].
In both directions precise modularization concepts, i.e. parametrization, extension and implementation, have been developed.
Our topic, the problem of error and exception handling in abstract
data types, has been treated in a series of papers. Some approaches only consider strict error propagation without recovery
[Go 78.1, Pl 82] or lead to an unpleasant amount of specification
overhead [ADJ 78]. In others, standard semantics for specifications do not always exist [BGP 82, Pl 82, Bi 84] or standard
algebraic constructions do not work and difficulties occur
[Go 78.2]. [BW 83] does not mention error and exception handling
explicitly, but treats algebras allowing different undefined elements. However, the approach presented here can handle other sets
of axioms and our final algebra construction is different from
the corresponding construction in [BW 83]. An operational treatment of errors has been given in [EPE 83] and an approach to
parametrization of exceptions can be found in [Po 84].

In this paper we modify our previous approach [GDLE 84, Go 84] to automatize the propagation of errors respecting error recovery, which before had to be done explicitly. Our equational specifications allow two different kinds of functions and variables, safe and unsafe ones. Implicitly we add inequations between ok elements mutually and ok and error values and choose a final algebra as a standard semantics. By this means we identify error elements behaving in the same way with respect to the ok values.

2. The basic idea

Consider the following simple specification of the natural numbers with equality.

    spec natural numbers with equality
    srts bool, nat
    opns false, true : ---> bool
        0 : ---> nat
        succ : nat ---> nat
        eq : nat x nat ---> bool
    vars n, m : nat
    axms eq(0,0)=true
        eq(0,succ(n))=eq(succ(n),0)=false
        eq(succ(n),succ(m))=eq(n,m)

    ceps

The initial model of the above specification is isomorphic to the booleans and the natural numbers, whereas the final one consists of singleton sets for bool and nat. But if one adds the axiom

    false$\neq$true

the above specification has a non-trivial final model, namely the booleans and the natural numbers. But what is missing in this situation, are rules to derive new inequations that hold in all models of the specification and therefore also in the final model. The usual rules of reflexivity, symmetry, transitivity and operational closure for the equality do not allow for example to conclude $0\neq$succ(0) in the above example. Therefore we additionally introduce the following rules to derive new inequations.

(1) Rule of symmetry :
    $a\neq b$ implies $b\neq a$

(2) Rule of equality multiplication :
    $a=b$ and $b\neq c$ implies $a\neq c$

(3) Rule of observability :
    $f(a_1...a_i...a_n)\neq f(a_1...a_i'...a_n)$ implies $a_i\neq a_i'$

91

In the above example all inequations that are valid can be derived using only these rules, but this does not hold for arbitrary
specifications for which final models exist. Nevertheless these
rules allow to formulate a criterion for the existence of final
algebras : If one can prove that for a given (perhaps already
derived) inequation a≠b and for a given c a≠c or b≠c holds, then
the final model of the specification exists.

Given these results, we can apply them to automatize error propagation in abstract data types. Consider the following specification of the natural numbers including error handling, formulated
within our approach to error and exception handling. The details
of this approach are explained in chapter 5 and in [GDLE 84,
Go 84].

> spec natural numbers with error handling
> srts bool, nat
> opns false, true : ---> bool ok
>   0 : ---> nat ok
>   succ : nat ---> nat ok
>   pred : nat ---> nat unsafe
>   error : ---> nat unsafe
>   if : bool x nat x nat ---> nat ok
> vars n : nat ok
>   n-, m- : nat unsafe
> axms pred(succ(n))=n
>   pred(0)=error
>   if(false,n-,m-)=if(true,m-,n-)=m-
>
> ceps

One important point to mention is that in our approach the above
variable n stands for ok elements only, e.g. terms that can be
built only from function symbols marked by ok in the signature.
But the variables n- and m- hold arbitrary elements, ok and error
values as well. So, for example if(true,0,error) evaluates to 0,
but pred(succ(error))=error does not hold in the initial model of
the above example. For this reason a lot of new, distinct error
elements are generated: succ(error),pred(error),succ(succ(error)),
etc. These new error elements behave in the same way with respect
to the ok part of the initial model, and therefore one can implicitly add inequations to distinguish between ok elements mutually
and ok and error elements. By this error elements behaving in the
same way are identified in the final model, and automatic error
propagation is achieved.

In the above example one would add implicitly the following inequations :

    0≠1   0≠2   0≠3   0≠4   0≠5   ...
    1≠2   1≠3   1≠4   1≠5   ...
    ...
    error≠0   error≠1   error≠2   ...
    succ(error)≠0   succ(error)≠1   succ(error)≠2 ...

But for example the inequation error≠succ(error) will not be added and in the final model error=succ(error)=pred(error)=... will be true. It can be shown that, if one proceeds in this way, final models for such specifications always exist and therefore they can be chosen as a standard semantics. In the above one would yield an algebra consisting of the natural numbers and exactly one error element.

3. Basic definitions and facts

This chapter introduces the basic definitions and some well known facts. For more details consult [ADJ 78, WPPDB 83, etc.].

A <u>signature</u> $(S,\Sigma,arity,sort)$ consists of sets S and Σ of sorts and operation symbols, respectively and mappings arity : $\Sigma \dashrightarrow S^*$ and sort : $\Sigma \dashrightarrow S$. arity and sort of function symbols are denoted by $\sigma : s1 \times ... \times sn \dashrightarrow s$. $(S,\Sigma,arity,sort)$ will also be denoted by Σ only. A <u>Σ-algebra</u> (A,F) consists of an S-indexed family of sets $A = \langle A_s \rangle_{s \in S}$ and a Σ-indexed family of operations $F = \langle \sigma_A \rangle_{\sigma \in \Sigma}$ with $\sigma_A : A_{s1} \times ... \times A_{sn} \dashrightarrow A_s$ for $\sigma : s1 \times ... \times sn \dashrightarrow s$. (A,F) will sometimes be abbreviated by A. A <u>Σ-algebra morphism</u> $f : A \dashrightarrow B$ is an S-indexed family of mappings $\langle f_s \rangle_{s \in S}$, that respects the operations.

A' is a <u>Σ-subalgebra</u> of A, if A'_s is a subset of A_s for $s \in S$, σ'_A is the restriction of σ_A for $\sigma \in \Sigma$ and A' is closed under all functions σ_A. For every algebra A there exists a least subalgebra sub(A) wrt set inclusion. An algebra is called <u>finitely generated</u>, if $A =$ sub(A). A is finitely generated, iff there is a surjective morphism $f_T : T_\Sigma \dashrightarrow A$, where T_Σ denotes the <u>term-algebra</u> (T_Σ, F_T), $T_\Sigma = \langle T_s \rangle_{s \in S}$ and $F_T = \langle \sigma_T \rangle_{\sigma \in \Sigma}$.

<u>Important remark</u> Because we want to investigate final models of specifications, we only consider finitely generated algebras. From now on the notion of algebra refers to finitely generated algebra with nonempty sets of terms.

If ALG_Σ denotes the category of all Σ-algebras with morphisms between them, then T_Σ is initial and $\underline{1}$ is final in ALG_Σ, where $\underline{1}$ is the algebra with all carriers consisting of singleton sets. Of course, in this category there is at most one morphism between two algebras due to the fact that they are finitely generated.

An <u>axiom</u> is a tuple [L,R] of terms with variables, which can be either an equation L=R or an inequation L≠R. An algebra <u>satisfies</u> an axiom [L,R], if for all substitutions α of variables $L_\alpha = R_\alpha$ or $L_\alpha \neq R_\alpha$ holds, depending on the form of the axiom. If EQ is a set of equations, $EQ(T_\Sigma)$ denotes the set of pairs of constant terms resulting from EQ by substituting terms for variables. Analogously, $NE(T_\Sigma)$ denotes the set of constant inequations resulting from given inequations NE. If equations EQ and inequations NE are given, $ALG_{\Sigma,EQ+NE}$ denotes the category of all algebras satisfying EQ and NE. $I_{\Sigma,EQ+NE}$ and $F_{\Sigma,EQ+NE}$ denote <u>initial</u> and <u>final</u> objects in $ALG_{\Sigma,EQ+NE}$, if they exist. If there are no inequations, $T_{\Sigma,EQ}$, the quotient of T_Σ by the least congruence generated by EQ, is initial and $\underline{1}$ is final in $ALG_{\Sigma,EQ}$. A signature together with a set of axioms $(\Sigma,EQ+NE)$ is called a <u>specification</u>.

4. Specifications with equations and inequations

<u>Simple observation 1</u> Inequations may lead to empty model categories. Let the signature consist only of the sort s and let {c≠c} be the set of axioms with c a constant. Then there is no algebra that satisfies the axioms.

<u>Simple observation 2</u> Inequations may lead to the non-existence of final algebras, although initial algebras may exist. Let the signature consist of the sort s and constants a, b and c and let {a≠b} be the axioms EQ+NE. T_Σ is initial in $ALG_{\Sigma,EQ+NE}$, but there is no final algebra, because both [a]=[c]≠[b] and [a]≠[b]=[c] are models.

In order to give a sufficient criterion for the existence of final models of specifications, we define the following relations $=_{EQ}$ and $\neq_{NE}$ on terms without variables.

<u>Definition 4.1</u> Let axioms EQ+NE be given. $=_{EQ}$ and $\neq_{NE}$ are the least (families of) relations on T_Σ satisfying the following conditions.

(EQ1) $EQ(T_\Sigma)$ is a subset of $=_{EQ}$.

(EQ2) $t=_{EQ}t$.

(EQ3) $t=_{EQ}t'$ implies $t'=_{EQ}t$.

(EQ4) $t=_{EQ}t'$ and $t'=_{EQ}t''$ implies $t=_{EQ}t''$.

(EQ5) $t_i=_{EQ}t_i'$ implies $\sigma(t_1..t_i..t_n)=_{EQ}\sigma(t_1..t_i'..t_n)$, $i\in\{1..n\}$.

(NE1) $NE(T_\Sigma)$ is a subset of $\neq_{NE}$.

(NE2) $t\neq_{NE}t'$ implies $t'\neq_{NE}t$.

(NE3) $t=_{EQ}t'$ and $t'\neq_{NE}t''$ implies $t\neq_{NE}t''$.

(NE4) $\sigma(t_1..t_i..t_n)\neq_{NE}\sigma(t_1..t_i'..t_n)$ implies $t_i\neq_{NE}t_i'$, $i\in\{1..n\}$.

A set of axioms is called <u>consistent</u>, if $(=_{EQ}\cap\neq_{NE})=\emptyset$. The axioms and $\neq_{NE}$ are called <u>covering</u>, if $t\neq_{NE}t'$ implies ($t\neq_{NE}t''$ or $t'\neq_{NE}t''$) for all $t''\in T_\Sigma$.

Please note that $\neq_{NE}$ is covering, iff the complement of $\neq_{NE}$, $comp(\neq_{NE})$ is transitive. If there are no inequations, $I_{\Sigma,EQ}$ is of course isomorphic to T_Σ factorized by $=_{EQ}$.

<u>Easy fact 4.2</u> (Characterisation of existence of models) Let $(\Sigma, EQ+NE)$ be an arbitrary specification. Then the following properties are equivalent.

(1) EQ+NE are consistent.

(2) $ALG_{\Sigma,EQ+NE}\neq\emptyset$.

(3) $I_{\Sigma,EQ}$ is initial in $ALG_{\Sigma,EQ+NE}$.

<u>Proof</u>

<u>(1) ===> (3)</u> If the axioms are consistent, then $=_{EQ}$ is a subset of $comp(\neq_{NE})$. $\langle t,t'\rangle\in NE(T_\Sigma)$ implies $\langle t,t'\rangle\in\neq_{NE}$, which implies $\langle t,t'\rangle\notin=_{EQ}$. But $[t]=[t']$ holds in $I_{\Sigma,EQ}$, iff $t=_{EQ}t'$, and therefore $\langle t,t'\rangle\in NE(T_\Sigma)$ implies $[t]\neq[t']$ in $I_{\Sigma,EQ}$. So $I_{\Sigma,EQ}$ satisfies the inequations NE as well.

<u>(3) ===> (2)</u> Trivial.

<u>(2) ===> (1)</u> Suppose EQ+NE are not consistent. Then there are terms t and t' with $t=_{EQ}t'$ and $t\neq_{NE}t'$. This would imply A]- t=t' and A]- t≠t' for an arbitrary $A\in ALG_{\Sigma,EQ+NE}$.   Q.E.D.

This lemma gives an easy method to test the consistency of a specification : Simply build $T_{\Sigma,EQ}$ (the quotient term algebra) and check whether it satisfies the inequations.

<u>Fact 4.3</u> (Sufficient criterion for the existence of final models) Let consistent axioms EQ+NE be given. If $\neq_{NE}$ is covering, then $ALG_{\Sigma,EQ+NE}$ has a final algebra, which is isomorphic to T_Σ factorized by the complement of $\neq_{NE}$.

Proof

If the axioms are consistent, then $=_{EQ}$ is a subset of comp($\neq_{NE}$). We first show that comp($\neq_{NE}$) is a <u>congruence</u>. comp($\neq_{NE}$) is <u>re-flexive</u> due to consistency, and <u>symmetry</u> holds because $\neq_{NE}$ is symmetric. <u>Transitivity</u> of comp($\neq_{NE}$) is equivalent to the cover-ing property of $\neq_{NE}$, and the <u>operational closure</u> is guaranteed by rule (NE4), which is equivalent to : $\langle t_i, t_i' \rangle \in$ comp($\neq_{NE}$) ===> $\langle \sigma(t_1 \ldots t_i \ldots t_n), \sigma(t_1 \ldots t_i' \ldots t_n) \rangle \in$ comp($\neq_{NE}$).

The quotient T_Σ/comp($\neq_{NE}$) <u>satisfies</u> the axioms. The equations EQ hold because $=_{EQ}$ is a subset of comp($\neq_{NE}$). If $\langle t, t' \rangle \in NE(T_\Sigma)$ are given, then $t \neq_{NE} t'$ and therefore $\langle t, t' \rangle \notin$ comp($\neq_{NE}$). But $[t]=[t']$ holds in T_Σ/comp($\neq_{NE}$), iff $\langle t, t' \rangle \in$ comp($\neq_{NE}$), and by this we have $[t] \neq [t']$ in T_Σ/comp($\neq_{NE}$).

Let A be an arbitrary (finitely generated) algebra satisfying EQ+NE. Then we have the following situation with unique morphisms f and g.

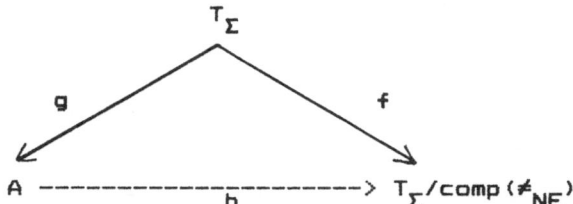

There can be at most <u>one morphism</u> h from A to T_Σ/comp($\neq_{NE}$), and if there is one, then f(t)=h(g(t)) has to be valid. Taking this as a definition we have to show the well-definedness of h : Let $t \neq t'$ with g(t)=g(t') be given. This implies $\langle t, t' \rangle \notin \neq_{NE}$ ($t \neq_{NE} t'$ would imply g(t)$\neq$g(t') in A). Therefore $\langle t, t' \rangle \in$ comp($\neq_{NE}$) and f(t)=f(t'). It is easy to see that h respects the operations and therefore we have a unique morphism. By this we know T_Σ/comp($\neq_{NE}$) is final in $ALG_{\Sigma, EQ+NE}$.   Q.E.D.

The reverse of the previous theorem is not true in general. Con-sider the following counter example.

```
    spec counter example
    srts nat
    opns 0 : ---> nat
         succ : nat ---> nat
         add : nat x nat ---> nat
    vars n, m : nat
```

<u>axms</u> add(O,n)=n

add(succ(n),m)=succ(add(n,m))

succ(succ(add(n,m)))≠n

<u>ceps</u>

The initial model of the specification is isomorphic to the natural numbers, and therefore other models can at most identify two
terms $succ^n(O)$ and $succ^m(O)$ with n≠m. The equalities that have to
be valid and the inequalities in all models determined by the
axioms and our rules can be pictured in the following table.

	0	1	2	3	4	5	...
0	=		≠	≠	≠	≠	...
1		=		≠	≠	≠	...
2	≠		=		≠	≠	...
3	≠	≠		=		≠	...
4	≠	≠	≠		=		...
5	≠	≠	≠	≠		=	...
⋮							

Now assume there is a model, where n=n+1 holds for some n. We know
n≠n+2 and then also n+1≠n+2 has to be true. Therefore n≠n+1 has to
be valid and this contradicts n=n+1. By this we know all spaces in
the above table have to be filled with inequalities ≠ and so the
initial and final models are isomorphic to the natural numbers.
Consider the inequation $0≠_{NE}2$. Neither $1≠_{NE}2$ nor $1≠_{NE}0$ is valid,
and therefore the specification is not covering although the final
model exists.

<u>Example 4.4</u>

<u>spec</u> bunch of natural numbers

<u>srts</u> bool, nat, bunch

<u>opns</u> false, true : ---> bool

if : bool × bool × bool ---> bool

O : ---> nat

succ : nat ---> nat

eq : nat × nat ---> bool

empty : ---> bunch

add : bunch × nat ---> bunch

in : bunch × nat ---> bool

<u>vars</u> x, y : bool

n, m : nat

b : bunch

axms false≠true

if(false,x,y)=if(true,y,x)=y

eq(0,0)=true

eq(0,succ(n))=eq(succ(n),0)=false

eq(succ(n),succ(m))=eq(n,m)

in(empty,n)=false

in(add(b,n),m)=if(eq(n,m),true,in(b,m))

ceps

It can be shown that the relation $\neq_{NE}$ induced by the above axioms is covering : First prove that bool and nat are monomorphic, i.e. in every model of the specification bool and nat are isomorphic to {false,true} and N_0, respectively. Then show that in(b,n) yields true, iff n appears in b seen as a string. By this we know $b\neq_{NE}b'$, iff there is a natural number n in b that is not in b' or vice-versa. Now test this n on a given b" and by this prove $b\neq_{NE}b"$ or $b'\neq_{NE}b"$. Therefore the specification has a final model, and it is isomorphic to finite sets of natural numbers, whereas the initial model represents finite strings of natural numbers.   ***

Remark One can additionally introduce the following rule to gene-rate new inequations :

$t\neq_{NE}c^n(t)$, n>=2 implies $t\neq_{NE}c(t)$

where c(x) is a term of sort s with a variable x of sort s.

The rule is correct : Suppose there is an algebra A such that t and $c^n(t)$ are different, but t and c(t) are equal. Then it follows that c(t) and $c(t)^n$ and therefore t and $c^{n-1}(t)$ are different. Thus by induction one can show that t and c(t) are different.

The rule is not needed in the above proofs, but excludes our counter example. We don't know whether the system including the above rule is complete.

5. Error and exception handling

In this chapter we first explain in short our approach to error and exception handling. More details of this approach can be found in [GDLE 84, Go 84]. Then we show how the preceding result can be used to automatize error propagation respecting error recovery.

A signature with ok predicates $(S,\Sigma,arity,sort,ok_\Sigma)$ adds to a usual signature an ok predicate $ok_\Sigma : \Sigma \longrightarrow BOOL$ and an algebra with ok predicates (A,F,ok_A) has additionally a family of predi-cates $ok_A=\langle ok_s\rangle_{s\in S}$, $ok_s : A_s \longrightarrow BOOL$, which expresses whether an element a is an ok ($ok_A(a)=TRUE$) or error element ($ok_A(a)=FALSE$).

By this the functions are classified into ok preserving ones ($ok_\Sigma(\sigma)$=TRUE) and functions, which may introduce errors when applied to ok values ($ok_\Sigma(\sigma)$=FALSE). The latter are also called unsafe functions.

This also gives a classification of terms : If there are only ok symbols in the term, one knows the term will always evaluate to an ok element, whereas terms with unsafe function symbols may evaluate to ok or error elements. Specifications now use equations, where two kinds of variables may be used: first, variables serving for the ok part only and second, variables for ok and error elements as well. For specifications of this kind initial models always exist and can be constructed as quotient term algebras as in the conventional case. In the quotient term algebras ok elements dominate the error elements, i.e. mixed classes with ok and error elements are ok classes. This approach allows to express all forms of error and exception handling : error introduction, error propagation and error recovery.

Example 5.1 Let us explain our ideas with the simple example of the natural numbers with error and exception handling already introduced in chapter 2. The carriers of the initial algebra of this specification can be described as a canonical term algebra using the following context-free productions.

    <bool>   ::= false / true
    <nat>   ::= <nat-ok> / <nat-err>
    <nat-ok>   ::= 0 / succ(<nat-ok>)
    <nat-err> ::= error / succ(<nat-err>) / pred(<nat-err>)

Here are some examples of operation applications.

$pred_{\Sigma,T}$[0] = error
$pred_{\Sigma,T}$[succ(0)] = 0
$pred_{\Sigma,T}$[error] = pred(error)
$succ_{\Sigma,T}$[succ(0)] = succ(succ(0))
$succ_{\Sigma,T}$[error] = succ(error)
$if_{\Sigma,T}$[true,0,error] = 0
$if_{\Sigma,T}$[true,error,0] = error

$succ_{\Sigma,T}$ is an ok function, because it yields an ok element when applied to an ok element. $pred_{\Sigma,T}$ is an unsafe function, because when applied to the ok element 0 it results in error, but when applied e.g. to succ(0) it yields the ok element 0. $if_{\Sigma,T}$ is in a sense an error recovery function, because for example $if_{\Sigma,T}$[true, 0,error] = 0.   ***

One flaw of this approach may be seen in the fact that there appear a lot of error elements behaving in the same way compared with ok elements. By this we mean that for two distinct error elements e and e' the following is valid : For all contexts ct (i.e. terms with exactly one variable of an appropriate sort) ct(e) = ct(e') or both ct(e) and ct(e') are error elements. The aim of this chapter is to identify these error elements that are in some sense observationally equivalent [ST 85] with respect to the ok part.

Definition 5.2 Let signature Σ with ok predicates, equations EQ (with both kinds of variables) be given and let $T_{\Sigma,EQ}$ denote the initial (Σ,EQ)-algebra with ok predicates $ok_{\Sigma,EQ}$. Then NE denotes the following set of inequations.

NE = { t≠t' | t,t'∈T_Σ, there is a context ct such that
$$[ct(t)]_{\Sigma,EQ} \neq [ct(t')]_{\Sigma,EQ} \text{ and}$$
$$ok_{\Sigma,EQ}([ct(t)]_{\Sigma,EQ}) \text{ or } ok_{\Sigma,EQ}([ct(t')]_{\Sigma,EQ}) \}$$

Fact 5.3 If EQ and NE (as above) is considered as a specification, then there exists a final model in $ALG_{\Sigma,EQ+NE}$.

Proof

We show $\neq_{NE}$ is covering, and to this end let $t_1 \neq_{NE} t_2$ be given. We have to prove $t_1 \neq_{NE} t_3$ or $t_2 \neq_{NE} t_3$ for an arbitrary $t_3 \in T_\Sigma$. In the following $[t]_{\Sigma,EQ}$ is abbreviated by $[t]$ and $ok_{\Sigma,EQ}([t])$ by $ok([t])$.

Case 1 : $ok([t_1])$ and $ok([t_2])$. If $[t_1]=[t_3]$, then $t_3 =_{EQ} t_1$ and $t_3 \neq_{NE} t_2$. If $[t_1] \neq [t_3]$, then $t_1 \neq_{NE} t_3$ by definition of NE.

Case 2 : not $ok([t_1])$ and $ok([t_2])$. If $ok([t_3])$, then $t_1 \neq_{NE} t_3$, and if not $ok([t_3])$, then $t_2 \neq_{NE} t_3$.

Case 3 : not $ok([t_1])$ and not $ok([t_2])$. If $[t_3]=[t_1]$, then $t_1 =_{EQ} t_3$ and $t_3 \neq_{NE} t_2$, and if $ok([t_3])$, then $t_1 \neq_{NE} t_3$. Therefore let distinct error classes $[t_1]$, $[t_2]$ and $[t_3]$ be given.

Case 3.1 : There is a context ct such that $[ct(t_1)] \neq [ct(t_3)]$ and ($ok([ct(t_1)])$ or $ok([ct(t_3)])$). Then $ct(t_1) \neq_{NE} ct(t_3)$ holds, and therefore also $t_1 \neq_{NE} t_3$.

Case 3.2 : For all contexts ct the following is valid : $[ct(t_1)] = [ct(t_3)]$ or (not $ok([ct(t_1)])$ and not $ok([ct(t_3)])$). We know $[t_1] \neq [t_2]$, but both are error classes. Therefore there has to be a context ct' such that $[ct'(t_1)] \neq [ct'(t_2)]$ and ($ok([ct'(t_1)])$ or $ok([ct'(t_2)])$), which implies $ct'(t_1) \neq_{NE} ct'(t_2)$.

Case 3.2.1 : $[ct'(t_1)]=[ct'(t_3)]$. This implies $ct'(t_1)=_{EQ}ct'(t_3)$ and $ct'(t_3)\neq_{NE}ct'(t_2)$, which implies $t_3\neq_{NE}t_2$.

Case 3.2.2 : $[ct'(t_1)]\neq[ct'(t_3)]$. This implies that $[ct'(t_1)]$ and $[ct'(t_3)]$ are both error classes. By this we know $[ct'(t_2)]$ has to be an ok class, and this implies $ct'(t_2)\neq_{NE}ct'(t_3)$ and $t_2\neq_{NE}t_3$.

Q.E.D.

Consequence 5.4 Given a specification with ok predicates (Σ,EQ) one can choose the final $(\Sigma,EQ+NE)$-algebra as a standard semantics.

Definition 5.5 Let signature Σ with ok predicates and Σ-algebra A be given. Two elements a and a' of A are called ok-distinguishable, iff there is a context ct such that $A \models ct(a)\neq ct(a')$ and $A \models$ (ok(ct(a)) or ok(ct(a'))). A is called error-minimal, iff all distinct error elements in A are pairwise ok-distinguishable.

Consequence 5.6 (Characterisation of the final $(\Sigma,EQ+NE)$-algebra) Let EQ and NE as above be given. A is final in $ALG_{\Sigma,EQ+NE}$, iff $A \in ALG_{\Sigma,EQ}$ and A is error-minimal.

Example 5.7 To demonstrate how our construction works when non-trivial error recovery is involved, we introduce yet another version of the obligatory stack example.

```
spec stack of natural numbers with error recovery
srts nat, stack
opns 0 : ---> nat ok
     succ : nat ---> nat ok
     empty : ---> stack ok
     push : stack x nat ---> stack ok
     pop : stack ---> stack unsafe
     underflow : ---> stack unsafe
     top : stack ---> nat unsafe
     topless : ---> nat unsafe
vars n : nat ok
     n- : nat unsafe
     s : stack ok
     s- : stack unsafe
axms pop(push(s,n-))=s
     pop(empty)=underflow
     top(push(s-,n))=n
     top(empty)=topless
ceps
```

In the initial (Σ,EQ+NE)-algebra for example the terms underflow and pop(underflow) as well as push(push(empty,topless),O) and push(underflow,O) represent different classes, respectively. But these terms are identified in the final (Σ,EQ+NE)-algebra. Again, we give a description of the final model in terms of a canonical term algebra using context-free productions.

```
<nat>       ::= <nat-ok> / <nat-err>
<nat-ok>    ::= O / succ( <nat-ok> )
<nat-err>   ::= topless
<stack>     ::= <stack-ok> / <stack-err>
<stack-ok>  ::= empty / push( <stack-ok> , <nat-ok> )
<stack-err> ::= underflow / push( underflow , <nat-ok> )
                          / push( <stack-err> , topless )
```

O_F : |---> O $underflow_F$: |---> underflow

$succ_F$: n |---> $\begin{cases} succ(n) \text{ if n ok} \\ topless \text{ otherwise} \end{cases}$

$empty_F$: |---> empty

$push_F$: (s,n) |---> $\begin{cases} push(s,n) \text{ if s ok and n ok} \\ push(underflow,n) \text{ if s not ok and n ok} \\ push(s,topless) \text{ if s ok and n not ok} \\ underflow \text{ otherwise} \end{cases}$

pop_F : s |---> $\begin{cases} s' \text{ if s=push(s',n'), s' ok and n' arbitrary} \\ underflow \text{ otherwise} \end{cases}$

top_F : s |---> $\begin{cases} n' \text{ if s=push(s',n'), n' ok and s' arbitrary} \\ topless \text{ otherwise} \end{cases}$

$topless_F$: |---> topless   ***

Acknowledgement

Scientific thanks to Hans-Dieter Ehrich and Udo Lipeck for draft reading. Special thanks to the Selmun Palace Beach, Malta for sandy sessions and to Peter Herr for even quiet moments. Calm thanks to Brigitte.

References

ADJ 78   Goguen,J.A./Thatcher,J.W./Wagner,E.G. : An initial al-
          gebra approach to the specification, correctness and imp-
          lementation of abstract data types. Current trends in
          programming methodology, Vol.IV, R.T.Yeh, ed. Prentice
          Hall, Englewood Cliffs, 1978, pp.80-149.
ADJ 81   Ehrig,H./Kreowski,H.-J./Thatcher,J.W./Wagner,E.G./Wright,
          J.B.: Parameter passing in algebraic specification lan-
          guages. Proc. Workshop on Program Specification, LNCS
          134, Berlin 1982, pp.322-369.

Bi 84   Bidoit,M. : Algebraic specification of exception handling
            and error recovery by means of equations and declara-
            tions. Proc. 11th ICALP, LNCS 172, pp.95-109, 1984.

BGP 82   Boisson,F./Guiho,G./Pavot,D. : Multioperator algebras.
            Report, L.R.I., Orsay, 1982.

BW 83   Broy,M./Wirsing,M. : Generalized heterogeneous algebras
            and partial interpretations. Proceedings 8th CAAP 1983,
            L'Aquila, pp.1-34.

Eh 82   Ehrich,H.-D. : On the theory of specification, implemen-
            tation and parametrization of abstract data types. JACM,
            Vol.29, 1982, pp.206-227.

EKMP 82   Ehrig,H./Kreowski,H.-J./Mahr,B./Padawitz,P. : Algebraic
            implementation of abstract data types. TCS, Vol.20, 1982,
            pp.209-263.

EPE 83   Engels,G./Pletat,U./Ehrich,H.-D. : An operational seman-
            tics for specifications of abstract data types with error
            handling. Acta Informatica 19, pp.235-253, 1983.

Ga 83   Ganzinger,H. : Parametrized specification : Parameter
            passing and implementation. ACM TOPLAS, Vol.5, No.3, pp.
            318-354, 1983.

GDLE 84   Gogolla,M./Drosten,K./Lipeck,U./Ehrich,H.-D. : Algebraic
            and operational semantics of specifications allowing ex-
            ceptions and errors. TCS, Vol.34, 1984, pp.289-313.

Go 84   Gogolla,M. : Partially ordered sorts in algebraic speci-
            fications. Proc. 9th CAAP Bordeaux, Cambridge University
            Press, B. Courcelle, ed. pp.139-153, 1984.

Go 78.1   Goguen,J.A. : Abstract errors for abstract data types.
            Proc. Conference on Formal Description of Programming
            Concepts, E.J.Neuhold, ed. North Holland, Amsterdam,
            1978.

Go 78.2   Goguen,J.A. : Order sorted algebras : Exception and error
            sorts, coercions and overloaded operators. Semantics and
            theory of computation report No.14, UCLA, 1978.

Gu 75   Guttag,J.V. : The specification and application to pro-
            gramming of abstract data types. Technical Report CSRG-59
            University of Toronto, 1975.

HR 80   Hornung,G./Raulefs,P. : Terminal algebra semantics and
            retractions for abstract data types. Proc. 7th ICALP,
            LNCS 85, pp.310-323, 1980.

Kl 84   Klaeren,H. : A constructive method for abstract algebraic
         software specification. TCS, Vol.30, No.2, pp.139-204,
         1984.

LZ 74   Liskov,B./Zilles.S. : Programming with abstract data
         types. SIGPLAN Notices, Vol.9, No.4, pp.50-59.

Pl 82   Plaisted,D. : An initial algebra semantics for error pre-
         sentations. Technical Report, 1982.

Po 84   Poigne,A. : Another look at parametrization using alge-
         bras with subsorts. Proc. MFCS 1984 Praha, LNCS 176.

ST 85   Sannella,D./Tarlecki,A. : On observational equivalence
         and algebraic specification. Proc. 10th CAAP, Berlin
         1985.

Wa 79   Wand,M. : Final algebra semantics and data type exten-
         sions. JCSS, Vol.19, No.1, pp.27-44, 1979.

WPPDB 83 Wirsing,M. /Pepper,P. /Partsch,H. /Dosch,W. /Broy,M. : On
         hierachies of abstract data types. Acta Informatica 20,
         pp.1-33, 1983.

OSI Transport Service
Considered as
an Abstract Data Type

Klaus Peter Hasler* , Jan de Meer**

* Technische Universitaet Berlin, Fachbereich Informatik
** Hahn-Meitner-Institut Berlin GmbH

Abstract

Due to the widespread use a precise definition of (the semantics of)
services and protocols used in Open Systems Interconnections (OSI) is
highly desirable. This paper reports on the experience gained in developing an algebraic specification of a transport service. A pragmatic
guideline for the development of a specification based on an abstract
model of the transport service is demonstrated and the relation of the
algebraic specification to other specification concepts used in the
field is discussed. We show especially how properties can be derived
from the specification and expressed in terms of OSI concepts. Finally
benefits and limitations of the algebraic specification with respect to
the general requirements for specifications in the field of Open
Systems Interconnections are reviewed.

1 INTRODUCTION

The aim of this article is not to provide just another specification
of the OSI transport service but to cope with the properties of the
service primitives which are generally hidden in the specification.
Nevertheless the specification developed in this article conforms to a
real implementation /dM 84/.

We were stimulated by the implementation of the local computer network HMINET2 /BHLM 83/ which runs in the Hahn-Meitner-Institute for
Nuclear Research in Berlin. During the periods of specification, implementation and testing we discovered that we had no reliable method for
the derivation of relevant system properties. This led us to algebraic
data type specification methods which appear suitable to satisfy our
requirements.

The algebraic specification language ACT ONE, which was selected for
this study, has a complete formal semantic. Also its basic concepts are
restricted enough to allow concentration on the points of interest.
ACT ONE provides concepts to write parameterized and unparameterized
specifications /EM 85/ in a structured manner built up in small parts.

A short introduction to ACT ONE is given in Section 3. Readers who
want to gain a detailed understanding are referred to the book of Ehrig
and Mahr /EM 85/.

Acknowledgement

Horst Hansen took part in the development of the specification.
Hartmut Ehrig, Werner Fey, and Bernd Mahr gave some valuable comments
on the topic of our article. Craig Smith and Horst Hansen read a draft
of this paper. Many thanks to all of them.

2 OPEN SYSTEMS INTERCONNECTION

2.1 Informal Introduction to Open Systems Interconnection

The system to be described is derived from the realm of Open Systems
Interconnection (OSI) /OSI 83/. The term *Open Systems Interconnection* refers to the public use of standardized procedures to perform
information exchange between systems, which are in this paper considered to be computers and their active processes.

For this environment with physically separated systems a Reference
Model (RM) was developed by the International Organization of Standardization (ISO). A system of this RM contains black boxes which are
called *entities* . They cooperate among each other by using a transmission medium. This cooperation is restricted by a set of rules and formats of data to be exchanged. Such rules and formats together form
a *protocol* .

The architecture of the Reference Model comprises seven layers which
represent different levels of abstraction. The entities of each layer
provide a set of services to the entities on the next upper layer via
so-called *Service Access Points* (SAP). For each layer all entities of
that layer must provide a uniform service throughout all interconnected
systems. The service providing entities realize the service by
exchanging information with the respective entities of the cooperating
systems in accordance to the protocol which is specific to the respective layer. This implementation makes use of the service provided by
the next lower layer.

In this article we focus on the *Transport Service* which is provided
to the *Transport Service User* (TSU) at the *Transport Service Access
Point* (TSAP). It offers a connection-oriented end-to-end data transmission service which enables the user to abstract from the underlying
network. The *Transport Service Provider* (TSP) realizes the service in
accordance to the *Transport Protocol* using the *Network Service* provided

at the *Network Service Access Point* (NSAP).   A complete informal
description is contained in the original ISO paper /ISO-TS 83/.

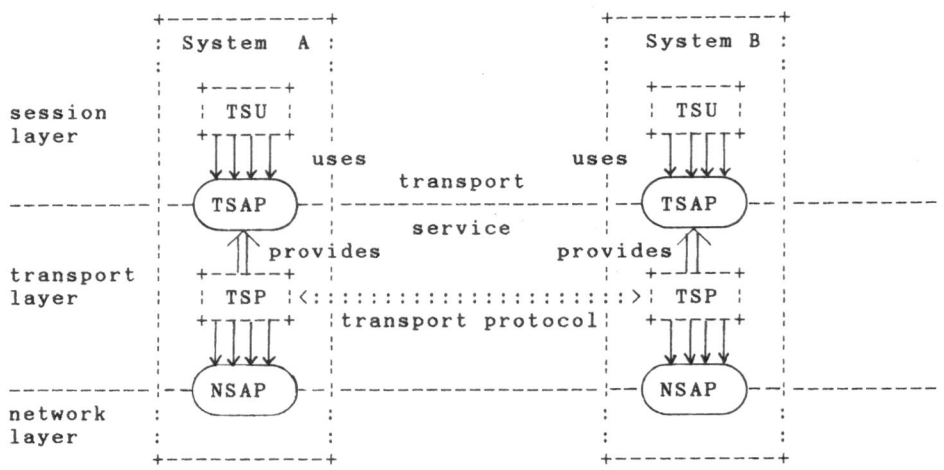

```
                 +----------+                 +----------+
                 : System  A :                 :  System B :
                 :          :                 :          :
                 : +-----+  :                 : +-----+  :
session          : : TSU :  :                 : : TSU :  :
layer            : +-----+  :                 : +-----+  :
                 :          :   uses      uses :          :
                 :      uses:   transport      :          :
      -----------:--(  TSAP )--:---------------------:--( TSAP )--:-----------
                 :          :    service        :          :
                 :       ^  : provides   provides ^       :
transport        : +-----+  :                 : +-----+  :
layer            : : TSP :<::::::::::::::::::::::::>: TSP :  :
                 : +-----+  : transport protocol : +-----+  :
                 :          :                 :          :
      -----------:--( NSAP )--:---------------------:--( NSAP )--:-----------
network          :          :                 :          :
layer            :          :                 :          :
                 +----------+                 +----------+
```

TSU: Transport Service User
TSP: Transport Service Provider
TSAP: Transport Service Access Point
NSAP: Network Service Access Point
Figure 1: Transport Service in the context of OSI architecture

2.2 Requirements on Service Specifications

   The service provided by the entities of each layer may be represented as a set of specific service primitives.   Each service primitive
defines a basic interaction between the service user and service provider which takes place at the service access point.   In addition to
the definition of the basic interactions all allowed sequences of
interactions must be given.   It is important to note that the sequences
of interactions on different SAPs are independent of each other. Nevertheless the specification of a service contains rules which relate the
interactions on interconnected SAPs to each other.   For example a message in transmission must not bypass another one which has been trans-
mitted in the same .direction.

   For a complete specification quantitative statements about the
throughput and delay of data,   probabilities of malfunctions e.g.
undected errors and release of a connection by the service-providing
layer are also necessary.

   Another general requirement for a service specification is that it
should capture the behaviour in time appropriately. This means that in
a network where the users of a transmission service reside in physically separated systems the provided service primitives may not be per-

formed as an indivisible whole without any time delay and incorporation
of other service users.

2.3 Property Specification Versus Abstract Model Specification

When using algebraic specification techniques there seem to be two
different approaches to service specifications. Using the first
approach one specifies the properties of the service primitives relative to each other only. This includes equations which define the
allowed sequences of interactions. In the second approach an abstract
model of the system including its internal state is specified as an
abstract data type and the effect of the service primitives is defined
with respect to this abstract data type. This approach is similar to
the one chosen in /Sun 80/. Using the first approach, which may be
called an axiomatic approach, only the types and sequences of interactions can be defined in a direct manner. But other properties of a service such as rules making assertions on more than one SAP as mentioned
above cannot be specified satisfactorally with this axiomatic approach.
Also it is very hard to decide whether a given set of properties is
sufficient to describe a service completely.

The approach which uses an abstract model provides the opportunity
to introduce necessary concepts e.g. states in order to express other
properties than sequences of interactions. On the other hand these
interaction sequences are not recognizable immediately as such. But one
can be sure that all possible sequences of interactions are contained
in the abstract (state transition) model. Therefore we give an abstract
model specification of the transport in this article and show how to
derive properties about sequences of interactions from this specification.

2.4 Correctness of Protocol Specification with Respect to Service
Specification

A complete specification of a layer contains both the specification
of the layer service and the layer protocol. Because the protocol
implements the service, one of the requirements for any protocol is
that it is compatible with the specified service properties. A protocol implements a service, if a set of properties derivable from the
service specification is also derivable from the protocol specification. In this way it is possible to verify a protocol specification
against its service specification. In this article we show a technique
to derive properties of a specification based on abstract data types.
This technique may be applied to the service specification as well as
to the protocol specification.

3 SPECIFICATION OF THE TRANSPORT SERVICE

After a short description of algebraic specifications in general and the specification language ACT ONE in particular we give some sample parts of the transport service specification and some pragmatics for its development.

3.1 Algebraic Specifications and ACT ONE

An *algebra* is a set of data carriers along with the operations on those carriers. A *signature* consists of names for data carriers (sorts) and operations and declares the domain and range of the operations, where operations with empty domains have to be interpreted as constants of their value sort. For an operation op:sl...sn-->s the operation call op(tl,...,tn) is called a term of sort s, if tl,...,tn are terms or variables of sort sl,...,sn respectively. Now an algebraic specification is a signature together with a set of equations, i.e. pairs of terms t=t', and defines the largest algebra where all data are operation-generated, i.e all data can be represented by a term without variables, and the equations are satisfied. For a more elaborate introduction to algebraic specifications we refer to /ADJ 76/ or /EM 85/.

The algebraic specification language ACT ONE (/EM 85/) provides concepts for structuring specifications adequately, since it is not possible to handle specifications of larger problems as one block of sorts, operations and equations only. On the uppermost level one may write an ACT ONE *text* which is a list of named *definitions* based on further definitions in a specification library. In a definition one may combine several other definitions using the *and* -construct, which is merely a set union of the respective components, and add new sorts, operations and equations if necessary. Furthermore ACT ONE allows parameterization of specifications and the replacement of formal parameters by actual ones. But these facilities will not be used here.

3.2 Some Pragmatics for Writing Specifications

Along with our specification of the transport service we demonstrate a simple procedure for the development of algebraic specifications in general. This procedure, which can be seen as a mixture between top-down and bottom-up specification design, has come out as a quite natural and efficient way of proceeding in several case studies. (cf. /HLR 82/ and /EFH 85/). Although it is certainly not the only way for developing specifications it shall be given here as a pragmatic guideline which may also help to read and understand the specification. A rough approximation of the procedure includes the following steps:

- define the signature of the user operations;
- define the basic data types for the system;
- refine the user operations over the basic types (possibly introducing auxiliary operations).

3.3 Structure of the Specification

The specification of the transport service consists of three levels (figure 2). The lowest level *Basic Types* contains the basic abstract data types necessary to describe the transport service. These basic abstract data types (from now on called basic types) describe the abstract model of the system. They include specifications for the system considered as a set of access points (tsapset), the transport service access point (TSAP), the transport connection (TC), a queue and simple data types called *state* and *address*. On top of these basic types elementary operations are defined, which consist of requests, write and read operations on that types. The highest level provides the user operations which are called primitives in the terminology of the RM. These primitives are devided into service and management primitives. Whereas the service primitives provide the bare transport service, the management primitives aid the service user to cooperate with the service providing entity.

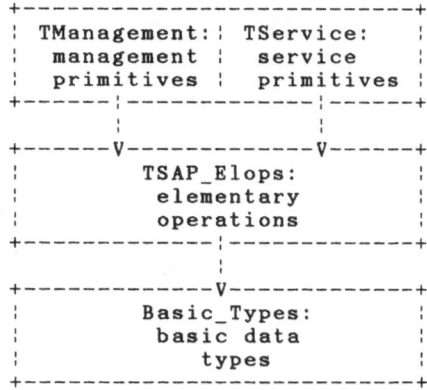

```
+---------------------------+
: TManagement:: TService:   :
:  management :  service    :
:  primitives :  primitives :
+------:-------------:------+
       :             :
+------V-------------V------+
:          TSAP_Elops:      :
:          elementary       :
:          operations       :
+-------------:-------------+
              :
+-------------V-------------+
:         Basic_Types:      :
:         basic data        :
:            types          :
+---------------------------+
```

Figure 2: components of the transport service specification

3.4 Signatures for the User Operations

In /EFH 85/ it is demonstrated that the set of user operations together with their informal description can be regarded as a part of an abstract user interface. Defining signatures for these operations relates the abstract user interface to the specification. We thus have the possibility to prove properties on the relation of the operations in the abstract user interface via this connection to the specification. In Section 4 we shall investigate the sequential independency of some operations. This property is of particular interest in the context of transport services.

The signatures for the operations define the domain and range of these operations, where in contrast to programming language-oriented descriptions (the state of) the whole system has to be included as an explicit input and output parameter of the top level operations. In our case this is also the main difference to the description of the operations in the abstract user interface.

According to our main abstraction the system is looked upon as a set of Transport Service Access Points (see Section 2) through which the communication between the Transport Service Users takes place, while the internal structure of the network is disregarded. Consequently we introduce the sort *tsapset* into the signatures to represent the system parameter.

As mentioned above the user operations include management as well as service primitives. The management primitives consist of four operations: *define TSAP* (DFTSAP) to create an access point, *delete TSAP* (DLTSAP) to delete an access point, *allocate TSAP* (TALLOC) to name a TSAP and thus make it addressable for others, and *de-allocate TSAP* (TDALOC) to discard the name. The service primitives include operations for establishing a connection – *connect request* (CONREQ) and *connect response* (CONRSP) to ask for a connection rsp. to respond on a request – for data transfer – *normal transport service request* (NTSREQ) to submit data and *normal transport service response* (NTSRSP) to acknowledge the receipt of data – and for disconnecting – *disconnect request* (DISREQ) – each of them given in a separate ACT ONE definition.

```
act text {Transport Interface Specification}

   def  Transport Interface  is
        TManagement   and   TService
   end of def

   def  TService  is
        Connection Establishment  and  Release
                                  and  Data Transfer
   end of def

   def  TManagement  is  TSAP Elops
        opns  DFTSAP: tsapset                      --> tsapset
              DLTSAP: tsapi  tsapset               --> tsapset
              TALLOC: tsapi  name  tsapset  --> tsapset
              TDALOC: name  tsapset               --> tsapset
        eqns  {"see 3.6 and /HHM 85/"}
   end of def
```

```
def  Connection Establishment  is  TSAP Elops
     opns  CONREQ: tsapi  name  data  tsapset   --> tsapset
           CONRSP: address  bool  data  tsapset --> tsapset
     eqns  {"see /HHM 85/"}
end of def

def  Release  is  TSAP Elops
     opns  DISREQ: address  tsapset --> tsapset
     eqns  {"see /HHM 85/"}
end of def

def  Data Transfer  is  TSAP Elops
     opns  NTSREQ: address  data  tsapset --> tsapset
           NTSRSP: address  tsapset       --> tsapset
     eqns  {"see /HHM 85/"}
end of def

uses from library  TSAP Elops

end of text
```

The equations omitted here will be partly developed in 3.6. The full set of equations as well as the specification *TSAP Elops* can be found in our long version /HHM 85/.

3.5 Definition of the Basic Types

At this point it becomes necessary to define the structure (an abstract model) of the system before we can describe the effects of the user operations. To find such a structure needs a thorough analysis of the problem or system concerned. Intuition and some experience will be very helpful for the selection of the adequate data types. In this case we have three different kinds of structures: list-like structures (*tsapset* , *tcset* , *queue*), tuples (*tsap* , *tc* , *address*) and enumeration types (*state*).

According to our main abstraction the system is modelled as a set of TSAPs , where a TSAP is a 4-tuple - <tsi,n,q,tcs> - of an internal address (tsapi), a (possibly empty) name, the set of connections running through that TSAP (tcset) and a queue, where all events happening on one of the connections are collected and can be requested by the user. Similarly a transport connection (TC) is a triple - [tci,st,a] - of its internal address (tci), a (connection) state and the address at the distant end of the connection. Since we don't want to extend the specification with the intricate details of naming and addressing we leave *tsapi* and *tci* as formal sorts, thus allowing any adequate realization for them. An address is then a pair consisting of a tsapi and a tci, written *t.tc* , which exactly locates one TC in the system.

To ease the understanding of terms we allow infix- and even mixfix-notation for the operations. The underscores in the definitions indicate the places of the arguments. The specifications *Bool* , *Name* and *Data* , which are used from the library, are standard and can be found e.g. in /ADJ 76/.

```
act text   {Basic Types}

    def  TSAP  is Queue  and  TC  and  Name
         sorts tsap, tsapset
         opns  <_,_,_,_>: tsapi  name  queue  tcset --> tsap
               EMPTYTS :                            --> tsapset
               _*_        : tsap  tsapset           --> tsapset
    end of def

    def  Queue  is  State  and  Data  and  Address
         sorts queue
         opns  EMPTYQ:                           --> queue
               ENQ  : tci  state  data  queue  --> queue
    end of def

    def  TC  is  Address  and  State
         sorts tc, tcset
         opns  [_,_,_] : tci  state  address --> tc
               EMPTYTCS:                          --> tcset
               _o_        : tc  tcset            --> tcset
    end of def

    def Address  is  Bool
        formal sorts tsapi, tci
        formal opns  EMPTYTSAPI: --> tsapi
                     EMPTYTCI   : --> tci
        sorts address
        opns  EMPTYADDR: --> address
              _._        : tsapi  tci --> address
        eqns  EMPTYADDR = EMPTYTSAPI.EMPTYTCI
    end of def

    def State  is
        sorts state
        opns  REQUESTED, INDICATED, D-T-READY,
              D-T-REQ, D-T-IND, D-T-REQ-IND,
              DISCONNECTED, REJECTED, EMPTYSTATE:   -> state
    end of def

    uses from library  Name, Data, Bool

  end of text
```

3.6 Refinement of the User Operations

To obtain a refinement the effect of the user operations has to be explained for any system (set of TSAPs). Since we now know the generating operations for the basic types we can achieve this by writing one (possibly recursive) equation for each of the generating operations (EMPTYTS and _*_ here). We shall demonstrate this technique along the definition of the operation TDALOC.

```
for all n,n' in name; t,t' in tsapi; q in queue;
        tcs in tcset; ts in tsapset:
TDALOC(n,EMPTYTS) = EMPTYTS
TDALOC(n,<t,n',q,tcs>*ts)
 = if n = n'
   then <t,EMPTYNAME,q,tcs>*ts)
   else <t,n',q,tcs>*TDALOC(n,ts)
```

Here the *for all* clause defines the sorts of the variables. The first equation defines that TDALOC applied to the empty set of TSAPs has no effect. In the second equation TDALOC removes the name from the first TSAP in the set, if it is the name to be discarded, otherwise the first TSAP remains unchanged, while TDALOC is applied recursively to the remaining set of TSAPs. The *if_then_else* is defined as a standard operation and can be read as in programming languages.

In some cases it is sufficient to give one equation for all cases of generating operations as the following equation for the TALLOC primitive shows

```
for all t in tsapi; n in name; ts in tsapset:
TALLOC(t,n,ts)
= if name-defined?(n,ts)
   then ts
   else set-name(t,n,ts)
```

Here *ts* is a variable for the sort tsapset and thus includes all cases of generating operations. The definition introduces two auxiliary operations and insures that a name is only given to a TSAP, if it is not already defined in the system, otherwise the primitive has no effect. The auxiliary operations *name-defined?* and *set-name* also have been refined recursively using the same technique as above.

3.7 Correctness of the Specification

The complete specification has been input into the ACT-System. Besides the usual syntactic checks the ACT-System also includes a Persistency-Checker /Lan 85/ which proved the completeness and consistency of the user-operations and the auxiliary operations with respect to the basic specifications given in 3.5. This means that all terms containing user operations can be uniquely reduced to a term consisting of the generating operations only.

4 DERIVATION OF SERVICE PROPERTIES

In this section some properties of the transport service will be derived from the specification. Along with the derivation we discuss the kind of properties that can be derived from the specification in general and the way this derivation can be achieved.

4.1 Writing Sequences of Interactions Instead of Terms

In Section 2 it was indicated that it is a general technique to express properties of the service by giving the allowed sequences of interactions. The construction of the signature for the user operations in 3.3 is analog to the usual BNF syntax for the user commands in the informal system description /ISO-TS 83/ except for the additional system parameter which represents the effect of the sequence of interactions before. Therefore we define a translation function *tra* from the terms of the specification to sequences of interactions.

tra(EMPTYTS) = Ø   where Ø denotes the empty sequence

tra(TS) = TS   for all variables of sort *tsapset*

tra(OP(t1,..,tn-1,tn) = tra(tn) ; OP(t1,..,tn-1)

where *tn* denotes the system parameter of OP and ';' the sequential composition of interactions. Obviously the inverse function from sequences of interactions to the respective terms can be defined similarly.

Generalizing this construction we obtain a way to express properties of the specification in a concept that is known to the users in the specific field. In this sense the informal description of the service operations together with the transformed properties presents an abstract user interface for the specification (cf. also /EFH 85/), which also allows people without an algebraic background to profit by the specification.

Among the properties that can be derived from the specification two groups will be treated in more detail. On one hand we can show that different sequences of interactions have the same effect. On the other hand we can designate certain sequences as the allowed ones, to obtain a certain effect.

4.2 Sequences of Interactions with Equal Effect

This first group of properties includes two relevant special cases which may be characterized by the following general expressions

(1)   seq ; op1 ; op2 = seq

(2)   seq ; op1 ; op2 = seq ; op2 ; op1

for arbitrary sequences *seq* and operations *op1* , *op2* .

In the first case it is expressed that op2 is inverse to op1. Thus the initial state can be recovered by applying the respective inverse operation. The second kind of expression indicates that op1 and op2 are sequentially independent.

In the following we give some examples of these properties for our specification and indicate how they have been proven correct.

1a) seq ; DFTSAP ; DLTSAP(t) = seq

where t is the address of the TSAP created by the *DFTSAP* primitive

1b) seq ; TALLOC(t,n) ; TDALOC(n) = seq

To prove these properties they have to be translated into equations of the specification according to 4.1. The equation for 1a could be derived directly from the equations for DFTSAP and DLTSAP. In the given case we added the assumption about the address t to the equations and then we could prove the property by simply deriving the lefthand side with the interpreter. In general one will need structural induction and a narrowing algorithm (cf. /Pad 83/ or /Hus 85/) in such proofs.

The proof of 1b shows that the property is only valid if the TSAP with address *t* has not been given a name before and the name *n* has not been assigned to another TSAP (i.e. in *seq*). Thus some properties are valid only in restricted cases while others are true for any previous sequence of interactions.

This is also true for the second case of properties: sequential independency of operations.

2a) seq ; conreq(t,n,d) ; conreq(t',n',d')
    = seq ; conreq(t',n',d') ; conreq(t,n,d)

2b) seq ; ntsreq(a,d) ; disreq(a')
    = seq ; disreq(a') ; ntsreq(a,d)

These properties have been proven correct in the same way as above by structural induction using automated tools as far as possible. Again the proof lead to some restrictions (t ≠ t' and n ≠ n' for 2a, and a ≠ a' for 2b). A more detailed description of the proofs can be found in /HHM 85/.

4.3 Allowed Sequences of Interactions

In 2.2 it was required that sequences of the allowed interactions should be given that have to be performed to obtain a certain effect e.g. to establish a connection, transmit a set of data etc. Other sequences will produce errors or lead to unintended effects. Since we have omitted an explicit error handling in our specification for reasons of simplicity and only said that operations have no effect in such cases, we now have to select those sequences of interactions where every interaction has some effect. In order to transmit a set of data {d1,...dn} from one user with TSAP t' to a user with TSAP n the following sequences will be adequate

    seq1 ; conreq(t,n,d1) ; conrsp(a,TRUE,d') ; ntsreq(a',d2)
           ; ntsrsp(a) ; ... ; ntsreq(a',dn) ; ntsrsp(a) ; disreq(a')

where a and a' are the distant rsp. local address of the connection.

The fact that every operation has an effect has been tested in the evaluation of the specification using an interpreter for algebraic specifications (e.g. /GMP 82/, /HLR 82/). By adding the translation from the user commands to the terms of the specification we have generated a complete simulation environment where user commands may be input successively to test their effects. The actual test of the service specification revealed one conceptual error which could be corrected easily.

5 CONCLUSION

In this paper we have presented the development of an algebraic specification of a transport service in networks. The specification describes an abstract model of the system where the interactions change an internal state. The specification does not include

- quantitative statements about the throughput and delay of data, probabilities of malfunctions etc, because we did not see any possibility to express these properties in the algebraic calculus;
- an explicit errorhandling, because specifying errorhandling tends to be as much work as writing errorhandling procedures in programs and we wanted to concentrate on the main problem of specifying primitives for Open Systems Interconnection;
- an explicit definition of the allowed sequences of interactions – but these can be derived from our abstract model as shown in Section 4.

Another major deficit of the algebraic specification is that the primitives provided by the specification are treated as an indivisible whole. The time spent to perform the primitive in a real-worlds environment with possible concurrency and interaction with primitives called by other service users cannot be captured in the algebraic semantics of the specification. Therefore it seems necessary to combine algebraic specification techniques which have been shown to be very useful in describing abstract data types with concepts that cope with concurrency e.g. Petri nets /Pet 80/ or CCS /Mil 80/. Within

the ISO the language LOTOS /LOTOS 85/ which combines algebraic specifications and CCS is being developed as a formal description technique
for OSI.

In spite of the deficiencies mentioned above we gained much insight
into the problem of the transport service by developing the specification. The ACT system as a specification environment has been of much
use in this process. Although still under development it provides a
syntax checker , a persistency checker (cf. /Pad 83/,/Lan 85/) and a
user-controlled interpreter (cf. /HLR 82/). Using these facilities we
could assure the syntactical correctness of the specification (not
trivial for some 30 pages of specification) and the completeness and
consistency of the user operations. Using the interpreter extended by
the translation of the user commands we generated a rapid prototype of
the system which was then used for various test of the user interface
of the transport service.

Besides the tests the specification also offered the possibility to
prove properties of the specified service. Proving these properties
was shown to be a straight-forward but sometimes rather tedious task,
because the proofs include recursive arguing over the definitions of
the auxiliary operations and much case reasoning. Because the interpreter can also handle terms with variables, it was used in some of the
proofs for automatic assistance. But in general the theorem proving
facilities of the system have to be extended further. A narrowing
algorithm like the one in the RAP system /Hus 85/ will be included
next. Also the interpreter will be extended in a way similar to the
OBJ system (cf. /GMP 82/).

6 REFERENCES

/ADJ 76/   J.A. Goguen, J.W. Thatcher, E.G. Wagner: An Initial Alge-
            bra Approach to the Specification, Correctness, and Imple-
            mentation of Abstract Data Types; in: Current Trends in
            Programming Methodology, IV: Data Structuring (ed.: R.
            Yeh), Prentice Hall, New Jersey, (1978)

/BHLM 83/   Butscher, Lausch, Henken, de Meer: Private lokale
            X.25-Netze mit Untervermittlung; Handbuch der modernen
            Datenverarbeitung, Heft 111, Mai 1983, Forkel Verlag

/dM 84/   J. de Meer: Konzepte zur Implementierung eines verbin-
            dungsorientierten Transport Dienstes auf der S7.8xx;
            internal paper, Hahn-Meitner-Institut Berlin

/EFH 85/   H. Ehrig,W. Fey, H. Hansen: Towards Abstract User Inter-
            faces for Formal System Specifications; this volume

/EM 85/   H. Ehrig, B.Mahr: Fundamentals of Algebraic Specification
               1:   Equations and Initial Semantics;   EATCS Monograph
               Series, Springer Verlag, Berlin, (1985)

/GMP 82/   J.A. Goguen, J. Meseguer, D. Plaisted: Programming with
               Parameterized Abstract   Objects in OBJ;   in: Theory and
               Practice of Software Technology (eds: Ferrari, Bolognani,
               Goguen), North Holland, (1982)

/HHM 85/   H. Hansen, K.P. Hasler, J. de Meer: Algebraic Specifica-
               tion of an OSI Transport Service using ACT ONE; TU Berlin,
               HMI Berlin, draft (1985)

/HLR 82/   K.P. Hasler, M. Loewe, M.Reisin: Algebraic Specification
               of an User-Controlled Interpreter for Algebraic Specifica-
               tions; Computer Science Report, TU Berlin (1982)

/Hus 85/   H. Hussmann: Unification in Conditional-Equational Theo-
               ries; Techn.Rep. MIP-8502, Univ. Passau (1985)

/ISO-TS 83/   ISO/TC97/SC16/N1435:   Information Processing Systems -
               Open Systems Interconnection - Transport Service Defini-
               tion

/Mil 80/   R. Milner: A Calculus of Communicating Systems; LNCS 92,
               Springer Verlag, Berlin 1980

/Lan 85/   A. Langen: Algorithmen zur Ueberpruefung der semantischen
               Kontextbedingungen der Spezifikationssprache ACT ONE; Com-
               puter Science Report 85-12; TU Berlin (1985)

/LOTOS 85/   ISO/TC 97/SC 21 N423:   Information Processing Systems -
               Open Systems Interconnection - LOTOS - A Formal Descrip-
               tion Technique Based on the Temporal Ordering of Observa-
               tional Behaviour

/OSI 82/   ISO/TC 97/SC 16 N1562E: Information Processing System -
               Open Systems Interconnection - Basic Reference Model

/Pad 83/   P. Padawitz: Corrrectness, Completeness, and Consistency
               of Equational Data Type Specifications; Ph.D.Thesis; Com-
               puter Science Report 83-15, TU Berlin, (1983)

/Pet 80/   C.A. Petri: Concurrency; in: Net Theory and Applications
               (ed: Brauer), LNCS 84, Springer Verlag, (1980) Informatik
               Fachberichte 60, Springer Verlag (1983)

/Sun 80/   C. A. Sunshine: Formal Modeling of Communication Proto-
               cols; Informatik Fachberichte 40, Springer Verlag (1980)

Observational Specification: A Birkhoff-Theorem[1]

Rolf Hennicker and Martin Wirsing

Universität Passau
Fakultät für Mathematik und Informatik
Postfach 2540
D – 8390 Passau

Abstract

"Observational specifications" are presented in order to provide a concept for determining the observable parts of algebraic specifications. Syntactically, equational specifications are extended to contain an "observability predicate" which allows to specify the "observable terms". Semantically, a notion of "observational homomorphism" respectively "full observational homomorphism" respecting only the observable objects of algebras is introduced.
A syntactic criterion is given for characterizing those classes of algebras which are closed under observational isomorphism. As a consequence a Birkhoff-like theorem can be proved which shows that any class of algebras closed under the formation of products, subalgebras and full observational homomorphism can be specified by a set of "observable" equations and observations. Vice versa, (the class of models of) any specification specified by a set of "observable" equations and observations is closed under the formation of products. subalgebras and full observational homomorphism.

---

[1] This work has been partially sponsored by the ESPRIT-project METEOR

1. Introduction

Observability plays an important role in program development. For example, the notion of implementation of abstract data types can be based on this concept (cf. e.g. [Goguen, Meseguer 82]. [Sannella, Tarlecki 84]), "experiments" on distributed processes (cf. e.g. [Broy 84]) or the abstraction from a single step transition relation to an input-output operational semantics [Astesiano et. al. 85] can be formalized using a notion of observable behaviour.

In the framework of algebraic specifications observability can be characterized as follows:
Given a Σ-algebra A one is interested in the observable behaviour of A with respect to an observability notion. This observable behaviour may be a class of Σ-algebras – those Σ-algebras which are "observationally" or "extensionally equivalent" to A (cf. [Broy et. al. 81]) or a special Σ-algebra, a so-called "fully abstract" algebra Z (in the sense of [Milner 77]) the equality relation of which is characterized by the fact that two (interpretations of) terms are identified in Z, iff they are indistinguishable with respect to the observable behaviour.
Starting with [Giarratana et. al. 76] there is a number of papers on observability, its use and its consequences. A way to classify them is their definition of the notion of observability. In [Giarratana et. al. 76] and in the papers of [Reichel 81], [Broy, Wirsing 81], [Goguen, Meseguer 82] and [Schoett 83] fixed sets of "observable" or "visible" sorts are considered as observable. As a consequence in "sufficiently complete" equational specifications the terminal algebra is fully abstract and represents the observable behaviour of all models of the specification (cf. e.g. [Broy et. al. 81]). The approach of visible sorts where all terms of any of the visible sorts are observable was generalized by [Sannella, Wirsing 83] by considering any (but fixed) set of terms as observable and again this approach was generalized by [Pepper 83] and [Sannella, Tarlecki 84] by dealing with fixed sets of observable formulas. With respect to this notion, observability of a fixed set of terms W is equivalent to observability of the set {t = t'| t $\in$ W} of equations. In this paper we deviate from the syntactic view of observability (as a fixed set of syntactic entities such as sorts, terms or formulas); our notion of observability is determined by a so-called "observability predicate" Obs which in the same way as the equality relation is considered as a basic predicate of every specification.
Hence, we adapt a "semantic view" of observability by considering observability as a part of the specification which is specified by the axioms. Such specifications are called "observational specifications"; Σ-algebras containing the observability predicate are called "observational algebras".

The fundamental tool for studying classes of algebras and the relationship between algebras is the notion of homomorphism. For observational algebras there are (at least) two possibilities for defining such a notion:
Either one does not give special importance to the observability predicate and therefore considers this predicate as one of the predicates of the algebra under consideration or the observability predicate is fundamental in the sense that only the observable objects and terms determine the (mathematically) interesting behaviour of an algebra.
The former case represents the "classical" view where a homomorphism between two Σ-algebras A and B is defined as usual for the function symbols of Σ and moreover it has to be compatible with the observability relations of A and B (cf. e.g. [Grätzer 68]). Then one gets the usual facts and theorems (such as Birkhoff theorems) about the fine structure of classes of algebras.

Motivated by the above mentioned applications in computer science we are in this work more interested in the latter case. Here an "observational homomorphism" from A to B should just require compatibility between the observable parts of A and B; nothing should be required for the nonobservable parts. Consequently, an observational homomorphism should be a mapping from the observable part of A to the observable part of B with some compatibility requirements.

In this paper such a notion of observational homomorphism is introduced (similar to [Broy, Wirsing 83]) and basic properties as well as relationships with the usual notion of homomorphism are studied. To show the mathematical adequacy of observational algebras closure properties for classes of observational algebras are studied. It turns out that closure properties concerning subalgebras and products generalize in a natural way from the "classical" case of total algebras to the case of observational algebras. What is really different to the "classical" case are closure properties with respect to observational isomorphism. Here "observationally complete" specifications (that are observational specifications such that their model classes are closed under observational isomorphism) are considered. An "observability condition" for the equations of an observational specification is introduced and it is shown that this observability condition is necessary and sufficient for observational specifications to be observationally complete.
As a consequence classes of observational algebras closed under the formation of products, subalgebras and full observational homomorphism are exactly those classes which are definable by "observable" equations and observations, where an axiom t = r is called observable if Obs(t) is an axiom as well. This is just the generalization of Birkhoff's theorem [Birkhoff 35] to observational algebras.

The paper is organized as follows:
In section 2 some basic notions of algebraic specifications are summarized.
In section 3 the underlying definitions of syntax and semantics of observational specifications are given and illustrated by examples. Especially a sound and complete proof system for observational specifications is presented and the notion of observational homomorphism is introduced.
In section 4 the definitions and results mentioned above concerning "observationally complete" specifications are presented and in section 5 the generalization of Birkhoff's theorem to classes of observational algebras is given. Finally, in section 6, some further aspects on observational specifications are discussed.

2. Basic Notions

A (many-sorted) <u>signature</u> Σ is a pair (S, F) where S is a set of <u>sorts</u> and F is a set of <u>function symbols</u>. To every function symbol $f \in F$ a functionality $s_1 x ... x s_n \to s$ with $s_1, ..., s_n, s \in S$ and $n \in \mathbb{N}$ is associated. If n = 0 then f is called a constant of sort s.
A <u>total Σ-algebra</u> $A = ((A_s)_{s \in S}, (f^A)_{f \in F})$ consists of a familiy of carrier sets $(A_s)_{s \in S}$ and a family of total functions $(f^A)_{f \in F}$ such that if f has functionality $s_1 x ... x s_n \to s$ then f^A is a total function from $A_{s_1} x ... x A_{s_n}$ to A_s (if n=0 then f^A is a constant object of A_s). In this paper we assume $A_s \neq \emptyset$ for all $s \in S$ (for a discussion see [Goguen, Meseguer 82a], [Padawitz, Wirsing 84]).
The <u>term algebra</u> $W_\Sigma(X)$ over a S-sorted family $X = (X_s)_{s \in S}$ of sets of (free)

variables of sort s has as carriers the sets $W_\Sigma(X)_s$ of terms of sort s and for
$f \in F$ with functionality $s_1 x \ldots x s_n \to s$ the interpretation $f^{W_\Sigma(X)}$ of f is defined
by $f^{W_\Sigma(X)} (t_1, \ldots, t_n) =_{def} f(t_1, \ldots, t_n)$. If $X = \emptyset$ then $W_\Sigma(\emptyset)$ is denoted by W_Σ
and W_Σ is called <u>ground term algebra</u>.
For a total Σ-algebra A a <u>valuation</u> $\alpha : X \to A$ is a family of maps
$(\alpha_s : X_s \to A_s)_s \in S$. The <u>interpretation</u> associated to α is a family
$\alpha^* = (\alpha^*_s)_s \in S$ of functions $\alpha^*_s : W_\Sigma(X)_s \to A_s$ inductively defined by

(1) $\alpha^*_s(x) = \alpha_s(x)$ if $x \in X_s$.

(2) $\alpha^*_s(f) = f^A$ if $f \in F$ is a constant of sort s.

(3) $\alpha^*_s(f(t_1, \ldots, t_n)) = f^A(\alpha^*_{s_1}(t_1), \ldots, \alpha^*_{s_n}(t_n))$
         if $f \in F$ has functionality $s_1 x \ldots x s_n \to s$.

For $t \in W_\Sigma(X)$ we write t^A_α for the interpretation $\alpha^*(t)$. If $X = \emptyset$ then the
interpretation is independent of the special choice of the valuation and we write
t^A for the interpretation of a term $t \in W_\Sigma$ in A. If the interpretation from W_Σ to
A is surjective then A is called <u>term generated</u>.
Let A and B be total Σ-algebras. A Σ-homomorphism $p: A \to B$ is a family of total
functions $(p_s: A_s \to B_s)_s \in S$ such that for all $s \in S$ and for all $f \in F$:

$p_s(f^A) = f^B$ if $f \in F$ is a constant of sort s.

$p_s(f^A(a_1, \ldots, a_n)) = f^B(p_{s_1}(a_1), \ldots, p_{s_n}(a_n))$ for all $a_1 \in A_{s_1}, \ldots, a_n \in A_{s_n}$
         if $f \in F$ has functionality $s_1 x \ldots x s_n \to s$.

3. Observational Specifications

3.1. Syntax

The syntax of observational specifications is based on the usual one for equational
specifications. There is given a signature Σ in the usual way and a set of axioms
which now consists of a set of equations and a set of formulas of the form Obs(t)
for axiomatizing the notion of observability. Obs is called observability predicate.

<u>Definition 1 :</u>
An <u>observational specification</u> is a pair (Σ, E) where Σ is a signature and E is a
set of <u>equations</u> and <u>observations</u>, called <u>axioms</u>.
An equation is of the form t = r; an observation is of the form Obs(t).
$(t, r \in W_\Sigma(X))$

The following example specifies properties of finite sets of natural numbers where
it is observable whether a natural number x belongs to a set S or not (The algebra
of finite sets of natural numbers with Obs = $\mathbb{B}$ is in the classical sense an initial
algebra of this specification, cf. e.g. [ADJ 76]):

Example 1

```
type NATSET = enrich BOOL, NAT by
    sorts  : set
    functs : Ø :  → set
             add : nat x set → set
              є : nat x set → bool
    axioms:
                  x є Ø = false
          x є add(y, S) = eq(x, y) or (x є S)
      add(x, add(y, S)) = add(y, add(x, S))
      add(x, add(x, S)) = add(x, S)
              Obs(x є S)
```

3.2. Observational Σ-Algebras and Model Classes

The semantics of an observational specification (Σ, E) is defined to be the class of all observational Σ-algebras satisfying the axioms E:

Definition 2 :
An observational Σ-algebra is a pair (A, Obs^A), where $A = ((A_s)_{s \in S}, (f^A)_{f \in F})$ is a total Σ-algebra and $Obs^A = (Obs^A_s)_{s \in S}$ is a family of subsets $Obs^A_s \subseteq A_s$. Obs^A is called the observable part of A.
The class of all observational Σ-algebras is denoted by Obs-Alg(Σ).
An observational Σ-algebra (A, Obs^A) is called term generated, if the total Σ-algebra A is term generated.

An observational Σ-algebra (B, Obs^B) is called observational subalgebra of (A, Obs^A), if the total Σ-algebra B is a subalgebra of A and $Obs^B_s = Obs^A_s \cap B_s$ for all $s \in S$, that is the observable objects of B are observable in A and the objects of B which are observable in A belong to the observable part of B.

The observational product $\prod_{i \in I} (A_i, Obs^{Ai})$ of a family $(A_i, Obs^{Ai})_{i \in I}$ of

observational Σ-algebras is the pair $(\prod_{i \in I} A_i, \prod_{i \in I} Obs^{Ai})$ where $\prod_{i \in I} A_i$ is the

usual product of total Σ-algebras and $\prod_{i \in I} Obs^{Ai}$ is the family $(\prod_{i \in I} Obs^{Ai}_s)_{s \in S}$
of set-theoretic products of the sets $(Obs^{Ai}_s)_{i \in I}$.

The satisfaction relation used here is the usual satisfaction relation of first order predicate calculus:

Definition 3 :
An observational Σ-algebra (A, Obs^A) satisfies:
   (1) an equation $t = r$ (written $(A, Obs^A) \models t = r$) iff $t^A_\alpha = r^A_\alpha$
        for all valuations $\alpha : X \to A$.
   (2) an observation Obs(t) (written $(A, Obs^A) \models Obs(t)$) iff $t^A_\alpha \in Obs^A$
        for all valuations $\alpha : X \to A$.

Definiton 4 :
An observational Σ-algebra is called a __model__ of the observational specification
(Σ, E) if it satisfies the axioms E.
The class of all models of (Σ, E) is denoted by Obs-Alg (Σ, E).

Example 2
Let (P, Obs^P) be the observational Σ-algebra with carrier sets

$P_{\underline{set}}$ = $\mathbb{P}_{\underline{fin}}$ ($\mathbb{N}$) (set of finite sets of natural numbers)
$P_{\underline{nat}}$ = $\mathbb{N}$
$P_{\underline{bool}}$ = $\mathbb{B}$ ($\mathbb{B}$ = {0, L})

with the usual functions and with observable part

$\text{Obs}^P_{\underline{set}}$ = $\text{Obs}^P_{\underline{nat}}$ = $\emptyset$, $\text{Obs}^P_{\underline{bool}}$ = $\mathbb{B}$.

(P, Obs^P) is the observational Σ-algebra of finite sets of natural numbers where
the boolean values are considered as observable.

Obviously (P, Obs^P) is a model of NATSET.

3.3. Proof System

Definition 5:
The proof system for observational specifications (Σ, E) is the usual proof system
(cf. e.g. [Ehrig, Mahr 85]) for equational specifications extended by the axiom
(0) E $\vdash$ Obs(t) for every observation Obs(t) $\in$ E and by the two rules:

  (1) E $\vdash$ t = r and E $\vdash$ Obs(t) then E $\vdash$ Obs(r)

  (2) E $\vdash$ Obs(t) then E $\vdash$ Obs(t[t'/x]) if t' and x are of the same sort.
       (t[t'/x] denotes the substitution of x by t' in t)

(1) gives the compatibility of the observability predicate with equality and (2)
extends the substitution rule of equational calculus to the observability
predicate.

Proposition 1:
The proof system for observational specifications is sound and complete.

Proof:
Soundness is obvious and completeness with respect to equations is well-known by
equational calculus.
Now let (Σ, E) be an observational specification and let for some term t
(A, Obs^A) $\models$ Obs(t) be true for all (A, Obs^A) $\in$ Obs-Alg(Σ, E). The algebra
($W_\Sigma(X)/\sim_E$, Obs^W) where $\sim_E$ is the congruence relation generated by E and
Obs^W = {[t'] | E $\vdash$ Obs(t')} is a model of (Σ, E) (Note that Obs^W is well-defined
by rule (1) and ($W_\Sigma(X)/\sim_E$, Obs^W) is a model of (Σ, E) since by axiom (0) and rule
(2) every observation of E is true in ($W_\Sigma(X)/\sim_E$, Obs^W)). Hence
($W_\Sigma(X)/\sim_E$, Obs^W) $\models$ Obs(t) and therefore by definition of Obs^W we have
E $\vdash$ Obs(t).   □

3.4. Observational Homomorphism

In this part a new notion of homomorphism is introduced. An observational homomorphism is required to be restricted to the observable parts of algebras and to be compatible with interpretations of terms.
First, observational homomorphisms are defined for term generated observational Σ-algebras:

Definition 6:
Let (A, Obs^A) and (B, Obs^B) be term generated observational Σ-algebras.
An <u>observational Σ-homomorphism</u>

$$p: (A, Obs^A) \longrightarrow (B, Obs^B)$$

is a family of total functions

$$(p_s: Obs_s^A \longrightarrow Obs_s^B)_{s \in S}$$

such that for all terms $t \in (W_\Sigma)_s$ the following holds:

$$t^A \in Obs_s^A \implies p_s(t^A) = t^B.$$

Hence the definition of observational homomorphism corresponds to the usual definition of homomorphism restricted to the observable parts. If $Obs^A = A$ and $Obs^B = B$ then the observational homomorphisms are exactly the usual ones. In the term generated case all elements of A and in particular of the observable part Obs^A can be represented by ground terms; for Σ-algebras which are not term generated this is not always true. But by introducing enough variables one can always get a surjective interpretation α^* from some term algebra $W_\Sigma(Y)$ onto A. Using this fact we generalize the notion of observational homomorphism to arbitrary observational algebras (cf. [Broy, Wirsing 83]):

Definition 7:
Let (A, Obs^A) and (B, Obs^B) be observational Σ-algebras.
An <u>observational Σ-homomorphism</u>

$$p: (A, Obs^A) \longrightarrow (B, Obs^B)$$

is a family of total functions

$$(p_s: Obs_s^A \longrightarrow Obs_s^B)_{s \in S}$$

such that there exists a family $Y = (Y_s)_{s \in S}$ of sets of free variables and there exist valuations

$$\alpha: Y \longrightarrow A, \quad \beta: Y \longrightarrow B$$

with surjective interpretation $\alpha^*: W_\Sigma(Y) \longrightarrow A$ such that for all terms $t \in W_\Sigma(Y)_s$ the following holds:

$$t_\alpha^A \in Obs_s^A \implies p_s(t_\alpha^A) = t_\beta^B$$

An observational Σ-homomorphism is called <u>full</u> if the associated interpretation wrt. β, $\beta^*: W_\Sigma(Y) \longrightarrow B$ is surjective.

A full observational Σ-homomorphism p: $(A, Obs^A) \rightarrow (B, Obs^B)$ is called
observational Σ-isomorphism if p is bijective and p^{-1} is a full observational
Σ-homomorphism.

Obviously for term generated algebras both definitions of observational
homomorphisms are equivalent.

Remarks:
Let (A, Obs^A), (B, Obs^B) be observational Σ-algebras, let p: $Obs^A \rightarrow Obs^B$ be a
map, let Y be a S-sorted family of sets of free variables and let α: $Y \rightarrow A$,
β: $Y \rightarrow B$ be valuations with surjective interpretation α^*: $W_\Sigma(Y) \rightarrow A$.

1.) If p is an observational Σ-homomorphism such that the homomorphism condition
is satisfied by p with respect to Y, α, β then p satisfies the homomorphism
condition for any S-sorted family of sets of free variables Y' and valuation
α': $Y' \rightarrow A$ by defining a suitable valuation β': $Y' \rightarrow B$; i.e. observational
homomorphism is independent of the special choice of variables and valuations for
which the homomorphism condition holds. This fact is ensured by the surjectivity
of α^*.

2.) If (A, Obs^A), (B, Obs^B) are term generated and p is an observational
Σ-homomorphism then p is a full observational Σ-homomorphism, i.e. in the term
generated case the concepts of observational Σ-homomorphism and full observational
Σ-homomorphism coincide. Consequently if p is bijective and p^{-1} satisfies the
homomorphism condition for ground terms then p is an observational Σ-isomorphism.

3.) If p: $(A, Obs^A) \rightarrow (B, Obs^B)$ and ψ: $(B, Obs^B) \rightarrow (C, Obs^C)$ are (full)
observational Σ-homomorphisms then $\psi \circ p$: $(A, Obs^A) \rightarrow (C, Obs^C)$ is a (full)
observational Σ-homomorphism. As a consequence observational isomorphism is an
equivalence relation on the class of all observational Σ-algebras.

4.) If $Obs^A = A$ and $Obs^B = B$ then p: $(A, Obs^A) \rightarrow (B, Obs^B)$ is an observational
Σ-homomorphism iff p is a Σ-homomorphism of total Σ-algebras; i.e. in this case
the concepts of observational Σ-homomorphism and "classical" Σ-homomorphism
coincide (The proof uses the surjectivity of α^*, cf. remark 1).

Example 3:
Let (P, Obs^P) be the observational Σ-algebra from example 2 and let (S, Obs^S) be
the observational Σ-algebra of sets of finite sequences of natural numbers where
the boolean values are observable; that is (S, Obs^S) has carrier sets

$S_{set} = Seq_{fin}(\mathbb{N})$ (set of finite sequences of natural numbers)
$S_{nat} = \mathbb{N}$
$S_{bool} = \mathbb{B}$

with the usual functions and observable part $Obs^S = Obs^P$.

Then p: $(P, Obs^P) \rightarrow (S, Obs^S)$

where p_{bool}: $\mathbb{B} \rightarrow \mathbb{B}$
              $p_{bool}(x) =_{def} x$

is an observational Σ-isomorphism.

Note that (S, Obs^S) is <u>not</u> a model of the specification NATSET since the last two equations of NATSET are not true in (S, Obs^S).

This leads to the following

FACT:
<u>Model classes of observational specifications are in general not closed under observational Σ-isomorphism</u>.

The reason for this is that in general an observational Σ-homomorphism does not preserve equations which are informally in no sense observable. So the question arises, whether there are conditions for the equations of observational specifications such that closure under observational Σ-isomorphism is available.

4. Observationally Complete Specifications

Observational Σ-isomorphism defines an equivalence relation between observational Σ-algebras (cf. remark 3):

(A, Obs^A) ~ (B, Obs^B) iff

there exists an observational Σ-isomorphism $\wp$: (A, Obs^A) $\longrightarrow$ (B, Obs^B).

Then for any class K of observational Σ-algebras

Beh(K) =$_{def}$ {(B, Obs^B)| $\exists$ (A, Obs^A) $\in$ K: (A, Obs^A) ~ (B, Obs^B) }

defines the class of all algebras which are observationally equivalent to some algebra in K. Beh(K) is called the <u>behaviour</u> of K.

A class K of observational Σ-algebras is called <u>observationally complete</u> if

Beh(K) = K.

An observational specification (Σ, E) is called <u>observationally complete</u> if the model class of (Σ, E) is observationally complete.

In the following we are interested in the characterization of observationally complete specifications. For that purpose a purely syntactic condition for the equations of observational specifications is formulated which is necessary and sufficient for model classes of observational specifications to be closed under full observational Σ-homomorphism as well as to be closed under observational Σ-isomorphism. Hence this condition is necessary and sufficient for proving the observational completeness of the specification under consideration.
Informally this condition (called observability condition) is satisfied by an axiom t = r of an observational specification (Σ, E) if the terms t and r coincide except for equivalent (wrt. E) observable subterms. To explain this condition more technically we call a term c $\in$ W$_\Sigma$(X $\cup$ {$x_1,...,x_n$}) where $x_1,...,x_n \notin$ X a context of the variables $x_1,...,x_n$. Then the observability condition is satisfied by t = r if t can be obtained by substituting terms $t_1,...,t_n$ for $x_1,...,x_n$ in a context c (i.e. t $\equiv$ c[$t_1/x_1,...,t_n/x_n$]) and if r can be obtained by substituting terms $r_1,...,r_n$ for $x_1,...,x_n$ in the same context c (i.e. r $\equiv$ c[$r_1/x_1,...,r_n/x_n$]) where the equations $t_i = r_i$ as well as the observability of the terms t_i (and hence the

observability of the terms r_i by definition 5, rule (1)) is provable from the axioms E.

Definition 8:
Let (Σ, E) be an observational specification.
An equation $t = r \in E$ (t, $r \in W_{\Sigma}(X)$) satisfies the observability condition if for some $n \geq 0$, $n \in \mathbb{N}$, there exist terms $t_1,\ldots,t_n,r_1,\ldots,r_n \in W_{\Sigma}(X)$ and there exists a context $c \in W_{\Sigma}(X \cup \{x_1,\ldots,x_n\})$ where $x_1,\ldots,x_n \notin X$ such that:

$c[t_1/x_1,\ldots,t_n/x_n] \equiv t$, $c[r_1/x_1,\ldots,r_n/x_n] \equiv r$
($\equiv$ stands for syntactic identity)

$E \vdash t_i = r_i$, $E \vdash Obs(t_i)$ for $i = 1,\ldots,n$.

Note that any trivial equation $t = t \in E$ satisfies the observability condition by choosing $n = 0$ and $c \equiv t$.

Example 4:
Let NATSET1 be the observational specification NATSET (see example 1) where the last two equations are omitted. Then the equations of NATSET1 satisfy the observability condition for $n = 1$ by taking the trivial context $c \equiv x_1$ and choosing $t_1 \equiv x \in \emptyset$, $r_1 \equiv$ false for the first equation and $t_1 \equiv x \in add(y, S)$, $r_1 \equiv eq(x, y)$ or $(x \in S)$ for the second one. Clearly in both cases $E \vdash t_1 = r_1$ and $E \vdash Obs(t_1)$.
On the other hand the last two equations of NATSET do not satisfy the observability condition since any subterm occurring in these equations is either of sort set or of sort nat. But only for terms of sort bool observability is provable from the axioms.

Theorem 1 gives a characterization of observationally complete specifications. For the proof of theorem 1 we use the following lemma which characterizes those axioms (of some observational specification) which satisfy the observability condition:

Lemma 1:
Let (Σ, E) be an observational specification and $E' = \{t' = r'| E \vdash t' = r'$, $E \vdash Obs(t') \}$.
Then for all equations $t = r \in E$ the following conditions are equivalent:

1.) $t = r$ satisfies the observability condition.
2.) $E' \vdash t = r$.

Proof:
1.) $\Rightarrow$ 2.):
Let $t = r$ satisfy the observability condition wrt. terms $t_1,\ldots t_n$, $r_1,\ldots,r_n$ and context c, i.e. $c[t_1/x_1,\ldots,t_n/x_n] \equiv t$, $c[r_1/x_1,\ldots,r_n/x_n] \equiv r$ and $E \vdash t_i = r_i$, $E \vdash Obs(t_i)$ for $i = 1,\ldots,n$. Then $t_i = r_i \in E'$ for $i = 1,\ldots,n$ and hence $E' \vdash t = r$.
2.) $\Rightarrow$ 1.):
By induction on the length of the proof:
If $t = r$ is an axiom of E' then the observability condition holds obviously.
The only induction step which is not simple is transitivity: Here it is to show that if $E \vdash t = s$, $E \vdash s = r$ for some term $s \in W_{\Sigma}(X)$ and $t = s$, $s = r$ satisfy the observability condition (by induction hypothesis) then $t = r$ satisfies the observability condition.

Now let $c[t_1/x_1,\ldots,t_n/x_n] \equiv t$, $c[s_1/x_1,\ldots,s_n/x_n] \equiv s$
$\quad\quad E \vdash t_i = s_i$, $E \vdash Obs(t_i)$ for $i = 1,\ldots,n$
and let $c'[s_1'/y_1,\ldots,s_m'/y_m] \equiv s$, $c'[r_1/y_1,\ldots,r_m/y_m] \equiv r$
$\quad\quad E \vdash s_i' = r_i$, $E \vdash Obs(s_i')$ for $i = 1,\ldots,m$.
We show that $t = r$ satisfies the observability condition by induction on the structure of s:
W.l.o.g. assume $n > 0$ and $m > 0$ since otherwise $t \equiv s$ or $s \equiv r$ and then clearly $t = r$ satisfies the observability condition.
1.) If s is a constant or a variable then $c \equiv x_1$ and therefore $E \vdash Obs(t)$. Since $E \vdash t = s$, $E \vdash s = r$ one has $E \vdash t = r$. Hence $t = r$ satisfies the observability condition.
2.) If $s \equiv f(s_1'',\ldots,s_k'')$ for some k-ary function symbol f, $k > 0$, and some terms $s_1'',\ldots,s_k'' \in W_\Sigma(X)$ then distinguish the following cases:
a) If $c \equiv x_1$ or $c' \equiv y_1$ then $E \vdash Obs(t)$ or $E \vdash Obs(s)$ and hence, similarly to 1.), $t = r$ satisfies the observability condition.
b) If $c \not\equiv x_1$ and $c' \not\equiv y_1$ then there exist contexts $c_1,\ldots,c_k \in W_\Sigma(X \cup \{x_1,\ldots,x_n\})$ and contexts $c_1',\ldots,c_k' \in W_\Sigma(X \cup \{y_1,\ldots,y_m\})$ such that $c \equiv f(c_1,\ldots,c_k)$ and $c' \equiv f(c_1',\ldots,c_k')$.
W.l.o.g. let for $i = 1,\ldots,k$ $c_i \in W_\Sigma(X \cup \{x_{n_{i-1}+1},\ldots,x_{n_i}\})$ where $0 = n_0 < n_1 \leq n_2 \leq \ldots \leq n_k = n$ and $c_i' \in W_\Sigma(X \cup \{y_{m_{i-1}+1},\ldots,y_{m_i}\})$ where $0 = m_0 < m_1 \leq m_2 \leq \ldots \leq m_k = m$.
Then $c_i[s_{n_{i-1}+1}/x_{n_{i-1}+1},\ldots,s_{n_i}/x_{n_i}] \equiv s_i''$ and $c_i[t_{n_{i-1}+1}/x_{n_{i-1}+1},\ldots,t_{n_i}/x_{n_i}] \equiv t_i''$
for $i = 1,\ldots,k$ where $f(t_1'',\ldots,t_k'') \equiv t$. Hence all $t_i'' = s_i''$ satisfy the observability condition.
Analogously one shows that $s_i'' = r_i''$ satisfies the observability condition for $i = 1,\ldots,k$ where $f(r_1'',\ldots,r_k'') \equiv r$.
Then by induction hypothesis (on the structure of s) all $t_i'' = r_i''$ satisfy the observability condition. Now it easily follows that $t = r$ satisfies the observability condition. $\quad\quad\quad\quad\quad\Box$

Theorem 1:
Let $K = Obs-Alg(\Sigma, E)$ be the model class of an observational specification (Σ, E). Then the following conditions are equivalent:

1.) All equations $t = r \in E$ satisfy the observability condition.
2.) K is closed under full observational Σ-homomorphism.
3.) K is closed under observational Σ-isomorphism.
4.) (Σ, E) is observationally complete.

Proof:
1.) $\Rightarrow$ 2.):
Let $(A, Obs^A) \in K$, $(B, Obs^B) \in Obs-Alg(\Sigma)$ and $p: (A, Obs^A) \to (B, Obs^B)$ be a full observational Σ-homomorphism such that the homomorphism condition holds with respect to a set of variables Y and valuations $\alpha: Y \to A$, $\beta: Y \to B$. It is to show that every axiom from E is true in (B, Obs^B).
Let $t = r \in E$ satisfy the observability condition wrt. terms $t_1,\ldots,t_n,r_1,\ldots,r_n$ and context c, i.e. $c[t_1/x_1,\ldots,t_n/x_n] \equiv t$, $c[r_1/x_1,\ldots,r_n/x_n] \equiv r$ and $E \vdash t_i = r_i$, $E \vdash Obs(t_i)$ for $i = 1,\ldots,n$. Let $\beta': X \to B$ be an arbitrary valuation (X contains the free variables occuring in E). It is to show that $t_{\beta'}^B = r_{\beta'}^B$. Since p is full there exists for every variable x occurring in $t = r$ a term $t'_x \in W_\Sigma(Y)$ such that $\beta'(x) = (t'_x)_\beta^B$. Let $t'_i \equiv t_i[t'_x/x]$, $r'_i \equiv r_i[t'_x/x]$ for $i = 1,\ldots,n$. Since $(A, Obs^A) \in K$: $(t'_i)_\alpha^A = (r'_i)_\alpha^A$ and $(t'_i)_\alpha^A \in Obs^A$. Therefore $(t_i)_{\beta'}^B = (t'_i)_\beta^B = p((t'_i)_\alpha^A) = p((r'_i)_\alpha^A) = (r'_i)_\beta^B = (r_i)_{\beta'}^B$ for $i = 1,\ldots,n$. Then $t_{\beta'}^B =$

$c[t_1/x_1,...,t_n/x_n]_{\beta'}^B = c[r_1/x_1,...,r_n/x_n]_{\beta'}^B = r_{\beta'}^B$. Analogously one shows that any observation $Obs(t) \in E$ is true in (B, Obs^B).

2.) $\Rightarrow$ 3.): trivial.

3.) $\Rightarrow$ 1.):

By contradiction: Assume there exists an equation $t_0 = r_0$ in E which does not satisfy the observability condition. By lemma 1 $t_0 = r_0$ is not deducible from E' where E' = {t = r | E $\vdash$ t = r , E $\vdash$ Obs(t)} $\cup$ {Obs(t) | E $\vdash$ Obs(t)} (in particular E $\nvdash$ Obs(t_0)). Since equational calculus is complete the algebra $W_\Sigma(X)/\sim_E$, which is initial wrt. E' does not satisfy $t_0 = r_0$.

Define A = $W_\Sigma(X)/\sim_E$, B = $W_\Sigma(X)/\sim_{E'}$, Obs^A = {[t] $\in$ A | E $\vdash$ Obs(t)} , Obs^B = {[t] $\in$ B | E' $\vdash$ Obs(t)}. Then (B, Obs^B) $\notin$ K (since K = Obs-Alg(Σ, E)) but the canonical map ρ: $Obs^A \rightarrow Obs^B$ which maps any congruence class of Obs^A to the corresponding congruence class of Obs^B is an observational Σ-isomorphism.

3.) $\Leftrightarrow$ 4.): obvious.   □

Example 5:

By theorem 1 NATSET1 (see example 4) is observationally complete but NATSET is not observationally complete.

The following corollary shows that any observationally complete specification can be axiomatized by a set of observations and equations such that for any equation t = r the observation Obs(t) is an axiom of the specification:

Corollary 1:

For an observational specification (Σ, E) the following conditions are equivalent:

  1.) (Σ, E) is observationally complete.
  2.) There exists a finite (if E is finite) set of axioms E' such that:
$$\forall \; t = r \in E': \quad Obs(t) \in E' \quad and$$
$$Obs-Alg(\Sigma, E) = Obs-Alg(\Sigma, E').$$

Proof:

1.) $\Rightarrow$ 2.):

Since (Σ, E) is observationally complete, by theorem 1 any equation t = r $\in$ E satisfies the observability condition. Now let E' consist of all the equations $t_i = r_i$ occurring in the observability conditions for the equations t = r $\in$ E, of all observations Obs(t_i) and of all observations Obs(t) $\in$ E. Then by construction of E' any axiom from E is deducible from E' and any axiom from E' is deducible from E. Hence Obs-Alg(Σ, E) = Obs-Alg(Σ, E').

2.) $\Rightarrow$ 1.):

Since any equation t = r $\in$ E' satisfies the observability condition, (Σ, E') is observationally complete by theorem 1. Hence (Σ, E) is observationally complete as well.   □

5. A Birkhoff-Like Theorem

The classical Birkhoff theorem (cf. e.g. [Birkhoff 35], [Grätzer 68]) says that any class of total Σ-algebras can be axiomatized by a set of equations iff it is closed under the formation of subalgebras, products and Σ-epimorphism.

As a consequence of theorem 1 here a theorem is presented which is in a natural way a generalization of Birkhoff's theorem to classes of observational Σ-algebras. It gives a characterization for classes of observational Σ-algebras to be definable by a set of observations and equations such that for any defining equation $t = r$ the observation $Obs(t)$ is an axiom as well. As a consequence we obtain a characterization of model classes of observationally complete specifications. The "generalized Birkhoff-theorem" shows that our definitions for observational specifications, in particular the definitions of observational Σ-algebras and observational Σ-homomorphisms, which are suggested by experience and practice in computer science lead to similar results as the classical definitions of universal algebra.

For the proof the following lemma providing a connection between classical Σ-homomorphism and observational Σ-homomorphism is used. Especially the connection between classical epimorpism and full observational homomorphism is turned out:

Lemma 2:
Let (A, Obs^A) and (B, Obs^B) be observational Σ-algebras.
If $p: A \longrightarrow B$ is a Σ-homomorphism of total Σ-algebras and $p_s(Obs_s^A) \leq Obs_s^B$ for all $s \in S$ then the restriction from p to the observable part of A is an observational Σ-homomorphism $p: (A, Obs^A) \longrightarrow (B, Obs^B)$.
If $p: A \longrightarrow B$ is a Σ-epimorphism then $p: (A, Obs^A) \longrightarrow (B, Obs^B)$ is a full observational Σ-homomorphism.
If $p: A \longrightarrow B$ is a Σ-isomorphism and $p_s(Obs_s^A) = Obs_s^B$ for all $s \in S$ then
$p: (A, Obs^A) \longrightarrow (B, Obs^B)$ is an observational Σ-isomorphism.

Proof:
Obvious, since the classical Σ-homomorphism p is compatible with interpretations of terms and the surjectivity of p induces a surjective valuation on B. ▫

Theorem 2:
Let $K \subseteq Obs\text{-}Alg(\Sigma)$ be a class of observational Σ-algebras.
Then the following conditions are equivalent:

  1.) There exists a set E of observations and equations such that:
        $K = Obs\text{-}Alg(\Sigma, E)$ and $\forall\ t = r \in E: Obs(t) \in E$.
  2.) K is closed under the formation of observational subalgebras, observational
       products and full observational Σ-homomorphism.

Proof:
1.) $\Rightarrow$ 2.):
Closure under the formation of observational subalgebras and observational products is simple. Closure under full observational Σ-homomorphism follows by theorem 1 since any equation $t = r \in E$ satisfies the observability condition.
2.) $\Rightarrow$ 1.):
Set $E1 = \{t = r \mid K \models t = r\} \cup \{Obs(t) \mid K \models Obs(t)\}$ where $t, r \in W_\Sigma(X)$ with a countably infinite set of free variables X. Then the equality $K = Obs\text{-}Alg(\Sigma, E1)$ is proved using lemma 2 by a simple generalization of the classical proof of Birkhoff's theorem. Since K is closed under full observational homomorphism $(\Sigma, E1)$ is observationally complete and therefore by corollary 1 $K = Obs\text{-}Alg(\Sigma, E)$ where E is chosen in the desired way. ▫

Corollary 2:
Let K ⊆ Obs-Alg(Σ) be a class of observational Σ-algebras.
Then the following conditions are equivalent:

1.) K is the model class of an observationally complete specification (Σ, E).
2.) K is closed under the formation of observational subalgebras, observational
    products and full observational Σ-homomorphism.

Proof:
1.) ⟹ 2.):
Corollary 1 shows that K = Obs-Alg(Σ, E') where ∀ t = r ∈ E': Obs(t) ∈ E'. Now
use theorem 2.
2.) ⟹ 1.):
By theorem 2 and theorem 1 (1. ⟹ 4.).   ☐

6.   Concluding   Remarks: Observational Implementations

The present study shows that observational specifications can be treated in a
mathematically sound way and that, moreover, classical theorems such as the
Birkhoff-theorem can be extended in a "natural way" to observational
specifications. Next consequent steps for reaching the goal of a mathematical
theory of observational specifications would be the proof of a Birkhoff-theorem
for specifications with Horn-formulas as axioms and the study of proof systems for
the behaviour Beh(Obs-Alg(Σ, E)) of a specification (Σ, E) (in the case where
(Σ, E) is not observationally complete and therefore Obs-Alg(Σ, E) ≠
Beh(Obs-Alg(Σ, E))).
One of the most important applications of observational specification is the notion
of observational implementation of specifications a variant of which has first been
studied by [Goguen, Meseguer 82]. An observational specification (Σ1, E1) is called
observational implementation of (Σ, E) if for every model (A, Obs^A) of (Σ1, E1)
some appropriately defined restriction of (A, Obs^A) to an algebra in Obs-Alg(Σ) is
in the behaviour of (the model class of) (Σ, E).
In the simplest case this restriction is just $(A|_\Sigma, Obs^A|_\Sigma)$ that is forgetting the
sorts and operation symbols of Σ1 which are not in Σ. Another possibility is to
allow also a restriction of Obs^A to a subset of Obs^A. These implementation
relations are both transitive and under appropriate conditions also monotone, hence
in the terminology of [Goguen, Burstall 80] they are vertically and horizontally.
The latter notion covers many examples known from the literature. E.g. it is
simple to prove that finite sequences implement finite sets if boolean terms of
the form x ∈ S (cf. example 1) are observable. As another example we consider
stacks over a set of elements $a_1,...,a_n$ and their array-pointer realization. It can
be proved that the following type ARRAY-POINTER is an observational implementation
of the observational specification STACK where STACK has the usual
"stack-equations" as axioms and specifies the top elements of stacks as
observable:

```
type STACK =
      sorts : elem, stack
      functs : aᵢ : → elem     for i = 1,...,n
            empty : → stack
            push : stack x elem → stack
            pop : stack → stack
            top : stack → elem

      axioms :
                  pop(push(s,e)) = s
                  top(push(s,e)) = e
                        Obs(top(s))
```

The type ARRAY-POINTER specifies stacks as tuples consisting of an array a (over $a_1,...,a_n$) and a natural number p (called pointer). The operations are specified by the axioms as follows: The push operation inserts an element in the p-th component of a and puts the pointer on the next ((p+1)-th) component. The pop operation moves the pointer down to the last ((p-1)-th) component and the top operation gets the (p-1)-th component if the pointer has value p. The product-operations (constructor cons, selectors selnat, selarray) are specified as usual and for simplicity only those array-operations are specified which are necessary for the example (vac for the empty array, put for putting a new element on the array and get for selecting an element of the array (cf. also the type GREX in [Bauer, Wössner 81])).

```
type ARRAY-POINTER = enrich BOOL, NAT by
     sorts : elem, array, stack
     functs : a_i  : → elem          for i = 1,...,n
              vac : → array
              put : array x nat x elem → array
              get : array x nat → elem
              cons : nat x array → stack
              selnat : stack → nat
              selarray : stack → array
              empty : → stack
              push : stack x elem → stack
              pop : stack → stack
              top : stack → elem
     axioms :
     get(put(a, n, e), m) = if eq(n, m) then e else get(a, m)
        selnat(cons(n, a)) = n
     selarray(cons(n, a)) = a
              push(s, e) = cons(selnat(s) + 1, put(selarray(s), selnat(s), e))
                 pop(s) = cons(selnat(s) - 1, selarray(s))
                 top(s) = get(selarray(s), selnat(s) - 1)
                 Obs(top(s))
```

(We assume that if-then-else for elem is specified as usual.)

Note that ARRAY-POINTER does not satisfy the STACK-axiom pop(push(s, e)) = s. But the behaviour of STACK is respected by ARRAY-POINTER, i.e. ARRAY-POINTER satisfies all equations between terms of sort elem which are satisfied by STACK. In particular the equations top(push(s, e)) = e and top(pop(push(s, e))) = top(s) hold in ARRAY-POINTER.

Another possible application for observational implementations are "many-level specifications" where the different levels contain more and more details. Consider e.g. a data structure for which first the context correct behaviour is specified (e.g. stacks without errors or interpreters for context correct programs). In a second level also the error behaviour of the structure is specified. For the correctness of such a pair of specifications it is necessary that the second specification is an observational implementation of the first.

Acknowledgement
We would like to thank Andrzej Tarlecki for interesting discussions and helpful comments. We gratefully acknowledge a number of useful suggestions made by the referee.

References

[ADJ 76]
J.A. Goguen, J.W. Thatcher, E.G. Wagner: An initial algebra approach to the specification, correctness, and implementation of abstract data types. IBM research report RC 6487, 1976. Also in: Current Trends in Programming Methodology, Vol. 4: Data Structuring (R.T. Yeh, ed.), Prentice-Hall, pp. 80-149 (1978).

[Astesiano et. al. 85]
E. Astesiano, G.F. Mascari, G. Reggio, M. Wirsing: On the parameterized algebraic specification of concurrent systems. In: H. Ehrig et. al. (eds.): Proc. of TAPSOFT Joint Conf. on Theory and Practice of Software Development, Berlin, March 1985. Springer Lecture Notes in Computer Science 185, pp. 342-358 (1985). Extended version: MIP 8403, Fakultät für Mathematik und Informatik, Universität Passau.

[Bauer, Wössner 81]
F.L. Bauer, H. Wössner: Algorithmische Sprache und Programmentwicklung. Berlin: Springer Verlag (1981).

[Birkhoff 35]
G. Birkhoff: On the structure of abstract algebras. Proc. Cambridge Philos. Soc. 31, pp. 433-454 (1935).

[Broy 84]
M. Broy: Extensional behaviour of concurrent, nondeterministic, communicating systems. In: M. Broy (ed.): Control Flow and Data Flow: Concepts of Distributed Programming, Int. Summer School Marktoberdorf 1984, NATO-ASI-Series Springer Berlin (1985).

[Broy et. al. 81]
M. Broy, C. Pair, M. Wirsing: A systematic study of models of abstract data types. TCS 33, pp. 139-174 (1984). Preliminary version: Centre de Recherche en Informatique de Nancy, Rapport 81-R-042 (1981).

[Broy, Wirsing 81]
M. Broy, M. Wirsing: On the algebraic extension of abstract data types. In: J. Diaz, I. Ramos (eds.): Formalization of Programming Concepts. Springer Lecture Notes in Computer Science 107, pp. 244-251 (1981).

[Broy, Wirsing 83]
M. Broy, M. Wirsing: Generalized heterogeneous algebras and partial interpretations. In Proc. CAAP 83, Springer Lecture Notes in Computer Science 159 (1983).

[Ehrig, Mahr 85]
H. Ehrig, B. Mahr: Fundamentals of algebraic specification 1: Equations and initial semantics. EATCS Monographs on Theoretical Computer Science. Berlin: Springer Verlag (1985).

[Giarratana et. al. 76]
V. Giarratana, F. Gimona, U. Montanari: Observability concepts in abstract data type specification. Proc. 5th MFCS, Gdansk. Springer Lecture Notes in Computer Science 45 (1976).

[Goguen, Burstall 80]
J.A. Goguen, R.M. Burstall: CAT, a system for the structured elaboration of correct programs from structured specifications. Technical report CSL-118, Computer Science Laboratory, SRI International (1980).

[Goguen, Meseguer 82a]
J.A. Goguen, J. Meseguer: Completeness of many-sorted equational logic. SIGPLAN Notices 16,7 , pp. 24-32 (1981) and 17,1 , pp. 9-17 (1982).

[Goguen, Meseguer 82]
J.A. Goguen, J. Meseguer: Universal realization, persistent interconnection and implementation of abstract modules. Proc. 9th ICALP, Aarhus, Denmark. Springer Lecture Notes in Computer Science 140, pp. 265-281 (1982).

[Grätzer 68]
G. Grätzer: Universal algebra. Princeton: Van Nostrad (1968).

[Milner 77]
R. Milner: Fully abstract models of typed λ-calculi. TCS 4, pp. 1-22 (1977).

[Padawitz, Wirsing 84]
P. Padawitz, M. Wirsing: Completeness of many-sorted equational logic revisited. Bull. EATCS 24, pp. 88-94 (1984).

[Pepper 83]
P. Pepper: On the correctness of type transformations. Talk at 2nd Workshop on Theory and Applications of Abstract Data Types, Passau (1983).

[Reichel 81]
H. Reichel: Behavioural equivalence -- a unifying concept for initial and final specification methods. Proc. 3rd Hungarian Computer Science Conf., Budapest, pp. 27-39 (1981).

[Sannella, Tarlecki 84]
D.T. Sannella and A. Tarlecki: On observational equivalence and algebraic specification. Draft report, Dept. of Computer Science, Univ. of Edinburgh (1984).

[Sannella, Wirsing 83]
D.T. Sannella and M. Wirsing: A kernel language for algebraic specification and implementation. Report CSR-131-83, Dept. of Computer Science, Univ. of Edinburgh; extended abstract in: Proc. Intl. Conf. on Foundations of Computation Theory, Borgholm, Sweden. Springer Lecture Notes in Computer Science 158, pp. 413-427 (1983).

[Schoett 83]
O. Schoett: A theory of program modules, their specification and implementation (extended abstract). Report CSR-155-83, Dept. of Computer Science, Univ. of Edinburgh (1983).

Fair Conditional Term Rewriting Systems :
Unification, Termination and Confluence

Stéphane Kaplan
LRI. Bât. 490
Université des Sciences
F-91405 Orsay (France)

Abstract :

In symbolic evaluation via general conditional term rewriting systems, recursive evaluation of the premisses of the rules is needed, which leads to intractability. In this paper, a new principle is introduced allowing to control that complexity. This enables the extension of several results for the classical rewriting to the conditional framework. In particular, results about correctness of evaluation procedures, unification in conditional theories, termination and confluence together with Knuth and Bendix procedures are obtained.

INTRODUCTION

Much attention has been devoted to term rewriting systems in several fields of computer science related with symbolic manipulation. In particular, rewriting is an operational framework that allows to simulate the action of a set of equations on a term algebra.

In this paper, we consider *conditional* term rewriting systems, where rules are under the form :
$$r : \bigwedge_{i=1}^{n} u_i = v_i \implies G \to D .$$
In the literature, this notion has been considered under two aspects:

- without further restrictions on the rules, as in [BK 82], [Kaplan 83]. This has been shown to lead to indecidability even for the rewriting process, and is therefore mainly of theoretical interest;
- strongly restricting the rules that are admitted, in order to avoid infinite recursive evaluation on the $\bigwedge_{i=1}^{n} u_i = v_i$ part (called the premisses).
In this approach, there is a hierarchy between the rules, and the premisses are evaluated at a lower layer of that hierarchy (cf. e.g. [PEE 81], [Drosten 83], [Pletat 83], [Remy 83]).

In this paper, we investigate the first approach, considering systems verifying the following condition :
$$\text{for every rule } r, \quad G > D \quad \text{and} \quad G > u_i , v_i$$
for a given *simplification ordering* <.
For such "fair" systems, we show that several important notions used in the case of purely equational rewriting carry over to our formalism, in a natural and systematical way. These results are richer than those obtained by the second approach and apply to much a larger class of rules, without the indecidability empeachments implied by the first approach.

The first part of the paper states results about general conditional equations and rewrite rules. The condition hereabove is introduced, and a *rewriting procedure* is shown to be totally correct. The problem of finite termination is considered.

In the second part, the procedure of *unification by narrowing* in equational theories presented by canonical rules is extended to our framework of fair conditional term rewriting systems.

In the third part, the question of the *confluence* of such systems is addressed, and a Knuth-Bendix-like completion procedure is presented and discussed.
Our notion of fair conditional term rewriting systems is compared to other works in the fourth part.

We assume the reader has basic knowledge on term algebra, classical rewriting, unification, finite termination, confluence. For general reference, cf. [HO 80].

1. BASIC RESULTS

Definition 1.1
A *conditional term rewriting system* (*conditional TRS*) is a finite set of formulas, called *conditional rewrite rules*, with the following form :
$$r : \bigwedge_{i=1}^{n} u_i = v_i \implies G \to D ,$$
satisfying the conditions :
  (*i*) $Var(u_i) \subseteq Var(G)$
  (*ii*) $Var(v_i) \subseteq Var(G)$
  (*iii*) $Var(D) \subseteq Var(G)$

Note : These conditions insure that no equation solving is needed to apply a rule. This would be the case with such an equation as :
$$f(x,y,z) = a \implies g(x,y) \to h(z)$$
which requires to look for a z such that $f(x,y,z)=a$, in order to reduce a term depending solely on variables x and y.
The part $(\bigwedge_{i=1}^{n} u_i = v_i) = Prem(r)$ is called the *premises* of the rule r, and the G→D part is called its *conclusion*.

Lemma 1.2
Given a conditional TRS R, there exists a smallest precongruence $\to_R$ such that :
  $t \to_R t'$ iff there is a rule $r : \bigwedge_{i=1}^{n} u_i = v_i \implies G \to D$ in R such that
    • there exists a substitution $\sigma : X \to T_{S,\Sigma}(X)$ and an occurence ω in t such that $t_{|\omega} = G\sigma$ and $t' = t[\omega \leftarrow D\sigma]$,
    • there exist $(\gamma_{i,\sigma})_{i \in [1,...,n]}$ such that $u_i\sigma \overset{\circ}{\to}_R \gamma_{i,\sigma}$ and $v_i\sigma \overset{\circ}{\to}_R \gamma_{i,\sigma}$.

So, a given step of rewriting G → D may be applied when the premises are *verified*-which is recursively determined by rewriting.
Note too that other interpretations of $\to_R$ are possible. This is discussed in [BK 82], [Kaplan 84], ...
Proof:
We provide an explicit construction of $\to_R$. Let $Congrs_\Sigma$ be the lattice of precongruences on $T_{S,\Sigma}(X)$, ordered by inclusion. Consider the functional $\partial : Congrs_\Sigma \to Congrs_\Sigma$ associating to any $\to_1 \in Congrs_\Sigma$ the smallest $\to_2 \in Congrs_\Sigma$ such

that :

- $\rightarrow_1 \subseteq \rightarrow_2$
- for any r : $\bigwedge_{i=1}^{n} u_i = v_i \implies G \rightarrow D$,
  if $\forall\, i$, $u_i\sigma\downarrow_1 v_i\sigma$, then $G\sigma \rightarrow_2 D\sigma$

It is shown in [Kaplan 83] that ∂ is continuous, and that its least fixpoint is precisely $\rightarrow_R$. As a consequence, $\rightarrow_R$ may be constructed iteratively :

$$\rightarrow_R = \cup_{i=1}^{\infty} \partial^{(i)}(\rightarrow_{id})$$

where $t \rightarrow_{id} t'$ iff $t = t'$. ■

This provides an induction principle for general conditional TRS.

Theorem 1.3

(i) When $\rightarrow_R$ is confluent, then
$$\equiv_R = (\rightarrow_R \cup \rightarrow_R^{-1})^* = \downarrow_R$$
(ii) When $\rightarrow_R$ is confluent and noetherian, then
$$\equiv_R = (\rightarrow_R \cup \rightarrow_R^{-1})^* = \downarrow_R = \perp_R$$

Here, by convention,

- $\equiv_R$ is the smallest *congruence* generated by the rules of R, *interpreted as axioms*,
- $t \downarrow_R t'$ iff there exists a term s such that $t \rightarrow_R^* s$ and $t' \rightarrow_R^* s$,
- $t \perp_R t'$ iff t and t' have the same *normal form* for $\rightarrow_R$ (denoted NF_R henceforth. The existence of NF_R comes from the hypotheses on $\rightarrow_R$).

The proofs are by ∂-induction and appear in [Kaplan 84].

The main problem regarding *general* conditional TRS is that in order to apply a rule, one intuitively has to recursively evaluate the premises of the rule by rewriting, which may lead to infinite loops *even for one step of rewriting*. For instance, let :

$$r_0 : f(f(x)) = \alpha \implies f(x) \rightarrow \alpha$$

It is not clear that an evaluator for conditional TRS could avoid going in the infinite loop of evaluating f(x), f(f(x)), ...
Actually :

Theorem 1.4

There exists a conditional TRS R such that $\rightarrow_R$ is *confluent and noetherian*, but such that the relation $\rightarrow_R$ is non decidable and NF_R is non computable.

Such an example appears in [Kaplan 84].
Nevertheless, suppose that there exists an oracle $Reduc?_R$ telling whether a term of $T_{S,\Sigma}(X)$ is reducible *or not*. Consider then the following procedure NF_R that captures the intuition of what computing a normal form for $\rightarrow_R$ should be :

```
proc y ← NF_R(t) ;
   y ← t ;
   if Not(Reduc?_R(t)) then STOP endif;
   for every rule r : ⋀_{i=1}^{n} u_i = v_i ⟹ G → D  of R
      if there is ω,σ such that y_ω = Gσ then
         if ( n = 0 ) ∨
            ( n > 0 and ∀i∈[1..n], NF_R(u_iσ)=NF_R(v_iσ) )
         then y ← NF_R(y[ω←Dσ]) endif endif endfor
endproc
```

It is assumed that the procedure stops if each rule $r \in R$ has been applied whithout succes in a "for ... endfor" block. Moreover, the rules must be marked in such a way that there be no interference during the recursive calls.

It should be noted that non-determinism is involved in the order of chosing rules in the "for ... endfor" blocks.

This procedure is shown to be correct in the following sense (cf. [Kaplan 83]) : any *angelic* non-deterministic execution of the procedure will eventually stop, producing the result $y = NF_R(t)$.

Now, in order to deal with termination of the premises, we come to the central idea of the paper.

Remind that the point is to avoid infinite calls to the evaluation procedure when the premises have to be evaluated. This may be achieved if the premises of each rule are "simpler", in some sense, than its conclusion. More precisely, we shall use *simplification orderings* to check this.

A *simplification ordering* is a well-founded ordering $<$ on $T_{S,\Sigma}(X)$ such that :

$f(...,t,...) > t$ (subterm property)

if $t > t'$ then $f(...,t,...) > f(...,t',...)$ (compatibility).

Now, one has the following theorem, which may be considered as extending Dershowitz's (cf. [Dersh 79]) :

Theorem 1.5

Given a conditional TRS R, and a simplification ordering $<$, such that for every rule r of R : $\bigwedge_{i=1}^{n} u_i = v_i \implies G \to D$,

$G\sigma > D\sigma$ and $\forall i, G\sigma > u_i\sigma$ and $G > v_i\sigma$, for all $\sigma : X \to T_{S,\Sigma}$,

then :

    (i) $\to_R$ is *globally terminating* (or noetherian),

    (ii) $\to_R$ is *one−step terminating* (which means that during the application of the procedure NF_R to any term t, there is no infinite sequence of calls to NF_R itself).

   Moreover,

    (iii) when $\to_R$ is confluent, $\to_R$ is totally decidable and the procedure NF_R computes correctly the normal form function associated to $\to_R$.

Proof :

(i) Identical to [Dersh 79].

(ii) Ad absurdum, let $t_1, t_2, ...$ such a sequence of infinite calls. One has : $t_{1|\omega_1} = G_1\sigma_1$, for a given rule $r_1 : \bigwedge_{i=1}^{n} u_{i,1} = v_{i,1} \implies G_1 \to D_1$, an occurence ω_1 and a substitution σ_1. Now,

    • either t_2 is one of the $u_{i,1}\sigma_1, v_{i,1}\sigma_1$.

    But $t_1 > G_1\sigma_1$, because $>$ is a simplification ordering.

    Now $G_1\sigma_1 > u_{i,1}\sigma_1, v_{i,1}\sigma_1$. By hypothesis on the rule r_1, $G_1\sigma_1 > t_2$. Thus, $t_1 > t_2$.

    • or $t_2 = t_1[\omega_1 \leftarrow D_1\sigma_1]$, and then again, $t_1 > t_2$.

So, $t_1 > t_2 > \cdots$ (by induction) which contradicts the well-foundedness of $>$. ∎

(Note actually that the one-step termination involves and requires the global termination of $\to_R$)

(iii) Under confluence hypothesis on $\to_R$, NF_R procedure is correct whenever it terminates (cf. *supra*). Now, (ii) proves termination of the procedure. ∎

The requirement on the rules is somehow minimal; nevertheless, it is sufficient to recover tractability for one-step rewriting and normal form function computation. We shall see in the following that it allows also to deal with several questions addressed in the field of term rewriting systems : unification in theories presented by canonical conditional TRS, Knuth and Bendix criterion for confluence and completion procedure,.... These questions have well-known answers in the non-conditional case. This paper proposes solutions in the larger framework of conditional TRS.

From now on, we restrict to conditional TRS under conditions of theorem 1.5, that we call **fair conditional TRS.** They have a natural induction principle, namely induction on $<$ (as shown in the previous proof). Most of the proofs will be conducted following this principle.

Note nevertheless that several results that we present for fair TRS are also true for non-fair ones; they would have to be proved by ∂-induction (cf 1.3), which is more difficult to manipulate than $<$-induction. Moreover, results obtained for non-fair TRS would often be of solely theoretical interest because of intractability.

Example 1 : Let R be the following term rewriting system :

$$\{ e_1 : s\, p\, x = x$$
$$e_2 : p\, s\, x = x$$
$$e_3 : 0 \leqslant 0 = T$$
$$e_4 : 0 \leqslant p\, 0 = F$$
$$e_5 : 0 \leqslant x = T \implies 0 \leqslant s\, x = T$$
$$e_6 : 0 \leqslant x = F \implies 0 \leqslant p\, x = F$$
$$e_7 : s\, x \leqslant y = x \leqslant p\, y$$
$$e_8 : p\, x \leqslant y = x \leqslant s\, y \qquad \}$$

R is clearly a fair conditional TRS. It is shown in [Kaplan 83] that R modelizes the integers with the "less or equal" predicate. Note that the specification is quite natural, due to the fact that recursive evaluation is allowed on the premises.

2– UNIFICATION IN CONDITIONAL THEORIES

In this section, we suppose that a *fair* conditional TRS R is given, to which the congruence $\equiv_R$ on $T_{S,\Sigma}(X)$ is associated. Given two terms $u, v \in T_{S,\Sigma}(X)$, we consider the following question :

$$\text{find all the substitutions } \sigma : X \to T_{S,\Sigma}(X) \text{ such that :}$$
$$u\sigma \equiv_R v\sigma$$

(Such a σ is called a *unifier* of u and v in the algebraic theory defined by R.)

This definition is extended to *clauses* :

given a clause $C : \bigwedge_{i=1}^{n} u_i = v_i$, C is R-unifiable iff there exists a substitution σ such that

$$u_1\sigma \equiv_R v_1\sigma \text{ and } \cdots \text{ and } u_n\sigma \equiv_R v_n\sigma.$$

For the case of *purely equational* theories, a satifying answer may be found in [Fay 77], [Hullot 80] (to which we refer for basic discussions and for notations). A semi-decision procedure, based on the notion of *narrowing*, is described, that gives a complete (and possibly infinite) set of such unifiers. The purpose of this part is to extend this method to the case of *fair* conditional TRS.

In the *purely equational case*, the central idea is the following (notations are from [Hullot 80]) :

given a rule $r : G \to D$, M is *narrowable* in M' at occurence ω using rule r and via a substitution σ, and we write : $M \leadsto_{\omega, r, \sigma} M'$

if $M_{|\omega}\sigma = G\sigma$ and $M' = M[\omega \leftarrow D]\sigma$ (σ being a minimal unifier for $M_{|\omega}$ and G).

Now, consider two terms M and N in $T_{S,\Sigma}(X)$ that are R-unifiable. There exists a substitution σ such that $M\sigma \equiv_R M'\sigma$. Thus,

• either σ is a unifier of M and M' (in the usual sense) and classical algorithms give a minimal unifier of M and M'.

• or one of the $M\sigma$, $M'\sigma$ is $\rightarrow_R$-reducible (otherwise, it would be impossible to have $M\sigma \equiv_R M'\sigma$).
In that case, suppose that $M\sigma$ may be reduced by the rule $r : G \rightarrow D$ (we assume that, after a possible renaming of the variables of G, $Var(M) \cap Var(G) = \emptyset$). For a suitable occurence ω in G and a substitution σ', one has $M\sigma_{|\omega} = G\sigma'$. Thus M is narrowable by the rule r, via $\sigma\sigma'$ at occurence ω.

Consider now the *conditional case*. As previously, suppose that $M\sigma$ is reducible by a rule $r : \bigwedge_{i=1}^{n} u_i = v_i \implies G \rightarrow D$ with $M\sigma_{|\omega} = G\sigma'$. The main difference with the equational case is that one has the additive following relation : $\bigwedge_{i=1}^{n} u_i\sigma' \equiv_R v_i\sigma'$ (°).
As previously, M and G are unifiable. Let μ be their least unifier. There exists ρ such that $\sigma' = \mu\rho$. The relation (°) may be interpreted as : $[Prem(r)\mu]$ *is R-unifiable* (via ρ). This leads to the following definition :

Definition 2.1
Given two clauses C and C', the couple (M,C) is **narrowable** into (M',C') at occurence ω using rule $r : \bigwedge_{i=1}^{n} u_i = v_i \implies G \rightarrow D$, via substitution μ, i.e.:
$$(M,C) \rightsquigarrow_{\omega,r,\mu} (M',C') ,$$
if   (1) $M_{|\omega}$ and G are unifiable (with least unifier μ)
     (2) $M' = M[\omega \leftarrow D]\mu$
     (3) $C' = C \cup Prem(r)\mu$

With respect with the equational case, only condition (3) is new. Note that it remains of syntactical order.
Now, we have the three following results, similar to those of [Hullot 80] but in the larger framework of conditional term rewriting systems :
(The reader not concerned with these rather technical results may skip to the unification procedure after lemma 2.5.)

Theorem 2.2
Given a fair conditional TRS R, a term T_0, a finite set of variables $V_0 \supseteq Var(T_0)$, a substitution η_0 such that $Dom(\eta_0) \subseteq Var(T_0)$. *Then,*
to every $\rightarrow$-derivation (1) issuing from $t_0 = \eta_0(T_0)$, a $\rightsquigarrow$-derivation (2) issuing from $(T_0, \emptyset)$ may be associated :

$$(1): \quad t_0 \xrightarrow{\quad} \omega_0, r_0 \quad t_1 \xrightarrow{\quad} \cdots \xrightarrow{\quad}_{\omega_{n-1}, r_{n-1}} t_n$$
$$\uparrow \eta_0 \qquad\qquad \uparrow \eta_1 \qquad\qquad\qquad \uparrow \eta_n$$
$$(2): (T_0, \phi) \rightsquigarrow_{\omega_0, r_0, \sigma_0} (T_1, C_1) \rightsquigarrow \cdots \rightsquigarrow_{\omega_{n-1}, r_{n-1}, \sigma_{n-1}} (T_n, C_n)$$

such that for every $i \in [1..n]$, there exist a substitution η_i, a set of variables V_i such that :
- $Dom(\eta_i) \subseteq V_i$
- $(\eta_0)_{|V_0} = (\eta_i \vartheta_i)_{|V_0}$ and $Im(\vartheta_i) \subseteq V_i$ where $\vartheta_0 = \varepsilon$ and $\vartheta_{i+1} = \sigma_{i+1}\vartheta_i$.
- $Var(T_i) \subseteq V_i$ and $\eta_i(T_i) = t_i$.
- C_i is R-unifiable
Conversely, to every $\rightsquigarrow$-derivation (2) issuing from T_0 such that
- there exists ρ s.t. $(\eta_0)_{|V_0} \leqslant_R (\rho\vartheta_n)[V]$
- C_{n-1} is R-unifiable
a $\rightarrow$-derivation (1) issuing from t_0 may be associated.

Notes :
- By definition, $\sigma \leqslant_R \sigma'[V]$ iff there exists ρ such that $\forall x \in V, \sigma(x) \equiv_R \rho(\sigma'(x))$.

- Requirements on the V_i are technical (preventing name conflicts on the variables). Proof (by induction on i) is similar to [Hullot 80], but taking into account the conditions on the clauses C_i. It is given in the technical report [Kaplan 84b].
- Note that $C_{i+1} = Prem(r_0)\sigma_0\sigma_1...\sigma_i \cup Prem(r_1)\sigma_1...\sigma_i \cup \cdots \cup Prem(r_i)\sigma_i$.

Corollary 2.3

Suppose a "new" binary functional symbol $\ominus$ is given.
(α) Given a $\leadsto\to$-derivation :
$$(\ominus(M_0,N_0),\emptyset) \leadsto\to ... \leadsto\to (\ominus(M_n,N_n),C_n)$$
such that M_n and N_n are unifiable, with least unifier μ, and such that the C_i are R-unifiable. Then $\mu\vartheta_n$ (with previous notations) is a R-unifier of M_0,N_0.
(β) Let M_0 and N_0 two R-unifiable terms, ρ a R-unifier, and $V_0 \supseteq Var(M_0) \cup Var(N_0)$. Then, there exists a $\leadsto\to$-derivation issuing from $\ominus(M_0,N_0)$:
$$(\ominus(M_0,N_0),\emptyset) \leadsto\to ... \leadsto\to (\ominus(M_n,N_n),C_n)$$
such that M_n and N_n are unifiable, with least unifier μ, and such that the C_i are R-unifiable. Moreover, $\mu\vartheta_n \leqslant \rho[V_0]$.

Proofs *(sketches)* :
(α) follows from the $<=$ part of Theorem 2.2 choosing η_0 to be ϑ_n.

(β) comes from the $=>$ part, with $\eta_0(x) = NF_R(x)$ for x in V_0. ∎
Note that we need the unifiability of the clauses C_i which may be (syntactically) large, in order to unify terms. Nevertheless, with **fair** TRS, the clauses happen to be *smaller* (w.r.t. $<$) than the two initial terms to unify (cf. proof of the following procedure). This is why the whole approach works.

Theorem 2.4

Let M and N be two terms. Let us consider the set of all the substitutions σ such that there exists a $\leadsto\to$-derivation
$$(\ominus(M_0,N_0),C_0) \leadsto\to_{r_1,\sigma_1} (\ominus(M_1,N_1),C_1) \leadsto\to \cdots \leadsto\to_{r_n,\sigma_n} (\ominus(M_n,N_n),C_n)$$
with $C_0 = \emptyset$ and $C_{i+1} = [C_i \cup Prem(r_{i+1})]\sigma_{i+1}$
and :
- $\forall i$, C_i is R-unifiable;
- M_n and N_n are unifiable, with minimal unifier μ ;
- $\sigma = \mu\sigma_n\sigma_{n-1} \cdots \sigma_1$.

This set is a complete set of R-unifiers of M and N.

Proof : Straigthforward from Corollary 2.3.

The previous theorem makes possible to give a (semi-)procedure computing a complete set of R-unifiers for two given terms. Before doing so, notice that the R-unification of two terms involves the R-unification of clauses. Let us add a new binary symbol $\otimes$. This symbol serves as a technical trick to map R-unification of clauses into simple R-unification.

Lemma 2.5

Let $C = \bigwedge_{i=1}^n u_i = v_i$ be a clause, and σ a substitution. The two properties are equivalent
- σ is a R-unifier for C   [i.e. $\bigwedge_{i=1}^n u_i\sigma \equiv_R v_i\sigma$]
- σ is a R-unifier of the two terms $u_1\otimes...\otimes u_n$ and $v_1\otimes...\otimes v_n$

We can now define the unification procedure :

```
Procedure Unif_R[M,N]
    0- i=0 ;  M_0=M ;  N_0=N ;
       T_0=⊖(M_0,N_0) ;  C_0 = ∅ ;  ϑ_0=ε          /* the empty substitution */
    1- If M_i and N_i are unifiable, with ζ as smallest unifier.
       then return ζϑ_i fi
    2- i = i + 1
    3- If possible then
             Choose an unmarked rule r : ⋀_{j=1}^{n} u_j = v_j  ⟹  G → D  such that :
                   T_{i|ω} and G are unifiable, with smallest unifier ζ;
             σ_i = ζ ;  C_i = (C_{i-1} ∪ ⋀_{j=1}^{n} u_j = v_j)σ_i ;
       else STOP.
    4- If Unif_R[C_i] then goto 5
       else goto 3 fi
    5- T_i = T_{i-1}σ_i[ω←Dσ_i];
       M_i = 1(T_i); N_i = 2(T_i);
       ϑ_i = σ_iϑ_{i-1}; go to 1
```

In the previous procedure :
• functions 1 and 2 are the "projections" $1[⊖(a,b)] = a$ and $2[⊖(a,b)] = b$;
• if $C = ⋀_{j=1}^{n} a_j = b_j$ is a clause, $Unif_R(C)$ (in step 4) is an alias for $Unif_R[a_1⊗...⊗a_n, b_1⊗...⊗b_n]$ (cf. Lemma 2.5).
• the procedure is non-deterministic. In particular, the "return" statement relies only to the current execution path.

Theorem 2.6

The previous procedure is a semi-decision procedure for the computation of the R-unifiers of M_0 and N_0. More precisely :
   - If M_0 and N_0 admit a complete finite set of R-unifiers, the procedure provides a complete finite set of unifiers after a finite amount of time, but may run forever.
   - If M_0 and N_0 admit no complete *finite* set of R-unifiers but are R-unifiable, then the procedure runs forever and provides an (infinite) complete set of R-unifiers.
   - If M_0 and N_0 are not R-unifiable, the procedure may run forever.

Proof (sketch) :
The correctness of the procedure stems from the following facts :
• when the procedure returns a substitution, this substitution is a R-unifier of the input (Corollary 2.3.α);
• consider a "winning" path described in Corollary 2.3.β leading to a R-unifier. Then an execution of the procedure will eventually follow the path, and produce the unifier :
   Ad absurdum, suppose that the unifier is *not* reached. Then, there must be a recursive call to the procedure that does not return. Now, by construction of the path, this recursive call is on a pair-argument of R-unifiable terms. Then, the only way this call cannot return its result is to induce in turn another call to the procedure itself, and so forth. Thus, there is an infinite sequence of recursive calls to the procedure.
   Assuming now that R is a *fair* conditional TRS, with order > on the rules. One proves that this sequence of infinite call should be strictly decreasing for >, which is impossible. Let us check it on a typical configuration :
     suppose that during evaluation of $Unif(M_i,N_i)$, the procedure is recursively called. This means that (for instance) $M_{i|ω}=Gσ_i$. Thus :

$$M_i > Gσ_i > u_jσ_i, v_jσ_i \ (\forall j) \text{ and thus } M_i > [⊗_j u_j]σ_i, [⊗_j v_j]σ_i. \ ■$$

Finally, this shows that the procedure will eventually produce every R-unifier given in Theorem 2.4. ∎

Examples of unification of termes and clauses are given in the next section (Example 3).

It is clear that the previous unification procedure may and should be optimized in order to be suitably implemented. One should first extend to our framework the optimizations commonly used in the equational case (s.a. normalization, basic narrowing). Moreover, some additive optimizations are relevant in our case . In particular, a unifier for G_{i+1} is also a unifier for G_i. Thus, a narrowing for G_i leading to no R-unifier should be discarded when unifying G_{i+1}.
The question of narrowing in conditinal theories has been considered also in [Fribourg 84],[Hussman 85],[Paul 85].

3—CONFLUENCE FOR FAIR CONDITIONAL TRS. EXTENDING KNUTH–BENDIX CRITERION

In section 1, the question of global and one-step termination is dealt with the use of simplification ordering; $fair$ conditional TRS are shown to have these two properties. It seems natural to consider the question of confluence for such systems.
First, for noetherian conditional TRS in their full generality (i.e. whithout the hypothesis of one $-step$ termination), the following result holds :

Theorem 3.1
The problem of confluence for noetherian conditional TRS is non- decidable.

Proof : cf. [Kaplan 84]. Note that it is always co-semi-decidable : if $\rightarrow_R$ is not confluent, one can exhibit an instanciated critical pair by enumeration.

This result justifies the consideration of $fair$ systems, for which we provide criterion $\grave{a}$ la $Knuth\text{-}Bendix$.

3.1 A naive Knuth—Bendix completion procedure
Let R a conditional TRS. Suppose that a classical Knuth-Bendix completion procedure is run on R, considering only the $conclusion$ $part$ of R :
    if the $G_i \rightarrow D_i$ parts of two rules :
$$r_1 : \bigwedge_{i=1}^{m_1} u_{1,i} = v_{1,i} \implies G_1 \rightarrow D_1 \text{ and } r_2 : \bigwedge_{i=1}^{m_2} u_{2,i} = v_{2,i} \implies G_2 \rightarrow D_2$$
generate a critical pair $\langle \lambda, \rho \rangle$ (oriented into $\lambda \rightarrow \rho$) via a substitution σ,
    then the new rule $(\bigwedge_{i=1}^{m_1} u_{1,i} = v_{1,i})\sigma \downarrow \wedge (\bigwedge_{i=1}^{m_2} u_{2,i} = v_{2,i})\sigma \downarrow \implies \lambda \rightarrow \rho$ is added.
[From now on, $(\bigwedge_i a_i = b_i) \downarrow$ will stand for $(\bigwedge_i a_i \downarrow = b_i \downarrow).$]
Suppose that this procedures eventually stops, yielding a system RR. Then RR is confluent and $\equiv_R = \equiv_{RR}$. In that sense, this completion procedure is correct. Nevertheless, it would generate too large systems of rules, would run forever too frequently, and produce non-orientable though irrelevant critical pairs (cf. next paragraph). We propose another approach taking into account the treatment of the premisses. It may be considered as an $optimisation$ of the procedure described hereabove.

3.2 Conditional Knuth—Bendix criterion
Consider the following example :
    R = { r_1 : even?(0) → True
            r_2 : even?(s 0) → False
            r_3 : even?(s s x) → even?(x)

$$r_4 : \text{even?}(x) = \text{True} \implies \text{odd?}(x) \rightarrow \text{False}$$
$$r_5 : \text{even?}(x) = \text{False} \implies \text{odd?}(x) \rightarrow \text{True} \ \}$$

r_1 through r_3 provide a (non-conditional) definition of the even? predicate on the integers. r_4 and r_5 form a (conditional) definition of odd? in term of the predicate even?.

Considering the confluence of R, there is just one critical pair (in the previous sense), namely the pair <True,False> [from the term odd?(x)]. The previous Knuth-Bendix completion procedure would thus fail in orienting this critical pair, and stop.

Actually, <True,False> is not a genuine critical pair : the term odd?(σx) cannot both rewrite into True and False (for a given instantiation σ), because there is no σ such that conditions even?(σx) = True and even?(σx) = False are both verified.

We shall say that :

- <True,False> is a *contextual* critical pair, in the *critical context*
$$\text{even?}(x) = \text{True} \wedge \text{even?}(x) = \text{False} .$$
- the critical context even?(x) = True $\wedge$ even?(x) = False is *non−feasible*, and thus the critical pair <True,False> is *non−feasible*.

When testing confluence, only *feasible* critical pairs are relevant. Let us make it more precise.

Definition 3.2

Given a *fair* conditional TRS R and two rules in R :
$$r_1 : \bigwedge_{i=1}^{m_1} u_{1,i} = v_{1,i} \implies G_1 \rightarrow D_1 \text{ and } r_2 : \bigwedge_{i=1}^{m_2} u_{2,i} = v_{2,i} \implies G_2 \rightarrow D_2$$
such that $G_{1|\omega}$ and G_2 are unifiable, of smallest unifier σ.

• The formula :
$$((\bigwedge_{i=1}^{m_1} u_{1,i} = v_{1,i}) \wedge (\bigwedge_{i=1}^{m_2} u_{2,i} = v_{2,i}))\sigma \implies <G_1[\omega \leftarrow D_2\sigma], D_1\sigma> .$$
is called a **contextual critical pair** [abbreviated CCP] in the **contextual critical context:**
$$((\bigwedge_{i=1}^{m_1} u_{1,i} = v_{1,i}) \wedge (\bigwedge_{i=1}^{m_2} u_{2,i} = v_{2,i}))\sigma .$$
• A critical context $(\bigwedge_{i=1}^{m} a_i = b_i)$ is called *feasible* iff it is R-unifiable (as a clause), which means that there exists a substitution τ such that
$$(\bigwedge_{i=1}^{m} a_i \tau \equiv_R b_i \tau) .$$
• A CCP is said to be **feasible** iff its associated critical context is feasible.

We can know formulate results stating connection between criteria on the CCP's, and notions of confluence of a fair conditional term rewriting system.

Theorem 3.3 [Knuth-Bendix theorem for fair conditional TRS]

Given a *fair* conditional TRS R, consider the two groups of properties :

(i) $\rightarrow_R$ is locally confluent, and thus confluent on $T_{S,\Sigma}(X)$.
(ii) $\rightarrow_R$ is locally confluent, and thus confluent on $T_{S,\Sigma}$.

and

(α) For every feasible CCP (C) $\implies$ <t,t'> ,
$$t\downarrow_R = t'\downarrow_R$$
(β) For every feasible CCP (C) $\implies$ <t,t'> ,
$$\forall \sigma : X \rightarrow T_{S,\Sigma}(X) \text{ with } \models_R(C)\sigma ,$$
$$t\sigma\downarrow_R = t'\sigma\downarrow_R$$
(γ) For every feasible CCP (C) $\implies$ <t,t'> ,
$$\forall \sigma : X \rightarrow T_{S,\Sigma}(X) \text{ with } \models_R(C)\sigma,$$
$$\forall \tau : X \rightarrow T_{S,\Sigma},$$
$$t\sigma\tau\downarrow_R = t'\sigma\tau\downarrow_R.$$

Then :

$$(\alpha) \quad \Rightarrow \quad \boxed{\begin{array}{c} (\beta) \\ \Updownarrow \\ (i) \end{array}} \quad \begin{array}{c} \Rightarrow \\ \\ \Rightarrow \end{array} \quad \begin{array}{c} (\gamma) \\ \Updownarrow \\ (ii) \end{array}$$

Moreover,

(i) $\iff \forall t, t' \in T_{S,\Sigma}(X)$
$$t \equiv_R t' \text{ iff } t{\downarrow}_R = t'{\downarrow}_R$$

(ii) $\iff \forall t, t' \in T_{S,\Sigma}(X)$
$$t \equiv_R t' \text{ iff } \forall \tau{:}X \to T_{S,\Sigma}, \ t\tau{\downarrow}_R = t'\tau{\downarrow}_R$$

Proofs :

• The last two equivalences are straightforward generalizations of the equational case. The congruence :
$$t \equiv_R^{(ind)} t' \iff_{def} \forall \tau{:}X \to T_{S,\Sigma}, \ t\tau{\downarrow}_R = t'\tau{\downarrow}_R$$
is sometimes called the inductional congruence generated by R. After a classical result, $t \equiv_R^{(ind)} t'$ if and only if the equation $t = t'$ is valid in $\text{Gen}_{S,\Sigma,R}$ (the set of the finitely generated models of R).

• The $(\alpha) \Rightarrow (\beta) \Rightarrow (\gamma)$ part is clear, by the definition of these criteria..

• The two implications (i) $\Rightarrow$ (β) and (ii) $\Rightarrow$ (γ) are applications of the definition of the confluence.

• In the two the implications (β) $\Rightarrow$ (i) and (γ) $\Rightarrow$ (ii) lie the difficult part of the theorem.

The proof of (β) $\Rightarrow$ (i) is given in Appendix A. The proof of the second implication is similar, restricting to instanciations of ground terms.

■

Notes :

• Implications in Theorem 3.3 are strict.

    • The fact that (ii) does not imply (i) is true in the equational case, and a fortiori in the conditional case.

    • It is easy to construct a counter-example showing that (β) does not imply (α).

• Among the results of Theorem 3.3, it is the equivalence (i) $\iff$ (β) that constitutes the extension of Knuth and Bendix theorem to the conditional case.

It is the theoretical point that justifies a possible Knuth and Bendix-like completion procedure (that we denote $\text{KBCP}_{(\beta)}$) for fair conditional term rewriting systems— yet to be described.

In $\text{KBCP}_{(\beta)}$, we shall use the fact that determining whether a contextual critical pair is feasible is exactly the problem of unifying a clause in $\equiv_R$. This was the question addressed in Section 2.

• Nevertheless, we feel that $\text{KBCP}_{(\beta)}$ would make a too intensive use of the R-unification procedure. Its use would thus be unrealistic in many practical cases. For this reason, we will focus in the sequel on a completion procedure based on criterion (α) (that we denote $\text{KBCP}_{(\alpha)}$).

Though discarded in the following, $\text{KBCP}_{(\beta)}$ is nevertheless considered in appendix B.

    Compared with the naive KBCP of section 3.1, $\text{KBCP}_{(\alpha)}$ is a very neat optimization, that remains realistic. Compared with $\text{KBCP}_{(\beta)}$, it is less powerful, but much more reallistic. This justifies to mainly focus on $\text{KBCP}_{(\alpha)}$.

• Criterion (γ) gives rise to no implementable completion procedure : one could not avoid examining the set of all closed substitutions $\tau{:}X \to T_{S,\Sigma}$, which is infinite. Actually, such a procedure would test confluence on closed terms, which is non decidable even in the equational case (by Theorem 3.3, this is equivalent to the question of the inductive congruence of two terms).

We can now give the following procedure :

Completion procedure KBCP$_{(\alpha)}$
Given a set E of conditional equations .
0. $E_0 \leftarrow E$
   $R_0 \leftarrow \emptyset$
   $i \leftarrow 0$
1. If $E_i = \emptyset$, then STOP-WITH-SUCCES.
2. Non-deterministically choose an equation $e_{loc} = (\bigwedge_{i=1}^{m} u_i = v_i \implies M = N)$ in E_i.
3. If *possible* then
   Normalize and orient e_{loc} into r_{loc} : $((\bigwedge_{i=1}^{m} u_i = v_i)\downarrow \implies \bar{\lambda} \to \bar{\rho})$
        with $(\bar{\lambda},\bar{\rho})$ being one of $(M\downarrow_{R_i}, N\downarrow_{R_i})$ or $(N\downarrow_{R_i}, M\downarrow_{R_i})$
        and so that $R_i \cup \{r_{loc}\}$ is a *fair* conditional TRS
   else STOP-WITH-FAILURE-2.
4. Let
        $R_{touched} \leftarrow \{r : (\bigwedge_{i=1}^{m} \mu_i = v_i \implies l \to r) \in R_i \mid l \text{ or } r \text{ contains an instance of } \bar{\lambda}\}$
        $R_{loc} \leftarrow R_i - R_{touched} + r_{loc}$
        CCP $\leftarrow$ the set of contextual critical pairs of R_{loc}
5.   /* R_i-feasible critical pairs of CCP are saved into CCP-OK : */
   CCP-OK $\leftarrow \emptyset$
   for $[(C) \implies <M,M'>] \in$ CCP **do**
        if (C) is R_i-unifiable **then** CCP-OK $\leftarrow$ CCP-OK $+ [(C) \implies <M,M'>]$ **od**
6. $R_{i+1} \leftarrow R_{loc}$
   $E_{i+1} \leftarrow E_i - e_{loc} + E_{touched} +$ CCP-OK
        /* $E_{touched}$ is $R_{touched}$ interpreted as a set of equations */
   $i \leftarrow i + 1$
7. Go to 1

This procedure takes a system of conditional equations E as input, and produces, whenever it stops, a system RR of conditional rewrite rules that is *fair and confluent*, and such that :

$$\equiv_E = (\to_{RR} \cup \to_{\bar{RR}})^*$$

Proof : The correctness of the procedure comes from the following facts :
   (i) For every step i, $\equiv_E = \equiv_{E_i \cup R_i}$
        [Shown by induction on i]
   (ii) R_i is a *fair* conditional TRS [because of step 4.].
   (iii) At STOP-WITH-SUCCES, R_i = RR is locally confluent
        [It admits no feasible critical pair any more]
Hence, RR is a fair (i.e. one-step and globally terminating)) and confluent TRS, such that $\equiv_E = \equiv_R$.   ∎

Notes :
1- This procedure is essentially similar to the one in [Huet Oppen 80], except that only *feasible* CCP's are retained.
2- Cases of failure are the following :
   - traditional failures of the Knuth-Bendix completion procedure.
   - additive cases introduced by our method :
        - possibility of infinite loop inside the R_i-unification procedure at step 5. This is inherent to the semi-completeness of the unification procedure.
        - the system may be compelled to orient a "harmless" CCP : $(C) \implies <M,M'>$ (with (C) feasible) and fail. This is the case whenever $M\downarrow_{R_i} = M'\downarrow_{R_i}$, though, for

every σ such that $|=_R(C)\sigma$, $M\sigma\downarrow_{R_i} = M'\sigma\downarrow_{R_i}$.

In that case, $KBCP_{(\beta)}$ would recognize that $(C) \Longrightarrow <M,M'>$ needs not be oriented, though $KBCP_{(a)}$ cannot.

3- To implement the procedure, one would have to use more efficient forms of it, - for instance the one of [Huet 80]- in which marking the rules would avoid recomputing useless critical pairs. Fairness in the choice of the rules should be carefully considered too.

4- Further optimizations :

• Let us consider step 2 (normalization and orientation) in the procedure $KBCP_{(a)}$. It is easy to construct a fair system generating a *non-normalized* contextual critical pair $(C) \Longrightarrow <M,M'>$, such that neither $M\downarrow > (C)\downarrow$ nor $M'\downarrow > (C)\downarrow$ for any simplification ordering $>$
[though it is always the case that $M > (C)$ or $M' > (C)$, for some $>$, by construction].
The completion procedure would thus fail at step 3 in attempting to transform $R_i \cup \{r_{loc}\}$ into a *fair* conditional TRS.
We see that, at the opposite of what happens in the equational case *normalization can be harmful*.
An optimization of $KBCP_{(\beta)}$ would consist in trying to add in such a failure case the non-normalized CCP, adding the rule $(C)\downarrow \Longrightarrow \lambda\to\rho$, with (λ,ρ) being one of the $(M,N),(N,M)$. But this might of course generate new problems of elimination further on in the procedure.
At the opposite, normalizing the premises is never harmfull, for if $\lambda > (C)$, then *a fortiori*, $\lambda > (C)\downarrow$.

• Moreover, a better notion of normalization might be defined. Let $(C) \Longrightarrow <T,T'>$ to "normalize", and a rule $r : (P) \Longrightarrow G\to D$ such that $T_{|\omega}=G\sigma$.
If $(P)\sigma$ is wrong, it is not allowed to reduce T by the rule r. But if $(P)\sigma$ may be detected as being a "consequence" of (C), it becomes correct to normalize T.
This is in general non-decidable, but we could restrict to detections of syntactic order, for instance if $(P)\sigma$ a subset of the clauses of (C) (up to the ordering). This still needs to be further investigated.

We now provide an example of the application of the completion procedure on a realistic example.

Example :
Consider the following set of equations :

$E = \{$ $e_1 : EQ(x,x) = True$
$e_2 : EQ(c_1,c_2) = False$
$e_3 : x \in \emptyset = F$
$e_4 : EQ(x,y) = True \Longrightarrow x \in ins(y,s) = True$
$e_5 : EQ(x,y) = False \Longrightarrow x \in ins(y,s) = x \in s$
$e_8 : x \in ins(y,s) = True \Longrightarrow ins(x,ins(y,s)) = ins(y,s) \}$

x,y are variables of sort *data*, c_1,c_2 are two distinct constants of sort *data*, and s is a variable of sort *set(data)*.
Equations are presented in order to be left-to-right oriented during the procedure.
The simplification ordering is associated with the weights of the terms.
• Equations e_1 to e_4 are oriented and added without creating critical pairs.
• Adding equation e_5 generates the critical pair $<x\in s,True>$ in the critical context C = (EQ(x,y)=True$\wedge$EQ(x,y)=False).
Then, C is passed to the unification procedure :

either C may be narrowed via r_1, yielding (True=True $\wedge$True=False) which is not unifiable, or C may be narrowed via r_2, yielding (False=True$\wedge$False=False) which is not unifiable neither.

Thus, the previous critical pair is discarded, as being non feasible. So e_5 is oriented and added.

- e_6 generates several critical pairs :
  - With r_4, the critical term $z\in ins(x,ins(y,s))$ generates the pair $<z\in ins(y,s),True>$ in the critical context $C' = (x\in ins(y,s)=True \wedge EQ(z,x)=True)$.

    C' may be narrowed via r_1, yielding $(x\in ins(y,s)=True\wedge True=True)$, that is in turn conditionally narrowed via r_4 into $(True=True\wedge True=True)$, in the context $C'' = \{EQ(x,y)=True\}$.

    C'' is (recursively) found unifiable when narrowed via r_1.

    Thus C' is unifiable and the critical pair $<z\in ins(y,s),True>$ is feasible.

The new rule

$$e_7 : x \in ins(y,s) = True \wedge EQ(z,x) = True \implies z \in ins(y,s) = True$$

is generated (stating the equivalence of two terms z and x that are EQual with respect to insertion and membership).

At this point, the procedure is supposed to stop, because e_7 does not verify the property Var(G) $\supseteq$ Var(Prem). On this example, we choose nevertheless to proceed further (though the rule system that will be generated will not probably fit into our formalism).

  - With r_5, the critical term $z\in ins(x,ins(y,s))$ generates the pair $<z\in ins(y,s),z\in ins(y,s)>$ in the critical context $C' = (z\in ins(y,s)=True\wedge EQ(z,x)=False)$. No new rule needs to be added.

Thus r_8 is added to the rules and e_7 to the equations.

- Then e_7 is oriented and added, generating no new critical pair.

Finally, the system is completed into :

$$R = \{\ r_1 : EQ(x,x) \to True$$
$$r_2 : EQ(c_1,c_2) = \to False$$
$$r_3 : x \in \emptyset \to F$$
$$r_4 : EQ(x,y) = True \implies x \in ins(y,s) \to True$$
$$r_5 : EQ(x,y) = False \implies x \in ins(y,s) \to x \in s$$
$$r_8 : x \in ins(y,s) = True \implies ins(x,ins(y,s)) \to ins(y,s)$$
$$r_7 : x \in ins(y,s) = True \wedge EQ(z,x) = True \implies z \in ins(y,s) \to True\ \}$$

Note :

R is not a *fair* conditional TRS, because of rule r_7.

In particular, the evaluation procedure of part 1. could not be used with such a system. Nevertheless, it should be emphasized that the completion procedure has generated a *canonical system*, though in a larger framework.

4- COMPARISON WITH OTHER WORKS

- As stated in the introduction, [BK 82] and [Kaplan 83] in a first group of authors, have considered *general* conditional rewrite rules, and investigated the indecidability that it involves. Most of these results are recalled in part 1.

- A second group has been considering restricted kinds of rules.
  - [BDJ 78] and [Lankford 79] have done the first researchs in the field. They showed in particular that different evaluation mechanisms were possible, and considered the concept of *hierarchical* evaluation.
  - [PEE 81], [BK 82] and [Drosten 83] have investigated rules verifying syntactical conditions such as left-linearity, non-overlapping,.... This lead to results extend-

ing those of [O'Donnel 77], concerned with confluence, correctness of evaluation strategies,...

These authors often use the concepts of *boolean* specifications in which the premisses consist in a single term of boolean type, and of *hierarchical* specification where premisses are evaluated in a lower layer of specification interpreted by non-conditional rewriting. [Pletat 83] considers specifications with any finite number of layers, the lowest one being interpreted too by non-conditional rewriting.

• [Remy 83], [RZ 84] in a restricted hierarchical and boolean framework, consider questions related with confluence and Knuth-Bendix procedures. A notion of "contextual confluence" is used, that is intermediate between criteria (i) and (ii) in Theorem 3.3.

The formalism presented here has the following characteristics :
- our conditions about fairness are syntactical (involving only simplification ordering) and non-restrictive : they just express that the premisses are in some sense less complicated than the conclusion. Doing so, we treat much a larger class of rules. For instance, it would be uneasy to specify the "≤" predicate (as we do in example 1) in the formalisms above. Moreover, the resulting specification would probably be less natural than ours;
- we obtain powerful results, naturally extending the ones about non-conditional rewriting. We treat the question of the evaluation process (which most authors do), the question of confluence (considered in [Remy 83], [RZ 84], in a more restricted framework), and the problem of unification in conditional theories.

Actually, we have the feeling that several other results obtained with classical rewriting may be extended to our formalism in a similar way (mastering the additive complexity introduced by recursivity on the premisses, through the use of *fair* conditional TRS).

5- CONCLUSION

We have shown that fair conditional term rewriting systems give rise to results similar to those for purely equational systems, enabling simpler and more powerful specifications. The additive recursivity introduced by the evaluation of the premisses is not harmful, as it is controlled by the use of our "fair" systems.

Compared with other formalisms, it seems at the same time more powerful (allowing for more rules) and more natural.

We think that the following points need some further research :
• Optimization of the procedures described in this paper, in order to implement them in a satisfying way. In particular, normalizing and marking rules should neatly enhance the unification procedure of part 2., and completion procedure of part 3.
• Proofs in conditional theories with constructors should be considered. We believe in particular that results in [HH 80], [Goguen 80] naturally extend to our formalism.
• Recall that we have dicarded of our discussion conditional rules such as :
$$f(x) = g(y) \implies h(x) \rightarrow i(x,y) ,$$
because evaluation of the premisses requires some kind of equation solving : find a y such that $f(x) = g(y)$.

Actually, evaluating the premisses would correspond to finding a R-unifier for the premisses instanciated by the substitution matching the LHS. For *fair* systems, this is possible through the use of the unification procedure. Thus, rewriting would involve

unification, and thus become only semi-decidable. It seems that all our results would extend : correctness of the evaluation procedure, of the unification procedure and of the completion procedure.
Such a rewriting would constitute a general treatment for equational Horn clauses, with some analogies with [Fribourg 84].

I thank M.-C. Gaudel, L. Fribourg and J.-L. Remy for fructful comments and discussions.

This work has been partially supported by the Gréco de Programmation (CNRS) and AdI contract N°639.

BIBLIOGRAPHY

[BD 81]   M. Bergman, P. Deransart,
Abstract data types and rewriting systems applications to the programmation of abstract data types in PROLOG, Proc. of 6th CAAP, Genes (1981).
[BDJ 78]   D. Brandt, J.A. Darringer, W.H. Joyner,
Completeness of conditional reductions, IBM Res. Center, Yorktown Heights (1978).
[BK 82]   J. Bergstra, J. Klop,
Conditional rewrite rules : confluence and termination, Report IW 198/82, Amsterdam (1982).
[Drosten 83]   K. Drosten,
Toward executable specifications using conditional axioms, Report 83-01, T.U. Braunschweig (1983).
[Dersh 79]   N. Dershowitz,
Orderings for term rewriting systems, Proc 20th Symposium on Foundation of Computer Science, pp.123-131 (1979).
[Fribourg 84]   L.Fribourg,
Oriented equational clauses as a programming language, Proc. 11th ICALP, Antwerpen (1984).
[Goguen 80]   J.Goguen,
How to prove algebraic inductive hypotheses without induction, 5th CAD, Les Arcs- France (1980).
[HH 80]   G. Huet, J-M. Hullot,
Proofs by induction in equational theories with constructors Report INRIA N.28, Rocquencourt (1980).
[HO 80]   G.Huet, D.C. Oppen,
Equations and rewrite rules : a survey , Formal languages : Perspective and open problems, R. Book Ed., Academic Press (1980).
[Kaplan 83]   S. Kaplan,
Un langage de specifications de types abstraits algebriques, These de 3eme cycle, Orsay-France(1983).
[Kaplan 84]   S. Kaplan,
Conditional rewrite rules, to appear in TCS (1984)
[Kaplan 84b]   S. Kaplan,
Unification, narrowing with fair conditional term rewriting systems, Internal L.R.I. Report (to appear).
[KB 70]   D.E. Knuth, P.B. Bendix,
Simple word problems in universal algebra, Computational problems in abstract algebra,

J.Leech Ed., Pergammon Press (1970).

[Lankford 79]   D.S. Lankford,
Some new approaches to the theory and applications of conditional term rewriting systems, (Aug. 79).

[O'Donnel 77]   M.J. O'Donnel,
Computing in systems described by equations, LNCS 58, Springer Verlag (1977).

[PEE 82]   U. Pletat, G.Engels, H-D. Ehrich,
Operational semantics of algebraic specifications with conditional equations, 7th CAAP, Lille (1981).

[Remy 82]   J-L. Remy,
Etude des systemes de recriture conditionnels et applications aux types abstraits algebriques, These d'Etat, Nancy-France (1982).

[RZ 84]   J-L. Remy, H. Zhang,
REVEUR4 : A system for validating conditional algebraic specifications of parameterized abstract data types, Proc of 2nd ECAI Conference, Pisa (1984).

[Hussman 85]   H. Hussman,
Unification in conditional-equational theories, Proc. of the EUROCAL Conf., Linz (1985)

[Paul 85]   E.Paul,
On solving the equality problem in theories defined by Horn clauses, Proc. of the EUROCAL Conf., Linz (1985)

Appendix A : Proof of the implication $(\beta) \Rightarrow$ (i)   [Theorem 3.3]

The hypothesis is that R is a *fair* conditional TRS such that :
    for every feasible CCP (C) $\Rightarrow$ <t,t'>,
    for every $\sigma{:}X{\to}T_{S,\Sigma}(X)$ such $\models_R(C)\sigma$, then
        $t\sigma{\downarrow}_R = t'\sigma{\downarrow}_R$
We wish to show that $\to_R$ is confluent on $T_{S,\Sigma}(X)$
Ad absurdum, suppose that there exists a term t such that :
  • $t{\to}_R t_1$ and $t{\to}_R t_2$
  • there exists no t' such that $t_1{\to}_{\overset{\circ}{R}}t'$ and $t_2{\to}_{\overset{\circ}{R}}t'$.
Such a term will be called a *lethal critical term*. There exist two rules :
$$C_i \implies G_i{\to}D_i \quad [i{\in}\{1,2\}]$$
such that, for instance :
$$t = G_1\sigma_1 \text{ and } t_{|\omega} = G_2\sigma_2 \text{ with } \models_R C_1\sigma_1{\wedge}C_2\sigma_2$$
There are two cases to consider :

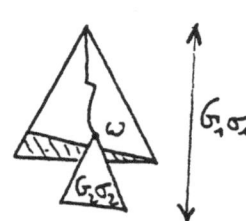

1- The path connecting ω to the root of t is a path of G_1.
Then, ω is the occurence of a node of G_1 that is a symbol of Σ. This implies easily that $t_1 \downarrow_R t_2$, which contradicts the hypothesis.

2- Else, ω occurs in t "under" the occurence of a variable x of G_1.
Then, $G_1\sigma_{1_{|_s}} = K[G_2\sigma_2]$.
Thus, $t \to_R t_1 = G_1\sigma_1[\omega{\leftarrow}D_2\sigma_2] \to_{\overset{\circ}{R}} G_1\sigma_1[x{\setminus}K[G_2\sigma_2]]$ (by successive applications of r_2).
Let $\sigma'_1 = \sigma_1.[x{\setminus}K[G_2\sigma_2]]$. The previous relations is reformulated in $t_2 \to_{\overset{\circ}{R}} G_1\sigma'_1$.
We are going to show that $\models_R C_1\sigma'_1$. Then, it will be possible to apply r_1 to $G_1\sigma'_1$, yielding
$$t_2 \to_{\overset{\circ}{R}} D_1\sigma'_1 = t' .$$
But on the other hand, it is clear that $t_1 \to_{\overset{\circ}{R}} t'$. This will prove that t was not a lethal critical term, and achieve the proof.

Proof that $\models_R C_1\sigma'_1$.
• If $C_1 = \emptyset$, then this is obvious.
• Else, $C_1 = \bigwedge_{i=0}^{n}u_i{=}v_i$. We need to show that $\forall i, u_i\sigma'_1 \downarrow v_i\sigma'_1$.
Suppose that this is wrong for a given i_0. We have :
$$u_{i_0}\sigma'_1 \not\downarrow v_{i_0}\sigma'_1 \text{ but : } u_{i_0}\sigma_1 \downarrow v_{i_0}\sigma_1.$$
Thus, there exist $\alpha^i{}_{i\in[1..n]}$ and $\beta^i{}_{i\in[1..m]}$ such that :
$$u_{i_0} \to_R \alpha_1 \to_R ... \to_R \alpha_n$$
$$v_{i_0} \to_R \beta_1 \to_R ... \to_R \beta_m$$

Consider now the following diagram (DIAG) :

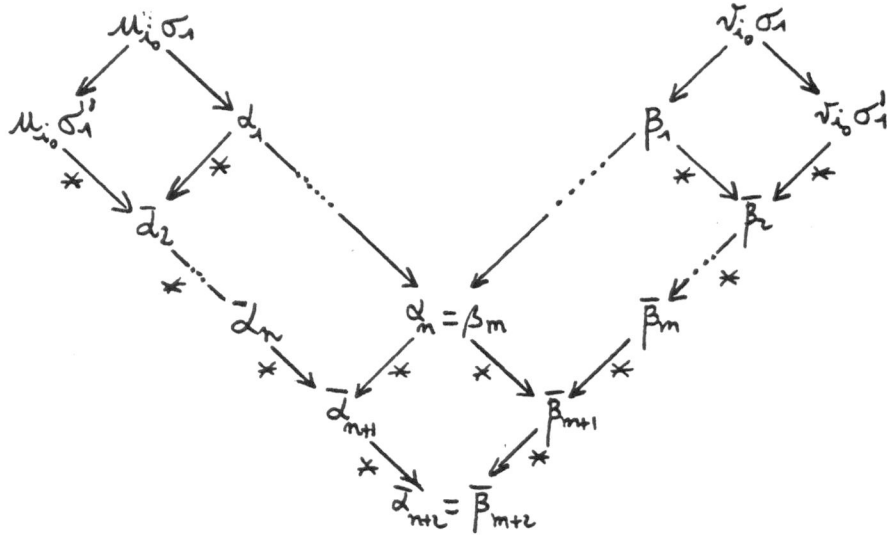

IF there exist no $\overline{\alpha}^2$ such as (DIAG), THEN $v_{i_0}\sigma_1$ is a lethal critical term, *smaller* (for the ordering <) *than the first lethal critical term t*,
ELSE IF there exist no $\overline{\alpha}^3$ such as (DIAG), THEN α^1 is a lethal critical term, *smaller* (for the ordering <) *than the first lethal critical term t*,
ELSE IF ...
. . .

ELSE IF there exist no $\overline{\alpha}^{n+1}$ such as (DIAG), THEN α^{n-1} is a lethal critical term, *smaller* (for the ordering <) *than the first lethal critical term t*,

IF there exist no $\overline{\beta}^2$ such as (DIAG), THEN $u_{i_0}\sigma_1$ is a lethal critical term, *smaller* (for the ordering <) *than the first lethal critical term t*,
ELSE IF there exist no $\overline{\beta}^3$ such as (DIAG), THEN β^1 is a lethal critical term, *smaller* (for the ordering <) *than the first lethal critical term t*,
ELSE IF ...
. . .

ELSE IF there exist no $\overline{\beta}^{m+1}$ such as (DIAG), THEN β^{m-1} is a lethal critical term, *smaller* (for the ordering <) *than the first lethal critical term t*,

ELSE IF there exist no $\overline{\alpha}^{n+2}=\overline{\beta}^{m+2}$ such as (DIAG), THEN $\alpha^n=\beta^m$ is a lethal critical term, *smaller* (for the ordering <) *than the first lethal critical term t*,
ELSE there exist $\overline{\alpha}^{n+2}=\overline{\beta}^{m+2}$ such as (DIAG), which implies that $u_{i_0}\sigma'_1 \downarrow_R v_{i_0}\sigma'_1$, which contradicts the previous hypothesis.

In any case, if the hypotheses are not contradicted, we managed to associate to any lethal critical term t another lethal critical term t'', such that t > t''. By induction, there exists therefore an infinite chain of lethal critical terms, that is descending w.r.t. to >. This contradicts the well-foundedness of >, and achieves the proof.

∎

Appendix B : Completion procedure $KBCP_{(\beta)}$

Procedure $KBCP_{(\beta)}$ is identical to procedure $KBCP_{(\alpha)}$ given in section 3., except for step 5., that must be substituted by the following :

```
5'. for [(C)  ⟹  <M,M'>] ∈ CCP do
        U = Unif_R_i(C) ;
        CCP-OK = ∅ ;
        if U ≠ ∅ then
            for σ ∈ U  do
                if Mσ↓_R_i ≠ M'σ↓_R_i
                then CCP-OK = CCP-OK + [ Cσ↓  ⟹  <Mσ↓_R_i,M'σ↓_R_i> ]
                endif
            endfor
        endif
    endfor
```

Thus, only feasible critical pairs instanciated by fitting substitutions are retained in $KBCP_{(\beta)}$. Recall at the opposite that in $KBCP_{(\alpha)}$, a (non-instanciated) critical pair was retained as soon as it was feasible.

Note too that in order to use $KBCP_{(\beta)}$, the R_i-unification procedure must return after a finite amount of time. This implies in particular that the set of unifiers is finite (which justifies the innermost "for-loop" in step 5'.).

That hypothesis is not realistic, which explains that we focused interest on $KBCP_{(\alpha)}$ in Section 3. Recall actually that in $KBCP_{(\alpha)}$, the existence of only *one* unifier for C was required, in order to add the rule : $C\downarrow \Rightarrow M\downarrow \rightarrow N\downarrow$ (up to the ordering).

Finally, note that informally speaking, whenever the procedure $KBCP_{(\beta)}$ terminates, it has the same power with respect to our framework of *fair* conditional TRS, as the usual Knuth and Bendix completion procedure in the equational case.

Transformation of Interface Specifications[1]

Bernd Krieg-Brückner

FB3 Mathematik und Informatik
Universität Bremen

Abstract

The relationship between different styles of interfaces in Ada and their formal specifications in Anna is defined by transformation rules: applicative packages with axiomatic specifications of Abstract Data Types, imperative packages with pre- and post-conditions, and stand-alone packages with an internally hidden state. The introduction of exceptions for such packages or the transition to monitor tasks in the concurrent case is defined as a derivation from the notion of partial functions. In all these cases, the original axiomatic or algebraic ADT specification is retained.

1. Introduction

This paper tries to give a solution to a practical problem in program development concerning various styles or levels of programming: applicative, imperative, with hidden global variables, with exceptions, with monitor tasks. Can a relationship between these styles be formalized? Can they, perhaps, be mapped into each other in a (semi-) automatic way? The problem is practical since we may wish to develop, for example, a more efficient and machine-oriented version from a program given in an applicative style, or we may wish to use a program module, whoes interface is given in an imperative style with exceptions, in a larger context at an applicative level with no exceptions at all.

The problem of conversion not only concerns executable program versions, of course. We would like to relate, say, an algebraic specification at the applicative level to a corresponding specification at the imperative level, or characteristic predicates in first order logic to Hoare-style pre-and post conditions.

Furthermore, it would be nice if the notion of errors or exceptions could be explained in algebraic terms. The relationship of such specifications to concurrency is open. Thus the problem also poses some interesting theoretical questions; they are only partially answered here.

A solution is presented in this paper by relating formal specifications and executable program versions in various styles by means of *transformation rules* that can be (semi-) automatically applied in a program transformation system. They are expressed in the linguistic framework of Ada/Anna: Ada [1] provides a notation for executable program versions and for signatures of operations at the abstract level, and Anna [2,3] complements Ada with a notation for formal specifications and annotations of executable program portions. Both together cover the whole spectrum from abstract specifications to machine-oriented programs.

The transformation rules given are definitional or axiomatic in the sense of a transformational semantics [2]. When a formal definition of Ada and Anna becomes available, the consistency of the transformation rules and the formal definition might be provable. For the purposes of this presentation, however, the semantics should be intuitive enough to allow a transliteration of the rules for other programming and specification languages as long as these have comparable expressive power.

2. Interface Specifications

The discussion concentrates on the transformation of interfaces of program modules; it is here that formal specifications have their place. Furthermore, interface specifications not only have their use in hierarchical decomposition for top-down program development, they are as important for generally and multiply usable components in a bottom-up development. The specification of an existing module must be precise; but it must also match the style of the using program, for example when use or non-use of exceptions is concerned.

---

[1]This work was partially supported by the Commission of the European Communities under the ESPRIT programme in the project PROSPECTRA, ref#390

2.1. Interfaces in Ada: the Signatures

In Ada, modularization can be achieved by decomposition into subprograms, i.e. functions or procedures, packages and tasks (embodying concurrency aspects); subprograms and packages can be statically parameterized as generics. The interfaces of such modules or "program units" are physically separate pieces of text and called "specifications"; in the sense of a formal specification, these only provide the signatures of the operations involved and must be complemented by Anna text.

Fig. 1 shows several styles of interfaces for subprograms in Ada/Anna. The Ada portion, respectively, contains information about the kind of subprogram (function with (constant) in-parameters only, procedure with in-, out- or in-out-parameters, or entry to a parallel task), its name, its parameter names, their mode and their types, and the result type (in the case of functions). This is about the information one would expect in a signature for an operation in an algebraic specification.

2.2. Formalization in Anna: the Abstract Specification

Ada thus provides only the structure of a specification; the meaning must be provided by a formal specification in Anna. These have the form of *annotations*, starting with --| on each line, or *virtual*, that is auxiliary and non-executable, *Ada text*, starting with --: . Since all specifications in Anna start with --, the Ada comment symbol, they are well separated from the executable underlying Ada text.

A formal specification of a subprogram may contain an in-annotation constraining the legal values of its parameters upon entry to the subprogram, thus making them partial operations. A function is specified completely by a result annotation, its characteristic predicate; see

    return Q:NATURAL => **exist** R: NATURAL => R < B **and** A=B*Q+R;

in "/" of fig. 2 as an example.

At the imperative level, an out-annotation may constrain the legal values of in-out- or out-parameters upon normal return from a procedure or entry; thus in- and out-annotations correspond to pre- and post-conditions in a Hoare-style logic.

```
function PUSH (S:STACK; E:ITEM) return STACK;
--| where LENGTH(S) < SIZE;
-- function with stack as parameter and result

procedure PUSH (S: in out STACK; E:in ITEM);
--|where LENGTH (in S) < SIZE;
-- procedure with stack as explicit in-out-parameter

procedure PUSH (E: in ITEM);
--|where STACK. LENGTH < SIZE;
-- procedure with stack as implicit parameter: global variable

procedure PUSH (E: in ITEM);
--|where not (STACK. LENGTH < SIZE) => raise OVERFLOW;
-- exception raised by subprogram

entry PUSH (E: in ITEM);
--| where not (STACK.LENGTH < SIZE) => delay;
-- entry to (monitor) task with resource variable
```

Fig. 1: Various Styles of Subprogram Interfaces

```
function "/" (A,B: NATURAL) return NATURAL;
--| where B > 0,
--|   return Q: NATURAL =>
--|     exist R: NATURAL => R < B and A=B*Q+R;

procedure DIV (A, B: in NATURAL; Q: out NATURAL);
--| where in B > 0;
--|   out (exist R : NATURAL => R < B and A=B*Q+R);
```

Fig. 2: Result-, in- and out-Annotations.

Propagation annotations specify exceptional situations: a strong propagation annotation as in fig. 1 specifies the condition under which the named exceptions will be raised by the operation. Exceptions will be discussed in section 4.

The delay annotation specifies the condition under which a delay or waiting state for the caller will occur; it is not presently included in Anna and must be considered to be an experimental notation in this paper. Delay annotations will be discussed in section 5.

2.3. Packages: Abstract Data Types

All these annotations referred to individual subprograms. In this paper we shall focus more on the formal specification of Abstract Data Types and various styles of expressing them.

Ada provides, again, the structure (or signature) of an ADT in the notation of a package specification, more precisely, its visible part; see the conventional example of a stack in fig 3 (It is assumed that SIZE and ITEM are given globally, or in a generic clause:

generic
SIZE: NATURAL;
type ITEM is private;

prior to the package specification. Parameterization issues are of no concern in this paper).

The meaning can be given in Anna by an axiomatic annotation, subsuming the case of an algebraic specification by universally quantified equations. We shall come to imperative styles of ADT specification in Anna in the sequel.

An aside on algebraic specifications: the Anna Logic underlying the semantics of Anna is a Hoare-style logic incorporating partial functions and the notion of undefinedness [5,6]. Quantifications are always defined even if constituent expressions become undefined for some value in its range. This has the nice consequence, that equations in an algebraic style can, in the first stages of development, specify an "ideal" type, for example an unbounded stack. The introduction of a constraint there after, for example LENGTH(S) < SIZE on PUSH in Fig.3 turns the whole specification into that of a bounded stack without having to change the equations by cluttering them with definedness premises as in

LENGTH(S) < SIZE → POP (PUSH (S,X)) = S

A similar example are, necessarily bounded, numeric types. Algebraicists may have to get used to the implicit influence of the in annotations on the functions, given in the signature portion of the specification, which make the respective functions partial.

3. Transformation Between Applicative and Imperative Styles

Let us first look at the transformation rules relating applicative and imperative styles of specifications. Although the transformation rules work on individually specified subprograms as well, we shall focus our attention on the specification of package interfaces to study the transformation of various styles of Abstract Data Type specification: the transition from an *algebraic* specification to an analogous "algebraic" *imperative* specification for procedures with explicit in-out-parameters, and the transition from a package specifying a type to a "*stand-alone*" package representing a single (variable) object of such a type; this corresponds to a specification style relating *states* of this object in an algebraic fashion.

```
package STACKS is
   type STACK is limited private;
--: function LENGTH (S: STACK) return NATURAL;

   function PUSH (S: STACK; E: ITEM) return STACK;
   --| where LENGTH(S) < SIZE;
   function POP (S: STACK) return STACK;
   --| where LENGTH(S) > 0;
   function TOP (S:STACK) return ITEM;
   --| where LENGTH(S) > 0;

--| axiom for all S:STACK; X: ITEM =>
--|    POP (PUSH (S,X)) = S,
--|    TOP (PUSH (S,X)) = X,
--|    LENGTH (STACK 'INITIAL) = 0,
--|    LENGTH (PUSH (S,X)) = LENGTH(S) + 1;
-- Private part irrelevant here
end STACKS;
```

Fig. 3: Applicative Package, Algebraic Specification.

We shall be mainly interested in the transformation of the interface specification, but the transformation rules for the use of the interface (subprogram calls to the ADT generations) and for its implementation (the package and subprogram bodies) shall also be presented.

3.1. Functions, Algebraic Specifications

The applicative style is characterized by functions that may be partial, as indicated by a respective in-annotation. Individual functions may be specified completely by a characteristic predicate in the form of a result annotation, see "/" in fig. 2. Alternatively, a set of functions may be characterized together by axiomatic annotations in, say, an algebraic style, cf. fig. 3 .

In trafo. 1 and 2a, a schema for a function, its in-annotation Q and characteristic predicate R is given on the left hand side of the transformation rule. In the case of an axiomatic annotation, the result annotation would, of course, be omitted, cf. fig. 3 (but cf. also fig. 5 below).

3.2. Procedures with Explicit Parameters

Trafo. 1,2a show the introduction of procedures and out- or in-out-parameters, respectively, by means of a definitional transformation rule. The result is transformed into an out-parameter (or "result"-parameter) or "folded" with an in parameter Y into an in-out-parameter (or "variable"-parameter): X stands for an arbitrary number of other parameters. Notice that the characteristic predicate R turns into an out- annotation ("post-condition").

With these transformation rules, the two versions of the division example in fig. 2 can be mapped into each other; the bodies would, of course, have to be transformed in an similar way. The operation **mod** can be specified analogously. Both procedures DIV and MOD could then be combined into one with two out parameters; such supplementary transformations shall not be discussed here.

Trafo. 1: Introduction of out-Parameter in Interface	
function F (X: S) **return** T; --| **where** Q (X), --| **return** Z: T => R(X,Z);	**procedure** F (X: **in** S; Z: **out** T); --| **where in** Q (X), --| **out** R (**in** X,Z);

Trafo. 2a: Introduction of in-out-Parameter in Interface	
function F (X: S; Y: T) **return** T; --| **where** Q (X,Y), --| **return** Z: T => R (X,Y,Z);	**procedure** F (X: **in** S; Y: **in out** T); --| **where in** Q (X,Y), --| **out** R (**in** X, **in** Y, Y);

```
package STACK_VARS is
    type STACK is limited private;
  --| function LENGTH (S:STACK) return NATURAL;

    procedure PUSH (S: in out STACK; E: in ITEM);
    --| where LENGTH (in S) < SIZE;
    procedure POP (S: in out STACK);
    --| where LENGTH (in S) > 0;
    procedure TOP ( S: in STACK; E: out ITEM);
    --| where LENGTH (in S) > 0;

  --| axiom for all S: STACK; X· ITEM =>
  --|  POP 'OUT (PUSH 'OUT(S,X)) = S,
  --|  TOP 'OUT (PUSH 'OUT(S,X)) = X,
  --|  LENGTH (STACK 'INITIAL) = O
  --|  LENGTH (PUSH 'OUT (S,X)) = LENGTH(S) + 1;
   private
  -- irrelevant here.
   end STACK_VARS;
```

Fig. 4: Imperative Package, Procedures with Explicit Paramenters.

Trafo 1, 2a can also be applied to constituent operations of packages, see fig. 3,4. In the axioms, F is replaced by F'OUT, see Trafo 2b. F'OUT is a notation in Anna to denote the 'OUT function associated to the procedure F, that is the function mapping from in-values of the parameters to out-values of the (in out-) parameters. In our case, F'OUT of the procedure F is the same as the original function F, before transformation.

3.3. Procedure Call

Trafo 2c shows the simultaneous transformation of a call to F, in an assignment context, to a procedure call of the transformed F in trafo 2a. So we assume that other transformation rules have already introduced variables, as auxiliary variables to transform nested calls into a sequence of assignments, or, for example, when transforming (tail-)recursion into iterative loops, see e.g. [7,8]. The assignment to V is now folded into the call to the procedure F and happens as a "side-effect" on the explicit in-out-parameter V. The characteristic predicate R on the result of the function F (and therefore the value of V after the assignment) has now become a post-condition on the procedure call. The notation in U and in V refers to the resp. values of U and V before the execution of the preceding statement.

3.4. Procedure and Package Body

Before we discuss further transformation ot the interface, let us look at the simultaneous transformation of the corresponding bodies of the operations.

Trafo. 2d shows how the assignment that used to be on the calling side has now migrated into the body of the procedure where the variable is an explicit in out-parameter. This transformation rule supports the view that the semantics of every procedure can be explained by an assignment, possibly a collective assignment to several variables passed as in-out- or out-parameters. Fig. 5 shows the complete implementation of the STACK example whose (visible) specification was given in fig. 3; because of Ada rules for separate compilation it is distributed over the (hidden) private part of the package specification, giving the type implementation, and the package body.

The correctness proof of the bodies against the specifications shall not be discussed in this paper. To give an example of a possible interaction of axiomatic/algebraic specification of the whole package and individual specification of operations, the implementation is specified using result annotations for the operations, and a specification of (virtual) equality to aid in the proving process. Note that these "specifications" are now given in terms of the particular implementation and its properties.

Trafo. 2b: Introduction of Associated 'OUT Function in Specifications	
--| **axiom for all** *U, W: S; V: T* => --| ... *G (F (U, V), W)* ...	--| **axiom for all** *U, W: S; V: T* => --| ...*G (F 'OUT(U,V), W)* ...

Trafo. 2c: Introduction of in-out-Parameter in Call	
--| *Q (U, V),* V:=F(U, V); -- V = F(**in** U, **in** V), thus --| *R (**in** U, **in** V, V);*	--| *Q (U, V);* F(U, V); -- V = F'OUT (**in** U, **in** V), thus --| *R (**in** U, **in** V, V);*

Trafo. 2d: Introduction of in-out-Parameter in Body	

function F (X:S; Y:T) **return** T
--| **where** *q(X,Y)*
--| **return** *Z:T* => *r(X,Y,Z);*
is
begin
  return g(X,Y);
end F;
	procedure F (X: **in** S; Y: **in out** T)
	--| **where in** *q(X,Y),*
	--| **out** *r (**in** X, **in** Y, Y);*
	is
	begin
	  Y:= g(X,Y);
	end F;

q, r, g are expressed in terms of the implementation of the operation in its body	

```
      package STACKS is
         ...   -- visible part as in Fig. 3
      private
        type ITEM_ARRAY is array (1..SIZE) of ITEM;
        type STACK is
          record
            SPACE: ITEM_ARRAY;
            INDEX: NATURAL := 0;
          end record;
      end STACKS;

      package body STACKS is
      --: function LENGTH(S:STACK) return NATURAL;
       --| where return S.INDEX;

          function PUSH (S:STACK; E:ITEM) return STACK
          --| where S.INDEX < SIZE,
          --|   return T:STACK =>
          --|   T.INDEX = S.INDEX + 1 and
          --|   T.SPACE = S.SPACE [T.INDEX=>E];
          is
             T:STACK;
          begin
             T.INDEX := S.INDEX + 1;
             T.SPACE(T.INDEX) := E;
             return T;
          end PUSH;
          -- analogously for POP and TOP;
      end STACKS;
```

Fig. 5: Annotated Package Body

In the body of the function PUSH in Fig. 5, a transition to an imperative style has already been made by introducing a result variable T and sequentializing the ("collective") assignment to T.INDEX and T.SPACE such that T.INDEX is assigned to first and can be used in the assignment to T.SPACE. Such transformations are documented elsewhere (e.g. in [8])and of no particular concern here.

The result of the application of trafo 2d, (or rather, a corresponding transformation rule incorporating a result variable) to example 5 is shown in fig. 6. Only the bodies of the operations are affected by the transformations.

```
      -- visible part as in Fig. 4, private part as in Fig.5
      package body STACK-VARS is
      --: function LENGTH(S:STACK) return NATURAL;
       --| where return S.INDEX;

        procedure PUSH(S: in out STACK; E: in ITEM);
        --| where in S.INDEX < SIZE,
        --|   out (S.SINDEX = in S.INDEX + 1),
        --|   out (S.INDEX = in S.SPACE [S.INDEX=>E]);
        is
        begin
           S.INDEX := S.INDEX + 1;
           S.SPACE(S.INDEX) :=E;
        end PUSH;
        ...
      end STACK_VARS;
```

Fig. 6: Explicit Parameter in Body

3.5. Stand-alone Package

The in-out- or out-parameters of the previous sections were always introduced as explicit formal parameters; the variables they worked on were passed as explicit actual parameters. We shall now look at the suppression of such variables as parameters: they become global to the subprogram body and serve as "implicit paramerers"; procedures have implicit side-effects on global variables. Transformation rules to suppress variable parameters by using a global variable directly can be defined for subprograms in analogy to trafos 2a-c. Instead, we shall combine the simultaneously applied rules for procedure specification, body and call to a system of rules for a whole package, see trafo. 3.

For packages, the transition corresponds to that from a package specifying an Abstract Data Type T with only one variable F representing a singular use of T, to a package representing a single "object" (in the sense of object-oriented languages) or "stand-alone module"; the single variable V from the using environment now becomes an "own" variable of the module, that is a local variable of the package, hidden in the package body. This variable is a global and implicit parameter of all those subprograms of the package that used to have it as an explicit actual parameter, for functions (cf. LENGTH) and procedures alike. This way, it is totally hidden from the users point of view.

The abstract specification in the axioms is now transformed into a corresponding specification about the package state, that is, implicitly, about the state of the localized variable V. In the abstract interface specification, the package state P represents the hidden variable; in the concrete implementation specifications of the body, the variable is visible as a local variable V and specifications are expressed in its terms, cf. trafo. 3.

Fig. 7,8 show the effects of trafo. 3 on our stack example from fig. 4,6. The two components of the local V, SPACE and INDEX, have been made explicit separate variables to avoid indirection.

This concludes the discussion of the transformation between applicative, imperative and "stand-alone" package interfaces and their formal specification. We might call these styles discrete *levels* when gradually transforming to machine-oriented programs.

4. Exceptions

In contrast to discrete levels of interface specification style, as presented in the previous chapter, we shall now look at a style transformation that can be applied somewhat orthogonally to any of these levels: the introduction of exceptions in interfaces, body and call.

Trafo. 3: Suppression of Parameter in Stand-alone Package	

package P **is**
   type T **is limited private;**
   procedure F(X: **in** S; Y: **in out** T);
 --| **where in** Q(X,Y),
 --| **out** R(**in** X, **in** Y, Y);
   -- analogously for other operations
 --|**axiom for all** U, W:S; V:T =>
 --| ... Q(F 'OUT (U,V), W) ...
   private
   type T **is new** t;
   end P;
 	
 package body P **is**
   procedure F (X : **in** S; Y: **in out** T)
 --| **where in** q(X,Y),
 --| **out** r(**in** X, **in** Y, Y);
   is
   begin
     Y:= g(X,Y);
   end F;
   -- analogously for the other operations
   end P;
 	
 V: T; -- single decaration of T
 ...
 --| Q(U,V);
 F(U,V);-- V = F'OUT(in U, in V), thus
 --| R(**in** U, **in** V,V);
	package P **is** -- stand alone
	
	   procedure F(X: **in** S);
	 --| **where in** Q(X, P),
	 --| **out** R(**in** X, **in** P, P);
	   -- analogously for other operations,
	 --| **axiom for all** U, W: S; V: P 'TYPE =>
	 --| ... P[F(U)]. Q(W)...
	   end P;
	
	 package body P **is**
	   type T **is new** t;
	   V: T;
	   procedure F (X: **in** S)
	 --| **where in** q(X, V),
	 --| **out** r(**in** X, **in** V, V);
	   is
	   begin
	     V:= g(X, V);
	   end F;
	   -- analogously for the other operations
	   end P;
	
	 ...
	 --| Q(U, P);
	 F(U); -- P = in P[F(in U)], thus
	 --| R(**in** U, **in** P, P);

```
package STACK is
--: function LENGTH return NATURAL;


   procedure PUSH(E: in ITEM);
   --| where in STACK.LENGTH < SIZE;
   procedure POP;
   --| where in STACK.LENGTH > 0;
   procedure TOP (E: out ITEM);
   --| where in STACK.LENGTH > 0;


--| axiom for all S: STACK 'TYPE; X: ITEM =>
--|    S[PUSH(X)][POP] = S,
--|    S[PUSH(X)]. TOP 'OUT = X,
--|    STACK 'INITIAL. LENGTH  = 0,
--|    S[PUSH(X)]. LENGTH =  S.LENGTH + 1;
end STACK;
```

Fig. 7: Stand-alone Package Specifications,
Procedures with Implicit Global Variable

```
-- package specification as in fig. 7
package body STACK is
   type ITEM_ARRAY is array (1..SIZE) of ITEM;
   SPACE: ITEM_ARRAY;
   INDEX: NATURAL:=0;
--: function LENGTH return NATURAL;
   --| where return INDEX;

   procedure PUSH (E: in ITEM)
   --| where in INDEX < SIZE,
   --|    out (INDEX = in INDEX + 1),
   --|    out (SPACE = in SPACE[INDEX => E]);
   is
   begin
      INDEX := INDEX + 1;
      SPACE (INDEX):= E;
   end PUSH;
   -- analogously for POP and TOP
end STACK;
```

Fig. 8: Stand-alone Package Body with Local Hidden Variable

As a representative of analogous transformation rules at all three levels, the trafos. 4a,b,c describe the introduction of exceptions at the level of procedures with global side-effects as described in section 3.5 above.

4.1. Introduction of Exceptions

Let us first look at the introduction of an exception in a subprogram interface, cf. trafo. 4a. So far, a subprogram was allowed to be partial: if the in annotation Q (if present) was not fulfilled, its result would be undefined.

Trafo. 4a: Introduction of Exception in Interface	
	E: exception;
procedure F(X: in S); --| where in Q(X,P), --| out R(in X, in P, P);	procedure F (X: in S); --| where not Q(X, P)=> raise E, --| out R(in X, in P, P);

At first glance, the introduction of an exception E achieves nothing else than naming such an exceptional situation or error explicitly. In the simple case of trafo. 2a, E will be raised by F if Q does not hold. Note that F remains to be partial: its value is still undefined if Q does not hold, but we now have an explicit name for this particular undefined situation.

In a transformation rule generalized from trafo. 4a, several exceptions E_i can be introduced by splitting up Q into conjuncts

$Q = Q_0$ **and** ... **and** Q_n

such that Q_i, Q_j, $1 \leq i,j \leq n$, are mutually disjoint, i.e.

not Q_i **and not** Q_j = FALSE, $1 \leq i,j \leq n$, or equal, for some i, j.

A subprogram specification is then a combination of in-annotation, propagation annotations and an out-annotation (or result-annotation):

```
--| where in Q₀ (x),
--|       not Q₁ (x) => raise E₁,
--|       ...
--|       not Qₙ (x) => raise Eₙ,
--|       out R(x);
```

If Q_0 holds, F will terminate normally or exceptionally. F will be defined, and its result characterized by R, if Q_0 **and** ... **and** Q_n holds. Each Q_i, $1 < i < n$, specifies a unique condition under which E_i will be raised by F. If Q_0 or a Q_i is omitted, it corresponds to TRUE.

This more general transformation requires user interaction to split up Q into conjuncts and to give names to the resp. exceptions.

As an example see fig. 9, as a transformation of fig. 7. Exceptions and propagate annotations have been introduced instead of the in-annotations, each exception with a distinct name.

Note that the axioms remain totally unchanged. The reason is that the definedness properties of the axioms have not changed. Each equation can still, as before, be considered to be prefixed by an implicit definedness premise, e.g. (cf. section 2.3):

S.LENGTH < SIZE → S[PUSH(X)] [POP] = S

This is very nice from the methodological point of view of gradual development: one can first specify an ADT in a "purely" algebraic fashion based on the concept of partial operations, and then introduce exceptions later on, without changing the axioms or their algebraic interpretation. Exceptions, as introduced here, are just a different notation for denoting partiality of an operation.

4.2. Raising of Exception in Body

When we look a trafo 4b, we now see an important aspect that distinguishes exception conditions Q_i from in-annotations Q_0 in general: exception conditions must be computable or, in our context, must be operational Ada expressions. The reason is that we have made a strong promise in the interface specification: if **not** Q_i holds then the exception E_i *will* be raised! Thus we must check for this condition in the body and, when it holds, raise the exception. Cf. also fig.

```
package STACK_EX is
   OVERFLOW, UNDERFLOW, NO_ITEM: exception;
--: function LENGTH return NATURAL;


   procedure PUSH (E: in ITEM);
--| where not (STACK. LENGTH < SIZE) => raise OVERFLOW;
   procedure POP;
--| where not (STACK. LENGTH > 0) => raise UNDERFLOW;
   procedure TOP (E: out ITEM);
--| where not (STACK. LENGTH > 0) => raise NO_ITEM;


--| axiom for all S: STACK TYPE; X: ITEM=>
--|    S[PUSH(X)][POP] = S,
--|    S[PUSH(X)]. TOP 'OUT = X,
--|    STACK 'INITIAL. LENGTH = 0,
--|    S[PUSH(X)]. LENGTH =  S.LENGTH + 1;
   end STACK_EX;
```

Fig. 9: Package Specification with Exceptions

Trafo. 4b: Raising of Exception in Body	

procedure F (X: in S)
--| where in q (X, V),
--| out r (in X, in V, V);
 	
is
begin
 V:= g (X, V);
end F;
	procedure F (X: in S)
	--| where not q (X, V) => raise E,
	--| out r (in X, in V, V);
	is
	begin
	 if q (X, V) then
	  V:= g(X, V);
	 else -- not q(X,V);
	  raise E;
	 end if;
	end F;

such that q is an operational Ada predicate	

10.

In terms of operational checking for definedness upon a call, an explicit check for secure calling, i.e.

```
if STACK.LENGTH < SIZE then
    PUSH (X);
else
    ... some other action or error report
end if;
```

has now migrated in to the body of PUSH; the exception OVERFLOW is then raised (instead of the general exception ANNA_ERROR for violation of consistency with annotations).

```
-- package specification as in fig. 9
package body STACK_EX is
    ...
    procedure PUSH (E: ITEM)
    --| where not ( in INDEX < SIZE) => raise OVERFLOW,
    --|     out (INDEX = in INDEX + 1),
    --|     out (SPACE = in SPACE[INDEX => E]);
    is
    begin
      if INDEX < SIZE then
        INDEX:= INDEX + 1;
        SPACE (INDEX):= E;
      else
        raise OVERFLOW;
      end if;
    end PUSH;
    -- analogously for POP and TOP
end STACK_EX;
```

Fig. 10. Raising of Exceptions in the Body

trafo. 4c: Introduction of Exception Handler at Guarded Call	

if Q(U,P) then
 F(U);
 	
 -- P = in P[F(in U)], thus
 --| R(in U, in P, P);
 G(U); -- optional continuation
else
 H(U);
end if;
	begin
	 F(U);
	--| not Q(X,P) => raise E;
	 -- P = in P[F(in U)], thus
	 --| R(in X, in P, P);
	 G(U); -- optional continuation
	exception
	 when E => -- not P(U,V);
	 H(U);
	end

If Ei always corresponds to an *erroneous* situation (this depends on the programming style and can be argued), then we would probably wish to avoid it alltogether and prove its absence, that is, that it will never be raised. In this case we had better remain with the original interface, prove that Q_i will always hold, and thus delete all explicit tests (if we trust over proof).

4.3. Exception Handlers

However, if we want to leave in the tests, or if Ei corresponds to an unusual situation which nevertheless may happen (or will happen eventually), then we should regard the introduction of exceptions and their handling as just another notation for explicit tests in conditionals. The notation using exception handlers has the advantage of visually emphasizing the usual (or normal) computation by eliminating the cluttered notation of (nested) conditionals.

Consider trafo. 4c: the explicit test for Q on the calling side is now implicit (it has migrated into the body of F); the conditional goes away and the exceptional situation(s) are collected towards the end of the sequence of statements and treated in corresponding exception handler(s).

5. Monitors

In chapter 3, partial operations were used, where partiality was defined by an in-annotation (or "pre-condition") Q on the parameters.

In chapter 4 we saw that partiality, or portions Q_i of it if Q is split up into conjuncts (see section 4.1), can be denoted by the raising and propagation of exceptions, as an alternative notation. Exception handling gives an alternative operational semantics for recovery from exceptions or "errors" one would otherwise give rise to under conditions that define such partial domains.

We shall now see that partiality of operations may often correspond to *partial availability of resources* in a concurrent context. A monitor, protecting a resource by synchronizing concurrent (possibly parallel) access to it, may block some access operations temporarily since the present state of the resource does not meaningfully allow such access. Here "temporarily" does not necessarily refer to (real) time; conditions under which unavailability may occur arise because of (different) relative speeds of the accessing processes. In an actual configuration, speeds may happen to be such that unavailability never occurs and no process has to wait.

It is desirable, both from a theoretical and a pragmatic point of view, to separate the purely sequential semantic aspects of the components of a concurrent system from those aspects that are inherent in concurrency: synchronization, scheduling, (real) time, deadlock, starvation, liveness etc.

The approach presented here is a first step in this direction, trying to separate out the sequential semantics of monitors from the concurrency aspect.

5.1. Monitor Task Specifications

Consider fig. 11 and compare it with fig. 7 (partial operations in a stand-alone package) and fig. 9 (exceptions). If the in-annotation is not fulfilled (cf. fig. 7) or, analogously, the condition for propagation holds (cf. fig. 9) then the operation will not terminate normally.

```
task STACK_MONITOR is
--: function LENGTH return NATURAL;

   entry PUSH (E: in ITEM);
   --|where not (STACK.LENGTH < SIZE) => delay;
   entry POP;
   --|where not (STACK.LENGTH > 0) => delay;
   entry TOP (E: out ITEM);
   --|where not ( STACK.LENGTH > 0) => delay;

--| axiom for all S: STACK TYPE; X: ITEM=>
--|    S[PUSH(X)][POP] = S,
--|    S[PUSH(X)]. TOP 'OUT = X,
--|    STACK 'INITIAL. LENGTH = 0,
--|    S[PUSH(X)]. LENGTH= S.LENGTH + 1;
 end STACK_MONITOR;
```

Fig. 11: Monitor Task Specification with Entries

In the concurrent case, the operations of the ADT correspond to entry operations in a monitor task (in the notation of Ada here). They are, of course, also partial, and only properly defined if the in-annotation (or its equivalents) Q holds. However if the converse of Q (or portions of it, similarly to the case for exceptions described in section 4.1) is true, the entry operation will be blocked but not abnormally terminated. This is stated by the resp. delay annotation: the calling task will have to wait (i.e. be delayed in its execution) if the delay condition holds. In this case, the protected resource is partially (or "temporarily") unavailable.

Here, as in the case of exceptions, the axioms describing the sequential semantics of the monitor remain unchanged. For the caller, the concurrent semantics aspects will be affected (waiting, possibly deadlock or starvation); its sequential aspects will not be affected since blocking ensures that a call is only successfully completed if the operation is properly defined (we disregard exceptions for a moment).

Thus, methodologically, monitor tasks can be gradually developed from (applicative) algebraic specifications by applying resp. transformation rules of chapter 3 and trafo. 5.

Note that (at least for the case of Ada) the condition Q must only depend on the state of the monitor task, i.e. the implicit, globalized resource variable parameters (cf. 3.5), and not on the explicit parameters of the entry operations. This way there is a clear separation of concerns: blocking depends only on the state of the (locally protected) resource and not on (explicit) parameters of the callers. On the other hand, scheduling decisions based on an inspection of parameters of the callers to an entry cannot be made. Families of entries are the only alternative, and have been introduced precisely for the purpose of allowing special scheduling tasks. This was a conscious design decision for Ada, probably primarily for efficiency reasons since conditions in a select statement are evaluated only once. Our approach would obviously work just the same if an inspection of the parameters was possible.

5.2. Monitor Task Bodies

Trafo. 5: Introduction of Monitor Task	

package P **is** -- stand alone
  procedure F(X: **in** S);
  --| **where in** Q(X, P),
  --| **out** R(**in** X, **in** P, P);
  -- analogously for other operations,
--| **axiom for all** U, W:S; V:P 'TYPE =>
--| ... P[F(U)]. G(W)...
  end P;
	task P **is**
	  entry F (X: **in** S);
	  --| **where not** Q(P) => **delay**,
	  --| **out** R (**in** X, **in** P, P);
	  -- analogously for other entry operations
	--| **axiom for all** U, W: S; V: P TYPE =>
	--| ... P [F(U)]. G(W) ...
	  end P;

package body P **is**
  type T **is new** t;
  V : T;
  procedure F (X: **in** S)
  --| **where in** q (V),
  --| **out** r (**in** X, **in** V, V);
  is
  begin
    V:= g(X, V);
  end F;
  -- analogously for the other operations
end P;
  ...
 	
--| Q(U, P);
  F(U);   -- P = in P[F(in U)], thus
--| R(**in** U, **in** P, P);
	task body P **is**
	  type T **is new** t;
	  V: T; -- protected resource
	begin
	  loop
	    select
	      when q(V) =>
	        accept F (X: **in** S)
	        --| **where out** r(**in** X, **in** V, V);
	        do
	          V:= g(X, V);
	        end F;
	      or
	        -- analogously for other entry operations
	      or
	        terminate;
	    end select;
	  end loop;
	end P;
	  ...
	  P.F (U);
	--| **not** Q (P) => **delay**;
	  -- P = in P[F(in U)], thus
	--| R(**in** U, **in** P, P);

The application of trafo. 6 to the package body in fig. 8 yields the task body of fig. 12. The
bodies of the entry operations are now given by so-called accept statements (for a rendez-vous
between caller and callee task). The rather imperative and explicit notation using loop, select
etc. in Ada points to the fact that monitors may, as an option, be regarded as, and implemented
by, active processes. For example, a monitor may have a separate, physical processor if it
denotes a peripherical device. However, it may be seen as a totally passive module (like a package), a collection of entry bodies executed on behalf of the calling process in a synchronized
fashion; so the notation should not deter us. Since monitors might be implemented in an
"active" way, it may be good to move those actions in a select alternative that do not depend on
the explicit entry parameters (i.e. only on the state of the monitor) to the sequence of statements after the end of the accept statement body (cf. [10] for the inverse transformation). In
fig. 12, we would then get

    accept POP;
  INDEX:= INDEX - 1;

Caution has to be exercised w.r.t. exceptions in this case.

6. Conclusion

6.1. Transformational Semantics

It has been shown in chapter 3 how applicative packages and subprograms, in particular
their abstract "data type" specifications, can be transformed to imperative style and to stand-
alone modules. Since the transformation rules given are (almost) context-free, the change may
appear to be "only" stylistic, as a kind of "notational extension" of the applicative sublanguage
of Ada/Anna. This is the approach of defining such other styles by Transformational Semantics
(cf. [4] based on earlier work in [11,12]).

The transformational semantics for exceptions given in chapter 4 defines the introduction of
concepts like exceptions, raising and handling of an exception, etc, by means of definitional
transformation rules,etc.

```
task body STACK_MONITOR is
  type ITEM_ARRAY is array (1..SIZE) of ITEM;
  SPACE: ITEM_ARRAY;         -- protected
  INDEX: NATURAL := 0;       -- resources
--: function LENGTH return NATURAL;
  --| where return INDEX;
begin
  loop
    select
      when INDEX < SIZE =>        -- STACK. LENGTH < SIZE
        accept PUSH (E: in ITEM)
        --| where out (INDEX = in INDEX + 1),
        --|       out (SPACE = in SPACE [INDEX => E]);
        do  INDEX:=INDEX + 1;
          SPACE (INDEX):= E;
        end PUSH;
    or when INDEX > 0 =>          -- STACK.LENGTH > 0
        accept POP do
          INDEX:= INDEX - 1;
        end POP;
    or when INDEX > 0  =>         -- STACK.LENGTH > 0
        accept TOP (E: out ITEM) do
          E:= SPACE (INDEX);
        end TOP;
    or
        terminate;
    end select;
  end loop;
end STACK_MONITOR;
```

Fig. 12: Monitor Task Body

6.2. Program Development by Transformation

By applying these transformation rules and those from the applicative to the imperative level of section 3 (and combinations of both), imperative program versions with exceptions can be derived from applicative ones without exceptions that are specified algebraically. If only such transformation rules are applied in a systematic way, the imperative versions are correct with respect to the original specification. This methodology is called *program development by transformation* (see [13] for an overview of ongoing projects). It is presently pursued in the PROSPECTRA Project (PROgram development by SPECification and TRAnsformation), it is carried out by the Universities of Bremen, Dortmund, Passau, Saarland, Strathclyde (at Glasgow), and SYSECA Logiciel (St. Cloud), and SYSTEAM KG (Karlsruhe), corrsponsored by the Commision of the European Communities under the ESPRIT Programme, see [14]. It is based on work done in the CIP-Project in Munich (see e.g. [15]).

In the PROSPECTRA Project, transformation rules such as those given here will be individually applicable by the user of the PROSPECTRA System that supports the development methodology. An attempt will also be made to automate sets of transformation rules to transformation scripts or methods.

6.3. Inverse Transformation

Since all the transformation rules given are equivalence transformation rules, they can also be applied backwards. By applying these rules and rules from the applicative to the imperative level, (such as in section 3) from right to left, most programs in Ada using exceptions should be reducible to equivalent applicative programs; their specifications in Anna to algebraic specifications without exceptions. It can, presently, not be guaranteed that all Ada programs are, in fact, covered; this is not even desirable for methodological reasons.

It might be interesting to apply inverse transformations to existing program (portions) to make their specification applicative .

6.4. Exceptions

Exceptions are by no means only "errors"; they may correspond to perfectly reasonable terminating conditions that do not occur under the normal, i.e. wishful, behaviour of a program, but under abnormal or "exceptional" circumstances. Operationally, the introduction of exceptions means pushing tests (for these rare conditions) "inwards" till the last point where their violation can be detected.

Thus if an exception really occurs rarely, then it pays to introduce them: repeated tests, possibly at many levels, are avoided until the innermost operation, which then raises the exception. Propagation of exceptions ("outwards") is comparatively inefficient, but negligable compared with the increase in efficiency when avoiding the tests.

If applied systematically or even (semi-)automatically, the introduction of exceptions may thus yield considerably more efficient program versions, quite apart from the usually desired effect of freeing the "normal" program text from cluttering with tests for exceptions.

6.5. Monitors and Concurrency

The introduction of monitor tasks and delay annotations is similar to the introduction of exceptions. It is perhaps a little exaggerated, at this point, to speak of transformational semantics until considerably more work on concurrency, and tasking in Ada, is done. Still, we can isolate the sequential aspects of monitors, considering them as special versions of stand-alone packages hiding an internal state (of the resource, in this case).

As in the case of exceptions, the importance lies in the preservation of the abstract axiomatic specification that is virtually unchanged. The only thing that changes is the interpretation of the partiality of the operations, i.e. those conditions under which the operations, and therefore the axioms, become undefined. Thus, as long as the axioms are well-defined, they define the sequential semantics of monitors. Some conditions under which the operations would become undefined have a reasonable semantic interpretation of delay conditions for the caller in a concurrency semantics.

So far, one can only speculate which conditions should be interpreted in this way, resulting in intentional, potentially nonterminating, iteration in the calling task. and which conditions should remain unchanged to denote "true" partiality or should indicate abnormal termination by exception. Also, one can only speculate how a similar development by transformation could be achieved for tasks in general, or in what kind of concurrency semantics and specification language extension of Anna it might be imbedded in the future.

It looks promising, however, that we have been able to identify a discrete transition from "bounded", usually finite, computations described by ADT's to infinite, concurrent computations, at least for the case of monitors. To seperate out the sequential semantic aspects, and to reason about them, it is sufficient to restrict attention to computations within the "bounds", i.e. while the delay conditions do not hold and, therefore, the axioms (or other abstract specifications) are well-defined.

Also, the sequential semantics can directly be related to an applicative style of specification, by a chain of inverse transformations. Will it be possible or desirable to develop an applicative style of specificiation for the concurrency aspects as well?

For the time being, monitors in our approach cannot handle scheduling, i.e. making decisions dependent on how many calling task are waiting to execute an entry operation (cf. the attribute E'COUNT for an entry E in Ada). This is no wonder since scheduling should have a semantic effect on concurrency aspects in smoothing relative speeds of tasks, ensuring fairness, and so on. It should not have any effect on the sequential aspects of a monitor, i.e. its ADT-behaviour when operating on the protected resource.

There is hope that the scheduling aspects can be separated out by interposing a so-called "agent task" between the caller and the " ADT"-monitor: the only purpose of the agent is scheduling. It may then be reasonable in a second step to combine both for efficiency reasons. It will be interesting to see to what extent e.g. path-expressions (cf. [16]) define only the scheduling behaviour or also (intentionally?) the sequential aspects; these should be specified separately.

7. Acknowledgements

I would like to thank H. Ganzinger and Z. Qian for helpful discussions, and A. Traser for her patient typing.

8. References

[1] The Ada Programming Language. ANSI / MIL-STD 1815 A. US Government Printing Office, 1983. Also in: Rogers, M. W. (ed.): Ada: Language, Compilers and Bibliography. Ada Companion Series, Cambridge University Press, 1984

[2] Krieg-Brückner, B., Luckham, D.C.: Anna: Towards a Language for Annotating Ada Programs. ACM SIGPLAN Notices 15:1 (1980), 128-138

[3] Luckham, D. C., von Henke, F. W., Krieg-Brückner, B., Owe, O: Anna, a Language for Annotating Ada Programs; Preliminary Reference Manual. Technical Report No. 84-248, Computer Systems Lab., Standford University, June 1984

[4] Pepper, P.: A Study of Transformational Semantics. in: Bauer, F.L., Broy, M.(eds.): Program Construction. LNCS 69 (1979) 322-405.

[5] Owe, O.: An Approach to Program Reasoning Based on a First Order Logic for Partial Functions. Research Report No. 89, Institute of Informatics, University of Oslo, 1985

[6] Owe, O: Formal Definition of the Anna Kernel. (in preparation)

[7] Broy, M., Krieg-Brückner, B.: Derivation of Invariant Assertions During Program Development by Transformation. ACM TOPLAS 2:3 (1980) 321-337

[8] Bauer, F.L., Wössner, H: Algorithmic Language and Program Development. Springer Verlag, 1982

[9] Engels, G., Pletat, V., Ehrich, H.-D: Handling Errors and Exceptions in the Algebraic Specification of Data Types. Osnabrücker Schriften zur Mathematik, Reihe Informatik, Heft 3, 1981

[10] Habermann, A. N., and Nassi, I. R.: Efficient Implementation of Ada Tasks. Carnegie Mellon University Technical Report CMU-CS-80-103, Jan. 1980

[11] Krieg-Brückner, B.: Concrete and Abstract Specification, Modularization and Program Development by Transformation. Dissertation. Technische Universität München, Institut für Informatik, TUM-INFO-7805, Jan 1978

[12] Laut, A.: Safe Procedural Implementations of Algebraic Types. Information Processing Letters 11: 4,5(1980) 147-151

[13] Partsch, H., Steinbrüggen, R.: Program Transformation Systems. ACM Computing Surveys 15 (1983) 199-236

[14] Krieg-Brückner, B., Ganzinger, H., Broy, M., Wilhelm, R., McGettrick, A.D., Campbell, I.G., Winterstein, G.: PROgram development by SPECification and TRAnsformation, Project Summary. Universität Bremen, 1985.

[15] Bauer, F. L., Berghammer, R., Broy, M., Dosch, W., Geiselbrechtinger, F., Gnatz, R., Hangel, E., Hesse, W., Krieg-Brückner, B., Laut, A., Matzner, T., Möller, B., Nickl, F., Partsch, M., and Wössner, H.: The Munich Project CIP, Vol. 1: The Wide Spectrum Language CIP-L. LNCS 183, Springer Verlag, 1985

[16] Goldsack, S.J., and Moreton, T.: Ada Package Specifications, Path Expressions and Monitors. IEE Proceedings part E, Vol 129, March 1982.

Axiomatising Specification Theory

Tom Maibaum
Martin Sadler

Department of Computing
Imperial College of Science and Technology
180 Queen's Gate, London SW7 2BZ

1. Introduction

In contrast to the more usual algebraic or model theoretic approaches we can try and capture our intuitions about specification on a purely syntactic or proof theoretic level. Such intuitions are, we feel, independent of any specific logic. So we can start with the general notion of a logic as something given by a consequence relation, ⊢, as opposed to by an institution say, and investigate what we need to add, by way of properties on ⊢, in order to support an account of specification. We don't regard such a "semantics-less" approach to be worthless but rather, in the spirit of Frege and more recently Martin-Lof, take meaning to be something that is given directly by such a proof theory.

This paper consists, primarily, of one result: that for a logic to support specification, that is where specifications are taken to be theories over the logic, it needs (at least) to satisfy the Craig interpolation property. Of course, what we take "to support" to mean might be disputed, however it is the general enterprise of establishing such "abstract" results for specification that we feel is important.

2. Specification

It is not unnatural to regard a specification as being a theory or theory presentation, and to consider a syntactic or proof theoretic notion of implementation, that is as a mapping between theories. Ideally we would like to structure our specifications in some fashion. Clearly one important mechanism is the idea of a conservative extension. See [MVS] for an account of specification based primarily on this mechanism. Now suppose we conservatively extend one specification, S say, for example by adding some definitions. Then if we implement S, by T say, we ought to be able to copy (*ie* avoid overloading symbols) the extension we have over S over T, and the new extension should still be conservative. It is not unreasonable to claim that to support an account of specification and implementation at least this much must be guaranteed.

An interesting question to ask then is what conditions do we need to impose on a logic and on a notion of mapping between theories over that logic in order that an account of specification and implementation be supported. There is of course no reason why we should regard the source and target specifications of some implementation as being theories over the same logic, so we look at this more general case. In what follows the special case where all activity is over the same logic is obtained by ignoring the superscripts on ⊢.

3. Logics and mappings

As we want to talk about different logics, we need to know when two different theories are to be understood as being over the same logic. One way of dealing with this is to regard logics as being defined or presented over an abstract or schematic language, with the language of each theory being a replacement of the symbols of the abstract language by appropriate "concrete" symbols. The actual formal mechanism for doing this is not relevant, as far as our results are concerned. And as with the idea of a logic, we operate only with suitable properties that the mechanism must satisfy. Further we will only concern ourselves with one kind of expression for such schematic languages. Such expressions are the ones that appear on the right of the ⊢ symbol, call them 'sentences' say. On the left of ⊢ will appear sets (or lists) of such sentences. We will use:

$L, M, ...$ as meta-variables over schematic languages.

And given a particular such schematic language, L, we will use:

$\phi, \psi, ...$ as meta-variables over sentences from L;

$\Gamma, \Delta, ...$ as meta-variables over sets of sentences from L;

and:

$L, L', ...$ as meta-variables over (concrete) languages for L.

So as a starting point we consider a logic over a schematic language, L, to be given by a consequence relation ⊢. We read $\Gamma \vdash \phi$ as: "ϕ follows from Γ". And require that the following conditions on ⊢ be satisfied:

Ref − For $\phi \epsilon \Gamma$: $\Gamma \vdash \phi$ (Ref for reflexivity);

Mon − If $\Gamma \vdash \phi$ then $\Gamma, \Delta \vdash \phi$ (Mon for monotonicity);

Cut − If $\Gamma \vdash \phi$ and $\Gamma, \{\phi\} \vdash \psi$ then $\Gamma \vdash \psi$ (Cut for cut);

Fin $-$ If $\Gamma \vdash \phi$ then $\Delta \vdash \phi$ for some finite subset Δ of Γ (Fin for finiteness).

(Here we have adopted the usual notational convenience of writing ',' for '$\cup$' on the left of $\vdash$.)

To relate our schematic languages to "concrete" languages we require that the replacement or substitution mechanism, $L:L \rightarrow L$ say, satisfies:

Sub $- \Gamma_L \vdash_L \phi_L$ iff $\Gamma \vdash \phi$ (Sub for substitution),

> where the subscripts denote the result of

> the substitution map L.

From now on we retain the subscript on $\vdash$, only where it is essential to remind ourselves where we are, and also drop the subscripts on the sentences.

So now we can regard specifications as structures: $<L,\Gamma,\vdash_L>$ and implementations as mappings: $i:<L,\Gamma,\vdash_L> \rightarrow <M,\Delta,\vdash'_M>$, where the superscript on the $\vdash$ reminds us that we may be using a different logic in the target. Again the actual mechanism for such i's is not important, all we require is that any such map induces a map from the sentences of L to the sentences of M ($i:\phi \rightarrow \phi^i$, $\Gamma_0 \rightarrow \Gamma_0{}^i$, say), and that the following conditions hold:

Trn $-$ If $\Gamma_0{}^i \vdash'_M \phi^i$ then $\Gamma_0 \vdash_L \phi$ (Trn for translation);

Imp $-$ If $\Gamma \vdash_L \phi$ then $\Delta \vdash'_M \phi^i$ (Imp for implementation).

The translation condition just demands that our logic cannot get any stronger - something that is plausible in moving in the direction: specification to program. Note also that i might be a complex mapping as with the case of first order logic where the notion of interpretation between theories involves the use of relativisation predicates, and the enforcing of certain closure and non-emptiness criteria.

We call a mapping i (satisfying Trn and Imp) an *extension* iff $\vdash = \vdash'$ and whenever ϕ is a sentence of L it is also a sentence of M. So: if $\Gamma \vdash_L \phi$ then $\Delta \vdash_M \phi$.

We call a mapping i (satisfying Trn and Imp) *conservative* iff if $\Delta \vdash'_M \phi^i$ then $\Gamma \vdash_L \phi$.

4. Results

Our basic requirement (for the support of specification) becomes:

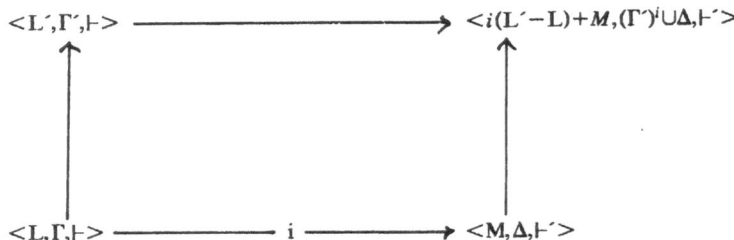

when can we guarantee the conservativeness of the right arm of the square, given the left arm is a conservative extension? The notation of the top right corner is to be interpreted as follows: the − and + denote the copying of whatever is in L′ but not in L, whilst avoiding the overloading of the symbols of M. (Note conservativeness will also guarantee consistency (at least for logics where this notion makes sense) of the top right corner, given the consistency of the bottom right corner.)

We will use the notation "$(\vdash,\vdash')$ preserves conservative extensions under implementation" for this situation.

Result: If $\vdash'$ satisfies the Craig interpolation property then $(\vdash,\vdash')$ preserves conservative extensions under implementations.

We will use the following general form of the Craig interpolation property:

Given Γ a set of sentences from L, Δ a set of sentences from L′, and ϕ a sentence of L′, if $\Gamma,\Delta\vdash\phi$ (*ie* at the schematic level), then there exists a finite set of sentences $\{\psi_j\}$ such that:

1) $\Gamma\vdash_L\psi_j$ for all j;

2) $\{\psi_j\},\Delta\vdash_{L'}\phi$.

That is each of the ψ's can be taken as belonging to both of the languages L and L′.

Proof: The proof is simple, the right hand arm of our square above is an extension by construction. All we need to check is conservativeness. So suppose ϕ a sentence of M is such that: $\Gamma^{\prime i},\Delta\vdash'\phi$ (dropping the long subscript on $\vdash'$ appropriate for the top right corner of the square). We need to show $\Delta\vdash'_M\phi$

Now factor $\Gamma^{\prime i},\Delta\vdash'\phi$ by the Craig interpolation property so there exists $\{\psi_j{}^i\}$ in L^i such that 1) $\Gamma^{\prime i}\vdash'\psi_j{}^i$ for each j and 2) $\{\psi_j{}^i\},\Delta\vdash'\phi$. Hence:

$\Gamma'\vdash\psi_j$ for each j (Trn)

$\Gamma\vdash\psi_j$ for each j (conservativeness)

$\Delta\vdash'\psi_j{}^i$ for each j (Imp)

$$\Delta \vdash' \phi \hspace{10cm} \text{(Cut)}$$

In fact the Craig interpolation property is not only sufficient it is, as far as preserving conservative extensions under implementations are concerned, necessary.

Result If $(\vdash,\vdash)$ preserves conservative extensions under implementations then $\vdash$ satisfies the Craig interpolation property.

Proof Suppose $\vdash$ doesn't satisfy the Craig interpolation property. So for some Γ a set of sentences of L, Δ a set of sentences of L´, and ϕ a sentence of L´, we have $\Gamma,\Delta \vdash \phi$. But there is no finite set of appropriate interpolants.

Consider the following square:

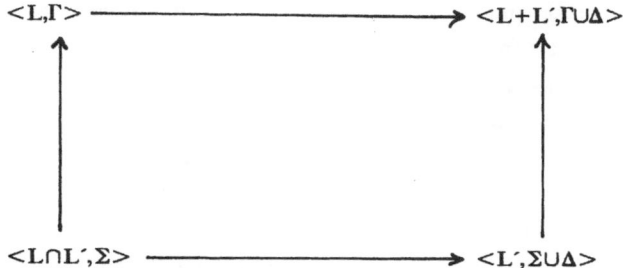

where $\Sigma = \{\sigma$ in $L \cap L'$ such that $\Gamma \vdash \sigma\}$. '∩' is used to indicate those sentences that can be taken as belonging to both languages.

Clearly the left arm is conservative by construction, but by appeal to finiteness (Fin) it is easy to verify that the right arm is not conservative.

5. The algebraic case

Interestingly equational logic, on which most accounts of specification are based, does not satisfy the Craig interpolation property. Consider the example suggested by the following diagram:

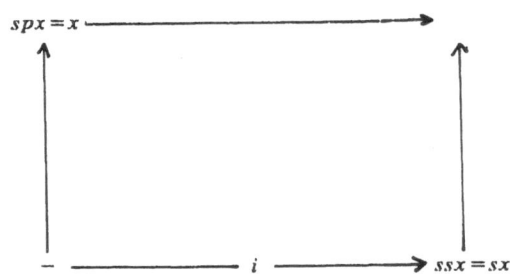

where the language of the bottom line is given by a constant 0 and a unary function s. The extension consists of adding a further unary function p and the equation in the top left hand corner. (Intuitively successor and predecessor functions). And i is just the identity map on languages, but where the target specification also has the equation $ssx = sx$.

The left arm of the square is conservative, there are no additional equations we can derive about s and 0 in the top left corner that we could not derive in the bottom left corner. But we can derive $sx = x$ in the top right hand corner, where we have both the equations $ssx = x$ and $spx = x$ available. [eg $x = spx = sspx = sx$] As $sx = x$ is not derivable in the bottom right corner the right arm of the square is not conservative.

The presence of either a conditional or an existential quantifier in the schematic language (and appropriate rules governing them) would mean that the left arm would no longer be conservative. For example, either $ssx = x \to sx = x$ or $\exists x . sx = 0$ would be derivable in the top left corner.

Algebraic approaches to specification get around this problem by imposing extra conditions, such as persistency, on extensions, something we feel is unsatisfactory. See [EM]. See also [POI] for a more detailed examination of related examples.

6. Conclusions

The moral, as far as specification languages are concerned, is perhaps: if the logic is weak we require strong conditions on structuring mechanisms, whereas we can adopt weaker conditions if the logic is stronger. As we need to verify such conditions when we construct specifications, perhaps we should prefer weaker conditions - so conservativeness and the Craig interpolation property.

However as we stated in the introduction, it is the emphasis on general, abstract considerations that we feel is of primary importance as far as specification theory is concerned.

Bibliography

[EM]

Ehrig, H. and Mahr B. *Fundamentals of Algebraic Specification 1*, EATCS Monographs on Theoretical Computer Science, Springer, 1985.

[MVS]

Maibaum, T. S. E. , Veloso, P. and Sadler, M. "A Theory of Abstract Data Types for Program Development: Bridging the Gap?", Springer LNCS 186.

[POI]

Poigne, A. "Error Handling in Parameterised Specifications", This volume.

On the Algebraic Specification of Domains

Bernhard Möller
Walter Dosch

Institut für Informatik
Technische Universität München
Postfach 20 24 20
8000 München 2

We explore the possibilities for the algebraic specification of semantic domains by continuous abstract types, that is, by abstract types with monotonicity, continuity and completeness constraints. In this framework, a domain results from the ideal completion of a term-generated algebra constituting its finite part. Then by construction, all finite elements of a domain can be denoted by finite terms. These finite elements are specified algebraically by conditional order relations describing the characteristic properties of the operations manipulating them. Properties of infinite elements can be inferred by continuity from the properties that hold for their finite approximations. The approach is illustrated by giving algebraic specifications of various domains and domain constructions.

1. Introduction

In denotational semantics the meaning of a program is modelled by an element of a semantic domain. Thus, the aims of domain theory are to provide spaces in which to interpret (results of) programs and to investigate their properties.

When ascribing meanings to programs, one inductively defines the semantics of a program following its syntactic structure. In this process the elements of a domain have to be denoted and to be manipulated; frequently used are constructions of composite elements and selections of their components. Since these operations are essential, a domain is not just a set but rather a semantic algebra.

In proofs about programs, the reasoning about syntactic objects often makes use of the properties of the semantic elements of the corresponding domain. In concrete domain models, however, such properties are not explicitly stated, but implicitly contained in the representation of the elements. This shows the need for specifying both the elements and operations as well as some fundamental properties of a domain in a rigorous, formal and convenient way.

One possible way of formalizing domain constructions is the category-theoretic approach: A domain is defined (up to isomorphism) using continuous functions from it into an external "trial domain" (see, for example, [Lehmann, Smyth 81], [Smyth, Plotkin 82]). Another

This work was carried out within the Sonderforschungsbereich 49, Programmiertechnik, Munich.

possibility is to give axioms and inference rules for domain categories [Dybjer 84].

In this paper we introduce an alternative way based on the specification methodology of abstract data types: The semantic elements of a domain are characterized by axioms for the operations manipulating them. To cope with fixpoints and algebraicity of domains as needed as essential concepts in denotational semantics, we employ the framework of continuous abstract types. Here a symbol for Scott's semantic approximation order replaces the equality sign used in conventional abstract types; as axioms we use conditional order relations.

In a first step we axiomatize the basis, that is, the finite elements, of a domain. The method ensures that all finite elements can be named by finite terms over the operations of the respective semantic algebra. In the second step, the domain itself results by taking the ideal completion of the basis, generally by adding certain limit points.

The resulting domains are countably algebraic. The infinite elements can easily be handled by manipulating the terms denoting their finite approximations; the operations then extend to the limit points by continuity. This proceeding follows [Scott 70, 82] in that domains are sets representable as completions of structures with finite information contents.

Throughout the paper, we try to fruitfully exploit concepts from the algebraic specification technique: We employ hierarchies of algebraic specifications to define composite domains in a modularized way; we specify parametrized types for the basic domain constructions such as forming direct product or direct sum. Different domain constructions, for example the separated and coalesced direct sums, turn out to be initial and terminal models of one and the same specification.

Moreover, the rich proof theory associated with algebraic types provides a powerful and flexible tool for proofs of correctness and further properties of such semantic specifications. The restriction to term-generated algebras as the bases of domains provides induction principles and stresses the constructive nature of the approach.

The paper is organized as follows: Section 2 suveys the theoretical foundations of continous types by recalling the basic notions and some important theorems. Section 3 contains sample specifications of some fundamental domains such as the Boolean values and natural numbers. In Section 4 follows the specification of various domain constructions, such as products, sums, streams, environments, and power domains.

2.   Theoretical Foundations

In this chapter we survey the theoretical foundations to the extent necessary in the following sections. For a more comprehensive treatment and detailed proofs we refer to [Möller 85].

2.1.   Ordered and Continuous Σ-Algebras

2.1.1.   Ordered Σ-Algebras

A **signature** Σ = (S, F) comprises a nonempty countable set S of **sorts** and a nonempty family F = $(F_{w \to s})_{w \in S^*, s \in S}$ of countable sets of **operators**. For w = $s_1 * ... * s_n$ with length $|w|$ = n, f $\in F_{w \to s}$ has the **argument sorts** s_i and the **result sort** s. A **(ordered)** Σ-algebra A consists of a family $(s^A, \subseteq_s^A)_{s \in S}$ of ordered **carrier sets** s^A and a family $(f^A)_{f \in F}$ of monotonic **operations** f^A: $s_1^A \times ... \times s_n^A \to s^A$ corresponding to the operators f $\in F_{s_1 * ... * s_n \to s}$. For n = 0, $f^A \in s^A$ is called a **constant**.

The orders $\subseteq_s^A$ are supposed to be **approximation orders** reflecting growth of "computational information". Thus a $\subseteq_s^A$ b means that "a approximates b", "a is less defined than b" or "a has less information contents than b". The **maximal (total)** elements in this order contain maximal information, whereas **partial** elements can be further refined.

The more conventional "unordered" Σ-algebras (see, for example, [Goguen et al. 78], [Wirsing et al. 83]) correspond to the case where all carrier sets s^A are trivially ordered by the identity relation; in this case all operations are automatically monotonic.

Let **Alg(Σ)** denote the class of all Σ-algebras. For every signature Σ there is the trivial Σ-algebra $\mathbb{1}_\Sigma$ having singleton carrier sets for all sorts and constant operations on these carrier sets; thus $\text{Alg}(\Sigma) \ne \emptyset$.

In the sequel we often treat sort-indexed families of objects as single entities; in this case all operations on them are understood componentwise.

2.1.2. Grounded Σ-Algebras

For every sort $s \in S$ we assume a constant symbol $\perp_s \in F_{\to s}$ and consider only **grounded** Σ-algebras A where $\perp_s^A$ is the least element of the carrier set s^A. This **bottom element** $\perp_s^A$ "contains no information"; it serves to model the values of computations that are erroneous or never produce any information. An operation f^A is called **strict** if $f^A(a_1,\dots,a_n) = \perp_s^A$ whenever $a_i = \perp_{s_i}^A$ for some $i \in \{1,\dots,n\}$.

A carrier set s^A is called **flat (discrete)** if for all $a, b \in s^A$
$$a \sqsubseteq_s^A b \iff a = \perp_s^A \lor a = b .$$
Thus in a flat carrier set s^A all elements different from $\perp_s^A$ are maximal and pairwise incomparable.

2.1.3. Σ-Homomorphisms

A (Σ-)**homomorphism** $\rho: A \to B$ between Σ-algebras A, B is a family
$$\rho = (\rho_s: s^A \to s^B)_{s \in S}$$
of monotonic mappings which respect the operations, that is,
$$\rho_s(f^A(a_1,\dots,a_n)) = f^B(\rho_{s_1}(a_1),\dots,\rho_{s_n}(a_n))$$
for all $a_i \in s_i^A$ if f $\in F_{s_1*\dots*s_n \to s}$ $(n \ge 0)$.

The homomorphism property implies that every ρ_s is strict:
$$\rho_s(\perp_s^A) = \perp_s^B .$$

If all ρ_s are bijective, ρ is called a (Σ-)**isomorphism.**

Define on Alg(Σ) the relations
A $\approx$ B iff A and B are Σ-isomorphic, and
A $\ll$ B iff there is a Σ-homomorphism
$$\rho : A \to B .$$

$\ll$ is a preorder on Alg(Σ) .

For a class $\mathbb{K} \subseteq \text{Alg}(\Sigma)$, a Σ-algebra A $\in \mathbb{K}$ is called **initial** in $\mathbb{K}$ if for all B $\in \mathbb{K}$ there is a unique Σ-homomorphism $\rho: A \to B$. Initial algebras are characterized up to isomorphism. Conversely, A is called **terminal** in $\mathbb{K}$ if for all B $\in \mathbb{K}$ there is at least one Σ-homomorphism $\rho: B \to A$.

2.1.4. Term-Generated Σ-Algebras

For a signature $\Sigma = (S, F)$ and a family $X = (X_s)_{s \in S}$ of **variables**, the **(finite)** $\Sigma(X)$-**terms** are defined as usual. For $\Sigma(X)$-terms t_1, t_2 of the same sort, $t_1 \equiv t_2$ denotes the **lexical (syntactic) identity.**

The **term algebra** $W\Sigma(X)$ is ordered by Nivat's **syntactic approximation order**; this is the least family $\sqsubseteq = (\sqsubseteq_s)_{s \in S}$ of orders $\sqsubseteq_s$ with
(1) $\perp_s \sqsubseteq_s t$ for all $t \in sW\Sigma(X)$;
(2) for f $\in F_{s_1*\dots*s_n \to s}$ $(n \ge 1)$
and $r_i, t_i \in s_i W\Sigma(X)$ with $r_i \sqsubseteq_{s_i} t_i$
we have $f(r_1,\dots,r_n) \sqsubseteq_s f(t_1,\dots,t_n)$.
The operations of $W\Sigma(X)$ are defined in the usual way as term constructors. For $X = \emptyset$ we get the **ground term algebra** $W\Sigma$ which is initial in Alg(Σ). In the sequel we only consider signatures Σ with $sW\Sigma \ne \emptyset$ for all $s \in S$.

The **interpretation** $i^A : W\Sigma \to A$ of Σ-ground-terms in a Σ-algebra A is defined inductively as follows:
(1) If $t \equiv f \in F_{\to s}$, then $i^A(t) := f^A$.
(2) If $t \equiv f(t_1,\dots,t_n)$ $(n \ge 1)$,
then $i^A(t) := f^A(i^A(t_1),\dots,i^A(t_n))$.
i^A forms (the only possible) Σ-homomorphism from $W\Sigma$ into A. In the sequel $i^A(t)$ is abbreviated by t^A.

If i^A is surjective, then A is called **term-**

generated. This means that every element of a carrier set of A can be denoted by a finite Σ-ground-term; in other words, every element can be obtained by applying finitely many operations of the algebra to some constants. We denote by **Gen(Σ)** the class of all term-generated Σ-algebras.

Theorem 1

Let Σ be a signature.
a. $W\Sigma$ is initial in Gen(Σ).
b. There is at most one Σ-homomorphism between two term-generated Σ-algebras.
c. For A,B $\in$ Gen(Σ), A $\ll$ B and B $\ll$ A implies A $\approx$ B .
d. The set Gen(Σ)/$\approx$ of isomorphism classes forms a complete lattice under the order induced by $\ll$.

2.1.5. Continuous Σ-Algebras

Recursive definitions are given a mathematical semantics by solving fixpoint equations in the respective domain. Thus we now head for continuous algebras in whose carrier sets such fixpoints exist. We use continuity wrt. limits of directed sets since the argument terms of a multiary operation may be refined independently according to the order; compare, for example, the refinement of a binary operation f:

A nonempty ordered set D is called **directed** if for any two elements a, b $\in$ D there is an element c $\in$ D with a $\sqsubseteq$ c and b $\sqsubseteq$ c. We call a Σ-algebra A (**directed-)complete**, if every directed subset D $\subseteq$ s^A has a **supremum** $\bigsqcup_s D \in s^A$. A **continuous Σ-algebra** is a complete Σ-algebra with **continuous operations**, that is with

$$f^A(\bigsqcup_{s_1} D_1, \ldots, \bigsqcup_{s_n} D_n) = \bigsqcup_s f^A(D_1, \ldots, D_n)$$

for all directed subsets $D_i \subseteq s_i^A$ and all operators $f \in F_{s_1 * \ldots * s_n \to s}$ $(n \geq 1)$.

The elements of a directed subset are all consistent wrt. the information contents order. Thus such a set D can be viewed as a set of approximations of one particular element, viz. its supremum $\bigsqcup$D which in a complete algebra

always exists. Continuity then ensures that the value of an operation at a point can be inferred as the limit (supremum) of the values at the approximations of that point.

Finally, we quote the well-known fixpoint theorem which is the basis for solving recursion equations.

Theorem 2 (Knaster, Tarski, Kleene)

Every continuous mapping f : M $\to$ M on a complete set M with least element $\bot$ has the least fixpoint

$$\mu(f) = \bigsqcup \{f^i(\bot) \mid i \in \mathbb{N}\} .$$

2.1.6. Inductively Generated Σ-Algebras

In order to use Theorem 2, we embed a Σ-algebra A into a complete Σ-algebra A^∞ by taking the ideal completion of its carrier sets.

An element m of an ordered set $(M, \sqsubseteq)$ is called **finite (isolated, compact)** if for all directed sets D $\subseteq$ M, m $\sqsubseteq$ $\bigsqcup$D implies m $\sqsubseteq$ d for some d $\in$ D. This means that any directed cover of m can be replaced by a finite subcover. M is called **inductive (algebraic)** if every element of M is **finitely approximable**, that is, the supremum of a directed set of finite elements. A set is called **limit-free** if all its elements are finite. A non-finite element of an inductive set is called a **limit point** or an **infinite element.**

An **ideal** of an ordered set $(M, \sqsubseteq)$ is a nonempty downward closed, upward directed subset of M. For a directed subset D $\subseteq$ M we denote by
$$\langle D \rangle := \{m \in M \mid \exists\, d \in D : m \sqsubseteq d\}$$
the ideal **generated** by D. Note that, if $\bigsqcup$ D exists, then $\bigsqcup$ D = $\bigsqcup$ $\langle D \rangle$.

Theorem 3

Let $(M, \sqsubseteq)$ be an ordered set and I(M) be the set of ideals of M.
a. The set (I(M), $\subseteq$) ordered by set inclusion is complete and inductive, the finite elements being the ideals $\langle m \rangle$ for m $\in$ M. M is embedded into I(M) by the mapping m $\mapsto$ $\langle m \rangle$.
b. For every monotonic mapping h : M $\to$ N into a complete set (N, $\subseteq$) there is a unique continuous extension h' : I(M) $\to$ N of h with h'($\langle m \rangle$) = h(m) for all m $\in$ M. Moreover, h'($\langle D \rangle$) = $\bigsqcup$ h(D) for all directed D $\subseteq$ M.

For the proof see, for example, [Wright et al. 78] or [Guesserian 81].

We call (I(M), $\subseteq$) the **ideal completion** M^∞ of the ordered set M. Every grounded Σ-algebra A may be embedded into its ideal completion A^∞ by setting

$$s^{A^\infty} := I(s^A) \quad \text{ordered by set inclusion, and}$$

$$f^{A^\infty}(I_1,\ldots,I_n) := \langle f^A(I_1,\ldots,I_n)\rangle \ .$$

This extends the operations of A in a continuous way to the newly added limit points.

Theorem 4

Let A be a grounded Σ-algebra.

a. A^∞ is an inductive continuous Σ-algebra. The mappings $a \mapsto \langle a\rangle$ form an injective monotonic Σ-homomorphism.

b. If B is a continuous Σ-algebra and $h : A \to B$ a monotonic Σ-homomorphism, then there is a unique continuous Σ-homomorphism $h' : A^\infty \to B$ with $h'|A = h$.

In particular, the ideal completion $W\Sigma(X)^\infty$ of $W\Sigma(X)$ yields the **algebra of finite and infinite terms** (compare the free complete magma [Courcelle, Nivat 76] or $CT_\Sigma(X)$ [Goguen et al. 77]).

We call a Σ-algebra **inductively generated** if it is (isomorphic to) the ideal completion of a term-generated algebra. For a class $\mathbb{K}$ of grounded Σ-algebras we define

$$\mathbb{K}^\infty := \{A^\infty \mid A \in \mathbb{K}\}.$$

Hence $\mathrm{Gen}(\Sigma)^\infty$ is the class of inductively generated Σ-algebras.

In the sequel we will concentrate on inductively generated algebras. They have the advantage that all their finite elements are denotable by finite ground terms; moreover, all information about the limit points may be inferred via continuity from the finite approximations. This means that the carrier sets of inductively generated algebras are countably algebraic; hence we may call them **domains**.

2.2. Algebraic Types and their Models

In this chapter we study continuous algebraic types as well as the existence and the properties of their models. These models are constructed in the following two steps:

(1) A premodel is an arbitrary term-generated ordered algebra satisfying the axioms of the type; it constitutes the "finite part" of a model.

(2) A model results from the ideal completion of a premodel. In this completion step limit points are added and the monotonic operations of the premodel are extended to continuous operations of the model.

2.2.1. $\Sigma(X)$-Formulas, Validity

The set of $\Sigma(X)$-**formulas** is defined inductively as follows:

(1) For $t_1, t_2 \in s^{W\Sigma(X)}$ every **order relation** $t_1 \sqsubseteq t_2$ is a $\Sigma(X)$-formula.

(2) For $\Sigma(X)$-formulas Φ_1 and Φ_2,

$$\neg\Phi_1 \ , \quad \Phi_1 \wedge \Phi_2 \ , \quad \Phi_1 \vee \Phi_2$$

are $\Sigma(X)$-formulas.

In writing $\Sigma(X)$-formulas, we use as abbreviations

equations $\quad t_1 = t_2$ for $t_1 \sqsubseteq t_2 \wedge t_2 \sqsubseteq t_1$

inequations $\quad t_1 \neq t_2$ for $\neg(t_1 = t_2)$, and

implications $\Phi_1 \Rightarrow \Phi_2$ for $\neg\Phi_1 \vee \Phi_2$.

A **valuation** v of X in a Σ-algebra A is a family $(v_s : X_s \to s^A)_{s \in S}$ of mappings that assign to every variable an element of the respective carrier set of A. Let V_A denote the set of all valuations $v : X \to A$.

For a $\Sigma(X)$-term t and a valuation $v \in V_A$ the **instantiation** $t[v]$ of t under v is inductively defined as follows:

(1) If $t \triangleq x \in X_s$ then $t[v] := v_s(x)$.

(2) If $t \triangleq f \in F_{\to s}$ then $t[v] := f^A$.

(3) If $t \triangleq f(t_1,\ldots,t_n)$

then $t[v] := f^A(t_1[v],\ldots,t_n[v])$ $(n \geq 1)$.

For a ground term $t \in W\Sigma$ instantiation and interpretation coincide, since we have for all valuations $v \in V_A$ that $t[v] = t^A$.

The order properties of a Σ-algebra A carry over to the set V_A of valuations: For a continuous Σ-algebra A, V_A is complete under the pointwise order of mappings; for an inductive Σ-algebra A, V_A is inductive as well. Moreover, the instantiation operation

$$\cdot[.] : W\Sigma(X) \times V_A \to A$$

is continuous.

The **validity** of a $\Sigma(X)$-formula Φ wrt. a valuation $v : X \to A$ (denoted by $v \models \Phi$) is defined inductively as follows:

(1) $v \models t_1 \sqsubseteq t_2$ iff $t_1[v] \sqsubseteq^A t_2[v]$.

(2) Validity of negations, conjunctions and disjunctions of $\Sigma(X)$-formulas is defined as usual.

Φ is **valid** in A (denoted by $A \models \Phi$) if $v \models \Phi$ for all $v \in V_A$. This means that the free variables of $\Sigma(X)$-formulas are implicitly universally quantified.

Note that in $\Sigma(X)$-formulas the metasymbol = denotes the (non-monotonic) **strong equality**, since $\bot_s = \bot_s$ is valid in every Σ-algebra A. It has to be kept well separate from the **weak equality** eq $\in F_{s*s \to bool}$ (for flat s), which denotes a strict and thus monotonic operation with Boolean result; therefore the operator eq can be part of the signature.

Similarly, the logical connectives, $\neg$, $\bigwedge$, $\bigvee$ occurring in $\Sigma(X)$-formulas and the Boolean operators $\neg$, $\wedge$, $\vee$ have to be well distinguished; the difference will always be clear from the context.

In the sequel we frequently use axioms that are (equivalent to) **conditional order relations** of the form $(m,n \geq 0)$

$$\bigwedge_{i=1}^{m} r_{i1} \sqsubseteq r_{i2} \Rightarrow \bigwedge_{j=1}^{n} t_{j1} \sqsubseteq t_{j2}$$

where r_{i1}, r_{i2} resp. t_{j1}, t_{j2} are $\Sigma(X)$-terms of pairwise equal sorts.

2.2.2. Types and Models

A (**continuous algebraic**) **type** $T = (\Sigma, E)$ consists of a signature Σ and a set E of Σ-formulas called its **axioms**. Let **Gen(T)** denote the class of all **premodels** of T, that is, of all term-generated ordered Σ-algebras validating E. Then the semantics of T is the class **Mod(T)** of all **models** of T, that is, of all inductively generated algebras validating E:

$$Mod(T) := \{ A \in Gen(\Sigma)^\infty \mid A \models E \} .$$

2.2.3. Existence and Properties of Premodels

The premodels of a type form a variety with least and greatest element if the form of the axioms is restricted to conditional order relations:

Theorem 5
Let $T = (\Sigma, E)$ be an algebraic type with conditional order relations as axioms. Then the isomorphism classes of premodels, that is the set Gen(T)/$\approx$, form a complete lattice. In particular, there exists an initial premodel. (The terminal premodels are isomorphic to the trivial algebra $\mathbb{1}_\Sigma$.)

In an initial premodel, ground terms are interpreted (as different and) as unordered as

possible; contrarily, in a terminal premodel ground terms are interpreted (as equal and) as ordered as possible:

Theorem 6
Let T be an algebraic type and $\mathbb{K} \subseteq Gen(T)$.
a. A premodel I is initial in $\mathbb{K}$, iff for all sorts s $\in$ S and for all ground terms t_1, t_2 $\in W\Sigma$ of the same sort s
$$I \models t_1 \sqsubseteq t_2 \Leftrightarrow$$
$$\forall A \in \mathbb{K} : A \models t_1 \sqsubseteq t_2 .$$
b. A premodel Z is terminal in $\mathbb{K}$, iff for all sorts s $\in$ S and for all ground terms t_1, t_2 $\in W\Sigma$ of the same sort s
$$Z \models t_1 \sqsubseteq t_2 \Leftrightarrow$$
$$\exists A \in \mathbb{K} : A \models t_1 \sqsubseteq t_2 .$$

In addition to validity we also need the notion of derivability. We say that an order relation $t_1 \sqsubseteq t_2$ is **derivable** in a type T, denoted $T \vdash t_1 \sqsubseteq t_2$, if it can be proved from the axioms of T using reflexivity, transitivity and antisymmetry of the order symbol, monotonicity of the operators, modus ponens, and induction over the structure of terms.

2.2.4. Existence and Properties of Models

We use the ideal completion of premodels to obtain models. This step needs some care, since even in inductively generated Σ-algebras a $\Sigma(X)$-formula may be valid for all finite elements but still be violated by the limit points.

We call a $\Sigma(X)$-formula ϕ **continuous**, if for all A $\in$ Gen(Σ) and all directed sets D $\subseteq V_A$ of valuations of X with finite elements of A we have
$$(\forall v \in D : v \models \phi) \Rightarrow \bigsqcup D \models \phi .$$
A conditional order relation is called **safe** for a type T, if the carrier sets of all result sorts of the terms in the premises are limit-free in all algebras in Gen(T)$^\infty$. Frequently the premises will be formulas over the flat domain of Boolean values and thus safe. Since safe conditional order relations are continuous, we get from Theorem 5:

Theorem 7
Let T be an algebraic type with safe conditional order relations as axioms.
a. The ideal completion of every premodel yields a model and thus Gen(T)$^\infty$ = Mod(T) holds.
b. The subalgebra of finite elements of every model is a premodel.

c. Mod(T)/≈ forms a complete lattice.
d. The ideal completion of an initial (terminal) premodel yields an initial (terminal) model.

2.3. Hierarchic Types

Up to now we have considered algebraic types as units without regarding their internal structure. However, aiming at modularized specifications, one frequently distinguishes "primitive" and "non-primitive" parts of types (compare, for example, [Bauer, Wössner 82], [Wirsing et al. 83]): it is then assumed that the primitive sorts and operations are characterized by another, "smaller" type which is extended by the non-primitive parts. The non-primitive elements are specified by their (extensional) behaviour wrt. the primitive parts. Additional semantic structure is imposed on such hierarchic types by constraints ensuring the soundness of a hierarchy.

Thus, a **hierarchic type** is either a type T or a pair (T, T') where T = (Σ, E) and T' = (Σ', E') are hierarchic types with Σ' $\subseteq$ Σ and E' $\subseteq$ E; in this case T' is called the **primitive type** of T with **primitive sorts** S', **primitive operators** F', and **primitive axioms** E'.

2.3.1. Consistency and Completeness

Let (T, T') be a hierarchic type with T = (Σ, E) and T' = (Σ', E') . T is called **sufficiently complete** wrt. T' (see [Guttag 75]), if for every ground term t $\in$ WΣ of primitive sort there is a primitive ground term p $\in$ WΣ' such that T $\vdash$ t = p . Furthermore T is called **consistent** wrt. T', if for all primitive ground terms p_1, p_2 $\in$ WΣ'

$$T \vdash p_1 \sqsubseteq p_2 \quad \Rightarrow \quad T' \vdash p_1 \sqsubseteq p_2 .$$

Thus in a sufficiently complete type the values of output operations leading into the primitive types are completely determined; in a consistent type no additional order (nor congruence) is imposed on the primitive subtype by the nonprimitive part of the specification.

2.3.2. Existence of Hierarchic Premodels

A premodel A $\in$ Gen(T) of a hierarchic type (T, T') is called **hierarchic**, if its reduct A|Σ' to the primitive signature Σ' is an initial premodel of T'. The notion of a hierarchic model is defined analogously.

HGen(T) and **HMod(T)** denote the classes of all hierarchic premodels and models of T. The semantics of a hierarchic type (T, T') is the class HMod(T) of hierarchic models of T.

The existence of hierarchic premodels widely depends on the form of the axioms.

Theorem 8
Let the hierarchic type (T, T') be sufficiently complete and consistent wrt. its primitive type T'.
a. If all axioms are order relations, then HGen(T)/≈ is a complete lattice; in particular there exists an initial and a terminal hierarchic premodel.
b. If all axioms are conditional order relations, then HGen(T)/≈ is a complete semilattice; in particular there exists an initial hierarchic premodel.
c. If all axioms are conditional order relations where all premises are of primitive sort, then HGen(T)/≈ is a complete lattice; in particular initial and terminal hierarchic premodels exist.

2.3.3. Existence of Hierarchic Models

For the existence of (initial or terminal) hierarchic models, one needs additional conditions.

Theorem 9
Let (T, T') be a hierarchic type with safe conditional order relations as axioms, all premises of which are of primitive sort. If T is sufficiently complete and consistent wrt. T', then HMod(T)/≈ is a complete lattice. In particular, there exist an initial and a terminal hierarchic model.

A (hierarchic) type is called **monomorphic** if all its (hierarchic) models are isomorphic.

2.3.4. Extensionality

Since the primitive part of a hierarchic (pre)model is fixed as the initial (pre)model of the primitive type, we can compare different (pre)models wrt. these primitives: Two hierarchic (pre)models A, B of a hierarchic type (T, T') are called **extensionally equivalent** if for all ground terms t_1, t_2 of T of primitive sort we have

$$A \models t_1 \sqsubseteq t_2 \Leftrightarrow B \models t_1 \sqsubseteq t_2$$

(compare [Broy, Wirsing 83]). In this case the ground terms of primitive sort behave equally in both hierarchic models A and B.

Theorem 10

Let (T, T') be a hierarchic type which is sufficiently complete and consistent wrt. its primitive type T'. Then all (pre)models of T are extensionally equivalent.

2.4. Parametrized Types

In a **parametrized type** (**type scheme**) λ Y.(T, Y), the primitive type Y of T is designated as exchangeable. In a **type instantiation** the type variable Y is replaced by a (primitive) type T' to yield a hierarchic type (T, T'). Following CIP-L (see [Bauer et al. 85]) we do not associate an independent a-priori semantics with parametrized types but explain their instantiations by textual substitution.

3. Sample Specifications of Some Fundamental Domains

In this section we apply the mathematical tools from the previous chapter to specify some fundamental domains by continuous algebraic types. In the notation for writing abstract types we widely follow CIP-L (see [Bauer et al. 85]). In particular, dots indicate the places of operands if we abandon the fully parenthesized function notation in favour of a more readable operator notation.

For every sort **s** in a domain we specify a **definedness predicate** δ_s, that is, a monotonic operator δ_s : s $\rightarrow$ **bool** with the following properties:

$\delta_s(x) \sqsubseteq$ true ;

if $\delta_s(x)$ = true then x $\neq \perp_s$.

In this way, δ_s reflects the positive semi-decidability of definedness: Either an element is defined (result true) or there is no information about its definedness (result $\perp_{\textbf{bool}}$). We say that δ_s is **sharp** if

$\delta_s(x)$ = $\perp_{\textbf{bool}}$ iff x = $\perp_s$.

Since δ_s already needs the Boolean values, we first specify this domain by a type.

3.1. The Boolean Values

The Boolean values consist of three constants $\perp_{\textbf{bool}}$, true, false; as operations we provide the negation $\neg$ and the definedness predicate $\delta_{\textbf{bool}}$.

type BOOL $\equiv$
  sort   **bool** ,
  operators $\perp_{\textbf{bool}}$, true, false : $\rightarrow$ **bool** ,
            $\neg$.   : **bool** $\rightarrow$ **bool** ,
            $\delta_{\textbf{bool}}$: **bool** $\rightarrow$ **bool** ,
  axioms $\perp_{\textbf{bool}} \sqsubseteq$ b ,
          true $\neq$ false ,
          $\neg$ true   = false ,
          $\neg$ false   = true ,
          $\delta_{\textbf{bool}}(\perp_{\textbf{bool}})$ = $\perp_{\textbf{bool}}$,
          $\delta_{\textbf{bool}}$(true) = true ,
          $\delta_{\textbf{bool}}$(false) = true
endoftype

Chains like $\perp_{\textbf{bool}} \sqsubseteq$ true $\sqsubseteq$ false are excluded by the axioms; thus all (pre)models of the type BOOL are flat. The strictness of the negation,

$\neg \perp_{\textbf{bool}} = \perp_{\textbf{bool}}$,

is derivable using monotonicity and term-generatedness. More detailed examples of derivations are given in section 4.2 on sums.

Proposition 1

The type BOOL specifies the flat domain $\mathbb{B}$

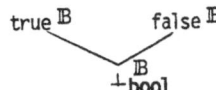

uniquely up to isomorphism.

The type BOOL can consistently be enriched by further Boolean operators:

operators
  $\cdot\wedge\cdot, \cdot\underset{\triangle}{}\cdot, \cdot\wedge\cdot.$: **bool** * **bool** $\rightarrow$ **bool** ,
  $\cdot\vee\cdot, \cdot\nabla\cdot, \cdot\forall\cdot$: **bool** * **bool** $\rightarrow$ **bool** ,
  if.**then**.**else**.**fi** : **bool** * **bool** * **bool** $\rightarrow$ **bool** ,
axioms
  a $\wedge$ b = b $\wedge$ a ,
  true $\wedge$ a = a ,
  false $\wedge$ a = $\neg$ $\delta_{\textbf{bool}}$(a) ,
  a $\triangle$ b = b $\triangle$ a ,
  true $\triangle$ a = a ,
  false $\triangle$ a = false ,
  a $\wedge$ b = (a $\wedge$ b) $\triangle$ a ,
  a $\vee$ b = $\neg$($\neg$a $\wedge$ $\neg$b) ,
  a ∇ b = $\neg$($\neg$a $\triangle$ $\neg$b) ,
  a $\forall$ b = (a $\vee$ b) ∇ a ,
  if a **then** b **else** c **fi** = (a$\wedge$b)∇($\neg$a$\wedge$c)

Here the operators $\wedge$, $\vee$ denote the **natural**

(**minimal**, **strict**) **extensions** of the usual Boolean operations conjunction and disjunction on the two-element set {true $\mathbb{B}$, false $\mathbb{B}$}; the operators $\wedge$, $\vee$ denote the **sequential conjunction** resp. **sequential disjunction**; like the **conditional if.then.else.fi** they are strict in their first arguments only. The operators $\triangle$ resp. $\triangledown$ denote the non-strict, non-sequential (see [Vuillemin 74]) **parallel-and** resp. **parallel-or**. This example shows how the algebraic approach copes well with the specification of strict, non-strict and even non-sequential operations.

From the definition of the conditional we can derive the properties
if $\bot_{\textbf{bool}}$ then a else b fi = $\bot_{\textbf{bool}}$,
if true then a else b fi = a ,
if false then a else b fi = b .
In the sequel we assume for every sort **s** occuring in a type an operator
if.then.else.fi : bool * s * s $\rightarrow$ s
with the analogous axioms.

In hierarchic types, BOOL is used as a primitive type to enforce non-trivial hierarchic (pre)models. Since true and false may not be identified nor put into any order relation, output operations into the sort **bool** can be used for keeping non-primitive elements apart.

3.2.   Enumerated Domains

Next we define for every $n \in \mathbb{N}$ an algebraic type ATOM_n that specifies a finite flat domain by enumerating the $n+1$ elements as constants together with a weak equality predicate eqat.

type ATOM_n $\equiv$
primitive   BOOL ,
sort   **atom** ,
operators $\bot_{\textbf{atom}}$, a_1, ..., a_n : $\rightarrow$ **atom** ,
         eqat : **atom * atom $\rightarrow$ bool** ,
         $\delta_{\textbf{atom}}$: **atom $\rightarrow$ bool** ,
axioms
 $\bot_{\textbf{atom}} \sqsubseteq x$,
 eqat(a_i, a_i) = true $(1 \le i \le n)$,
 eqat(a_i, a_j) = false $(1 \le i \neq j \le n)$,
 eqat(x, $\bot_{\textbf{atom}}$) = eqat($\bot_{\textbf{atom}}$,x) = $\bot_{\textbf{bool}}$,
 $\delta_{\textbf{atom}}(x)$ = eqat(x, x)
endoftype

In particular, ATOM_0 specifies the **singleton domain** $\mathbb{U}$ where **atom** $\mathbb{U}$ consists just of $\bot_{\textbf{atom}}^{\mathbb{U}}$. Furthermore, ATOM_1 defines the two-element domain $\mathbb{O}$ where **atom** $\mathbb{O}$ is a chain. $\mathbb{O}$ arises as the result domain of the definedness predicates.

Proposition 2
For every $n \in \mathbb{N}$ the type ATOM_n is sufficiently complete and consistent wrt. BOOL. All its hierarchic models $\mathbb{A}$ are isomorphic, and the carrier set **atom** $\mathbb{A}$ is the flat domain

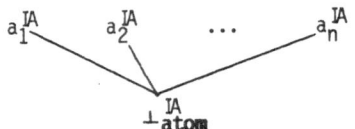

with $n+1$ elements.

3.3.   Natural Numbers

As an example of an infinite flat domain we specify the natural numbers. They are generated from 0 using a strict successor operation succ; pred denotes the predecessor and iszero the test on zero.

type NAT $\equiv$
primitive   BOOL ,
sort   nat ,
operators $\bot_{\textbf{nat}}$, 0   : $\rightarrow$ nat ,
         succ, pred : nat $\rightarrow$ nat ,
         iszero, $\delta_{\textbf{nat}}$: nat $\rightarrow$ bool ,
axioms
 $\bot_{\textbf{nat}} \sqsubseteq n$,
 succ($\bot_{\textbf{nat}}$) = $\bot_{\textbf{nat}}$,
 pred(0) = $\bot_{\textbf{nat}}$,
 pred(succ(n)) = n ,
 iszero(0) = true ,
 iszero(succ(n)) =
    if $\delta_{\textbf{nat}}(n)$ **then** false **else** $\bot_{\textbf{bool}}$ fi ,
 $\delta_{\textbf{nat}}(\bot_{\textbf{nat}})$ = $\bot_{\textbf{bool}}$,
 $\delta_{\textbf{nat}}(0)$ = true ,
 $\delta_{\textbf{nat}}(\text{succ}(n))$ = $\delta_{\textbf{nat}}(n)$
endoftype

The second axiom specifies the strictness of the successor operation; the strictness of pred and iszero are derivable. In hierarchic (pre-) models the ground terms $\bot_{\textbf{nat}}$, 0, and $\text{succ}^m(0)$ $(m \ge 1)$ have to be interpreted pairwise distinct due to the output operation iszero . Furthermore $\text{succ}^m(0)$ and $\text{succ}^n(0)$ $(m \neq n)$ cannot be related by the order. This establishes

Proposition 3

The type NAT is sufficiently complete and consistent wrt. BOOL. All its hierarchic models N are isomorphic, and the carrier set nat^N is the infinite flat domain

$$0^N \diagdown \quad succ(0)^N \quad succ^2(0)^N \quad \cdots$$

$$\perp^N_{nat} = succ^m(\perp_{nat})^N$$

4. Sample Specifications of Some Domain Constructions

In this section we specify various domain constructions by parameterized types. The sorts and operators to be provided by the parameter types are described informally in the enclosing text.

4.1. Products of Domains

For the instantiations of the following type schemes we assume that the n constituent domains $\mathbb{D}_i$ of an n-ary product are specified by monomorphic types D_i, each providing a sort d_i with least element $\perp_i$ and sharp definedness predicate δ_i .

4.1.1. Direct Product

For every $n \in \mathbb{N}$ the **direct (Cartesian) product** of n domains $\mathbb{D}_i$ is specified by the following type scheme $DPRODUCT_n$ where dcomp denotes the construction of tuples and π_i the projection onto the i-th component.

type $DPRODUCT_n \equiv$
parameters $D_1, \ldots, D_n$,
primitives $D_1, \ldots, D_n$, BOOL ,
sort   dprod ,
operators
  $\perp_{dprod}$: $\to$ dprod ,
  dcomp   : $d_1 * \ldots * d_n \to$ dprod $(n \geq 1)$,
  π_i : dprod $\to d_i$ $(1 \leq i \leq n)$,
  δ_{dprod} : dprod $\to$ bool ,
axioms
  $\perp_{dprod} \sqsubseteq p$,

$\pi_i(dcomp(x_1, \ldots, x_n)) = x_i$ $(1 \leq i \leq n)$,
$\delta_{dprod}(\perp_{dprod}) = \perp_{bool}$,
$\delta_{dprod}(dcomp(x_1, \ldots, x_n)) =$
$$\delta_1(x_1) \bigtriangledown \ldots \bigtriangledown \delta_n(x_n) \quad (n \geq 1)$$
endoftype

From these axioms the strictness of the projections,

$\pi_i(\perp_{dprod}) = \perp_i$ $(1 \leq i \leq n)$,

can be derived. Note that, using structural induction, also recombination property

$\delta_{dprod}(p) = true \Rightarrow$
$$dcomp(\pi_1(p), \ldots, \pi_n(p)) = p \quad (n \geq 1)$$

can be derived. If the restriction to term-generated algebras is abandoned in favour of a first order theory, then an axiom of this kind must explicitly be included into every particular axiomatization (compare [Plotkin 81]).

Proposition 4

For every $n \in \mathbb{N}$ the type $DPRODUCT_n$ is sufficiently complete and consistent wrt. BOOL and $D_1, \ldots, D_n$. For $n \geq 1$ it has exactly the following two isomorphism classes of hierarchic models:

a. An initial hierarchic model I is the **separated direct product**

$dprod^I := d_1^I \times \ldots \times d_n^I \cup \{\perp_{dprod}\}$
with

$$dcomp(\perp_1, \ldots, \perp_n)^I$$

$$\perp^I_{dprod} \cdot$$

b. A terminal hierarchic model Z is the **coalesced direct product**

$dprod^Z := d_1^Z \times \ldots \times d_n^Z$
with

$$dcomp(\perp_1, \ldots, \perp_n)^Z = \perp^Z_{dprod} \cdot$$

Since $dcomp(\perp_1, \ldots, \perp_n)$ and $\perp_{dprod}$ cannot be distinguished by δ_{dprod} and the π_i, they are identified in the terminal hierarchic model Z. This model can be specified up to isomorphism by adding the axiom
$dcomp(\perp_1, \ldots, \perp_n) = \perp_{dprod}$ $(n \geq 1)$,
the initial hierarchic model by changing the second axiom of the definedness predicate into
$\delta_{dprod}(dcomp(x_1, \ldots, x_n)) = true$ $(n \geq 1)$.

For n = 1 the terminal hierarchic model Z of DPRODUCT_1 is order-isomorphic to $\mathbb{D}_1$, whereas the initial hierarchic model I originates from $\mathbb{D}_1$ by adjoining a new bottom-element (**lifting** of $\mathbb{D}_1$ to $\mathbb{D}_1^{\perp}$):

For n = 0, DPRODUCT_0 monomorphically specifies the singleton domain $\mathbb{U}$ with $\textbf{dprod}^{\mathbb{U}} = \{\perp^{\mathbb{U}}_{\textbf{dprod}}\}$. Of course, by construction the finite elements of the direct product, different from $\perp_{\textbf{dprod}}$, are the products of the finite elements of the constituent domains. Furthermore, suprema of nontrivial directed sets are determined coordinatewise, that is, in every hierarchic model A we have for all nontrivial directed sets $D \subseteq \text{dprod}^A$

$$\bigsqcup D = \text{dcomp}^A(\bigsqcup\nolimits_1 \pi_1^A(D), \ldots, \bigsqcup\nolimits_n \pi_n^A(D)).$$

This **internal axiomatization** in terms of elements and operations refers to the constituent domains; it can be shown to be equivalent to an **external axiomatization** using continuous functions from an external trial domain (see, for example, [Plotkin 81]).

The direct product of n domains is used, for example, in the call-by-name semantics for n-ary routines.

4.1.2. Smash Product

For a call-by-value semantics of n-ary routines, however, the **smash** (**strict**) **product** is needed.

type SPRODUCT_n ≡
parameters $D_1, \ldots D_n$,
primitives $D_1, \ldots, D_n$, BOOL ,
sort sprod ,
operators
$\perp_{\textbf{sprod}}$: $\rightarrow$ **sprod** ,
scomp : $d_1 * \ldots * d_n \rightarrow$ **sprod** $(n \geq 1)$,
π_i : **sprod** $\rightarrow d_i$ $(1 \leq i \leq n)$,
$\delta_{\textbf{sprod}}$: **sprod** $\rightarrow$ **bool** ,
axioms
$\perp_{\textbf{sprod}} \subseteq p$,
$\delta_1(x_1) \wedge \ldots \wedge \delta_n(x_n) = \text{true} \Rightarrow$
$\quad \pi_i(\text{scomp}(x_1, \ldots, x_n)) = x_i$ $(1 \leq i \leq n)$,
$\delta_1(x_1) \wedge \ldots \wedge \delta_n(x_n) = \perp_{\textbf{bool}} \Rightarrow$
$\quad \pi_i(\text{scomp}(x_1, \ldots, x_n)) = \perp_i$ $(1 \leq i \leq n)$,
$\delta_{\textbf{sprod}}(\perp_{\textbf{sprod}}) = \perp_{\textbf{bool}}$,
$\delta_{\textbf{sprod}}(\text{scomp}(x_1, \ldots, x_n)) =$
$\quad \delta_1(x_1) \wedge \ldots \wedge \delta_n(x_n)$ $(n \geq 1)$
endoftype

Again, the strictness of the projections,
$$\pi_i(\perp_{\textbf{sprod}}) = \perp_i \qquad (1 \leq i \leq n) ,$$
is derivable, and, by structural induction, we obtain
$$\delta_{\textbf{sprod}}(p) = \text{true} \Rightarrow$$
$$\text{scomp}(\pi_1(p), \ldots, \pi_n(p)) = p \qquad (n \geq 1) .$$

Proposition 5

For every n ∈ $\mathbb{N}$ the type SPRODUCT_n is sufficiently complete and consistent wrt. BOOL and $D_1, \ldots, D_n$. Now let $n \geq 1$.

a. An initial hierarchic model I is the **separated smash product** which has the same carrier set as the initial hierarchic model of DPRODUCT_n , only the output operations π_i^I and $\delta_{\textbf{sprod}}^{I}$ behave differently.

b. A terminal hierarchic model Z is the **coalesced smash product** with
$$\text{sprod}^Z :=$$
$$(d_1^Z \backslash \{\perp_1^Z\}) \times \ldots \times (d_n^Z \backslash \{\perp_n^Z\}) \cup \{\perp_{\textbf{sprod}}\}$$
where all tuples containing at least one $\perp_i$ are identified with $\perp_{\textbf{sprod}}$.

The terminal hierarchic model of SPRODUCT_n can be uniquely specified by adding the **strictness axioms** $(1 \leq i \leq n)$
$$\text{scomp}(x_1, \ldots, x_{i-1}, \perp_i, x_{i+1}, \ldots, x_n) = \perp_{\textbf{sprod}}$$
to the type. Note that in hierarchic models A with $I \ll A \ll Z$ a certain subset of tuples containing at least one $\perp_i$ is identified.

Again, the initial hierarchic model I of SPRODUCT_1 defines the lifting $\mathbb{D}_1^{\perp}$ of $\mathbb{D}_1$, the terminal hierarchic model Z is order-isomorphic to $\mathbb{D}_1$. Also, SPRODUCT_0 defines the singleton domain $\mathbb{U}$.

4.2. Sums of Domains

The **direct sum** of n domains $\mathbb{D}_i$ is specified by the type SUM_n below. There in_i denotes the **injection**, π_i the **projection** and is_i the **discrimination** for the i-th summand $(1 \leq i \leq n)$.

type SUM_n ≡
parameters $D_1, \ldots, D_n$,
primitives $D_1, \ldots, D_n$, BOOL ,
sort sum ,

operators $+_{sum}$: $\rightarrow$ sum ,

$\quad\quad in_i$: $d_i \rightarrow$ sum ,

$\quad\quad is_i$: sum $\rightarrow$ bool

$\quad\quad \pi_i$: sum $\rightarrow d_i$, $\quad\Big\}$ $(1 \le i \le n)$,

$\quad\quad \delta_{sum}$: sum $\rightarrow$ bool ,

axioms

$\perp_{sum} \sqsubseteq s$,

$$is_i(in_k(x_k)) = \begin{cases} \delta_k(x_k) & (i=k) \\ \\ \neg\delta_k(x_k) & (i \ne k) \end{cases} \quad (1 \le i,k \le n)$$

$$\pi_i(in_k(x_k)) = \begin{cases} x_i & (i=k) \\ \\ \perp_i & (i \ne k) \end{cases}$$

$\delta_{sum}(\perp_{sum}) = \perp_{bool}$,

$\delta_{sum}(in_i(x_i)) = \delta_i(x_i)$ $(1 \le i \le n)$

endoftype

Again, the strictness properties

$is_i(\perp_{sum}) = \perp_{bool}$ $(1 \le i \le n)$,

$\pi_i(\perp_{sum}) = \perp_i$ $(1 \le i \le n)$

are derivable from the axioms, and, by structural induction, we obtain

$is_i(s) = true \Rightarrow s = in_i(\pi_i(s))$ $(1 \le i \le n)$.

Proposition 6

For every $n \in \mathbb{N}$ the type SUM_n is sufficiently complete and consistent wrt. BOOL and $D_1, \ldots, D_n$. Now let $n \ge 1$.

a. An initial hierarchic model I is the **separated direct sum** with

$sum^I :=$

$(d_1^I \times \{1\}) \cup \ldots \cup (d_n^I \times \{n\}) \cup \{+_{sum}\}$

where the order is inherited from the summands and the bottom-elements are kept separate:

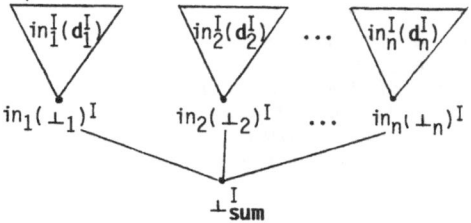

b. A terminal hierarchic model Z is the **coalesced (amalgamated) direct sum**

$sum^Z := ((d_1^Z \backslash \{+_1^Z\}) \times \{1\}) \cup \ldots$

$\quad\quad \cup ((d_n^Z \backslash \{+_n^Z\}) \times \{n\}) \cup \{+_{sum}\}$

where the order is also inherited from the summands, but the bottom-elements are

identified:

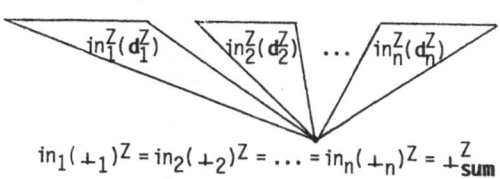

$in_1(\perp_1)^Z = in_2(\perp_2)^Z = \ldots = in_n(\perp_n)^Z = \perp_{sum}^Z$

Thus the separated and coalesced direct sums only differ in whether the summands share the least informative element or not. The separated direct sum being the initial hierarchic model can be specified monomorphically by modifying the axioms for the discriminations is_i in the following way:

$$is_i(in_k(x_k)) = \begin{cases} true & if \ i=k \\ \\ false & if \ i \ne k \end{cases} \quad (1 \le i,k \le n)$$

Then the terms $in_i(x_i)$ and $in_k(x_k)$ $(i \ne k)$ cannot be identified in hierarchic models, since by applying is_i this would result in the contradiction true = false , nor can they be put in an order relation, since this would imply true $\sqsubseteq$ false or false $\sqsubseteq$ true . This shows the monomorphicity of the modified specification.

Conversely, the terminal hierarchic model Z is distinguished by adding the strictness axioms

$in_i(\perp_i) = \perp_{sum}$ $(1 \le i \le n)$

for the injections.

Note that in hierarchic models A of SUM_n with $I \ll A \ll Z$ arbitrary (congruences and) order relations may hold in sum^A between the elements $in_i(\perp_i)^A$: they may be partially identified and be arranged in arbitrary order (**semi-separated sums**). However, the injections of the defined elements of the summands $\mathbb{D}_i$ must not be identified nor related by the order: Assume for example

$in_i(x_i)^A \sqsubseteq in_k(x_k)^A$ for $i \ne k$

and

$\delta_i(x_i)^A = \delta_k(x_k)^A = true^A$.

By monotonicity of is_i^A and definition of δ_{sum}^A we get

$true^A = \delta_i(x_i)^A = is_i(in_i(x_i))^A$

$\sqsubseteq^A is_i(in_k(x_k))^A = \neg\delta_k(x_k)^A = false^A$,

a contradiction in an hierarchic model A.

In every hierarchic model A of SUM_n any

directed set lies - apart from $\perp_{\text{sum}}^A$ - completely within one component $\text{in}_i^A(d_i^A)$.

In particular, SUM_1 defines either the lifting $\mathbb{D}_1^{\perp}$ of $\mathbb{D}_1$ or $\mathbb{D}_1$ itself, and SUM_0 again specifies the singleton domain $\mathbb{U}$. Finally note that the carrier set sum^I of the initial hierarchic model I of $\text{SUM}_2(\mathbb{U},\mathbb{U})$ is order-isomorphic to $\text{bool}^{\mathbb{B}}$; the same holds for carrier set sum^Z of the terminal hierarchic model Z of $\text{SUM}_2(\mathbb{D}, \mathbb{D})$.

4.3. Streams

As an example of a non-flat domain with limit points we specify streams of data atoms. Streams are a basic notion in the description of loosely coupled processes, for example, in data flow programming. For the domain $\mathbb{D}$ of data objects we assume a monomorphic type D defining a sort d together with a sharp definedness predicate δ_d.

4.3.1. Non-Strict Streams

The type STREAM comprises finite and infinite sequences of the elements of a sort d which are built from the empty stream empty and the undefined stream $\perp_{\text{stream}}$ using an operation for appending d-elements to the stream. The operators first and rest decompose a stream into its first element and the remaining stream.

```
type STREAM ≡
  parameter   D ,
  primitives  D, BOOL ,
  sort        stream ,
  operators   ⊥stream, empty :  → stream ,
              append : d * stream → stream ,
              first  : stream → d ,
              rest   : stream → stream ,
              δstream : stream → bool ,
  axioms
    ⊥stream ⊑ s ,
    first(empty) = ⊥d ,
    first(append(d, s)) = d ,
    rest(empty) = ⊥stream ,
    rest(append(d, s)) = s ,
    δstream(empty) = ⊥bool ,
    δstream(append(d, s)) = δd(d) ▽ δstream(s)
endoftype
```

The strictness properties
$$\text{first}(\perp_{\text{stream}}) = \perp_d ,$$
$$\text{rest}(\perp_{\text{stream}}) = \perp_{\text{stream}} ,$$
$$\delta_{\text{stream}}(\perp_{\text{stream}}) = \perp_{\text{bool}} ,$$
are derivable by monotonicity; by structural induction we get the recombination property
$$\delta_{\text{stream}}(s) = \text{true} \Rightarrow$$
$$\text{append}(\text{first}(s), \text{rest}(s)) = s .$$

Proposition 7

The type STREAM is sufficiently complete and consistent wrt. D and BOOL.

a. In an initial hierarchic model I the carrier set
$$\text{stream}^I := (d^I)^\star \cup ((d^I)^\star \times \{\perp_{\text{stream}}\})$$
$$\cup (d^I)^\infty$$
is composed of finite streams $(d^I)^\star$, partial streams $(d^I)^\star \times \{\perp_{\text{stream}}\}$ ending with $\perp_{\text{stream}}$, and infinite streams $(d^I)^\infty$ (that is, mappings from $\mathbb{N}$ to d^I). It is ordered by $s \sqsubseteq_{\text{stream}}^I t$ iff

(1) s, t are finite streams with $|s| = |t|$ and $s_i \sqsubseteq_d^I t_i$ for $1 \le i \le |s|$;

(2) $s = (s', \perp_{\text{stream}})$ is a partial stream with $s' \& s'' = t$ for some $s'' \in \text{stream}^I$;

(3) s, t are infinite streams with $s_i \sqsubseteq_d^I t_i$ for all $i \in \mathbb{N}$.

b. A terminal hierarchic model Z has the carrier set
$$\text{stream}^Z :=$$
$$\{ s \in (d^Z)^\star \cup (d^Z)^\infty \mid$$
$$\exists i \in \mathbb{N}: s_i = \perp_d^Z \Rightarrow \exists j > i: s_j \neq \perp_d^Z \}$$
with the order $s \sqsubseteq_{\text{stream}}^Z t$ iff $|s| \le |t|$ and $s_i \sqsubseteq_d^Z t_i$ for $1 \le i \le |s|$.

Thus, in an initial model a stream s approximates a stream t iff s and t are both finite streams of the same length or both infinite streams and approximation is componentwise, or s is a partial stream which, after dropping $\perp_{\text{stream}}$ at the end, is a componentwise less-defined prefix of t .

In the terminal hierarchic model Z two streams s, t are identified, iff for all $n \in \mathbb{N}$ $\text{first}(\text{rest}^n(s))^Z = \text{first}(\text{rest}^n(t))^Z$. In particular all streams s with $\delta_{\text{stream}}(s) = \perp_{\text{bool}}$ are identified, especially we have
$$\text{empty}^Z = \perp_{\text{stream}}^Z = \text{append}^Z(\perp_d^Z, \perp_{\text{stream}}^Z) .$$

As a consequence, in Z every finite stream is partial.

The initial and the terminal hierarchic models are extensionally equivalent. The terminal hierarchic model can be uniquely specified by adding the strictness constraints

$$\text{empty} = \perp_{\textbf{stream}} \text{,}$$

$$\text{append}(\perp_{\textbf{d}}, \perp_{\textbf{stream}}) = \perp_{\textbf{stream}} \text{.}$$

For an equational characterization of the initial hierarchic model one has to enrich the signature of STREAM by further output operations, for example by a length operation.

The streams specified above are "lazy" in that their elements need not be known ("evaluated") when they are adjoined to the sequence.

4.3.2. Semi-Strict Streams

Often a more specific stream domain STREAM1 is used which orginates from STREAM by identifying, as in the terminal hierarchic model of STREAM, the empty and the undefined streams and by additionally imposing left-strictness on the operation append.

```
type STREAM1 ≡
parameter   D ,
primitives  D, BOOL ,
sort        stream ,
operators   empty  : → stream ,
            append : d * stream → stream ,
            first  : stream → d ,
            rest   : stream → stream ,
            δ_stream : stream → bool ,
axioms
  empty ⊑ s ,
  append(⊥_d, s) = empty ,
  first(empty) = ⊥_d ,
  first(append(d, s)) = d ,
  rest(empty) = empty ,
  δ_d(d) = true ⟹ rest(append(d, s)) = s ,
  δ_stream(append(d, s)) = δ_d(d)
endoftype
```

Again the strictness property

$$\delta_{\textbf{stream}}(\text{empty}) = \perp_{\textbf{bool}}$$

is derivable. Furthermore we obtain by structural induction the recombination property
append(first(s), rest(s)) = s .

Proposition 8

The type STREAM1 is sufficiently complete and consistent wrt. D and BOOL. All its hierarchic models are isomorphic to the stream domain $\mathbb{IS}$ of finite and infinite sequences

$$\text{stream}^{\mathbb{IS}} := (d^{\mathbb{IS}} \backslash \{\perp_{\textbf{d}}^{\mathbb{IS}}\})^* \cup (d^{\mathbb{IS}} \backslash \{\perp_{\textbf{d}}^{\mathbb{IS}}\}) \infty$$

with the order $s \sqsubseteq_{\textbf{stream}}^{\mathbb{IS}} t$ iff

$$|s| \leq |t| \text{ and } s_i \sqsubseteq_{\textbf{d}}^{\mathbb{IS}} t_i \text{ for } 1 \leq i \leq |s| \text{ .}$$

Thus a stream s approximates a stream t iff s is a componentwise less-defined prefix of t .

4.3.3. Strict Streams

If one requires that the operation append is strict in both arguments then the stream domain collapses to the flat domain of (finite) sequences which has no limit points. In this border-line case the domain corresponds to a traditional data structure. This shows how error algebras can be retrieved as a particular case of this approach. Of course, this limit-free data structure of finite sequences can also be treated adequately in the setting of partial algebras exploiting the implicit error propagation of partial operations.

4.3.4. Comparison with the Standard Approach to Abstract Data Types

Since streams are our first domain with limit points, a comparison with the standard approach to abstract types seems appropriate. At first glance, the axioms of STREAM or STREAM1 just look like those for (finite!) stacks; however, in the framework of continuous types, they can be extended to infinite streams via continuity.

This essential difference becomes more obvious if we solve a recursion equation in a model B of STREAM1(NAT). For example, take the recursion equation

s = append^B(1, s)

for the infinite constant stream <1,1,1,...> . Assuming the standard semantics for abstract types, B would contain only finite streams and thus have no solution of this equation. In order to get a solution, the type STREAM1 would have to be enriched by an additional constant symbol $\overline{I}$ with the axiom

$\overline{I}$ = append(1, $\overline{I}$) .

From this, one could derive the properties

first($\overline{I}$) = 1   and   rest($\overline{I}$) = $\overline{I}$.

However, in the framework of continuous types, the infinite sequence <1,1,1,...> arises as the least solution of the fixpoint equation above, as the following shows:

In a hierarchic premodel A of STREAM1 the partial streams

<>, <1>, <1,1>, <1,1,1>, ...

are ordered by the prefix relation (left side of the figure):

$$1^\infty = \langle 1,1,1,\ldots\rangle$$

$$
\begin{array}{ccc}
\vdots & & \vdots \\
\langle 1,1,1\rangle & & \langle 1,1,1\rangle \\
| & & | \\
\langle 1,1\rangle & & \langle 1,1\rangle \\
| & & | \\
\langle 1\rangle & & \langle 1\rangle \\
| & & | \\
\langle\rangle & & \langle\rangle
\end{array}
$$

By ideal completion we get the hierarchic model $B = A^\infty$ where the limit point 1^∞ is added (right side of the figure above).

4.4. Environments

As an example for one of the auxiliary domains used in denotational semantics we specify environments, that is, **finite mappings (tables)** that associate values with identifiers. For the identifiers we assume a domain IID - isomorphic to the flat domain N of natural numbers - specified by a monomorphic type ID providing a sort **id**, a weak equality predicate eqid and a sharp definedness predicate δ_{id} . For the entries we assume a domain ID defined by a monomorphic type D providing a sort **d** and a definedness predicate δ_d.

In the type ENV below environments are constructed from the undefined environment $\perp_{env}$ using a ternary update operation $.[.\leftarrow.]$. The operator $.[.]$ yields the value associated with an identifier if there is one; otherwise it yields $\perp_d$ as a "default" value.

```
type ENV ≡
  parameter   D ,
  primitives  D, ID, BOOL ,
  sort        env ,
  operators   ⊥env   :  → env ,
              .[.←.] : env * id * d → env ,
              .[.]   : env * id → d ,
  axioms
    ⊥env ⊑ e ,
    ⊥env[j] = ⊥d ,
    eqid(i,j) = true  ⟹ e[i ← d][j] = d ,
    eqid(i,j) = false ⟹ e[i ← d][j] = e[j] ,
    eqid(i,j) = ⊥bool ⟹ e[i ← d][j] = ⊥d
endoftype
```

Proposition 9
The type ENV is sufficiently complete and consistent wrt. BOOL, ID and D.
a. An initial hierarchic model I represents environments with "history"

$$\text{env}^I := (\text{id}^I \times d^I)^* \ \cup\ (\text{id}^I \times d^I)^\infty$$

where $e_1 \sqsubseteq^I_{env} e_2$ iff e_1 is a componentwise less-defined suffix of e_2 .

b. A terminal hierarchic model Z represents environments without "history" where

$$\text{env}^Z := \{f: \text{id}^Z \to d^Z \mid f(\perp^Z_{id}) = \perp^Z_d\}$$

with the pointwise order of functions.

It is possible to enrich ENV by a (lengthy) specification of a definedness predicate that is sharp for the terminal model: it yields true only for environments with at least one defined entry.

Note that env^Z is the space of all strict (and thus continuous) functions from identifiers to data values. The terminal hierarchic models can be uniquely specified by forgetting multiple entries for the same identifier,

$$e[i \leftarrow d_1][i \leftarrow d_2] = e[i \leftarrow d_2] ,$$

by forgetting the order of entries for different defined identifiers,

$$\text{eqid}(i,j) = \text{false} \ \Rightarrow$$
$$e[i \leftarrow d_1][j \leftarrow d_2] = e[j \leftarrow d_2][i \leftarrow d_1] ,$$

and by setting environments that are updated with undefined identifiers equal to the undefined environment,

$$e[\perp_{id} \leftarrow d] = \perp_{env} .$$

Since the update operation is non-strict in its environment argument, **env** always is a non-flat domain. In particular, in every model E the carrier set env^E contains chains like

$$
\begin{array}{c}
d^\infty{}^E \\
\vdots \\
\perp_{env}[i_2 \leftarrow d][i_1 \leftarrow d]^E \\
| \\
\perp_{env}[i_1 \leftarrow d]^E \\
| \\
\perp_{env}{}^E
\end{array}
$$

Therefore recursion equations over environments have non-trivial least solutions. For example, the limit point $d^\infty{}^E$ is obtained as the least solution of the fixpoint equation

$$e = \text{updateall}^E(e, d)$$

where the functions

$$\text{updateall}^E : \text{env}^E \times d^E \to \text{env}^E ,$$
$$\text{uda}^E \qquad : \text{env}^E \times d^E \times \text{id}^E \to \text{env}^E ,$$

are given by

$$\text{updateall}^E(e, d) = \text{uda}^E(e,d,\text{firstid}^E) ,$$
$$\text{uda}^E(e, d, i) = \text{uda}^E(e,d,\text{nextid}^E(i))[i\leftarrow d]$$

Thus $d^\infty{}^E$ is an environment associating d with all defined identifiers.

4.5. Power Domains

Power domains are used in the description of nondeterministic processes; they serve to model the sets of possible values of such processes. For the domain $\mathbb{D}$ of objects we assume a monomorphic type D providing a sort **d** with definedness predicate δ_d.

4.5.1. The Power Domain for Erratic Nondeterminism

In the type POW below sets are generated from the undefined set $\perp_{set}$ using the operation {.} of forming a singleton set and the set union .U. . We exclude the empty set of values, since even a process without "proper" possible semantic values still has the pseudo-value $\perp_d$.

type POW $\equiv$
  parameter   D ,
  primitives D, BOOL ,
  sort   set ,
  operators $\perp_{set}$: $\to$ set ,
              {.}   : **d** $\to$ set ,
              .U. : set * set $\to$ set ,
              δ_{set} : set $\to$ **bool** ,
  axioms $\perp_{set} \sqsubseteq$ s ,
             s U t = t U s ,
             (r U s) U t = r U (s U t) ,
             s U s = s ,
             $\{\perp_d\} = \perp_{set}$,
             $\delta_{set}(\perp_{set}) = \perp_{bool}$,
             $\delta_{set}(\{x\}) = \delta_d(x)$,
             $\delta_{set}(s \; U \; t) = \delta_{set}(s) \; \nabla \; \delta_{set}(t)$
endoftype

Proposition 10

The carrier set $\mathbf{set}^{IE}$ of an initial hierarchic model IE of POW is the power domain of $\mathbb{D}$ first described in [Plotkin 76].

For the proof see [Winskel 83].

The domain IE models the nondeterminism in which branches of a choice may be taken "erratically", that is, indepedently of each other. Since there are almost no output operations for distinguishing sets, the terminal hierarchic model Z of POW(D) has as its carrier set again the set $\mathbb{D}$ whenever there is a d $\in \mathbb{D}$ with $\delta_d(d)$ = true : all ground terms s with $\delta_{set}(s)$ = true are identified to a point a; all ground terms t with $\delta_{set}(t)$ =

$\perp_{bool}$ are identified with $\perp_{set}^Z$; finally, by the first axiom of POW we get $\perp_{set}^Z \sqsubseteq$ a, whereas δ_{set} forces $\perp_{set}^Z \neq$ a.

It appears that for non-flat domains $\mathbb{D}$ the addition of "natural" output operations like the membership relation .$\in$. or the subset relation .$\sqsubseteq$. is impossible, because they would either be non-monotonic or not reflect the intuitive understanding. For example, the axiom x $\in$ s = true would imply y $\in$ s = true for all y with x $\sqsubseteq$ y if the element relation $\in$ is monotonic.

As is observed in [Hennessy, Plotkin 79], the two other "classical" power domains can be obtained from the erratic one by imposing additional axioms, that is, by passing to homomorphic images of the initial hierarchic model.

4.5.2. The Power Domain for Angelic Nondeterminism

The "angelic" power domain models a choice that always takes the branch with the larger information contents. In terms of operational semantics this can be rephrased that nontermination is avoided whenever possible.

For this purpose we enrich the type POW by the axiom
  s $\sqsubseteq$ s U t
to a type ANGPOW.

Proposition 11

An initial hierarchic model IA of the type ANGPOW constitutes the power domain for angelic nondeterminism.

To see that this actually models the choice described above, take two elements x, y $\in \mathbf{d}^{IA}$ with x $\sqsubseteq$ y. By monotonicity of the operations {.} and .U. we have
  {x} U {y} $\sqsubseteq$ {y} U {y} = {y} .
By the additional axiom we also get
  {y} $\sqsubseteq$ {y} U {x}
and hence, by antisymmetry,
  {x} U {y} = {y} ,
which means that the smaller elements are "swallowed" by the larger ones.

4.5.3. The Power Domain for Demonic Nondeterminism

Dually the "demonic" power domain is the initial model ID of the type that results from POW by adding the axiom
  s U t $\sqsubseteq$ s .

It models a choice that always takes the branch with the smaller information contents. Operationally, a program will diverge if there is a change for diverging. In this case, the third axiom for the definedness predicate has to be adjusted as well, viz. to

$$\delta_{set}(s \cup t) = \delta_{set}(s) \wedge \delta_{set}(t) \ .$$

Particularly these examples of different power domains shows that the algebraic specification technique provides a probably easier way of handling domains than explicit domain constructions.

5. Concluding Remarks

The attempt to specify domains algebraically is motivated by the hope to achieve comprehensible formal descriptions through simple axiomatizations. Moreover, this approach also tries to relate denotational and algebraic semantics within the framework of abstract types.

This proceeding is also advantageous for bridging the gap to operational semantics: After suitably restricting the class of the axioms, the equations can be interpreted as left-to-right rewrite rules and endowed with a safe strategy; then the resulting interpreter is by construction correct wrt. the denotational semantics (see [Möller 83], [Dosch, Möller 84]).

The approach tries to combine in a balanced way axiomatization and constructiveness: The essential properties of a domain are used to characterize the operations axiomatically. However, for the semantic elements we do not assume a universe of abstract mathematical objects, but we construct the semantic values: Finite elements are term-generated by the operations of the domain; infinite elements are added as limit points. This proceeding ensures that all domains specified are countably algebraic.

However, such a constructive specification of domains also faces a variety of problems: It is not always obvious what are the right operations to generate the semantic values, in particular for the space of continuous functions. Also, in general the constructiveness conflicts with full abstraction (for another approach compare [Tarlecki, Wirsing 85]).

The next step in utilizing the algebraic approach to domain description will be to carry over the "recursive" type instantiations of CIP-L (see [Bauer et al. 85]) to the continuous case. Experiments have shown that this leads to a simple semantics for recursive domain equations (compare, for example, [Smyth, Plotkin 82], [Ehrich, Lipeck 83]) that replaces the inverse limit construction (or equivalents thereof) by the layers of generation in a term-generated algebra. Since, however, the details still need to be worked out, we have not tried to give an account of this approach in the present paper.

Finally we want to hint at connections to Mosses' idea of using "abstract semantic algebras" [Mosses 83] as standard building blocks for language definitions. Together with a suitable notion of implementations of types by other types, specifications of the kind discussed here can be used for the concretization of the abstract semantic algebras, thus allowing a stepwise and modular approach to the semantic specification of programming languages.

Acknowledgements

We gratefully acknowledge stimulating discussions with Prof. F.L. Bauer. Thanks go to F. Nickl and P. Pepper for valuable comments on drafts of this paper.

Literature

[Bauer, Wössner 82]
Bauer, F.L., Wössner, H.: Algorithmic Language and Program Development. Berlin: Springer 1982

[Bauer et al. 85]
Bauer, F.L., Berghammer, R., Broy, M., Dosch, W., Gnatz, R., Geiselbrechtinger, F., Hangel, E., Hesse, W., Krieg-Brückner, B., Laut, A., Matzner, T., Möller, B., Nickl, F., Partsch, H., Pepper, P., Samelson, K., Wirsing, M., Wössner, H.: The Munich Project CIP. Volume I: The Wide Spectrum Language CIP-L. Lecture Notes in Computer Science 183. Berlin: Springer 1985

[Broy, Wirsing 83]
Broy, M., Wirsing, M.: Algebraic Definition of a Functional Programming Language and its Semantic Models. R.A.I.R.O. Informatique théorique 17:2, 137-161 (1983)

[Courcelle, Nivat 76]
Courcelle, B., Nivat, M.: Algebraic Families of Interpretations. 17th Annual IEEE Symposium on Foundations of Computer Science, 1976, 137-146

[Dosch, Möller 84]
Dosch, W., Möller, B.: Busy and Lazy FP with

Infinite Objects. Proceedings 1984 ACM Symposium on LISP and Functional Programming, Austin, Texas, August, 5-8, 1984, 282-292

[Dybjer 84]
Dybjer, P.: Domain Algebras. In: J. Paredaens (ed.): Automata, Languages and Programming, 11th Colloquium, Antwerp, Belgium, July 16-20, 1984. Lecture Notes in Computer Science 172. Berlin: Springer 1984, 138-150

[Ehrich, Lipeck 83]
Ehrich, H.D., Lipeck, U.: Algebraic Domain Equations. Theoretical Computer Science 27, 167-196 (1983)

[Goguen et al. 77]
Goguen, J.A., Thatcher, J.W., Wagner, E.G., Wright, J.B.: Initial Algebra Semantics and Continuous Algebras. Journal ACM 24, 68-95 (1977)

[Goguen et al. 78]
Goguen, J.A., Thatcher, J.W., Wagner, E.G.: An Initial Algebra Approach to the Specification, Correctness, and Implementation of Abstract Data Types. In: Yeh, R.T. (ed.): Current Trends in Programming Methodology. Vol. 3: Data Structuring. Englewood Cliffs, N.J.: Prentice Hall 1978, 80-149

[Guessarian 81]
Guessarian, I.: Algebraic Semantics. Lecture Notes in Computer Science 99. Berlin: Springer 1981

[Guttag 75]
Guttag, J.V.: The Specification and Application to Programming of Abstract Data Types. Ph. D. Thesis, University of Toronto, Department of Computer Science, Report CSRG-59, 1975

[Hennessy, Plotkin 1979]
Hennessy, M., Plotkin, G.: Full Abstraction for a Simple Parallel Programming Language. Proc. Mathematical Foundations of Computer Science 1979. Lecture Notes in Computer Science 74. Berlin: Springer 1979, 108-120

[Lehmann, Smyth 81]
Lehmann, D.J., Smyth, M.B.: Algebraic Specification of Data Types: A Synthetic Approach. Math. Systems Theory 14, 97-139 (1981)

[Möller 83]
Möller, B.: An Algebraic Semantics for Busy (Data-driven) and Lazy (Demand-driven) Evaluation and its Application to a Functional Language. In: Diaz, J. (ed.): Automata, Languages and Programming, 10th Colloquium, Barcelona, Spain, July 18-22, 1983. Lecture Notes in Computer Science 154. Berlin: Springer 1983, 513-526

[Möller 85]
Möller, B.: On the Algebraic Specification of Infinite Objects - Ordered and Continuous

Models of Algebraic Types. Acta Informatica (to appear)

[Mosses 83]
Mosses, P.D.: Abstract Semantic Algebras! In: Bjørner, D. (ed.): Formal Description of Programming Concepts - II. Proc. IFIP TC2 Working Conference, Garmisch-Partenkirchen, June 1-4, 1982. Amsterdam: North-Holland 1983, 45-70

[Plotkin 76]
Plotkin, G.D.: A Powerdomain Construction. SIAM Journal on Computing 5:3, 452-487 (1976)

[Plotkin 81]
Plotkin, G.D.: Algebraic Domains. Lecture Notes, Department of Computer Science, University of Edinburgh, 1981

[Scott 70]
Scott, D.S.: Outline of a Mathematical Theory of Computation. Proc. 4th Annual Princeton Conference on Information Sciences and Systems, 1970, 169-176. Also: Technical Monograph PRG-2, Oxford University, Computing Laboratory, Programming Research Group, 1970

[Scott 82]
Scott, D.S.: Domains for Denotational Semantics. In: Nielsen, M., Schmidt, E.M. (eds.): Automata, Languages and Programming, 10th Colloquium, Aarhus, Denmark, July 12-17, 1982. Lecture Notes in Computer Science 140. Berlin: Springer 1982, 577-613

[Smyth, Plotkin 82]
Smyth, M.B., Plotkin, G.D.: The Category-Theoretic Solution of Recursive Domain Equations. SIAM Journal on Computing 11:4, 761-783 (1982)

[Tarlecki, Wirsing 85]
Tarlecki, A., Wirsing, M.: Continuous Abstract Data Types - Basic Machinery and Results. Manuscript, Fakultät für Informatik, Universität Passau, January 85

[Vuillemin 74]
Vuillemin, J.: Correct and Optimal Implementation of Recursion in a Simple Programming Language. J. Computer Systems Sc. 9, 332-354 (1984)

[Winskel 83]
Winskel, G.: Non-deterministic Recursive Program Schemes and Powerdomains. Carnegie-Mellon University, Deptartment of Computer Science, Report CMU-CS-83-169, December 1983

[Wirsing et al. 83]
Wirsing, M., Pepper, P., Partsch, H., Dosch, W., Broy, M.: On Hierarchies of Abstract Data Types. Acta Informatica 20, 1-33 (1983)

[Wright et al. 78]
Wright, J.B., Wagner, E.G., Thatcher, J.W.: A Uniform Approach to Inductive Posets and Inductive Closure. Theoretical Computer Science 7:1, 57-77 (1978)

PASSING COMPATIBILITY IS ALMOST PERSISTENCY

F. Orejas (*)
C.R.I. Nancy
Campus Scientifique, B.P. 239
54506 Vandoeuvre-les-Nancy Cedex
FRANCE

Parameterized data types or program modules have been a step forward on the way of providing more powerful abstract constructs for software design.

From a theoretical (algebraic) point of view, parameterized data types were introduced in /13,2,3,4/. /13/ defined semantics of parameterizations at the model level, by means of free functors, while /3,4/ worked at the specification level, by means of pushouts. Later, the two approaches were combined in /7,8/.

In /13/ (strong) persistency was established as the condition of correctness for parameterized data types. Intuitively, it meant the protection of the actual parameters after applying the parameterization. Later, in /9/, persistency was characterized proof-theoretically in terms of consistency and sufficient completeness properties.

As a consequence of the unified (model/specification) view, in /8/ correctness of parameterized specifications was established in terms of two conditions concerning parameter passing: actual parameter protection (essentially, a re-statement of persistency) and passing compatibility, a property that guarantees the compatibility of the two semantic constructs (free functors and pushouts) used to define parameter passing.

Actual parameter protection or persistency has sometimes been considered as a too strong correctness condition for parameterizations, since in some cases non-sufficiently complete parameterizations seem to be of interest, for instance to deal with errors.

(*) On leave from Facultat d'Informàtica, Universitat Politècnica de Catalunya, Barcelona, SPAIN.

However, the compatibility of the two ways of handling parameter passing (at the specification level through pushouts, and at the model level through free functors) guaranteed by the passing compatibility property, and more explicitly stated through the so-called "Extension Lemma" /8/, should be considered in any case due to its importance when defining semantics of algebraic specification languages at the proof-theoretic and model levels.

Up to now, the characterization of passing compatibility has been an open problem. In /8/ it was proved that persistency was a sufficient condition, and also an example of non-persistent (non-sufficiently complete) specification not satisfying passing compatibility was given; but it was left unanswered the question of whether persistency would be equivalent or strictly stronger than passing compatibility.

In this paper, we shall show that a parameterized specification satisfies passing compatibility for all parameters iff it is persistent or trivially inconsistent. Which means that passing compatibility is almost persistency. In particular, it will be proved that sufficient completeness is a necessary condition for passing compatibility. Moreover, this result is a (in some sense) stronger version of the so-called Extension Lemma.

The organization of this paper is as follows: in section 1 we shall present the basic definitions concerning parameterizations and some basic results from /8,9/; in section 2 the results stated above shall be presented; finally, in section 3 we will propose some conclusions.

ACKNOWLEDGEMENTS

The first version of this paper was written during a stay in Nancy on leave from Barcelona's Facultat d'Informàtica. Following versions were written in Barcelona. The author would like to thank both centres for the facilities provided.

Part of the proof of the main result was inspired in a counter-example from U. Lipeck to be found in /4/.

The author would also like to thank H. Ehrig for some talks and encouragement.

This work has been partially supported by the Comision Asesora de Investigación Científica y Técnica (ref. 2704-83).

1. Preliminaries

Familiarity with the usual notions concerning (parameterized) algebraic specifications is assumed (for detail, see /11,8/). Also, some knowledge of elementary category theory is required (see, for example, /1/).

A specification SP is a triple (S, Σ, E), where S is the set of sorts or data domain names, Σ is the signature, i.e. an indexed family of sets of operation symbols, $\Sigma = \{\Sigma_{w,s}\}_{w \in S^*, s \in S}$, and E is a set of equations.

A Σ-algebra A consists of a family of sets (carriers or data domains) $\{A_s\}_{s \in S}$, and a family of operations $\sigma_A: A_{s1} \times \ldots \times A_{sn} \to A_s$, for every σ in $\Sigma_{s1 \ldots sn, s}$. A Σ-homomorphism $h: A \to A'$, where A and A' are Σ-algebras is a family of functions $\{h_s: A_s \to A'_s\}_{s \in S}$ which commute with the operations.

Σ-algebras together with their homomorphisms form the category Alg_Σ, having as initial object (up to isomorphism) the term algebra T_Σ.

$T_\Sigma(X)$ stands for the algebra of terms with variables in X, i.e. the free Σ-algebra generated by X. Given an assignment a: X → A, there is a unique Σ-homomorphism $\bar{a}: T_\Sigma(X) \to A$, extending a. A Σ-algebra A satisfies an equation t1=t2, t1,t2 in $T_\Sigma(X)$ iff for every assignment a: X → A, $\bar{a}(t1) = \bar{a}(t2)$. A satisfies a set of equations E iff it satisfies every equation in E. Given a specification SP = (S, Σ, E), a Σ-algebra satisfying E is called a SP-algebra. SP-algebras together with their homomorphisms form the category Alg_{SP} with initial object $T_{SP} = T_\Sigma/\equiv_E$, where $\equiv_E$ stands for the congruence generated by E.

Along this paper, initial algebra semantics will be considered, i.e. the data type defined by SP will be T_{SP}.

Given a specification SP = (S, Σ, E), a combination of SP and SP0 = $(S0, \Sigma0, E0)$, denoted SP+SP0, is defined:

$$SP+SP0 = (S+S0, \Sigma+\Sigma0, E+E0)$$

where + denotes disjoint union. Note that SP0 does not need to be a specification (for instance, there may be a σ in $\Sigma0_{w,s}$ with ws not in S0, but ws must be in $(S+S0)^*$), but SP+SP0 does.

A specification morphism h: SP1 → SP2 consists of a function $h_S: S1 \to S2$ and a family of functions $\{h_{w,s}: \Sigma1_{w,s} \to \Sigma2_{h_S(w), h_S(s)}\}_{w \in S1^*, s \in S1}$ (where $h_S(s1 \ldots sn)$ denotes $h_S(s1) \ldots h_S(sn)$), such that $h(E1) \subseteq E2$, i.e. every equation in E1 when translated through h belongs to E2. Specifications, together with their morphisms, form the category CATSP.

Every specification morphism h: SP1 → SP2 induces a functor U_h: Alg_{SP2} → Alg_{SP1} called the <u>forgetful functor associated to h</u>, defined $U_h(A2)$ = A1 iff

$s \in S1$ $A1_s = A2_{h(s)}$

$\sigma \in \Sigma 1_{w,s}$ $\sigma_{A1} = (h_{w,s}(\sigma))_{A2}$

U_h has a left adjoint F_h: Alg_{SP1} → Alg_{SP2}, called the <u>free functor associated to h</u>.

A <u>parameterized data type</u> PDT is a triple (SP1,SP2,H), where SP1 = (S1,Σ1,E1) is the <u>parameter declaration</u>, SP2 = SP1 + (S2,Σ2,E2) is called the <u>target specification</u> and H is a functor, H: Alg_{SP1} → Alg_{SP2} (we assume H equiped with a natural family of homomorphisms I_A: A → $U_i \cdot H(A)$, where i is the inclusion morphism from SP1 to SP2). PSP is <u>persistent</u> (<u>strongly persistent</u>) iff for every A in Alg_{SP1}, I_A is an isomorphism (the identity).

A <u>parameterized specification</u> PSP is a pair (SP1,SP2), where SP1 and SP2 are as in the previous definition. The semantics of PSP is considered to be the parameterized data type (SP1,SP2,F_i), where F_i is the free functor associated to the inclusion morphism i. We shall say that a parameterized specification is persistent if its semantics it is so.

In /9/ it is proved that PSP is persistent iff the following two conditions hold:

1. <u>Consistency</u>: for every t1, t2 in $T_{\Sigma 1}(X)$, SP2 |- t1=t2 implies SP1 |- t1=t2 (where SP |-t1=t2 means that t1=t2 is deducible from SP).

2. <u>Sufficient Completeness</u>: for every t1 in $T_{\Sigma 1 + \Sigma 2}(X)$, such that the sorts of t1 and the variables occurring in it are in S1, there is a t2 in $T_{\Sigma 1}(X)$ such that SP2 |- t1=t2.

In order not to make notation too heavy we have avoided to explicitly mention the variables occurring in equations when talking about deduction. However, explicit naming of variables should not alter the results of this paper.

Now, we may define (standard) parameter passing at the specification level: given a parameterized specification PSP = (SP1,SP2), with SP2 =

SP1 + (S2, Σ2,E2), a specification SP3 called <u>actual parameter specifi-</u>
<u>cation</u> and a morphism h1: SP1 → SP3, <u>called parameter passing mor-</u>
<u>phism</u>, the mechanism of parameter passing may be described by the fo-
llowing pushout diagram:

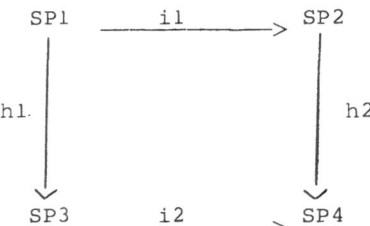

where i1 is the inclusion morphism. SP4 is called the <u>value specifica-</u>
<u>tion</u>. More concretely, SP4 = SP3 + (S4,Σ4,E4), with S4=S2, Σ4=h2(Σ2)
and E4 = h2(E2), i2 is the inclusion morphism and h2 is defined:

$h2_s(s)$ = <u>if</u> s∈S2 <u>then</u> s <u>else</u> $h1_s(s)$

$h2_{w,s}$: $Σ1+Σ2_{w,s}$ → $Σ3+Σ4_{h2_s(w),h2(s)}$

with

$h2_{w,s}(σ)$ = <u>if</u> σ∈Σ2 <u>then</u> σ <u>else</u> $h1_{w,s}(σ)$

Parameter passing is said to be correct iff the following two conditions hold:

1) <u>Actual parameter protection</u>: $U_{i2}(T_{SP4}) = T_{SP3}$

2) <u>Passing compatibility</u>: $F_{i1} \cdot U_{h1}(T_{SP3}) = U_{h2}(T_{SP4})$

A parameterized specification is correct if for all possible actual
parameter specifications parameter passing is correct. In /8/ it is
proved that PSP is correct iff it is persistent. Moreover, for proving
this statement it is used the following "extension lemma":

Given a (strongly) persistent parameterized data type PDT = (SP1,SP2,
,H), an actual parameter specification SP3, a parameter passing morphism h1 and the corresponding pushout diagram (as above), there is a
(strongly) persistent functor H2: Alg_{SP3} → Alg_{SP4}, called extension of
H1 via (h1,i1) satisfying for every A in Alg_{SP3}:

$$U_{h2}(H2(A)) = H1(U_{h1}(A))$$

moreover, H2 is uniquely determined by A and B = $H1(U_{h1}(A))$, in the following sense:

For every C in Alg_{SP4} satisfying $U_{i2}(C) = A$ and $U_{h2}(C) = B$, we have $H2(A) = C$.

If in addition $H1 = F_{i1}$, then $H2 = F_{i2}$.

This extension lemma should be considered important, not only because it is highly helpful in proving several properties about parameter passing, but because it establishes (under persistency) the equivalence of the two semantic constructs associated to parameterizations (pushouts and free functors).

2. Characterizing Passing Compatibility

In this section, we shall present the results of this paper, i.e. the characterization of parameterized specification correctness with respect to passing compatibility, together with a (in some sense) stronger version of the Extension Lemma.

Definition 2.1

A parameterized data type PDT = (SP1,SP2,H) is <u>extensible</u> iff for every actual parameter specification SP3, parameter passing morphism h1, and corresponding pushout diagram:

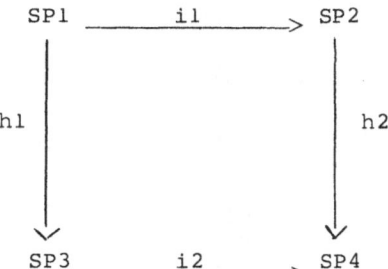

there is a functor H2: $Alg_{SP3} \rightarrow Alg_{SP4}$, called extension of H1 via (h1,i1), satisfying:

$$U_{h2} \cdot H2 = H1 \cdot U_{h1}$$

Moreover, if H1 is free, then PDT is <u>freely extensible</u> iff the extensions are free. As usual, we shall say that a parameterized specification is (freely) extensible iff PDT = (SP1,SP2,F_{i1}) it is so.

Definition 2,2

A parameterized specification $PSP = (SP1, SP2)$ is <u>trivially inconsistent</u> iff for all sorts s in S1:

$$SP2 \vdash X_s = Y_s$$

where X_s and Y_s are two distinct variables of sort s.

Lemma 2.3

If PSP satisfies passing compatibility then PSP is sufficiently complete.

Proof

Assume PSP is not sufficiently complete, then there is a term t1 in $T_{\Sigma1+\Sigma}(X)$ with its sort and the sort of its variables in S1, such that there does not exist a term t2 in $T_{\Sigma1}(X)$ with $SP2 \vdash t1=t2$. Let var(t1) be the set of variables occurring in t1 and let SP3 be the specification $SP1 + (S1', \Sigma3, E3)$, where S1' is a copy of S1 (i.e. S1' = {s'/s $\in$ S1}), $\Sigma3$ consists of var(t1) (taken as constants of the appropriate sorts) plus two operations, $c_s: s \rightarrow s'$ and $u_s: s' \rightarrow s$, for every s in S1, and E3 consists of the equations:

$$u_s(c_s(t)) = t$$

for every s in S1 and every t in $T_{\Sigma1+\Sigma3}$ of sort s.

Now, let h1 be the inclusion morphism, $h1: SP1 \rightarrow SP3$, and let SP4 be the corresponding value specification, then:

$$F_{i1} \cdot U_{h1}(T_{SP3}) \neq U_{h2}(T_{SP4})$$

The reason is the following: F_{i1} generates some junk on $U_{h1}(T_{SP3})$ (at least the term t1, if we consider its variables as constant symbols from $\Sigma3$, would be junk), but on $U_{h2}(T_{SP4})$ we have generated, at least, the double of junk: for every junk element t of sort s generated by F_{i1}, in T_{SP4} we have the same element plus $u_s(c_s(t))$.

Theorem 2.4

The following statements are equivalent:

i)   PSP is freely extensible.

ii)   PSP satisfies passing compatibility.

iii) PSP is persistent or trivially inconsistent.

Proof

We will prove i) $\Rightarrow$ ii) $\Rightarrow$ iii) $\Rightarrow$ i).

i) $\Rightarrow$ ii)   Trivial, since passing compatibility is a special case of free extendibility.

ii) $\Rightarrow$ iii)   According to lemma 2.3, if PSP satisfies passing compatibility then PSP is sufficiently complete. Suppose PSP is inconsistent but not trivially inconsistent. Then there should be terms t1, t2 (of sort s1) and t3, t4 (of sort s2) in $T_{\Sigma 1}(X)$ such that:

  a) $SP2 \vdash t1=t2$

  b) $SP1 \nvdash t1=t2$

  c) $SP2 \nvdash t3=t4$

Let V be the set of variables occurring in t1, t2, t3, and t4, and let SP3 be the specification SP1 + $(\emptyset, \Sigma3, E3)$, where $\Sigma3$ consists of V (taken as constants of the appropriate sorts) plus an operation c: s1 $\rightarrow$ s2, and E3 is the pair of equations:

$$c(t1^{*}) = t3$$
$$c(t2^{*}) = t4$$

(where ti˘ (i=1,2) is the term obtained from ti by substituting its variables by their associated constants in $\Sigma3$.

Now, let h1: SP1 $\rightarrow$ SP3 be the inclusion morphism, and let SP4 be the corresponding value specification, then:

$$F_{i1} \cdot U_{h1}(T_{SP3}) \neq U_{h2}(T_{SP4})$$

The reason is the following: in $F_{i1} \cdot U_{h1}(T_{SP3})$ t1* and t2* would be congruent terms and t3˘ and t4*would not, but in T_{SP4} t1* and t2˘, and t3* and t4*would be congruent terms, due to the operation c and the equations in E3.

iii) $\Rightarrow$ i)   If PSP is persistent according to the extension lemma PSP is freely extensible. Assume PSP is trivially inconsistent and let SPj' (j=1,4) be SPj $(\emptyset, \emptyset, \dot{E})$, with E being the set of equations $X_s = Y_s$ (where X_s and Y_s are variables of sort s) for every s in S1. Let also be i1' and i2' the inclusion morphisms from SP1' to SP2' and from SP3' to SP4' respectively; i the inclusion morphism from SP3 to SP3'; and h1' and h2' the morphisms from SP1' to SP3' and from SP2' to SP4' defined extending h1 and h2, respectively. Then we have the following facts:

1) For every A in Alg_{SP3} $F_{i1} \cdot U_{h1}(A) = F_{i1} \cdot \cdot U_{h1} \cdot \cdot F_i(A)$ (with an appropriate choice of the free functors, otherwise they would be isomorphic).

2) SP2' is persistent with respect to SP1', thus for every A in $\text{Alg}_{SP3'}$

$F_{i1} \cdot \cdot U_{h1'}(A) = U_{h2'} \cdot F_{i2'}(A)$.

3) For every A in Alg_{SP3} $F_{i2'} \cdot \cdot F_i(A) = F_{i2}(A)$.

Hence:

$F_{i1} \cdot U_{h1}(A) = F_{i1} \cdot \cdot U_{h1} \cdot \cdot F_i(A) = U_{h2'} \cdot \cdot F_{i2'} \cdot \cdot F_i(A) = U_{h2} \cdot F_{i2}(A)$.

The proofs of the previous facts are the following:

1) $F_{i1} \cdot U_{h1}(A) = T_{\Sigma 1 + \Sigma 2}(U_{h1}(A)) / \equiv_{E1+E2+E(U_{h1}(A))}$ where $E(U_{h1}(A))$ is the set of all ground term equations satisfied by $U_{h1}(A)$. Also, we have:

$$T_{\Sigma 1 + \Sigma 2}(U_{h1}(A)) / \equiv_{E1+E2+E(U_{h1}(A))} = T_{\Sigma 1 + \Sigma 2}(U_{h1}(A)) / \equiv_{E1+E2+E}$$

since E is deduced from E1 and E2 and all equations on $E(U_{h1}(A))$ are deduced from E. But:

$$T_{\Sigma 1 + \Sigma 2}(U_{h1}(A)) / \equiv_{E1+E2+E} = T_{\Sigma 1 + \Sigma 2}(1_{\Sigma 1}) / \equiv_{E1+E2+E}$$

where $1_{\Sigma 1}$ is the final $\Sigma 1$-algebra (i.e. the one point $\Sigma 1$-algebra), since, from E, all values in $U_{h1}(A)$ are congruent.

On the other hand $U_{h1} \cdot \cdot F_i(A)$ is $1_{\Sigma 1}$, then:

$$F_{i1} \cdot \cdot U_{h1} \cdot \cdot F_i(A) = T_{\Sigma 1 + \Sigma 2}(1_{\Sigma 1}) / \equiv_{E1+E2+E}$$

2) SP2' is consistent with respect to SP1', <u>all</u> equations are deducible from SP1'. Also SP2' is sufficiently complete with respect to SP1' since all SP2'-terms of sort s in S1 are equivalents to X_s , according to E.

3) $F_{i2'} \cdot \cdot F_i(A) = T_{\Sigma 3 + \Sigma 4}(A) / \equiv_{E3+E4+E+E(A)}$ = (since E may be deducible from E3 and E4) = $T_{\Sigma 3 + \Sigma 4}(A) / \equiv_{E3+E4+E(A)}$ = $F_{i2}(A)$.

Corolary 3.5

If PSP is freely extensible then PSP is sufficiently complete.

3. Conclusion

The results obtained in this paper may be considered quite disappoint-
ing. The original aim was to find under which conditions non-persistent (and,especially, non-sufficiently complete) parameterizations
could satisfy passing compatibility, in order to see if certain forms
of error handling, which suppose a violation of the condition of "actual parameter protection" when being parameterized, could have a compatible proof-theoretic/model semantics.

The results show, precisely, that sufficient completeness is a necessary condition for passing compatibility. Moreover, it is proved that
this condition is almost equivalent to persistency. Hence, this would
show, at least from a theoretical point of view, the inadequacy of
these forms of error handling.

4. References

/1/   Arbib, M.E.; Manes, E.G.: "Arrows, structures and functors: the
        categorical imperative", Academic Press 1975.

/2/   Burstall, R.M.; Goguen, J.A.: "Putting theories together to ma-
        ke specifications", Proc. 5th IJCAI, Cambridge Mass., 1977, pp.
        1045-1058.

/3/   Burstall, R.M.; Goguen, J.A.: "The semantics of Clear, a speci-
        fication language", Proc. Copenhagen Winter School on Abstract
        Software Specification, Springer LNCS 86, pp. 292-332, 1980.

/4/   Ehrich, H.-D.: "On the theory of specification, implementation
        and parameterization of abstract data types", JACM 29,1 (1982),
        pp. 206-227.

/5/   Ehrig, H.: "Algebraic theory of parameterized specifications
        with requirements", Proc. 6th CAAP, Springer LNCS 112, 1981,
        pp. 1-24.

/6/   Ehrig, H.; Fey, W.; Hansen, H.: "ACT ONE: an algebraic specifi-
        cation language with two levels of semantics", TU Berlin, FB 20
        Tech. Rep. No 83/03, 1983.

/7/   Ehrig, H.; Kreowski, H.-J.; Thatcher, J.W.; Wagner, E.G.; Wright
        J.B.: "Parameterized data types in algebraic specification lan-

guages", Proc. 7th ICALP, Springer LNCS 85, 1980, pp. 157-168.

/8/ Ehrig, H.; Kreowski, H.-J.; Thatcher,J.W.; Wagner, E.G.; Wright
     J.B.: "Parameter passing in algebraic specification languages",
     Proc. Aarhus Workshop on Program Specification, Springer LNCS
     134, 1981.

/9/ Ganzinger, H.: "Parameterized specifications: parameter passing
     and implementation with respect to observability", TOPLAS 5,3
     (1983), pp. 318-354.

/10/ Goguen, J.A.; Meseguer, J.: "Universal realization, persistent
     interconnection and implementation of abstract modules", Proc.
     9th ICALP, Springer LNCS 140, 1982, pp. 265-281.

/11/ Goguen, J.A.; Thatcher, J.W.; Wagner, E.G.: "An initial algebra
     approach to the specification, correctness and implementation
     of abstract data types", in 'Current Trends in Programming
     Methodology, Vol IV: Data Structuring', R.T. Yeh (ed.), Prenti-
     ce Hall 1978, pp. 80-149.

/12/ Sannella, D.; Wirsing, M.: "A kernel language for algebraic
     specification and implementation", Proc. FCT-83, Springer LNCS
     158, 1983, pp. 413-427.

/13/ Thatcher, J.W.; Wagner, E.G.; Wright,J.B.: "Data type specifi-
     cation: parameterization and the power of specification techni-
     ques", Proc. 10th STOC, San Diego Ca., 1978.

Automatic Prototyping of Algebraic Specifications using Prolog

H. Petzsch

Lehrstuhl für Informatik II, RWTH Aachen
Büchel 29-31, D-5100 Aachen

Abstract : We propose the translation of algebraic specifications into Prolog for the purpose of automatic prototyping. If the algebraic specification allows the automatic generation of a canonical term algebra, proofs by structural induction can be carried through with the interactive support of a small dialog program written in Prolog. Nonterminating reduction rules can be added to the database and evaluated with the help of a hierarchical ordering of reductions and Prolog's backtracking facility.

1. Introduction

Algebraic specifications have been proposed as a formal language for problem description during the last decade by an impressive number of authors. There seem to be two major advantages connected with the use of algebraic specifications :
- the fundamental idea in abstract data type specification is to present a data type precisely but independent of any concrete choice of the data objects and independent of any implementation of the operators of the types. Many-sorted (heterogeneous) algebras correspond exactly to this view of an abstract data type.
- an algebraic description of an abstract data type is sufficiently precise to be used for automatic prototyping. Although algebraic specifications tend to be easier to understand than descriptions of the same type at an operational level, the formal specification of a nontrivial data type tends to be nontrivial too. Automatic prototyping provides a necessary tool for testing the implications of a large specification.

The usual approach to prototyping is the implementation of a term rewriting system and to interpret the defining equations of the specifications as rewrite rules for simplifying terms. This has led to research on interesting questions concerning e.g. the treatment of nonterminating rewrite rules or sufficient conditions for termination. Given the term rewriting system as as basis to work on, a number of recent papers have discussed methods for proving inductive properties of the specified data types without induction. Since it is not possible in the general case to construct a canonical term algebra for an algebraically specified data type, the proof principle of structural induction does not seem to be directly applicable to automatically generated prototypes.

Our work starts from a subset of algebraic specifications which has been introduced by [Klaeren80] : structural recursive specifications. These specifications use the elements of a term algebra over a restricted set of 'constructors' as representations for data objects and allow only structural recursion as a method for specifying 'operations' over these terms. We feel that this method is sufficiently powerful to be used as a tool for system design. A more detailed discussion of the advantages and drawbacks of this method can be found in [Klaeren83].

After giving a short introduction to SRDL, our formal language for algebraic specifications, we discuss in chapter 3 the translation of SRDL specifications to Prolog. The proposed translation is in fact not restricted to SRDL specifications, but could be easily addapted to general algebraic specifications; as long as all equations describe terminating rewrite rules the resulting Prolog clauses will define a prototype for the given specification.

Chapter 4 discusses the incorporation of the 'proof by induction' principle into an interactive environment, where specifications may be tested. Proven equalities can be included into the systems data base and used as reductions at a later time. Since these equalities may be nonterminating when viewed as reduction rules, we propose their evaluation via a hierarchical ordering of reductions and Prolog's backtracking facility. A medium sized example of proving properties of a simple specification will be found in the appendix.

2. Structural recursive algebraic specifications

For this section we assume some familiarity with standard algebraic concepts and notations. Usually, algebraic specifications are given by triples (S,Σ,E), where S is a set of sorts, Σ is a set of operations over S and E is a set of Σ-equations, also called algebraic axioms, explaining the semantics of the operations and their relations to each other. A specification (S,Σ,E) determines a category $Alg(\Sigma,E)$ of models of this specification, consisting of all S-sorted Σ-algebras which satisfy the equations E. This category contains an initial model $T(\Sigma,E)$, the so-called abstract software module specified by (S,Σ,E).

$T(\Sigma,E)$ can be thought of as consisting of congruence classes of Σ-terms $t \in T(\Sigma)$, where $T(\Sigma)$ denotes the word algebra on the empty generator set and the congruence is generated by E. It is well known that in $T(\Sigma)$ we can prove assertions by induction on the structure of terms; furthermore, the freeness property garantees the unique existence of certain recursively defined operations on $T(\Sigma)$. Both results are based mainly on the unique decomposition of terms in $T(\Sigma)$; in $T(\Sigma,E)$ however, and all the more in other Σ-algebras, both facts are not true.

To overcome this difficulty we restrict Σ to a small set of 'constructing operations' (or 'constructors') and use $T(\Sigma)$ as a model of our data elements. All nonconstructing operations ('operations' in contrast to 'constructors') needed in our algebra are introduced by structural recursive definitions; for a more formal treatment see [Klaeren83]. Any equation over constructors, which we expect to be valid in our algebra, may be proved via the concept of 'observability' : given a specification (S,Σ,O) (where O are the operations defined by structural recursion) we regard two terms t1 and t2 $\varepsilon\, T(\Sigma)$ as equivalent iff we can show that for all operations f:s1,...,sn -> s

   f(... t1 ...) = f(... t2 ...)

is always true.

In this paper we use a subset of the language SRDL [Klaeren83] for abstract software specification. The constructor statement declares the formal constructors , at the same time attributing source and target sorts to them. In the operations clause all nonconstructing operations are defined by structural recursion. We hope that the following example will suffice to make the discussion in the following paragraphs understandable :

```
MODULE set_of_int =
INCLUDE boolean(bool,true,false);
        integer(int,zero,succ);
CONSTRUCTORS
   set = (empty, ins(int,set));
OPERATIONS
   element(I:int;S:set) : bool =
      CASE S OF
         empty : false;
         ins(X,S1) : IF X=I THEN true
                     ELSE element(I,S1)
      ESAC;
   delete(I:int;S:set) : set =
      CASE S OF
         empty : empty;
         ins(X,S1) : IF X=I THEN delete(I,S1)
                     ELSE ins(X,delete(I,S1))
      ESAC;
   card(S:set) : int =
      CASE S OF
```

```
          empty : zero;
          ins(X,S1) : IF element(X,S1)=true THEN card(S1)
                         ELSE succ(card(S1))
     ESAC
END
```

The equality used in the IF-expression is the strict term equality of T( ); in other
words, all parameters for an operation (and all operations occuring within the
predicate of a conditional expression) have to be evaluated to -terms before the
result of applying the operation to its parameters can be computed. Instead of
explicitly listing all possible costructors for a given sort, an OTHERWISE clause may
be included in a CASE-expression when appropriate.

3. Translation of SRDL into Prolog

In the following chapters a basic knowledge of Prolog is assumed; for more
information about Prolog compare [Clocksin81].

To translate an algebraic specification into Prolog, we have to specify a 'reduction
rule' corresponding to the semantic definition of an operation and, additionally, the
order of applying these reductions has to be defined. There exist at least three
approaches to this problem :
- Togashi and Noguchi (see [Togashi84]) translate algebraic equations $f(\underline{x})$=e into
  predicates $f(\underline{x},e)$:- ...; since this approach implies in the general case an
  extension of Prolog (namely to allow clauses with multiple head formulae), no
  automatic prototyping with existing Prolog interpreters is possible. For this
  reason we didn't follow their proposal.
- Bergman and Deransart (see [Bergman81]) produce from a specification three kinds
  of Prolog predicates :
  a) analyse($f(\underline{x}),y$) expressing that $f(\underline{x})$ is reducible to y
  b) normalize(x,y) yielding equality if no rule is applicable to x and starting
  reduction with a rule on the outermost level otherwise
  c) rule(x,y) stating that there is a rule x = y in the specification.
- Bandes (see [Bandes82]) produces from a specification the following three kinds of
  predicates :
  a) rule(x,z) :- reduce(y,z) expressing that x = y is a rule of the specification
  b) inner($f(\underline{x}),z$) expressing that iff $\underline{x}$ reduces to $\underline{x}'$ with $\underline{x} \neg=\underline{x}'$, then $f(\underline{x}')$
  reduces to z
  c) reduce(x,y), defined in terms of rule and inner, which specifies the order of
  applying reductions.

Our proposal extends of Bandes method to SRDL, because the distinction between rules
representing the equations, rules applying reduction to inner terms and a global rule
defining the reduction strategie allows an easy introduction of hierarchically
ordered reduction systems.

To improve readability we define in Prolog the following three infix operators :
x => y   : x may somehow be reduced to y (the global reduction
             operator)
x ==> y : starting with a rule at the outermost level x reduces to y
x ===> y : x reduces to y by inner reductions

We can now describe the basic translation from SRDL to Prolog. For each constructor
and each operation of our specification we generate a Prolog rule

```
f(X1,...,Xn) ===> f(Y1,...,Yn) :-
    X1 => Y1,
       ...
    Xn => Yn.
```

For each definition of an operation
    f(x1,...,xn) = e
we generate a Prolog rule
    f(X1,...,Xn) ==> Z_ :- e'.
where e' is defined recursivly following the structure of expressions as follows :

- if e is a simple expression (i.e. does not contain an IF or CASE), then
  e' ≡ e =>Z_

- if e is an IF-expression of the form
      IF s1 = s2 THEN e1 ELSE e2
  then e' stands for
      (s1 => Z_n,
       s2 => Z_m,
       (Z_n = Z_m, !, e1'
       ;e2'))
  where n and m are integer constants which avoid name conflicts between variables
  within one definition; the cut operator '!' avoids the inclusion of the negated
  test not(Z_n=Z_m) into the code

- if e is a CASE-expression of the form
      CASE s OF
          c1 : e1;

```
          ...
        cn : en;
        OTHERWISE e0
     ESAC
   then e' stands for
      (s => Z_m,
       (Z_m = c1, !, e1'
       ;Z_m = c2, !, e2'
          ...
       ;Z_m = cn, !, en'
       ;e0'))
```

The general reduce operator => is defined as

```
   X>>Y :- X==>Y,!.        /* use a rule if possible          */
   X>>X.

   X=>Y :-
      X===>Z,              /* reduce inner terms              */
      Z>>Y.                /* outermost reductions or identity */
```

Note that the rules introduced for ===> are included only for efficiency reasons; the ===> operator could have been globally defined as well as the => operator. This amounts to having an interpreter for algebraic specifications consisting only of about 10 lines of Prolog code (and one rule for each reduction specified by the specification). If no other tools are available, a hand translation of one's specification into Prolog seems to be the quickest possible way to generate a working prototyp of the specification.

For a possibility to prove the correctness of a translation as the one above compare [Drosten84].

4. Proving facts by structural induction

The translation from algebraic specifications to Prolog described in the last chapter is sufficient only for prototyping purposes; in order to prove interesting equalities within our specification we have to include the treatment of variables.

Translating our 'algebraic' variables to Prolog-variables would instruct the interpreter to look for an instantiation of this variable such that a reduction of the input term can be performed. This corresponds to an existential quantification of

our 'algebraic' variable. The depth-first strategie of existing Prolog interpreters
implies that a successful instantiation of such a variable will only be found if the
underlying term algebra, which describes the objects of the sort under consideration,
is build up using only one constant and one constructor with at most one argument of
the same sort. The treatment of existentially quantified variables therefore seems
to be possible only with 'fifth-generation' Prolog interpreters implementing a
breadth-first computation strategie on highly parallel machines; in this case Prologs
backtracking facility and its multidirectional interpretation of predicates might
lead to a generation of all possible terms for the variable.

Easier to implement is the treatment of universally quantified 'algebraic' variables.
If these variables are replaced by constants not appearing elsewhere in the
specification, any reductions of a term containing such constants will remain valid
with any data objects substituted for these constants.
The translation described in the last chapter has to be modified only in two points
to allow the correct reduction of terms containing 'unknown' constants :

- if e is an IF-expression of the form
    IF s1 = s2 THEN e1 ELSE e2
  then e' stands for
    (s1 => Z_n,
     s2 => Z_m,
     (Z_n = Z_m, !, e1'
     ;ground([Z_n,Z_m]), !, e2'))
  where ground is a predicate which succeeds if no 'unknown' constants appear in the
  list of terms given as the argument. The reason for this restriction is that a
  term 'eq(x,y)' denoting equality may be evaluated neither to true or false if x
  and y stand for universally quantified variables.

- if e is an CASE-expression of the form
    CASE s OF
       c1 : e1;
         ...
       cn : en;
       OTHERWISE e0
    ESAC
  then e' stands for
    (s => Z_m,
     (Z_m = c1, !, e1'
     ;Z_m = c2, !, e2'
         ...
     ;Z_m = cn, !, en'

```
   ;ground([Z_m]), !, e0'))
(ground has to be introduced for the same reason as above).
```

With this extention it is possible to prove that

   delete(x,ins(x,s)) = delete(x,s)

by reducing the first terms to delete(x,s). Note that the reduction delete(x,ins(x,s)) => delete(x,s) depends on the fact that x = x, which remains valid for all substitutions of data objects for x.

Given the modified reductions the implementation of dialog system supporting induction proofs becomes quite easy. Additional clauses have to be generated for the prolog interpreter specifying the constructors of each sort and the argument sorts of each operation. Such a system tries to proof equalities by reduction; if it does not succeed the user is asked for help. There are two basic choices in this situation : either a lemma has to be proved first, or the proof has to be carried through by induction. If the user chooses to prove a lemma, the system retries reduction on the original terms after the proof of the lemma has been completed. It seems to be more natural to proove equation with the help of induction and lemmas than by application of a modified version of the Knoth-Bendix algorithm [Goguen80], since the system simulates more closely the approach of a mathematically trained user to prooving equations correct. An example of a proof of commutativity of addition is presented in the appendix.

Equalities prooved by induction have to be entered into the system as reduction rules to allow their application within further proofs. Some equalities however lead to nonterminating reductions, because they do not simplify terms (e.g. commutativity of addition). We propose to handle these equations by the backtracking facility of Prolog : in order to proove an equality, first all terminating reduction rules are applied. If this is not successfull, applications of nonterminating rules are examined. If our reduction predicate guarantees that no rule is applied more than once in a row, but that on the other hand every possible order of applying several nonterminating rules is examined, all possible reductions of a given term will be checked without the danger of nontermination.

Because there may be several nonterminating reduction rules applicable to a term (e.g. add(X,Y) =>> add(Y,X) and add(add(X,Y),Z) =>> add(add(X,Z),Y) are both applicable to add(add(a,b),c); '=>>' is our notation for nonterminating reductions) it is not sufficient to distinguish just the two classes of terminating and nonterminating reduction rules; instead we introduce a hierarchie of reductions, where at the lowest level all terminating rules are collected, and each upper level contains reductions which do not have superpositions (a decidable property). We can now redefine the reduce operator => for a correct treatment of the two commutativity rules for addition mentioned above :

```
X=>X :- atomic(X), !.   /* treatment of constants               */
X=>Y :-
   X===>Z,              /* reduce inner terms                   */
   (Z>>Y                /* terminating reductions or identity   */
   ;use(1,Z,Z1),        /* or reduction on a higher level       */
    Z1===>Z2,           /* followed by inner reductions         */
    Z2>>Y               /* and possibly terminating reductions  */
   ).

use(N,X,Y) :-
   (reduce(N,X,Y)       /* reductions of level N, or            */
   ;reduce(N,_,_),      /* are there any level-N rules ?        */
    N1 is N+1,
    use(N1,X,Z1),       /* then reduction on a higher level     */
    Z1===>Z2,           /* followed by inner reductions         */
    (reduce(N,Z2,Y)     /* and possibly level-N reductions      */
    ;Z2=Y)              /* or identity                          */
   ).
```

reduce(N,X,Y) means that X =>> Y is a reduction at level N. The example in the appendix shows the automatic inclusion of the commutativity rules at different levels.

5. Concluding remarks

An examination of our translation algorithm shows that it is not only applicable to SRDL but to most other algebraic specification methods too. Even conditional equations of the form
    (p implies t1 = t1)
may be evaluated by the clause
    t1 ==> Z_ :- p=true, t2 => Z
as long as p can be evaluated within the term reduction system. Our choice of SRDL has been motivated only by the possibility of structural recursive proofs of equalities.

The translation of our specifications to Prolog is with regard to efficiency at the moment inferior to a direct implementation of specifications in a operational programming language like PASCAL; compare e.g. [Petzsch83]. This stems mostly from the fact that the Prolog clauses are interpreted and not compiled before evaluation.

Given a highly parallel computer architecture and Prolog compilers with the ability
to exploit this architecture, we can expect our prototyping method to be at least as
efficient as other implementations : the inherent perallelity of functional programming languages is retained by the translation to Prolog (e.g. parallel evaluation of
arguments). Nevertheless it would be worth while to increase efficiency by
inhibiting reevaluation of arguments which are unchanged by an application of a
reduction rule (compare the application of the '===>' operator within the definition
of the 'use' predicate). The decision which arguments to reevaluate can be made
statically by inspection of the specification.

Another important improvement would be the generalization of our translation to
hierarchical and parameterized specifications. A method for including type-checking
of arguments has been proposed by [Gaube84]; this is a prerequisite for truely
hierarchical specifications. How to handle parameters and their instantiation seems
to be still an open question.

The dialog system for proving equalities is a first step in the direction of
semi-automatically proving that one specification implements another one. Such a
system should be able to extract from two specifications all neccessary assertions
which, when verified, guarantee the 'compatibility' of the two specifications.

The work presented in this report has been partly supported by IBM Deutschland GmbH.

References

[Bandes82]   R. Bandes
             'Algebraic Specification and Prolog'
             Tech.Rep.#82-12-02, Dept. of Comp. Science,
             University of Washington, Seattle

[Bergman81] M. Bergman, P. Deransart
             'Abstract Data Types and Rewriting Systems :
             Application to the Programming of Algebraic
             Abstract Data Types in Prolog'
             in Astesiano,E;Böhm,C:CAAP81, LNCS 112,
             Springer Verlag Berlin-Heidelberg-New York, 1981

[Clocksin81] W. Clocksin, C. Mellish
             'Programming in Prolog'
             Springer Verlag Berlin-Heidelberg-New York, 1981

[Drosten84]   K. Drosten, H.-D. Ehrich
                 'Translating algebraic specifications to
                  Prolog programs'
                 Report 84-08, Institut für Informatik,
                 TU Braunschweig, Germany

[Gaube84]   W. Gaube, P. Lockemann, H. Mayr
                 'ORS-Spezifikationslabor : Generierung von
                  Prolog-Programmen aus Definitionen abstrakter
                  Datentypen'
                 Int.Report 15/84, Fakultät für Informatik,
                 Universität Karlsruhe, Germany

[Goguen80]   J. Goguen
                 'How to prove inductive hypotheses without induction'
                 Proc. 5. Conf.Automated Deduction, LNCS 87,
                 Springer Verlag Berlin-Heidelberg-New York, 1980

[Klaeren80]   H. Klaeren
                 'Eine Klasse von Algebren mit struktureller Rekursion
                  und ihre Anwendung bei der abstrakten Software-
                  Spezifikation'
                 Dissertation, RWTH Aachen, 1980

[Klaeren83]   H. Klaeren
                 'Algebraische Spezifikation'
                 Springer Verlag Berlin-Heidelberg-New York, 1983

[Petzsch83]   H. Petzsch
                 'INTAS V2.0 : Ein System zur Interpretation
                  algebraischer Spezifikationen'
                 Report 5/83, Lehrstuhl für Information II,
                 RWTH Aachen

[Togashi84]   A. Togashi, S. Noguchi
                 'A Program Transformation from Equational Programs
                  into Logic Programs'
                 Proc.Int.Conf.Fifth Generation Computer Systems 1984,
                 OHM * North Holland, Amsterdam

Appendix
========

This appendix shows the proof of commutativity of addition based on the following
short specification :

```
MODULE natural =
SORTS nat;
CONSTRUCTORS nat  = (0,suc(nat));
OPERATIONS
    add(X,Y : nat) : nat =
        CASE Y OF
            0        : X;
            suc(Y1) : suc(add(X,Y1))
        ESAC
END
```

Compiling the SRDL-specification generates the following Prolog clauses :

```
/* Module natural */
cons(nat,[0,suc(nat)]).
params(add,[nat,nat]).
add(X,Y) ==> Z_ :-
    Y => Z_1,
    ((Z_1=0),!,X => Z_
    ;(Z_1=suc(Y1)),!,suc(add(X,Y1)) => Z_
    ).
suc(X1) ===> suc(Y1) :-
    X1 => Y1.
add(X1,X2) ===> add(Y1,Y2) :-
    X1 => Y1,
    X2 => Y2.
```

(our compiler does not check if the reduction of the term specifying the CASE-part to
be used is neccessary)

In the following example all inputs of the user are underlined;
comments are marked with (* ... *) :

?- consult(dialog).

Prolog-version of the specification : prove

Do you want to :

```
 s - simplify a term
 p - prove the equivalence of two terms
 a - assert a new fact
 r - save results
 e - return to Prolog
 d - return to DOS ?
p
enter  t1 = t2 .  : add(add(x,y),z)=add(add(x,z),y).

add(add(x,y),z) => add(add(x,y),z)
add(add(x,z),y) => add(add(x,z),y)
The terms are not equivalent after reduction.
```

(* No reduction rule can be applied, since x,y and z are unknown constants. *)

Do you want to :

```
 b - return to the main menu
 c - continue
 i - prove equivalence by induction
 n - assert a new fact and retry reduction
 a - assert that add(add(x,y),z) ==> add(add(x,z),y)
 r - assert that add(add(x,z),y) ==> add(add(x,y),z)
 y - prove an other equivalence first
i
```
induction on : <u>x</u>

we have to prove :
add(add(0,y),z) = add(add(0,z),y)

add(add(0,y),z) => add(add(0,y),z)
add(add(0,z),y) => add(add(0,z),y)
The terms are not equivalent after reduction.

(* add is recursivly defined on the 2. argument : still no reduction rule applies *)

Do you want to :

```
 b - return to the main menu
 c - continue
 i - prove equivalence by induction
 n - assert a new fact and retry reduction
 a - assert that add(add(0,y),z) ==> add(add(0,z),y)
 r - assert that add(add(0,z),y) ==> add(add(0,y),z)
 y - prove an other equivalence first
y
```
enter t1 = t2 . : <u>add(0,x)=x.</u>

add(0,x) => add(0,x)
x => x
The terms are not equivalent after reduction.

Do you want to :

```
 b - return to the main menu
 c - continue
 i - prove equivalence by induction
 n - assert a new fact and retry reduction
 a - assert that add(0,x) ==> x
 r - assert that x ==> add(0,x)
 y - prove an other equivalence first
i
```
induction on : <u>x</u>

we have to prove :
add(0,0) = 0

add(0,0) => 0
0 => 0
The terms are equivalent
we have to prove :
add(0,suc(xx)) = suc(xx)
assuming
add(0,xx) = xx

add(0,suc(xx)) => suc(xx)
suc(xx) => suc(xx)
The terms are equivalent

```
Do you want to :

 c - continue
 a - add as a fact add(0,x) ==> x
 r - add as a fact x ==> add(0,x)
 d - add as a fact add(0,x) =>> x
a

add(0,x)==>x
Do you want to change constants to variables (y,n) ?
y

(* All unknown constants have to be replaced by Prolog-variables *)
(* if add(0,X) ==> X is to be used as a general reduction rule   *)

name of constant : x

add(0,_4159)==>_4159
Do you want to change constants to variables (y,n) ?
n

(* Now the system retries the last step of the proof : *)

add(add(0,y),z) => add(y,z)
add(add(0,z),y) => add(z,y)
The terms are not equivalent after reduction.

Do you want to :

 b - return to the main menu
 c - continue
 i - prove equivalence by induction
 n - assert a new fact and retry reduction
 a - assert that add(add(0,y),z) ==> add(add(0,z),y)
 r - assert that add(add(0,z),y) ==> add(add(0,y),z)
 y - prove an other equivalence first
y

(* Proving the proposition directly by induction would lead to a  *)
(* reduction rule of the form add(add(0,Y),Z) ==> add(add(0,Z),Y) *)
(* We prefer instead the more general rule :                      *)

enter  t1 = t2 .  : add(x,y)=add(y,x).

add(x,y) => add(x,y)
add(y,x) => add(y,x)
The terms are not equivalent after reduction.

Do you want to :

 b - return to the main menu
 c - continue
 i - prove equivalence by induction
 n - assert a new fact and retry reduction
 a - assert that add(x,y) ==> add(y,x)
 r - assert that add(y,x) ==> add(x,y)
 y - prove an other equivalence first
i
Induction on : x

we have to prove :
add(0,y) = add(y,0)
```

```
add(0,y) => y
add(y,0) => y
The terms are equivalent
(* Note that the rule add(0,X) ==> X has been used again *)
we have to prove :
add(suc(xx),y) = add(y,suc(xx))
assuming
add(xx,y) = add(y,xx)

add(suc(xx),y) => add(suc(xx),y)
add(y,suc(xx)) => suc(add(y,xx))
The terms are not equivalent after reduction.

Do you want to :

 b - return to the main menu
 c - continue
 i - prove equivalence by induction
 n - assert a new fact and retry reduction
 a - assert that add(suc(xx),y) ==> add(y,suc(xx))
 r - assert that add(y,suc(xx)) ==> add(suc(xx),y)
 y - prove an other equivalence first
y
enter  t1 = t2 .  : add(suc(x),y)=suc(add(x,y)).

(* Using induction directly would lead again to the *)
(* reduction add(suc(X),Y) ==> add(Y,suc(X))        *)

add(suc(x),y) => add(suc(x),y)
suc(add(x,y)) => suc(add(x,y))
The terms are not equivalent after reduction.

Do you want to :

 b - return to the main menu
 c - continue
 i - prove equivalence by induction
 n - assert a new fact and retry reduction
 a - assert that add(suc(x),y) ==> suc(add(x,y))
 r - assert that suc(add(x,y)) ==> add(suc(x),y)
 y - prove an other equivalence first
i
induction on : y

we have to prove :
add(suc(x),0) = suc(add(x,0))

add(suc(x),0) => suc(x)
suc(add(x,0)) => suc(x)
The terms are equivalent
we have to prove :
add(suc(x),suc(xy)) = suc(add(x,suc(xy)))
assuming
add(suc(x),xy) = suc(add(x,xy))

add(suc(x),suc(xy)) => suc(suc(add(x,xy)))
suc(add(x,suc(xy))) => suc(suc(add(x,xy)))
The terms are equivalent

Do you want to :
```

```
 c - continue
 a - add as a fact add(suc(x),y) ==> suc(add(x,y))
 r - add as a fact suc(add(x,y)) ==> add(suc(x),y)
 d - add as a fact add(suc(x),y) =>> suc(add(x,y))
a

add(suc(x),y)==>suc(add(x,y))
Do you want to change constants to variables (y,n) ?
y
name of constant : x

add(suc(_6443),y)==>suc(add(_6443,y))
Do you want to change constants to variables (y,n) ?
y
name of constant : y

add(suc(_6443),_6663)==>suc(add(_6443,_6663))
Do you want to change constants to variables (y,n) ?
n

add(suc(xx),y) => suc(add(y,xx))
add(y,suc(xx)) => suc(add(y,xx))
The terms are equivalent

Do you want to :

 c - continue
 a - add as a fact add(x,y) ==> add(y,x)
 r - add as a fact add(y,x) ==> add(x,y)
 d - add as a fact add(x,y) =>> add(y,x)
d

(* adding the reduction as add(x,y) ==> add(y,x) *)
(* would lead to nonterminating computations    *)

add(x,y)=>>add(y,x)
Do you want to change constants to variables (y,n) ?
y
name of constant : x

add(_7229,y)=>>add(y,_7229)
Do you want to change constants to variables (y,n) ?
y
name of constant : y

add(_7229,_7411)=>>add(_7411,_7229)
Do you want to change constants to variables (y,n) ?
n

reduction inserted into database at level 1

add(add(0,y),z) => add(y,z)
add(add(0,z),y) => add(z,y)
add(add(0,z),y) => add(y,z)
The terms are equivalent
we have to prove :
add(add(suc(xx),y),z) = add(add(suc(xx),z),y)
assuming
add(add(xx,y),z) = add(add(xx,z),y)

add(add(suc(xx),y),z) => suc(add(add(xx,z),y))
add(add(suc(xx),z),y) => suc(add(add(xx,z),y))
```

The terms are equivalent

Do you want to :

```
 c - continue
 a - add as a fact add(add(x,y),z) ==> add(add(x,z),y)
 r - add as a fact add(add(x,z),y) ==> add(add(x,y),z)
 d - add as a fact add(add(x,y),z) =>> add(add(x,z),y)
 d
```

add(add(x,y),z)=>>add(add(x,z),y)
Do you want to change constants to variables (y,n) ?
y
name of constant : x

add(add(_8517,y),z)=>>add(add(_8517,z),y)
Do you want to change constants to variables (y,n) ?
y
name of constant : y

add(add(_8517,_8777),z)=>>add(add(_8517,z),_8777)
Do you want to change constants to variables (y,n) ?
y
name of constant : z

add(add(_8517,_8777),_9037)=>>add(add(_8517,_9037),_8777)
Do you want to change constants to variables (y,n) ?
n

reduction inserted into database at level 2

(* Level 2 since there is already the reduction *)
(* add(X,Y) =>> add(Y,X) at level 1 and   *)
(* add(X,Y) and add(add(X,Y),Z) are overlapping *)

Do you want to :

```
 s - simplify a term
 p - prove the equivalence of two terms
 a - assert a new fact
 r - save results
 e - return to Prolog
 d - return to DOS ?
 r
```

Please enter file name : newprove

The file newprove.pro contains now all clauses of prove.pro and the following
additional reductions :

```
    reduce(1,add(X,Y),add(Y,X)) .
    reduce(2,add(add(X,Y),Z),add(add(X,Z),Y)) .
    add(0,X)==>Z_ :-
            X=>Z_ .
    add(suc(X),Y)==>Z_ :-
            suc(add(X,Y))=>Z_ .
```

If at a later time further equations have to be proved, all reductions can be used by
starting the dialog program with the file newprove.pro instead of prove.pro.

ERROR HANDLING FOR PARAMETERIZED DATA TYPES

Axel Poigné
Dept. of Computing
IMPERIAL COLLEGE
London SW7 2BZ

0. MOTIVATION

The merit and the problems of the initial algebra approach to data type specification
are widely discussed (e.g. [ADJ 78], [EKTWW84], [EKMP 82], [Or 82]), a prevailing view
being that the foundations are settled enough to define specification languages based
on this approach [EFH 83]. We somewhat disagree with this view, not so much as we favour other approaches [SW 83], [BG 80], [MV 83] - in fact we believe that the initial
algebra approach has the advantage clearly to distinguish between syntactical constructions and correctness criteria on the semantical level - but for reasons being inherent
in the method.

In order to explain our position a few general remarks about specification may be
appropiate. A specification method provides a language for specifications and states
which kinds of facts may be deduced from a specification. Algebraic specifications, for
instance, consist of a signature and a finite set of open equations (equations with
variables). In the simple case of non-parameterized specifications the semantics is
given by the initial algebra [ADJ 78] which exactly characterizes the set of closed
equations (equations without variables) derivable from the equations of the specifications. The closed equations are the provable facts or properties the initial algebra
approach is interested in. Such semantical properties have the objective to establish
certain correctness criteria by which a designer can judge if a specification satisfies
the more or less formal requirements.

In addition, a specification method has to provide modularization techniques which allow
to construct compound specifications from given ones, or which relate given specifications, like parameterization and implementation. Modularization techniques are motivated by pragmatics in that big programming systems can be split in comprehensible units,
thus easing the task of the designer and of the user. A less addressed consequence is
that responsibility is distributed and that bugs and design errors can be exactly
attached to a specific unit or subset of units. We claim that, for this reason, the very
question of data type theory is to prove that modularization techniques, which act on
the syntactical level, preserve the correctness criteria, or, in other words, that any

property achieved at some stage of the specification process should hold as well at
later stages. Simply, efforts should not be spent for nothing from the designer/program-
mers point of view, while the project management would like to keep responsibility
traceable (we certainly do not exclude that properties and/or requirements may change
during the process of specification but claim that this should happen only as the consequence of an explicit (re-) design, and not as a consequence of an (automated) application of modularization techniques). Hence modularization is not only a tool to split
specifications into smaller units but modularization techniques may be seen as well as
automated proof procedures which generate correct specifications under the assumption
that correct specifications are given as input.

With regard to the initial algebra approach we cannot avoid to detect a few flaws in
that modularization techniques do not always satisfy the properties sketched above.
Let us consider the parameterized specification

```
spec NAT- is
sorts $nat-
ops   $0, -1: → nat-
      $suc: nat- → nat-
eqns  suc(-1) = 0
```

where '$' indicates the parameter data. If we update by the specifications (according
to the definition in [EKTWW 84])

```
spec CLNAT1 is                      spec CLNAT2 is
sorts clnat                         sorts clnat
ops  0: → clnat                     ops  0: → clnat
     suc:clnat → clnat                   suc:clnat → clnat
var  n:clnat                        eqns suc(suc(0)) = suc(0)
eqns  suc(suc(n)) = suc(n)
```

which have the same initial algebra of two elements, we obtain result specifications
with different properties. In both cases updating adds the equations of the actual
parameter. If we update by CLNAT1, we can prove $0 = suc(-1) = suc(suc(-1)) = suc(0)$,
while in the second case $0 \neq suc(0)$. This well known phenomenon is rather unsatisfactory as preservation of the semantics seems to be the least property to hold for a
construction on specifications. Analysis of the example shows that the problems are
caused by an imbalance of the specification language of open equations and the proof
theory of closed equations linked to it; the specifications CLNAT1 and CLNAT2 state
the same facts about the terms generated by '0' and 'suc' but after updating the
equation 'suc(suc(n)) = suc(n)' states as well a fact about '-1' while 'suc(suc(0))
= suc(0)' does not.

Initial algebra semantics would certainly object to our example as the parameterized
specification NAT- is not persistent [EKTWW 84]. The condition of persistency reflects
the afore mentioned imbalance of language facilities in that persistency ensures in-

dependence of the equations of the parameterized specification and the actual parameter.
We hasten to agree that our example is not a particularly reasonable specification
(except that it nicely demonstrates why persistency is needed in the initial algebra
 approach) but we believe that there are reasonable parameterized specifications which
are not persistent. We apologize that we use the well known array once again.

```
spec ARRAY is
BOOL with
sorts $index, $data, array
ops   new: → array                        $derr: → data
      get: array index  →  data           aerr:  → array
   update: array index data → array       $dok: data → bool
      ifd: bool data data  →  data
      ifa: bool array array → array
   $_ = _ : data data → bool

var  d,d':data, i,j:index, a:array
eqns  get(update(a,i,d),j) = ifd(aok(a),ifd(i = j,d,get(a,j)),derr)
      update(update(a,i,d),j,d') = ifa(i = j, update(a,j,d'),
                                         update(update(a,j,d'),i,d))

      get(new,i) = get(aerr,i) = derr
      update(aerr,i,d) = update(a,i,derr) = aerr
    + " if- and  _ = _ -equations"
```

where Bool is a shared specification of booleans. 'derr' has to be a part of the parameter in order to obtain a persistent specification. Moreover parts of the error handling, namely the definition of the ok-predicate, has to be provided by the actual parameter. In contrast,we believe that the error handling is an inherent part of the
specification ARRAY which cannot and should not be anticipated by the designer of a
specification which is a possible actual parameter. To our opinion such a proceeding
contradicts the intention of modularization in that a specification then has to reflect the possible contexts in which it may be used. To retain modularity as well as
persistency,the only alternative of the initial algebra approach is to add a suitable
error handling to an actual parameter when updating, but with the obvious disadvantage
that in each case consistency of the extension with the original actual parameter is
to be proved seperately. Even this proceeding does not really agree with the spirit
of modularization as the error handling is definitely caused by the specification
ARRAY, hence it being the task of the designer of ARRAY to prove the appropiate facts
about the stack and especially the error handling.
We have yet to face another problem:
Assume that both the index and the data component are updated by the same sort, for
instance natural numbers. As 'derr' is parameter data to ensure persistency an error
element is to be added to the natural numbers (if one wants to preserve the error

message). In consequence we obtain an index error, and we have to take care of this
error in that the equation 'update(a,inerr,d) = aerr' is introduced and that a suitable
relativization of the other equations is considered. Therefore the designer of the specification ARRAY must take in account that his error handling on the <u>data</u> component may
have side effects with regard to the <u>index</u> component (The observation is due to [Schnei-
der 84]). If he decides to add an 'inerr', updating must be restricted to ensure that
the data error and the index error are identified. A way out may be to add an error
element to any sort and to assume that specification morphisms preserve error elements.
This procedure becomes somewhat obsolete if more than one error message is introduced
(say a bounded array with error messages 'overflow' and 'underflow'), or if some kind
of error recovery is intended.

To be fair we admit that the problems outlined above are mainly caused by error handling which is out of the scope of the initial algebra approach so far (except for
[ADJ 78] where only flat specifications are considered. The method to use ok-predicates
is due to this reference). Thus our remarks about the initial algebra approach may be
taken as a criticism of the lack of a suitable error handling for parameterized types,
and the subsequent may be understood as a proposal how to extend the initial algebra
approach. Nevertheless we believe that we have pointed out only a few of the deficits –
other kinds of side effects can be observed when implementations are considered (which
due to space are out of the scope of the paper) – and that a lot of work has to be spent
an a careful analysis of modularization techniques in order to match the requirements of
a practice of software engeneering.

We assume familiarity with [ADJ 78], [EKTWW 84], [EKMP 82] from where we borrow the
notation. Full proofs of our results are given in [Poigné 85].

1. ON THE USE OF SUBSORTS AND OVERLOADING FOR SPECIFICATION

Subsorting and overloading are introduced by [Goguen 78] and extended by[Gogolla 83].
We have used subsorting and overloading for parameterized specification in [Poigné 84]
where we prove correctness of parameter passing. In comparison to [Poigné 84] this paper focusses on the pragmatical aspects in that a parameter passing mechanism is proposed which is less powerful but considerably simpler to apply.

Subsorting introduces the subset relation to specification. If s is a *subsort* of s'
(s ≤ s') we assume that the carrie A_s of sort s is a subset of the carrier $A_{s'}$ of
sort s' ($A_s \subseteq A_{s'}$). Inclusion of carriers almost automatically induces the concept of
overloading. For instance,the same symbol is used for addition on natural numbers and
on integers, the typing of the operators being determined by the context. Informally
overloading distinguishes between the names of operators and elements and the corresponding typing in that operators and elements may have several typings. Clearly the condition should be satisfied that the same operator name applied to elements with the same
names have the same results independent of typing (exact definitions are given in the
next chapter).

Subsorting and overloading have the advantage that they allow to define partial functions as total functions on subsorts and that equations can be restricted to subsorts.
Especially the last feature turns out to be extremely useful for the applications we
have in mind, namely to seperate the parameter and the error handling.

```
          spec ARRAY is
          BOOL with
          sorts $index, $data ≤ data+, array ≤ array+
          ops  derr: → data+
          new: → array
          aerr: → array+
          get: array+ index → data+
          update: array index data → array
          update: array+ index data+ → array+
          ifa: bool array array → array
          ifd: bool data data → data
          $ _=_: index index → bool
     var  i,j:index, a,a':array, d,d':data,a+:array+, d+:data+
     eqns get(new,i) = get(aerr,i) = derr
          update(aerr,i,d+) = update(a+,i,derr) = arr
          get(update(a,i,d),j) = ifd(i=j,d,get(a,j))
          update(update(a,i,d),j,d')) = ifa(i=j,update(aj,d'),
                                            update(update(a,j,d'),i,d))
            + "if-equations"
```

Parameter data and error handling are strictly seperated, and no side effects can be
caused by updating. Moreover a reasonable error handling may be obtained if a little
syntactical sugar is added. Another advantage is that an error handling may be added
at each stage of the specification process without changing too much of the kernel specification.

The intuition of subsorting seems to be twofold: If $s \leq s'$, an interpretation may be that
we have two different types s and s', but there is a coercion of s-data to s'-data. Another interpretation may be that s-data are in fact s'-data, but certain conditions are
restricted to the subtype. There are specifications to which neither view applies:

```
          pres STRANGE is
          sorts s,s'
          ops f:s → s, fs' → s'
```

A possible interpretation is that only one operation f is specified with the semantics

$$f: A_s \cup A_{s'} \rightarrow A_s \cup A_{s'} \ , \quad a \rightarrow \begin{cases} f_a^{s,s}(a) & \text{if } a \in A_s \\ f_A^{s',s'}(a) & \text{if } a \in A_{s'} \end{cases}$$

(the mapping is well defined as $f_A^{s,s}$ and $f_A^{s',s'}$ coincide on the intersection). We exclude such signatures as well for conceptual as for technical reasons, and accept only those specifications such that for all operator names σ there exists a *maximal* operator $\sigma:w \to s$ with $w' \leq w$ and $s' \leq s$ for all operators $\sigma:w' \to s'$ (the subsort ordering is canonically extended to sort words). We reserve the word *presentation* if this property is not satisfied, and use the keyword 'pres' to distinguish presentations from specifications. The intuition is that the semantics of an overloaded operator $\sigma:w_i \to s_i$, $i \in \underline{n}$, which is given by

$$\sigma_A: \bigcup_{i \in \underline{n}} A_{w_i} \to \bigcup_{i \in \underline{n}} A_{s_i} \quad , \quad \bar{a} \to \sigma_A^{w_i, s_i}(\bar{a}) \quad \text{if} \quad \bar{a} \in A_{w_i}$$

should be explicitly represented by the maximal operator.

This assumption is essential for parameter passing.

```
pres ONE is                          pres TWO is
sorts s,s"                           sorts $s,s',$s"
ops    a: → s                        ops    $a: → s, a → s"
       f:s → s                              f:s' → s'
       f:s" → s"                            $f:s" → s"
```

If we update TWO by ONE (anticipating the next chapters) it may be taken for granted that parameter passing yields

```
pres THREE is
ops    a: → s, a: → s"
       f:s → s, f:s' → s', f:s" → s"    .
```

Now assume that we have a ONE-algebra such that $a \notin A_{s''}$ and $f(a) = a$. Let us accept that the free construction from the formal parameter to the body (see next chapter) yields $f(a) \neq a$. But $f(a) = a$ in the free THREE-algebra over A, and the same holds if we restrict to the TWO-part of it. We conclude that passing compatibility [EKTWW 84] is violated.

Unfortunately the above observation is not the only difficulty which we encounter when parameterized specifications with subsorting are considered. We shall resume the discussion in section 3 but at first state the basic definitions and facts about

2. ALGEBRAS AND THEORIES WITH SUBSORTS AND OVERLOADING

2.1 _Definition_: (i) A _signature_ SIG consists of
- a partially ordered set $S = (S, \leq)$ of _sorts_, and
- a $S^* \times S$-sorted set of _operators_ such that $|w| = |w'|$ if $\sigma:w \to s$, $\sigma:w' \to s' \in \Sigma$.

We say that s is a _subsort_ of s' if $s \leq s'$.
The set of _operator names_ is $\Sigma := \bigcup_{w \in S^*, s \in S} \Sigma_{w,s}$

(ii) A SIG-_algebra_ A consists of
- a S-sorted set $A = (A_s | s \in S)$ of elements, and
- a mapping $\sigma_A^{w,s}: A_w \to A_s$ for each $\sigma:w \to s \in \Sigma$.
These data are to satisfy the axioms

(a) $s \leq s'$ $\Rightarrow$ $A_s \subseteq A_{s'}$

(b) $\sigma:w \to s$, $\sigma:w' \to s' \in \Sigma$, $\bar{a}:w$, $\bar{a}:w' \in A$ $\Rightarrow$ $\sigma_A^{w,s}(\bar{a}) = \sigma_A^{w',s'}(\bar{a})$

(ii) A SIG-_homomorphism_ $f:A \to B$ is a S-sorted mapping such that

(a) $h_s(\sigma_A^{w,s}(\bar{a})) = \sigma_B^{w,s}(h_w(\bar{a}))$ for $\sigma:w \to s \in \Sigma$ and $\bar{a}:w \in A$

(b) $a:s$, $a:s' \in A$ $\Rightarrow$ $h_s(a) = h_{s'}(a)$

The category of SIG-algebras and SIG-homomorphisms is denoted by SIG^b.

Remark: (i) We indicate the typing of operators and elements by $\sigma:w \to s \in \Sigma$ and $x:s \in X$. For tuples we use $\bar{x}:w \in X$ instead of $\bar{x} \in X_w$ where $X := \underline{1} := \{0\}$, $X_{sw} := X_s \times X_w$. S-sorted relations $R = (R_s \subseteq X_s \times X_s | s \in S)$ are canonically extended to tuples using $\bar{x} R \bar{y}$ as notation.

(ii) Our definition differs from that of [Gogolla 83] in that we have omitted the condition $s \leq s'$, $w' \leq w$ $\Rightarrow \Sigma_{w,s} \subseteq \Sigma_{w',s'}$ which seems to be superfluous, but have added the necessary condition $|w| = |w'|$ if $\sigma:w \to s$, $\sigma:w' \to s' \in \Sigma$.

(iii) An equivalent (and maybe mathematically smoother) approach is to use mono-morphisms via a conditional specification, i.e. operators $m:s \to s'$ such that $m(x) = m(y) \Rightarrow x = y$. But notationally 2.1 is more comfortable as for instance

```
        sorts  nat ≤ int
        ops    +:nat nat → nat
               +:int int → int
```

is a signature in the sense of 2.1, while an equation $m(x) + m(y) = m(x + y)$ is to be added if we use a monomorphism $m:\underline{nat} \to \underline{int}$.

As in case of standard algebra we discuss the existence of SIG-algebras which are 'free' relative to 'S-ordered sets'.

2.2 _Definition_: Let S = (S, ≤) be a partially ordered set. A S-_ordered set_ X consists
of a S-sorted set X such that $X_s \subseteq X_{s'}$ if s ≤ s'. The set of _elements_ of X is
$X := \bigcup_{s \in S} X_s$. A _morphism_ f:X → Y of S-ordered sets is a S-sorted mapping f:X → Y
such that $h_s(x) = h_{s'}(x)$ if x:s, x:s' ∈ X. The category of S-ordered sets is denoted by <u>S-set</u>.
There is a forgetful functor $V:SIG^b$ → <u>S-set</u> of SIG-algebras to the underlying S-
ordered set where S is the set of sorts of SIG.

Notation: S-ordered sets may be specified by listing the elements by $\{x_i:s_i \mid i \in I\}$.
This denotes the S-ordered set $\{x_i:s \mid s \in S, i \in I, s_i \leq s\}$.

Similar to [Gogolla 83] we state

2.3 _Proposition_: The canonical free SIG-algebra $T_{SIG}(X)$ over a S-ordered set X
(w.r.t $V:SIG^b$ → <u>S-set</u>) is inductively defined by

(i) $X_s \subseteq T_{SIG}(X)_s$

(ii)   σ:w → s ∈ Σ, s ≤ s', $\bar{t}:w \in T_{SIG}(X)$ => $\sigma(\bar{t}):s' \in T_{SIG}(X)$

with operations

$$\sigma^{w,s}: T_{SIG}(X)_w \rightarrow T_{SIG}(X)_s , \quad \bar{t} \rightarrow \sigma(\bar{t})$$

and unit $X\eta: X \rightarrow T_{SIG}(X), \quad x \rightarrow x$

(We assume without restriction of generality that $\tilde{X} \cap \tilde{\Sigma} = \emptyset$).

2.4 _Definition_: (i) A _presentation_ PRES consists of a signature SIG and a set of
equations of the form

$$[\bar{x}:w] \; l =_s r$$

with $l,r:s \in T_{SIG}(\{\bar{x}:w\})$ for some s ∈ S, w ∈ S* where x̄:w is used to denote the
sequence '$x_0:s_0, x_1:s_1, \dots, x_{n-1}:s_{n-1}$'.
(ii) An equation $[\bar{x}:w] \; l =_s r$ is _satisfied_ by a SIG-algebra A if $I_s^\phi(l) = I_s^\phi(r)$
for all <u>S-set</u>-morphisms $I:\{\bar{x}:w\} \rightarrow A$ where $I^\phi: T_{SIG}(\{\bar{x}:w\}) \rightarrow A$ is the unique
extension.
(iii) A PRES-algebra is a SIG-algebra which satisfies all the equations of PRES.
With SIG-homomorphisms this defines a category $PRES^b$.

Remarks & Notation :(i) As we deal with heterogeneous algebras we have to be careful
about the typing of the equations (compare [GM 81]).

(ii) The same variable may occur in x̄:w with different typings. Observe that substitution replaces x by the same elents which has to be of corresponding typings.

(iii) For practical purposes we use presentation schemes of the form

```
pres 'name' is
sorts 'sorts & generating order'
ops 'operator'
var 'typing of the variables'
eqns 'equations'
```

and we assume that each equation is abstracted by the list of variables occuring
on both sides of the equation. By this convention we forbid equations of the form
$[x:s,\bar{x}:w]$ $l =_s r$ in which x does not occur in l or r.

2.5 _Definition_: A _morphism_ h:SIG → SIG' of signatures consists of a monotone sort mapping h:S → S' (h(s) ≤ h(s') if s ≤ s') and a $S^* \times$ S-sorted mapping h:Σ → Σ' such that

    (a) $h_{w,s}: \Sigma_{w,s} \to \Sigma'_{h(w),h(s)}$

    (b) $\sigma: w \to s$, $\sigma: w' \to s' \in \Sigma$ $\Rightarrow$ $h_{w,s}(\sigma) = h_{w',s'}(\sigma)$.

We call $\tilde{h}: \tilde{\Sigma} \to \tilde{\Sigma}'$, $\sigma \to h_{w,s}(\sigma)$ with $\sigma: w \to s \in \Sigma$ the _renaming_ mapping.
For convenience we use $h(\sigma: w \to s) = h(\sigma): h(w) \to h(s)$ for notation.

For the definition of presentation morphisms we need that renaming extends to terms.

2.6 _Lemma_: Let h:(S,≤) → (S',≤') be a monotone mapping. Then $Y_h := \{y:s| y:h(s) \in Y\}$
defines a forgetful functor $_{-h}$: S'-set → S-set. For a S-ordered set X we define
$h(X)_{s'} := \bigcup\limits_{s \in S, h(s) \leq s'} X_s$ and $u:X \to h(X)_h$, x → x. Then (h(X),u) is a free S'-
ordered set over X.

2.7 _Definition_: A _morphism_ h:PRES → PRES' of presentations is a signature morphism
h: SIG → SIG' of the underlying signatures such that
$[\bar{x}:h(w)]h(l) =_{h(s)} h(r) \in E'$ if $[\bar{x}:w]l =_s r \in E$
where the renaming h: $T_{SIG}(\{\bar{x}:w\}) \to T_{SIG'}(\{\bar{x}:h(w)\})_h \in SIG^b$ is defined by universal properties in the diagram

$$\begin{array}{ccc}
\{\bar{x}:w\} & \xrightarrow{\quad \eta \quad} & T_{SIG}(\{\bar{x}:w\}) \\
\downarrow & & \downarrow h \\
h(\{\bar{x}:w\})_h = \{\bar{x}:h(w)\}_h & \xrightarrow[\eta'_h]{} & (T_{SIG'}(\{\bar{x}:h(w)\})_h
\end{array}$$

The category of presentations and presentation morphisms is denoted by pres.

2.8 _Definition_: A presentation PRES is called _specification_ if for every operator
name $\sigma \in \tilde{\Sigma}$ there exists a _maximal_ operator $\sigma:a(\sigma) \to c(\sigma) \in \Sigma$, i.e. $w \leq a(\sigma)$, $s \leq c(\sigma)$
if $\sigma: w \to s \in \Sigma$. A presentation morphism is a _specification morphism_ if maximal
operators are mapped to maximal operators, i.e. h(a(σ)) = a(h(σ)), h(c(σ)) =
c(h(σ)).

Each presentation morphism induces a forgetful functor in the usual way. To obtain free construction relative such a forgetful functor we factorize a free term algebra by a suitable congruence relation. The notion of congruence is rather specific for algebras with subsorts.

2.9 _Definition_ [Gogolla 83]: A S-sorted relation R is called a SIG-_congruence_ on a
   SIG-algebra A if
   - $\tilde{R} \subseteq \tilde{A} \times \tilde{A}$ is the least equivalence with $\underset{s \in S}{\cup} R_s \subseteq \tilde{R}$ $(\tilde{A} = \underset{s \in S}{\cup} A_s)$
   - $R_s = \tilde{R}_s := \{(a,a') \in \tilde{R}| \ a:s,a':s \in A\}$,
   - for all $\sigma:w \to s, \ \sigma:w' \to s' \in \Sigma, \ \bar{t}:w, \ \bar{t}':w' \in A$ such that $\bar{t} \ \tilde{R} \ \bar{t}'$ it holds that $\sigma(\bar{t}) \ \tilde{R} \ \sigma(\bar{t}')$.

   The _quotient_ $A/_R$ is defined by

   $(A/_R)_s := \{[a] \ |a:s \in A\}$ where $[a] := \{a' \in \tilde{A}| \ a' \ \tilde{R} \ a\}$, and

   $\sigma^{w,s}_{A/_R}([\bar{a}]) = [\sigma^{w,s}_A(\bar{a})]$ with $\bar{a}:w \in A$.

2.10 _Proposition_ [Gogolla 83]: (i) $A/_R$ is a SIG-algebra, and $\pi:A \to A/_R$, $a \to [a]$ is
   a SIG-homomorphism.
   (ii) Given a SIG-homomorphism f: $A \to B$ such that
   $\tilde{R} \subseteq \text{Ker } f := \{(a,a') \in A_s \times A_{s'}| \ f_s(a) = f_{s'}(') \text{ in } B, \ s,s' \in S\}$
   for all $s \in S$, then there exists a unique SIG-homomorphism f': $A/_R \to B$ such that
   $f' \circ \pi = f$.

This prerequisite essentially allows to prove existence of free construction. In our context we are only interested in free constructions for presentation embeddings e: PRES $\subseteq$ PRES'. In this case a free PRES'-algebra $T_{PRES'}(A)$ over a PRES-algebra A can be constructed as follows:

Let (slightly ambiguously) A denote the S'-sorted set $A_{s'} := \underset{s \in S, s \leq s'}{\cup} A_s$

On $\tilde{T}_{SIG'}(A) := \underset{s \in S}{\cup} T_{SIG'}(A)_s$ we define a relation

t $\tilde{\curvearrowright}$ t'   iff (i) t = $\sigma(\bar{a})$ and t' = $\sigma^{w,s}_A(\bar{a})$ with $\sigma:w \to s \in \Sigma, \ \bar{a}:w \in A$, or

         (ii) t = $I^\phi_s(1)$, t' = $I^\phi_s(r)$ with $[\bar{x}:w] \ 1 =_s r \in E'$ and I: $\{\bar{x}:w\} \to T_{SIG'}(A)$,or

         (iii) t = $\sigma(\bar{t})$, t' = $\sigma(\bar{t}')$ with $\sigma:w \to s, \ \sigma:w' \to s' \in \Sigma', \ \bar{t}:w, \ \bar{t}':w' \in$
                 $T_{SIG'}(A)$ and $\bar{t} \ \tilde{\curvearrowright} \ \bar{t}'$, or

         (iv) t = t' or t' $\tilde{\curvearrowright}$ t.

Let t $\curvearrowright$ t' be the transitive closure of t $\tilde{\curvearrowright}$ t'.

2.11 _Theorem_: $T_{PRES'}(A) = T_{SIG'}(A)/_\curvearrowright$ is a free PRES'-algebra over the PRES-algebra A
   (the general case is obtained via renaming as in 2.6)

3. PARAMETERIZED DATA TYPES

We argued in the first section that parameterization should allow to add data to a parameter sort and that consequently the condition of persistency is to be abandoned. We favour to replace persistency by consistency (i.e. no parameter datas are identified by the semantics of a parameterized data type), and to use preservation of consistency as correctness criterium. Moreover we retain the correctness criterion of passing compatibility [EKTWW 84] which states that the actual parameter is extended exactly as prescribed by the parameterized specification.

In our examples for parameterized specifications with subsorts we have used the subsorting to seperate the parameter data from the data added by the parameterized specification in order to avoid interference of the added data with equations of the actual parameter. We formalize this policy by the notion of parameter completeness.

3.1 *Definition* : (i) A *parameterized specification* SPEC = (S,Σ,E) is a specification
with a *formal parameter* PSPEC = (PS,PΣ,PE) such that the following syntactical
and semantical requirements are satisfied:

- PSPEC is a specification and PSPEC ⊆ SPEC in <u>pres</u> (PSPEC is a subrepresentation
  of SPEC)

- *parameter completeness*, i.e.
    - s ∈ S, s' ∈ PS, s ≦ s' (in S) => s ∈ PS
    - σ:w → s ∈ Σ, s ∈ PS   =>   σ:w → s ∈ PΣ

- *parameter protection*, i.e. PSPEC ⊆ SPEC is consistent

where a presentation embedding PRES ⊆ PRES' is *consistent* if the units
Aη: A → (T$_{PRES'}$(A))$_{PRES}$ of the corresponding adjunction (2.11) are injective. If
the Aη's are isomorphisms (identities) the embedding is called (*strongly*) *persistent*.

(ii) Given a parameterized specification SPEC with formal parameter PSPEC and a
parameterized specification ASPEC a *parameter passing* (*morphism*) is a specification morphism h: PSPEC → ASPEC. ASPEC is called the *actual parameter*.

Remark: It is essential that PSPEC is only a subrepresentation of SPEC. As a subspecification PSPEC must be closed under maximal operator which excludes our use of subsorts.

Notation: We assume that SPEC is a fixed parameterized specification. PSIG and SIG are the underlying signatures of PSPEC and SPEC.

In order to model parameter paasing we proceed in analogy to [EKTWW 84] and use pushouts in the category <u>pres</u> of presentations. According to the nature of our presentations renaming must take place on operator names. To avoid unnecessary complications we only discuss pushouts of specific structure.

Throughout this chapter we consider a fixed parameterized specification SPEC with formal parameter PSPEC and an actual parameter specification ASPEC such that

PSPEC = (PS,PΣ,PE) , SPEC = (S,Σ,E) and ASPEC =(AS,AΣ,AE)

where S = (PS + BS,$\leqq$), Σ = PΣ+Σ and E = PE + BE ('B' stands for body). Let h: PSPEC $\rightarrow$ ASPEC be a specification morphism. Without restriction of generality we assume that BS$\cap$AS = $\emptyset$ and B$\Sigma$$\cap$A$\Sigma$ = $\emptyset$.

Let SPEC = (RS,RΣ,RE) be defined by

RS = (AS + BS, $\leqq$), RΣ = AΣ + h'(BΣ), RE = AE + h'(BE)

where h': SPEC $\rightarrow$ RSPEC is given by

h'(s) = if sϵ PS then h(s) else s

h'$_{w,s}$(σ) = if $\sigma \epsilon$ PΣ then $\tilde{h}$(σ) else σ

(for $\tilde{\Sigma}$, $\tilde{h}$ compare 2.1,2.5, the renaming of equations is defined as in 2.7), and the ordering of RS is given as the transitive closure of

$s_0 \leqq s_1$ iff (i) $s_0 \leqq s_1$ in AS, or

(ii) s_0 = h'(s'$_0$) and s_1 = h'(s'$_1$) and s'$_0 \leqq$ s'$_1$ in S.

3.2 <u>*Proposition*</u>:

PSPEC $\subseteq$ SPEC

h $\downarrow$ $\downarrow$ h'

ASPEC $\subseteq$ RSPEC

is a pushout diagram in <u>pres</u>.

3.3 <u>*Definition*</u>: The *syntax* of parameter passing is given by the diagram

PSPEC $\overset{p}{\subseteq}$ SPEC

h $\downarrow$ $\downarrow$ h'

PASPEC $\overset{p_A}{\subseteq}$ ASPEC $\overset{p'}{\subseteq}$ RSPEC

the square being the pushout in <u>pres</u>. The *result specification* is RSPEC with formal parameter PASPEC.

Parameter passing is called *correct* if

– RSPEC with formal parameter PASPEC is a parameterized data type, and if

– *passing compatibility* holds, i.e. $F_p \circ V_h \circ F_{p_A} = V_{h'} \circ F_{p'} \circ F_{p_A}$

(where the F's and V's denote the corresponding free and forgetful functors).

Parameter passing may be not correct if operators are identified.

```
spec IDENTIFY is           spec NOGOOD is
sorts s                    sorts $s ⩽ s'
ops  a,b: → s              ops  $a,$b: → s
     f: s → s                   $f,$g: s → s
                                c: → s'
                                f,g:s' → s'
                           eqns a = f(c)
                                b = g(c)
```

Identification of f,g:s → s extends to f,g:s' → s'. a ≠ b in the initial
IDENTIFY-algebra but a = b in the initial algebra of the result specification.

Parameter passing not necessarily yields a specification, but

Fact: Parameter passing is *syntactically correct* (i.e. the result is a specification)
iff it is *syntactically safe* (i.e. the sorts of maximal operators are identified by parameter passing if the names are identified).

In [Poigné 84,85] we give sufficient, proof-theoretic conditions for *safeness* of parameter passing in that updatings satisfying these conditions are correct. Even if there
may be some algorithmic procedures guaranteeing safeness, safeness appears to be a rather
awkward condition for practical purposes. Hence it might be useful critically to recon-
sider the situation.

Apart from the fact that only a few examples occur to us where identification of operators is natural , second order equations (on operators) are introduced implicitly thus
extending the language of first order equations. The initial algebra approach neutra-
lizes possible problems by the semantical condition of persistency. Though technically
sound, conceptually there may be objections:
We believe - may be in contrast to other views on abstract data type theory - that a
specification has a certain intensional character in that it encodes operational and
proof theoretic aspects. The designer will for instance take advantage of these aspects
in proofs of correctness, and the user will rely on them in order to comprehend a specification. We suspect that names and the specific properties attached to them take a
rather great part in the 'understanding' of a data type. Renaming of parameter data
may be accepted because parameter data is considered as renamable from the start. But
practical experience proves that renaming is applied in a rather restricted way in that
often names are kept or slightly modified. We claim that the motivation is to preserve
as much of the intensional aspects as possible (simply, changing names may destroy
the intuitive understanding). Identification of operators is even more subtle as the
operators to be identified must carry the same intuition, for instance being an
'order predicate' _< _: data data → bool. Not properly used identification of opera-

tors may cause confusion in that the acquired 'intensional knowledge' about a parameterized specification and an actual parameter is not preserved because there is no obvious decomposition of the result specification into actual parameter and body (as a worst case assume that all parameter sorts and all parameter operators with the same number of arguments are identified). We have to admit the difficulty to find a reasonable example to support our view, but all reasonable examples only identify very specific types of operators like the already mentioned order predicates.

One may try as usual to prevent abuse of a concept by syntactical criteria. We hesitate to put forward our proposal to ban identification of operators by parameter passing as there seem to be sound examples of identification. On the other side our examples demonstrate that identification of operators may interfere with correctness of parameter passing, and we have the experience that safeness conditions often turn out to be unpractical. As a compromise, we suggest to single out 'reasonable' identifications. We claim that identification of operators is reasonable if they have the same intensional character in that, intuitively, the 'same' equations hold for identified operators.

Definition: A parameter passing is _sufficiently faithful_ if for all $[\bar{x}:w]$ $l =_s r \in E$ and all $t, t' \in T_{SPEC}(\{\bar{x}:w'\})_{s'}$ such that $h(w) = h(w')$, $h(t) = h(r)$ and $h(t') = h(l)$ it holds that $[\bar{x}:w']$ $t =_{s'} t' \in E$.

The definition allows to identify 'order predicates' which satisfy the 'same' equations of reflexivity, antisymmetry and transitivity. A more liberal definition would be to state that $SPEC \vdash [\bar{x}:w']$ $t =_{s'} t'$, in fact our

Main Theorem: Parameter passing is correct if the updating morphism is sufficiently faithful.

holds for the more liberal definition. But the conditions of the definition suggested are easy to check, hence appear to be more suitable for applicatons.

A proper result does not necessarily justify a restriction. But identification of operators can be simulated by duplication of operators in the actual parameter. If $\sigma:w \to s$, $\sigma':w' \to s'$ are operators of the formal parameter which are identified by parameter passing $h(\sigma:w \to s) = h(\sigma':w' \to s') = \sigma'':w'' \to s''$ one may add an operator $\bar{\sigma}'':w'' \to s''$ to the actual parameter plus the equation $\sigma''(\bar{x}) = \bar{\sigma}''(\bar{x})$, and then use a faithful parameter passing. One should note that duplication of operators in this way does not affect the 'knowledge' about the actual parameter as the same properties hold as before but there is a new copy of the operator $\sigma'':w'' \to s''$.

Duplication of operators may appear to be cumbersome, so it might be helpful to provide an automatic mechanism. One may modify parameter passing to the effect that only definitorial equality is stated: $\sigma:w \to s$ is not replaced by $\sigma':w' \to s'$ if $h(\sigma:w \to s) = \sigma':w' \to s'$ but the sum of the specification is taken (modulo a suitable

identification of sorts) and the equation $\sigma(\bar{x}) = \sigma'(\bar{x})$ is added. This is the procedure
of the logical approach of [MV 83]. The advantage is that the (intensional) information
of both the parameterized specification and the actual parameter are kept and that the
equality of operators is explicitly expressed in the result specification. As a disadvantage the result specification is slightly more complex, and the push-out property of
parameter passing is lost (wnat might not be too serious as the only application
of the push-out property we have seen so far is in the proof of associativity of parameter passing which can easily be computed explicitly. In fact faithfulness of updating
plus duplication of operators allows to retain the pushout property).

The (to our opinion) most convincing solution for practical purposes allows as well
sufficiently faithful renaming as definitorial equality for parameter passing. In a
scheme this may be expressed by

> update SPEC
> by ACTUAL
> rename $\sigma' \to \sigma$ "σ' is renamed to σ"
> define $\sigma' = \sigma$ "σ' and σ'' are definitorial equal to v
> $\sigma'' = \sigma$ (σ', $\sigma'' \in P\Sigma, \sigma \in A\Sigma$)

(If names are replaced identically an explicit statement may be omitted).

Formally an updating consists of a specification morphism $h:PSPEC \to ASPEC$ and a *renaming set* $P\Sigma r \subseteq F\Sigma$ such that h is sufficiently faithful on $P\Sigma r$.
Parameter passing then yields the

> $RSPEC = ((RS, \leq), R\Sigma, RE)$.

where $(RS, \leq)$ is defined as in our original parameter passin concept, and where
$R\Sigma = A\Sigma + h'(B\Sigma)$, $RE = AE + h'(BE) + \{[\bar{x}:h'(w)] \; \sigma(\bar{x}) =_{h'(s)} h(\sigma)(\bar{x}) | \sigma:w \to s \in P\Sigma \; P\Sigma r\}$
and where $h': SPEC \to RSPEC$ is given by

> $h'(s) = $ if $s \in PS$ then $h(s)$ else s
> $h'(\sigma) = $ if $\sigma \in P\Sigma r$ then $\tilde{h}(\sigma)$ else σ.

If we define correctness of parameter passing in the same way as above we obtain

Theorem: Parameter passing is correct for the modified updating.

via some minor computations from the main theorem. Quite clearly, the modified updating
is associative if the compositions of updatings are defined.

REFERENCES

[ADJ 78]   J.A.Goguen, J.W.Thatcher, E.G.Wagner, An initial algebra approach to
                the specification, correctness and implementation of abstract data
                types, in: R.Yeh, Fd., Current Trends in Programming Methodology, IV:
                Data Structuring (Prentice-Hall, Englewood Cliffs,NJ) 1978

[BG 80]   R.M. Burstall, J.A.Goguen, Semantics of CLEAR, a specification language,
                Proc. 1979 Copenhagen Winter School on Abstract Software Specification,
                Lecture Notes in Computer Science 86, 1980

[EFH 83]   H.Ehrig, W.Fey, H.Hansen, ACT ONE: An Algebraic Specification Language
                with two Levels of Semantics, Techn. Rep. No. 83-03, Dept. of Computer
                Science, Techn. University Berlin, 1983

[EKMP 82]   H.Ehrig, H.-J.Kreowski, B.Mahr, P.Padawitz, Algebraic Implementation of
                Abstract Data Types, TCS 20, 1982

[EKTWW 84]   H.Ehrig, H.-J.Kreowski, J.W.Thatcher, E.G.Wagner J.B.Wright, Parameter
                Passing in Algebraic Specification Languages, TCS   , 1984, also
                Proc. of the Aarhus Workshop on Program Specification, LNCS 134, 1982

[GM 81]   J.A.Goguen, J.Meseguer, Completeness of many-sorted equational logic,
                ACM SIGPLAN Notices 16.7, 1981

[Gogolla 83]   M.Gogolla: Algebraic Specifications with Partially Ordered Sorts and
                Declarations, Techn. Rep. 169, Abt. Informatik, Univ. Dortmund, 1983

[Goguen 78]   J.A.Goguen, Order sorted algebras: Exception handling and error sorts,
                coercions and overloaded operators, Semantics and Theory of Computation
                Report No. 14, UCLA, 1978

[Guttag 76]   J.V.Guttag, Abstract data types and the development of data structures,
                Proc. Conf. on Data Abstraction, Definition, and Structure, SIGPLAN
                Notices, Vol. 8, 1976

[MV 83]   T.S.E.Maibaum, P.A.S.Veloso, A logical approach to abstract data types,
                Techn. Rep. Dept. of Computing, Imperial College London, 1983

[Or 82]   F.Orejas, Characterizing composability of abstract implementations,
                Rep. RR 82/08, Univ. Barcelona, 1982

[Poigné 84]   A.Poigné, Another look at parameterization using algebraic specifications
                with subsorts, Proc. MFCS'84, LNCS 176, 1984

[Poigné 85]   A.Poigné, Modularization techniques for algebraic specifications with
                subsorts, revised version, in preparation

[Schneider 84] M.Schneider, Zur Beziehung syntaktischer und semantischer Konstruktionen
                auf Datentypen, Diplomarbeit, Abt. Informatik, Univ. Dortmund, 1984

[SW 83]   D.T.Sannella, M.Wirsing, A kernel language for algebraic specification
                and implementation, Proc. Int. Conf. of Foundations of Computation Theory,
                LNCS 158, 1983

MODEL THEORY OF DENOTATIONAL SEMANTICS

Thomas Streicher

University of Passau , BRD

ABSTRACT: The category of complete partial orders (cpo-s) has been suggested as the category where to interpret programs, expressions, declarations etc. One usually restricts oneself to certain subcategories such as $\tilde{\omega}$-algebraic cpo-s, Scott domains or Plotkins SFP objects (sequences of finite partial orders). A quite different category is the category of sequential algorithms on concrete data structures introduced by Berry and Curien. Thus we can conclude that the model we choose to interpret a programming language depends on certain additional assumptions. There does not exist a unique model and so it is worthwhile to find a general definition of a notion of model for the metalanguage of denotational semantics.

1. The method of denotational semantics

In denotational semantics one usually translates programs, expressions, declarations etc. into terms of a typed λ-calculus which is enriched by a fixpoint operator, an if-then-else-fi construct and several nonlogical operations of the basic datatypes. Now the real problem of semantics consists in defining what a model of this enriched typed λ-calculus is.

In model theory of (typed) λ-calculus it has been proposed that a model is just a cartesian closed category. This definition of model has been extended to enriched typed λ-calculus by A. Poigné [5] and by P. Dybjer [2] in the frame - work of order-enriched categories.

In the present paper we extend this definition to cpo-enriched categories and show that the (least) fixpoint operator is a derived notion.

Furthermore we show that there exists an initial model in the category of order-enriched models where the fixpoint operator is the least fixpoint operator.

Moreover we shall prove that there also exist initial extensional models.

2. Specification of Domain Categories

Our point of view is that categories can be considered as many-sorted algebras, where the sorts are pairs of objects $((A,B)$ stands for the sort of morphisms from object A to object $B)$, id_A can be considered as a constant of type (A,A) and composition can be considered as a binary operation of type $(A,B)(B,C) \to (A,C)$ for any objects A,B,C.

As we have additional structure on our categories we shall have additional operations. Thus the specification of domain categories is a two-step process: first we have to define the set of objects of the category, in the second step we have to axiomatise the operations on the hom-sets.

All axioms will have the form of pointwise implicational formulas, i.e. formulas of the form $A_1 \wedge \ldots \wedge A_n \to A$ where A_i, A are positive atomic formulas (equalities or inequalities).

By the special syntactic form of our axioms we can guarantee
the existence of initial models and initial ordered models.

2.1. The objects of a domain category

The objects of a domain category are not only a set but have
some structure. As they can be considered as types we have
some type forming operators such as +,x,→. Thus the objects
(=types) of a domain category form an algebra with the following specification.

Dom =

sorts: dom

opus: nat, bool: → dom

       +,x,→: dom dom → dom

Let I_{Dom} denote the free continuous Dom-algebra. The objects
of I_{Dom} can be considered as partial, infinite terms over
the signature of Dom. By allowing infinite terms we have an
elegant solution of the problem of representing infinite types.

For example consider the unique object d = nat + (d → d)
which corresponds to the infinite tree

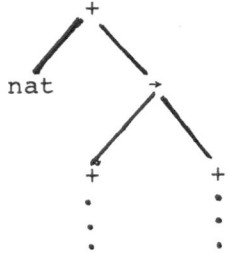

<u>Notation:</u> Let 1 denote the bottom element in $I_{\underline{Dom}}$.
There exists a canonical interpretation I of $I_{\underline{Dom}}$ in
the category of ω-algebraic cpo-s.

$I[\![1]\!] = \bot \quad I[\![nat]\!] = N_{\bot} \quad I[\![bool]\!] = Bool_{\bot}$

$I[\![d_1 + d_2]\!] = I[\![d_1]\!] + I[\![d_2]\!]$

$I[\![d_1 \times d_2]\!] = I[\![d_1]\!] \times I[\![d_2]\!]$

$I[\![d_1 \to d_2]\!] = I[\![d_1]\!] \to I[\![d_2]\!]$

for finite objects of $I_{\underline{Dom}}$.

If $d_1 \sqsubseteq d_2$ in $I_{\underline{Dom}}$ then there exists an embedding of
$I[\![d_1]\!]$ into $I[\![d_2]\!]$. If d is the lub of $d_0 \sqsubseteq d_1 \sqsubseteq \ldots$ in
$I_{\underline{Dom}}$ then $I[\![d]\!]$ is defined as the colimit of
$I[\![d_0]\!] \triangle I[\![d_1]\!] \triangle \ldots$

2.2. Specification of the operations of the domain category

The set of sorts of a domain category is $I_{Dom} \times I_{\underline{Dom}}$. As we
have infinitely many sorts we also shall have infinitely many
operations. This is possible as we shall use <u>polymorphic</u>
operations, i.e. families of operations indexed by tuples of
types.

The operations of the domain category are given in the following list:

id : $\to$ (A,A)

o : (A,B)(B,C) $\to$ (A,C)

! : $\to$ (A,1)

<-,-> : (A,B)(A,C) $\to$ (A,B $\times$ C)

π_1 : $\to$ (A $\times$ B,A) $\qquad$ π_2 : $\to$ (A $\times$ B,B)

ev : $\to$ ((A $\to$ B) $\times$ A,B)

curry : (A × B,C) → (A,B → C)

in$_1$:→ (A,A+B)   in$_2$: (B,A+B)

[-,-] : (A,C)(B,C) → (A+B,C)

fix :→ (B → B,B)

true, false :→ (1,bool)

zero :→ (1,nat)

succ :→ (nat,nat)

if-then-else-fi :→ (bool × A × A,A)

In standard terminology we could say that a domain category
should be a category with a terminal object, finite products,
exponentiation, weak sums and a fixpoint morphism for each
object and some other primitive objects and morphisms depending on our choice.

These properties can be expressed by the following axiom
schemes:

Category Axioms

(1)   id o f = f o id = f

(2)   (f o g) o h = f o (g o h)

Uniqueness of the Terminal Objects

(3)   ! = f

Axioms for Products

(4.1) <f,g> o π_1 = f   (4.2) <f,g> o π_2 = g

(5)   <h o π_1, h o π_2> = h

Axioms for Exponentiation

(6)   (curry (f) x id) o ev = f

(7)   curry ((g x id) o ev) = g

Axioms for (weak) Sums

(8.1) in_1 o [f,g] = f   (8.2) in_2 o [f,g]

(9) $\bot$ o h = $\bot$ $\Longrightarrow$ [in_1 o h, in_2 o h] = h

(10)   [in_1 o h, in_2 o h] $\subseteq$ h

Axioms for the Fixpoint Morphism

(11)   <id,fix> o ev = fix

Axiomas for the Data Types

(12) $\bot$ o succ = $\bot$

(13.1)   if ! o true then f else g fi = f

(13.2)   if ! o false then f else g fi = g

We can introduce additional data types by adding additional
constants (for morphisms) and additional equations.
If we delete axioms (9),(10) and (12) the specification is
purely equational and therefore has an inital model.

If we want to include the axioms (9),(10) and (12) it is a
specification of order-enriched algebras, i.e. algebras
where the carrier sets are partial orders with a least element and the operations are monotonic. (We substitute an
equation t = t' by t $\subseteq$ t' and t' $\subseteq$ t).

In specifications of order-enriched algebras we implicitly
assume the following logical axioms and rules:

(i) $\perp \sqsubseteq x$

(ii) $x \sqsubseteq x$

(iii) $x \sqsubseteq y \wedge y \sqsubseteq x \Rightarrow x = y$

(iv) $x \sqsubseteq y \wedge y \sqsubseteq z \Rightarrow x \sqsubseteq z$

(v) $x_1 \sqsubseteq y_1 \wedge \ldots \wedge x_n \sqsubseteq y_n \Rightarrow f(x_1, \ldots, x_n) \sqsubseteq f(y_1, \ldots, y_n)$
        for all operation symbols f

(vi) $\dfrac{t = t'}{\sigma[t] = \sigma[t']}$ for all substitutions σ.

As proved by Möller [4] any specification of order-enriched
algebras consisting of positiv implicational formulae only
admits an initial model. In both cases (equational and order-
enriched) the axioms can be understood as rules of an inductive definition of a binary relation on the set of variable
free terms over the underlying signature. Of course, if we
delete the axioms for the fixpoint operator (axiom (11)) initial models still exist.

3. Continuous domain categories

We are interested in continuous models of the theory of domain
categories, i.e. categories where the hom-sets are (ω-algebraic)
cpo-s and composition (and the additional operations) are
continuous.

As shown by Möller [4] specifications by positive implicational formulae do not admit initial continuous models in general.
Atomic formulae are not problematic.

We shall briefly outline the construction of initial continuous models: first construct the initial order enriched
model and then take the ideal completion of the carrier sets,

for the operations choose the unique continuous extensions. Then it remains to show that the algebra obtained in this way still satisfies the axioms.

Let $t[x] \sqsubseteq t'[x]$ be an axiom and d an infinite object of the same type as the variable x. If d is infinite then there exists an ascending chain $e_0 \sqsubseteq e_1 \sqsubseteq \ldots \sqsubseteq e_n \sqsubseteq \ldots$ such that $d = \bigsqcup_n e_n$, where the e_i's are finite elements, i.e. objects of the initial order enriched model.

As $t[x]$ and $t'[x]$ are continuous in x $t[d] = \bigsqcup_n t[e_n]$ and $t'[d] = \bigsqcup_n t'[e_n]$. But as the relation $\sqsubseteq$ restricted to finite objects is inherited from the initial order-enriched model, we can conclude that $t[e_n] \sqsubseteq t'[e_n]$. Therefore $t[d] = \bigsqcup_n t[e_n] \sqsubseteq \bigsqcup_n t'[e_n] = t'[d]$.

The only crucial point in our axiomatization is axiom (9): $\bot \circ h = \bot \implies [in_1 \circ h, in_2 \circ h] = h$. Let h be an infinite object of appropriate sort which is the lub of the ascending chain of finite objects $e_0 \sqsubseteq e_1 \sqsubseteq \ldots \sqsubseteq e_n \sqsubseteq \ldots$ Assume that $\bot \circ h = \bot$ then $\bot \circ e_n \sqsubseteq \bot \circ h \sqsubseteq \bot$ for all n by monotony of composition.

As $\bot \circ e_n = \bot$ for all n we have $[in_1 \circ e_n, in_2 \circ e_n] = e_n$ for all n. Thus we have $[in_1 \circ h, in_2 \circ h] =$ $= \bigsqcup_n [in_1 \circ e_n, in_2 \circ e_n] = \bigsqcup_n e_n = h$ as $\lambda h.[in_1 \circ h, in_2 \circ h]$ is a continuous function. Thus we have shown that the specification of a domain category admits an initial continuous model I. If we delete axiom (11) from our specification it still has an initial continuous model I'.

As pointed out by D. Scott in a discussion at this conference I shall show that in continuous cartesian closed
categories the fixpoint morphism is a derived notion.

Theorem: Let $\underline{C}$ be a continuous cartesian closed category
then for every object B of $\underline{C}$ there exists a least mor-
phism fix : $(B \rightarrow B) \rightarrow B$ such that $\langle id, fix \rangle \circ ev = fix$.

Proof: $\lambda h.\langle id, h \rangle \circ ev$ is a continuous function from
$Hom_{\underline{C}} (B \rightarrow B, B)$ to $Hom_{\underline{C}} (B \rightarrow B, B)$ thus it has a least fixpoint
fix. fix $= \bigsqcup_{n} \alpha_n$ where α_n is defined recursively as
$\alpha_o = \perp$ and $\alpha_{n+1} = \langle id, \alpha_n \rangle \circ ev$. $\qquad\qquad \square$

So we can associate with every morphism $f : B \rightarrow B$ an object
curry $(\pi_2 \circ f) \circ fix$, where $\pi_2 : 1 \times B \rightarrow B$, and it satisfies the following property.

curry $(\pi_2 \circ f) \circ fix = $ curry $(\pi_2 \circ f) \circ \langle id, fix \rangle \circ ev = $
$= \langle$curry $(\pi_2 \circ f),$ curry $(\pi_2 \circ f) \circ fix \rangle \circ ev.$

Notice that curry is a continuous isomorphism between
$Hom_{\underline{C}} (A \times B, C)$ and $Hom_{\underline{C}} (A, B \rightarrow C)$, especially we have
$Hom_{\underline{C}} (B, B) \cong Hom_{\underline{C}} (1 \times B, B) \cong Hom_{\underline{C}} (1, B \rightarrow B)$.

This observation leads to the following theorem:

Theorem: Let $\underline{C}$ be a continuous cartesian closed category
and $f : A \rightarrow (B \rightarrow B)$ a morphism of $\underline{C}$ then $f \circ fix$ is
a fixpoint of $\lambda h.\langle f, h \rangle \circ ev$. Moreover if $f \circ \perp = \perp$ the
morphism $f \circ fix$ is the least fixpoint of $\lambda h.\langle f, h \rangle \circ ev$.

Proof: $f \circ fix = f \circ \langle id, fix \rangle \circ ev = \langle f, f \circ fix \rangle \circ ev$.

Assume that $f \circ \bot = \bot$. The least fixpoint of $\lambda h.\langle f,h \rangle \circ ev$

is the lub of the chain $(\beta_n)_{n \in \omega}$, where β is defined re-

cursively as

$$\beta_0 = \bot \quad \text{and} \quad \beta_{n+1} = \langle f, \beta_n \rangle \circ ev.$$

By continuity of $\circ$ it holds that $f \circ fix = f \circ (\bigsqcup_n \alpha_n) =$

$= \bigsqcup_n (f \circ \alpha_n)$. If we can prove that $f \circ \alpha_n = \beta_n$ for all n

we have proved that $f \circ fix$ is the least fixpoint of

$\lambda h.\langle f,h \rangle \circ ev$. But this can be proved by induction.

$f \circ \alpha_0 = f \circ \bot = \bot = \beta_0$ by assumption. Assume that $f \circ \alpha_n = \beta_n$

for arbitrary fixed n. Then $f \circ \alpha_{n+1} = f \circ \langle id, \alpha_n \rangle \circ ev =$

$= \langle f, f \circ \alpha_n \rangle \circ ev = \langle f, \beta_n \rangle \circ ev = \beta_{n+1}$.

$\square$

4. Domain categories where fixpoints are least fixpoints

Definition: A domain category with least fixpoints is an order-

enriched model of the axioms (1) - (13) with the additional

property that $fix = \bigsqcup_n \alpha_n$ (where $\alpha_0 = \bot$ and $\alpha_{n+1} = \langle id, \alpha_n \rangle \circ ev$)

for all objects and for any term $t[x_1, \ldots, x_n]$ not containing

occurrences of fix

$$t[fix^{(1)}, \ldots, fix^{(n)}] = \bigsqcup_i [\alpha_i^{(1)}, \ldots, \alpha_i^{(n)}]$$

Theorem: There exists an initial domain category with least

fixpoints.

Proof: Interpret the terms of the theory of domain categories

in I' where the constant fix is interpreted as $\bigsqcup_n \alpha_n$. If we

take the "congruence order" $\sqsubseteq$ on the set of terms T, given

by the interpretation above, then $T/\subsetsim$ is a domain category with least fixpoints. It remain to show that $T/\subsetsim$ is
initial. Let M be any domain category then there exists
at most one homomorphism from $T/\subsetsim$ to M, as $T/\sim$ is
finitely generated. For existence we have to prove that for
any variable-free terms $t_1[\text{fix}^{(1)},\ldots,\text{fix}^{(m)}] \subsetsim$
$\subsetsim t_2[\text{fix}^{(1)},\ldots,\text{fix}^{(m)}]$ implies that $t_1[\text{fix}^{(1)},\ldots,\text{fix}^{(m)}]$
$\sqsubseteq t_2[\text{fix}^{(1)},\ldots,\text{fix}^{(m)}]$ in M. By construction of $T/\subsetsim$
$t_i[\text{fix}^{(1)},\ldots,\text{fix}^{(m)}]$ is the least upperbound of
$(t_i[\alpha_n^{(1)},\ldots,\alpha_n^{(m)}])_{n\in\omega}$ in $T/\sim$ and in M for $i = 1,2$.
If $t_1[\text{fix}^{(1)},\ldots,\text{fix}^{(m)}] \subsetsim t_2[\text{fix}^{(1)},\ldots,\text{fix}^{(m)}]$ then for
all n_1 there exists an n_2 such that

$$t_1[\alpha_{n_1}^{(1)},\ldots,\alpha_{n_1}^{(m)}] \subsetsim t_2[\alpha_{n_2}^{(1)},\ldots,\alpha_{n_2}^{(m)}].$$

But as $t_1[\alpha_{n_1}^{(1)},\ldots,\alpha_{n_1}^{(m)}] \subsetsim t_2[\alpha_{n_2}^{(1)},\ldots,\alpha_{n_2}^{(m)}]$ implies

$t_1[\alpha_{n_1}^{(1)},\ldots,\alpha_{n_1}^{(m)}] \sqsubseteq t_2[\alpha_{n_2}^{(1)},\ldots,\alpha_{n_2}^{(m)}]$ in M,

$t_1[\text{fix}^{(1)},\ldots,\text{fix}^{(m)}] \sqsubseteq t_2[\text{fix}^{(1)},\ldots,\text{fix}^{(m)}]$ in M.

$$\square$$

Notice that this class of order-enriched algebras can be
specified by adding infinitely many positive implicational
formulae with countably many premisses. For any term
$t[\text{fix}^{(1)},\ldots,\text{fix}^{(n)}]$ introduce the axiom

$$\{t[\alpha_i^{(1)},\ldots,\alpha_i^{(n)}] \sqsubseteq x \mid i \in \omega\} \rightarrow t[\text{fix}^{(1)},\ldots,\text{fix}^{(n)}] \subsetsim x$$

which just expresses that $t[\text{fix}^{(1)},\ldots,\text{fix}^{(n)}]$ is the least
upperbound of the chain $(t[\alpha_i^{(1)},\ldots,\alpha_i^{(n)}])_{i\in\omega}$. As these
axioms can be understood as generating rules of an inductive

definition, see Aczel [1], the existence of an initial
model can be proved in an alternative way. By the fact
that the class of domain categories with least fixpoints
is axiomatisable we can prove that the class of extensional,
finitely generated domain categories with least fixpoints
admits an initial model. This can be done by adding for
any terms t_1, t_2 of the same sort (A,B) the axiom

$$\{t \circ t_1 = t \circ t_2 \mid t \text{ a term of sort } (1,A)\} \to t_1 = t_2$$

which expresses that 1 is a cogenerator for finitely generated models. As these axioms are positive implicational
this specification admits an initial model, which is also
initial in the category of extensional (not necessarily
finitely generated) domain categories with least fixpoints.
(This category is a full sub-category of the category of
models satisfying the specification above, as morphisms
are considered equal iff they behave in the same way on
all finitely generated arguments, not necessarily on all
arguments). We should remark that the axiomatization of
least fixpoints and of extensionality are inconstructive
and do not have a r.e. axiomatization by finite quantifierfree
formulae.

5. Outline of future research

It is shown from Scott [6] that models of domain categories
are isomorphic to full subcategories of topoi, i.e. models
of higher order intuitionistic logic. This can be achieved
by a Yoneda embedding $\underline{C} \to \underline{Set}^{C^{op}}$ or by considering certain

subcategories of realizability topoi, as pointed out by
D. Scott in his talk at this conference. Of course, the
investigation of these models can and probably will give
us new insights into the structure of certain domain categories.

From a more general point of view it might be worthwhile
to consider a notion of free topos over a domain category.
It would be interesting whether the domain category is a
full subcategory of the free topos over it and how it relates to the syntactic model existing for any consistent
theory in higher order intuitionistic logic.

Another problem which is still open is to extend the appa-
ratus of this paper to handle powerdomains. In Hennessy/
Plotkin [3] the powerdomain functor is constructed as an
adjunction between the category of cpo-s and the category
of nondeterministic cpo-s (and big union $\bigcup$ is the counit
of this adjunction). As adjunctions can be characterised
equationally this might be a starting point.

REFERENCES

[1] P. ACZEL: "An Introduction to Inductive Definitions"
        in: "Handbook of Mathematical Logic", ed.
        Barwise, North-Holland, 1977.

[2] P. DYBJER: "Category - Theoretic Logics and Algebras
        of Programs", Ph. D. Thesis, Gotenburg, 1983.

[3] M. HENNESSY/ G. PLOTKIN: "Full Abstraction for a Simple
        Parallel Programming Language", Springer,
        LNCS 74, 1979.

[4] MÖLLER: "Unendliche Objekte und Geflechte", Ph.D.
        Thesis, Univ. of München, 1983.

[5] A. POIGNE: "On Semantic Algebras", Techn. Univ. Dort-
        mund, 1983.

[6] D. SCOTT: "Relating Theories of the λ-calculus"
        in: "Curry Festschrift", ed. Hindley, Seldin,
        Academic Press, 1981.

Informatik – Fachberichte